PSYCHOLOGICAL TESTING

An Inside View

Edited by

Moshe Zeidner
and
Robert Most

Consulting Psychologists Press, Inc.

Myers-Briggs Type Indicator and MBTI are registered trademarks of Consulting Psychologists Press, Inc.

Printed in the United States of America.

Credits appear on page 465, which constitutes a continuation of the copyright page.

Cover design by Don Taka.

Psychological testing : an inside view / editors, Moshe Zeidner, Robert Most
   p. cm.
  Includes bibliographical references and index.
  ISBN 0-89106-051-0
  1. Psychological tests. I. Zeidner, Moshe. II. Most, Robert.
BF176.P776 1992
150'.28"7--dc20   91-30493
                             CIP

For our partners and children

Eti, Omer, and Yair
and
Timi, William, and James

CONTENTS

PREFACE

Psychological Testing: An Inside View is designed as a supplement to introductory textbooks on psychological and educational testing and as the next book a test user would consult to gain a deeper understanding of the issues and pragmatics of test use. Our hope is that the book will inform both the professional and academic communities about the realities of testing and that it will serve as a foundation for the informed and critical interpretation and use of tests. It is our tacit assumption that the sound and intelligent use of tests rests on knowledge of how tests are constructed, distributed, used, and evaluated.

The editors of this volume saw the need for a supplementary reference text on testing through their work and testing experience. Moshe Zeidner is an academic psychologist who specializes in differential psychology, better known as testing. Robert Most is a publishing executive at Consulting Psychologists Press.

In teaching both undergraduate and graduate level courses and seminars focusing on assessment-related issues in education and psychology, Moshe Zeidner saw the need for a reference book on testing that was somewhere between basic introductory texts and more advanced texts on test theory and applied psychometrics. Although most introductory level measurement texts provide students with a heavy dose of psychometric theory and computational procedures, or with a comprehensive treatment of particular tests and measures, what seemed lacking was information and guidelines on several practical issues, such as how to choose and evaluate tests, what to look for in test manuals, how tests are constructed on the basis of particular test philosophies, how to interpret test profiles, how to make sense of multivariate analyses of test data, and how to go about gathering feedback from examinees. This book was designed to help fill a void in the literature for a practical second text or reference book on testing in psychology and education.

Robert Most saw the need for this book while serving on the Test User Qualifications Working Group (TUQWoG), an interassociation working committee whose mission was to develop a method for test publishers to qualify customers for test purchase. While serving on this committee, he discovered that the few courses universities and colleges did offer were insufficient to train the variety of individuals who wanted to use tests responsibly. At numerous professional conferences he talked to practitioners who wanted to use tests responsibly but who were unable to take the time for an advanced course on testing. Even members of the American Psychological Association did not always have training in testing as part of their academic course work. A supplement was needed to train people in using tests. To address the training problem, a second working group was formed, the Test User Training Working Group (TUQWoG). Lorraine Eyde, Allen Hammer, and Gary Robertson, three chapter authors, are members of TUQWoG.

There are several excellent textbooks on testing available, including Anastasi (1988), Cronbach (1990), and Kaplan and Saccuzzo (1989). Although these should be read by anyone who wants to use tests responsibly, *Psychological Testing: An Inside View* provides information and ways of thinking about tests for people who plan to use tests on a frequent basis. It tries to answer important questions about test use by focusing chapters on specific issues relevant to test selection, quality, results, evaluation, development, statistical analysis, feedback, and use.

There are two audiences for this book. First, as a supplement to existing textbooks it can provide individuals new to testing with useful information not found in these textbooks. Second, experienced test users can refer to this book as a refresher and for new perspectives on testing.

Test use has many stakeholders, who are represented among the authors of this book. Bruce Bracken, Harrison Gough, and Allen Hammer are test authors. Allen Hammer, Robert Most, and Gary Robertson currently work for test publishers, and Kevin Moreland and Baruch Nevo have previously done so. Lorraine Eyde works for the U.S. Office of Personnel Management, which develops tests. Bruce Bracken, Pamela Bradley, Mark

Davison, Harrison Gough, Patricia Jones, V. L. Schwean Kowalchuk, Kevin Moreland, Baruch Nevo, Ernest Primoff, Darrell Sabers, D. H. Saklofske, Richard Valencia, and Moshe Zeidner all are in academic institutions. Rubin Lopez is a test user, and, of course, all of the authors use tests and try to see the user's perspective.

The format of this book reflects our belief that it is difficult for one person to treat adequately all of the topics that should be included. Consequently, the chapter authors also represent respected authorities in each of the respective areas. Each was invited to contribute a chapter introducing a particular area of expertise, focusing on the practical aspects of testing.

Because of the diversity of authors and the range of issues discussed, some chapters are more advanced than others. We have arranged the chapters into four sections to allow readers to concentrate on issues that are of the most interest. The first section presents an overview of testing and matters of general interest to any test user. The second section deals with issues in test development from a refreshingly practical perspective. The third section concerns statistics and test measurement. The fourth section is a grabbag of special topics, including computer-administered testing, examinee feedback, assessment of multiethnic students, and ethics and responsible test use.

Each chapter is independent of the others, which makes it possible to satisfactorily read only a single or a few chapters. Understandably, there is some overlap between chapters. A new test user might want to read only a chapter that deals with a specific problem or testing issue. An experienced user may read about topics of particular interest or may read to gain a fresh perspective on a topic. The introductory chapter was written to give an overview of test logic but also to provide a slightly different perspective than that found in text books.

Each chapter was selected to address the *process* of test development and use rather than the content of particular tests. In the first chapter, Zeidner and Most give readers a general understanding of testing and a framework in which to think about testing. In the second chapter, Hammer discusses the next step, selecting a test. In the third chapter, Saklofske and Kowalchuk cover practical concerns in administering the test; and in chapter 4, Bracken follows through with issues in test interpretation.

One problem for psychological tests is the test user's belief that information from tests is fact rather than a given probability of particualr meaning. To deal with this, the realities of test development are discussed in chapters 5 and 6. In chapter 5, Robertson looks inside a test publishing company at how a test is developed. And in chapter 6, Gough and Bradley show how a scale is developed from two different methods.

The foundation of testing is statistics, so any understanding of testing must include knowledge of the mathematics of how tests work. Chapter 7 by Davison is an excellent exposition of the statistical methods that are the basis of testing. In chapter 8, Jones and Sabers show the practical utility of sophisticated statistical analysis and clarify the methods by applying powerful tools to analyze one instrument.

Testing is multifaceted and the chapters in part 4 address various facets. In chapter 9, Moreland deals with computerized test results. What test takers think of the test is discussed by Nevo in chapter 10. In chapter 11, Valencia and Lopez present some issues that must be dealt with when testing across ethnic cultures. Finally, in chapter 12, Eyde and Primoff deal with the ethics of testing.

We are indebted to the following individuals who provided us with their valuable suggestions during the early stages of preparing this book: Bruce Bracken, Lee J. Cronbach, Harrison Gough, Ed Haertel, Arthur Jensen, Baruch Nevo, Tom Oakland, Jerry Sattler, and Frank Schmidt. Special thanks are due to David Budesco and Burt Westbrook for reviewing chapters of this book. The editors take full responsibility, however, for any shortcomings herein.

As editors of this volume, we hope you will be able to make a more informed selection of tests for your particular needs, better understand and apply basic testing concepts and principles, and help readers interpret test scores more competently and use them more efficiently in decision making. In addition, we hope you will be sufficiently stimulated to continue learning about psychological testing and sound testing practice.

Anastasi, A. (1988). *Psychological testing* (6th ed.). New York: Macmillan.

Cronbach, L. J. (1990). *Essentials of psychological testing* (5th ed.). New York: HarperCollins.

Kaplan, R. M., & Saccuzzo, V. P. (1989). *Psychological testing: Principles, applications, and issues* (2nd ed.). Monterey, CA: Brooks/Cole.

PART I

BASIC CONCEPTS
IN PSYCHOLOGICAL TESTING

CHAPTER 1

AN INTRODUCTION
TO PSYCHOLOGICAL TESTING

Moshe Zeidner & Robert Most

The Context of Psychological Testing

Contemporary society may be described as test-oriented and test-consuming. Testing is widely used in education and by the military, industrial, and government sectors to help in making decisions about people, and tests are administered, interpreted, and used by such professionals as school psychologists, guidance counselors, organizational psychologists, personnel officers, clinical psychologists, and social workers. It is almost impossible to grow up without encountering some type of psychological test, whether a standardized achievement test, a vocational test of occupational interest or aptitude, a military placement or mechanical aptitude test, a scholastic aptitude test for college application, or an industrial occupational placement test.

Psychological test data provide objective and reliable information that directly affects the choices made in vocational guidance and counseling, selection, classification and placement, and screening and diagnosis—all of which help shape an individual's upbringing, school, and career. Given their ubiquity, their many uses and functions, and their critical impact, a knowledge of psychological tests is essential to an understanding of most fields of modern psychology. Knowledge of testing principles and practices may indeed be necessary in order to be informed in a society in which many crucial decisions are based on test score results.

The purpose of this book is to help readers understand the logic and method of psychological testing as well as how to use psychological tests in an informed and ethical manner. This introductory chapter provides a general overview of psychological testing, its basic rationale and functions. We define and distinguish among several key concepts and explain the logic of the field and some of the assumptions underlying tests and measurement. We discuss major uses and functions of psychological tests and some common ways of classifying and differentiating among them. We also address misuse, examine criticisms raised against standardized tests, and discuss the issue of when it is appropriate to test or not to test.

Key Concepts in Testing

PSYCHOLOGICAL TESTS

A *psychological test* is a standard procedure designed to obtain a sample of behavior from a specified set of measurable behaviors (Crocker & Algina, 1986). Observations made in natural (i.e., nontest) settings may vary from person to person, may extend over an indefinite time period, and are usually not perceived as evaluations. In contrast, test situations are generally based on a uniform series of tasks, are circumscribed in time and place, and are perceived as evaluations (Anastasi, 1988). Information provided by tests is unique compared to nontest information, in that it is explicit, quantitative, and reproducible, making it possible to check both the validity of interpretations and the decisions based on test scores (Nunnally, 1978).

A psychological test may be defined as any systematic procedure in which a person is presented with a uniform set of stimuli (tasks, questions, or problems) intended to elicit particular responses, which are then scored and interpreted according to a specified criterion or performance standard. Accordingly, the critical hallmarks of a psychological test (Thorndike, Cunningham, Thorndike, & Hagen, 1991) include the following:

- A set of tasks (usually test items) administered to examinees under uniform conditions

- Responses to the test stimuli

- Scores based on the responses that have desirable psychometric properties and are interpretable according to an appropriate standard of performance

Based on the responses of examinees to test stimuli, a quantitative value or *test score* is assigned to the behavior sample by some systematic procedure, such as counting or tallying scored or numerically weighted responses to inventory items, which allows generalizations to be made about examinee performance with respect to the domain or construct being measured.

To show the major elements in the testing process, take the example of an anxiety test. The test may contain a uniform series of statements (e.g., I am worried, I am frightened, I am tense) presented to examinees under uniform conditions. Examinees must rate the extent to which the statements characterize their present feelings on a scale of four (very characteristic) to one (not characteristic). Responses are scored according to uniform standards and are converted to a final summary score.

These summary scores are used to draw inferences about how much of the theoretical construct typifies the individual and to place them on a scale from low to high on a continuum representing that construct. The scores will most likely be interpreted by comparing examinees' anxiety scores to typical scores obtained by normative groups of examinees with similar characteristics. Inferences can be made about the amount of that construct (anxiety) the examinee shows. Since the behaviors are elicited in a consistent manner, the performance of the same test taker across time or of different test takers at any given point of time can be compared.

PSCYHOLOGICAL MEASUREMENT

Psychological tests are typically used to place individuals on a continuum representing differing levels of the designated trait or construct that the test attempts to measure. In its broadest sense, *measurement* can be understood as an operation in the real world, physical or social, in which a number or symbol is assigned to objects or events according to an explicit rule (Stevens, 1946). Accordingly, measurement has been defined as "rules for assigning numbers to objects in such a way as to represent quantities of attributes" (Nunnally, 1978, p. 3). This succinct definition embodies several important notions about the measurement process.

First, the definition of measurement includes three distinct components:

- A category or group of *objects to be measured* or assessed

- A category or group of *symbols representing various values* of the scale employed

- An explicit *rule of correspondence* relating elements of these two categories

Second, since numbers or symbols assigned to objects according to an explicit rule designate the amount of an attribute present in an object, measurement is actually concerned with attributes or properties of objects, rather than with objects themselves (Torgerson, 1956).

For a measure to be useful, the rules for relating objects to numbers or symbols must be explicit, clear, and practical to apply. Whereas this is implicit in the measurement of physical objects, such as a ruler, tape, or yardstick used to measure width or length, these rules are not intuitively obvious in assessing most psychological attributes, such as mathematical ability, deductive reasoning, shyness, self-related cognition, and depression.

Third, measurement itself is neither good nor bad, but depends heavily on the accuracy or validity of the rules used in assigning numbers to objects. In fact, any set of rules that unambiguously quantifies properties of objects constitutes a legitimate measurement method. For example, in calculating the *gender* of visitors to Disneyland on a given Sunday, one possible rule would be the following: Assign a person wearing pants to the *male* category; assign a person wearing a dress to the *female* category; if it is impossible to discern the exact nature of the clothing worn, place that person in the *problematic case* category. Obviously, this rule will incorrectly classify females who wear pants as well as kilt-wearing Scotsmen. A better rule is to simply ask what gender appears on the person's identity card or passport and use that information for classification purposes, which would result in a more accurate measurement of gender.

The anxiety test, shown in Figure 1, illustrates the elements of psychological measurement. In this test, the objects to be measured are feelings of anxiety; the symbols representing various values of the scale are numbered (1 to 4) responses to the items; and the rule of correspondence is the formula used to determine the score. Try taking this test. The responses are "scored," that is, they are evaluated according to certain rules in order to adduce numerical values. The values are added to produce a score, which is then interpreted. The meanings shown in Figure 1 are sample results only; Figure 1 shows the responses of a hypothetical examinee to the test.

TYPES OF TEST SCALES

Measurement is basically a procedure for assigning numbers to objects in order to represent the amounts of certain properties or values present in the group of objects. A scale is a set of numbers or symbols whose properties are designed to mirror the real-world properties of the objects being measured.

FIGURE 1. Overview of a Test

Items	Responses*	Rule for Combining Values to Get a Test Score	Interpretation of Final Scores
I am worried.	3	Sum values	3–4 = not anxious
I am frightened.	2	(3 + 2 + 4) = 9	5–7 = not very anxious
I am tense.	4		8–10 = anxious
			11–12 = very anxious

* Response categories: 4 = very characteristic of you now; 3 = somewhat characteristic of you now; 2 = somewhat not characteristic of you now; 1 = not characteristic of you now

Psychological measurement amounts to systematically assigning numerical values to objects.

Scales are distinguished according to the information actually conveyed by the numbers assigned to objects. Thus, various scales convey different kinds of information and allow the numbers to be interpreted differently. A brief discussion of the most used measurement scales in ascending order of precision is given. Note that in common use the word *scale* means a set of items on the test that measures a single psychological construct. In the discussion below we describe types of scales.

Nominal Scales
Nominal scales are used to name, label, classify, and describe individuals or groups. Some nominal scales serve mainly to label individual objects in order to identify and help keep track of them (i.e., the license-plate number of a car and the social security number of an employee). Nominal scales do not indicate rank or importance. Thus, player number 33 (Larry Bird) of the Celtics is not necessarily a better player than number 32 (Magic Johnson) of the Lakers. They are simply two different players, whose numbers identify them. Furthermore, it makes no mathematical sense to add up numbers on the jerseys of one team (the Celtics) and compare them with the sum of the numbers on the jerseys of a rival team (the Lakers) to determine which team is stronger. A sample nominal scale is depicted in Figure 2.

FIGURE 2. A Sample Nominal Scale

Each team simply represents a category and the nominal relationship between them is represented by different colored uniforms. The nominal relationship between players is represented by the different numbers on their jerseys, which identify them but imply no real mathematical or hierarchical relationship, as is evident from Figure 2.

Some nominal scales place objects into exhaustive and mutually exclusive categories based on common identifying properties, without implying any order to the groups. The categories composing the scale are determined in advance and persons assigned to the same category are thought to have similarities. Common examples are diagnostic categories, such as normal, neurotic, or psychotic, or occupational types, such as artistic, social, or enterprising.

Thus, it is meaningless to add, subtract, or divide the numerals assigned to identify a category because their only function is to identify them. Similarly, artistic and social occupational types may be identified by 1 and 2 respectively, without implying that one group is inferior to the other. It is not possible to specify the quantitative differences between scale categories. That is, we cannot say 1 = Artistic, 2 = Social, 3 = Enterprising, therefore Enterprising minus Social equals Artistic. We can only enumerate the number of objects in each category. For this reason, nominal scales do not provide as much information as other forms of measurement.

Ordinal Scales
Ordinal scale values rank objects on a continuum representing the property being measured. Common examples are letter grades in school, military rank,

FIGURE 3. Ordinal Relationships

Basketball Team	Final Standing
Celtics	First
Lakers	Second
Pistons	Third

and academic rank. The numbers assigned to objects indicate relative differences among them; adjacent numbers on the scale indicate higher or lower values on the continuum. Generally, the person or object with the greatest amount of the attribute ranks 1, the one with the next greatest amount ranks 2, and so on until all individuals are ranked with respect to the attribute under consideration.

Figure 3 shows the final standing of three basketball teams. Note that no matter how many points each scored or how many games they won or lost, one team came in first, another team second, and so forth. Ordinal scales specify the relative differences among objects on the continuum without accounting for the absolute amount of difference among objects. Also, ordinal scales give no indication of average performance since, as a group, all the scores could be high or low.

Interval Scales

In addition to the features of nominal and ordinal scales, numbers on an interval scale have equal intervals between adjacent points. No information is available, however, about the absolute magnitude of the attribute of the objects measured. Consider the realm of physical measurement of temperature in degrees centigrade, where the magnitude of the differences between any two adjacent points on the scale is the same, though the zero point is arbitrarily defined. Thus, the difference between 33 and 34 degrees centigrade equals the difference between 34 and 35 degrees centigrade. The same is true of psychological measurement on interval scales.

Figure 4 shows four individual scores on the three-item anxiety measure. The difference between each score is two, indicating an approximately equal difference in the stated anxiety level of each as measured by the three items. With respect to psychological measurement, since interval scales assume equal differences between successive categories in the attribute being measured, the performance differences between examinees have meaning. If we

FIGURE 4. Interval Relationships

Person Taking Anxiety Measure	Score on Anxiety Measure
Michael	10
Joanna	8
William	6
Jenny	4

assume, for example, that each raw score point that makes up a student's anxiety score is of the same value, then the test total is on an interval scale. This requires us to accept the notion that the difference between 8 and 7 points is the same as that between 11 and 10 points (or between any other pair of adjacent points). A five-point difference on the test is assumed to be the same along the scale. Adjacent points on the scales are equal regardless of the number of people at different points on the scale. However, without an absolute logical zero we cannot make a ratio comparison; that is, we cannot say that a score of 12 indicates twice the anxiety as a score of 6.

For practical purposes, most psychological measures are presently regarded as rough approximations of equal interval scales, enabling the use of sophisticated statistical mathematics for the analysis and interpretation of test data (Nunnally, 1978). In contrast, measurement in the physical sciences is a straightforward matter; if a measurement can be agreed upon, actual physical measures are relatively precise and uncontroversial (Green, 1981). Few people would argue over physical concepts of length, volume, mass, and so on, and there is little disagreement about how these concepts should be measured. In the behavioral sciences, the situation is fundamentally different. Not only is there controversy about how a concept should be measured but also considerable debate about the precision of psychological measurement and the meaning of the measurement units.

Ratio Scales
Although ratio scales are frequently found in the biological and physical sciences (length, time, distance, etc.) they are virtually nonexistent in the behavioral sciences. A ratio scale is a particular type of equal interval scale with an absolute zero point; that is, distances on the scale are stated with respect to a rational zero point. Since there cannot be a zero amount of a psychological construct, ratio scales do not truly relate to psychological measurement.

FIGURE 5. Ratio Relationships

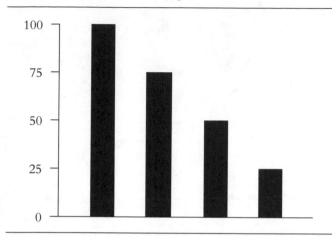

A classic example of a ratio scale is the measurement of length by a ruler or tape. There exists an absolute zero point in gauging length and the differences between intervals are also equal in length. Essentially, all mathematical operations can be performed meaningfully on a ratio measurement scale and ratios have meaning and can be directly interpreted. Figure 5 represents the ratio relationship of lengths of rectangles. One rectangle can be half the length of another and still another can be half the length of that rectangle (and thus one-fourth the length of the first). Conceptually, you could also have a rectangle of zero length.

Now that we have described the basics of a psychological scale and the general types of scales, we can move on to some broader issues.

PSYCHOLOGICAL ASSESSMENT

Psychological assessment is a multifaceted process designed to help appraise individuals in their current life settings. Although assessment includes psychological testing, measurement, and judgment in evaluating an individual or group, it is a more comprehensive and encompassing process as well. Tests, measurements, and judgments are merely elements of the overall process (Salvia & Ysseldyke, 1991).

Broadly speaking, psychological assessment aims to evaluate people in their present life situation, against the background of their past life. Assessment is an evaluative and interpretive appraisal of an individual's present level

FIGURE 6. The Temporal Context of Testing

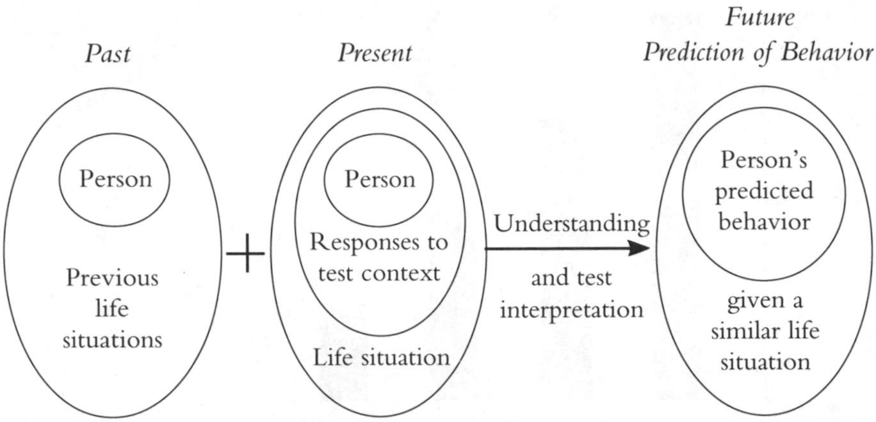

of performance. It recognizes that both test and nontest performance are influenced by many factors, including the past and present life situation and the conditions inherent in the setting. Factors typically considered in the course of the psychological assessment process (Salvia & Ysseldyke, 1991) include:

- Current life circumstances (physical and psychological health and well-being, financial and social situation, attitudes, values, motives, and expectations)

- Developmental history (overall health, ailments, traumas, stressful events, sensory limitations)

- Extrapersonal factors (context of examination, theoretical persuasion of tester)

- Assessor's interpretation and explanation of an individual's current performance

- Prognosis or inference of future performance based on past and present performance

Thus, assessment is both an evaluative and interpretive process. In it meaning is given to an individual's performance based on the subject's total functioning, and possible explanations of this performance are sought. Figure 6 depicts the total context of testing, including past, present, and future.

As an example of the assessment process, let's consider the case of a school psychologist assessing a student's scholastic ability. In addition to intelligence tests, the psychologist may consider the student's present and past medical status; physical, emotional, social, and cognitive home environment; past and present learning problems and adjustment difficulties in school; feelings, expectations, anxieties, attitudes, and behavioral styles expressed in interviews with the psychologist; and possible contextual effects on test and nontest performance, such as lack of motivation, poor rapport with examiner, and test anxiety. In addition, the psychologist may wish to examine previous test scores and obtain opinions about the student's abilities from others, such as teachers, counselors, and parents.

In other words, the school psychologist would go beyond merely obtaining test scores or other samples of human behavior (see Kleinmutz, 1985). The psychologist strives to understand the student in his or her present social ecology, in order to make a comprehensive diagnosis and prognosis about overall cognitive functioning. The psychologist would try to decide how the student would do in various class environments in order to find an optimal place for the student. Thus, in the overall picture, testing is the most narrow among the terms defined and is nothing more or less than a data-gathering tool used in the course of measurement or assessment.

The Conceptualization of Psychological Testing

Scientific Constructs

Psychology is typically described as the scientific study of behavior. It aims at gathering systematic data on key attributes, traits, and behaviors in order to describe, predict, understand, and improve the state of humanity. Much of psychology is the mapping out and illumination of human attributes or concepts and the establishment of systematic or lawful relationships among them.

A *construct* is a particular type of concept, a product of the informed imagination of scientists in a given field who use them for descriptive or explanatory purposes (Crocker & Algina, 1986). When constructs are measured, they can vary over a range of values and are often referred to as *variables*. Constructs are the building blocks of theory. They are *constructed* or *construed* on the basis of both informal and systematic observations of similarities in human behavior, which are then summarized and labeled. This labeling of behavioral similarity is often the scientific construct.

FIGURE 7. Anxiety Behaviors in Context

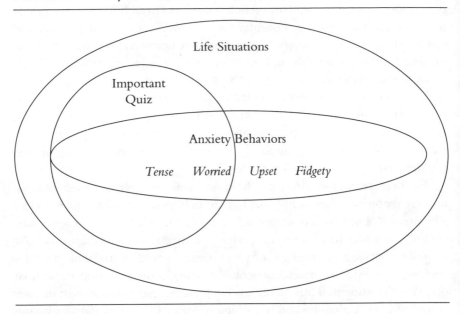

For example, if we observe a student to be excessively fidgety, upset, worried, and unduly tense in the course of an important exam, we may infer that the person is characterized by a trait that we label test anxiety. Through the use of constructs such as test anxiety (or aggression, optimism, scholastic aptitude, coping resources, etc.), observers try to classify a group of instances of similar behavior and communicate in concise terms the essence of the observation. Thus, psychologists may classify a variety of behaviors (e.g., worry and physiological arousal during classroom quizzes, tension and emotionality when performing a gymnastics exercise, apprehensive and disturbing thoughts when speaking before an audience, and so forth) as belonging to a similar category of behaviors and they would communicate the critical features of that concept by the term *test anxiety*. The construct may then be formally defined as a situation-specific trait involving apprehension, worry, and arousal of the autonomic nervous system when that person is being evaluated (Spielberger et al., 1978). Figure 7 presents a summary schematic of the anxiety construct in context.

OPERATIONS FOR MEASUREMENT

Before using a construct for research, theoretical, or practical purposes, it is essential to find an appropriate measurement operation in order to relate target objects to various values of the construct. Obviously, the first step before constructing a useful measurement procedure is to carefully define and limit the construct or attribute under consideration. The way a construct is construed is expressed generally by the label we attach to it, which helps define and limit the domain of the construct or its universe (Thorndike, 1982). However, we need to go beyond a formal or nominal definition of a construct to specify the operations or steps to be taken toward measuring it.

Accordingly, once a construct has been named, we need to operationalize it by looking for observable behaviors that would be valid indicators of the construct in order to learn more about its key attributes and relationships with other constructs. In other words, observable behaviors are the raw materials of construct formation, but once the construct exists it needs to be operationalized and measured by establishing rules of correspondence between the abstract construct and observable, measurable behaviors. In fact, much of the history of psychological testing during this century may be portrayed as the invention of instruments and procedures for eliciting, in a standard way and under uniform conditions, the behaviors that serve as valid indicators of the attributes of the individual that relate to the construct being measured.

In trying to operationalize measurement of a given construct, say, test anxiety, we can do one of several things: (a) observe, record, and rate the trait as it occurs in natural contexts (e.g., the evaluation); (b) set up a situation designed to elicit the behavior under controlled conditions (e.g., giving examinees an important test or causing anxiety by achievement-oriented instructions) and rate behaviors; (c) ask the target individuals to report their own feelings and reactions (e.g., the degree of anxiety experienced under testing conditions); (d) ask others (e.g., teachers, peers, psychologists, parents) to report about the specific behaviors of the targets studied; or (e) rely on objective physiological measures (heart rate, pulse, muscle tension, and so forth).

One way to define a measure of test anxiety would be: "Self-reports of target individual(s) about the frequency in which they typically experience anxiety-related behaviors in various evaluative situations, along a five-point scale (1 = almost never, 5 = almost always). Another definition could be based on a teacher's ratings of the target individual(s) on a ten-point scale, ranging from highly anxious (10) to not anxious at all (1). In any case, in order to gather data bearing on the extent, scope, and magnitude of the construct in the individual(s) under study, some systematic procedure for eliciting the behavior and gauging it is required.

Basic Steps in the Testing Process

Three basic steps, briefly described below, may be identified in any measurement procedure (Thorndike et al., 1991).

Construct Identification and Definition
This first step involves the identification and definition of the attribute of interest and ascertaining that it is relevant to what is trying to be accomplished. For example, if we want to select members of a sumo wrestling team, it would be inappropriate to measure candidates' verbal proficiency or artistic ability. Other factors (athletic ability, physical prowess, coordination) would be more useful in selecting the team.

As we deal with such complex, intangible concepts as need for achievement, social anxiety, sociability, verbal aptitude, and so on, considerable diversity in definition is inevitable. For example, to what extent should a definition of test anxiety include physiological reactions, irrelevant thoughts, and worry? Thus, a number of problems may arise at this stage in selecting constructs useful for a given purpose and in defining them clearly and unambiguously.

Operational Procedures
The next stage in any measurement process involves determining the set of operations that will expose the attributes and behaviors associated with the hypothetical construct we want to measure. That is, we need to isolate the attribute and find a set of operations suitable for measuring it. In selecting sumo wrestling team members, for instance, we might want to measure hand grip with a spring compression instrument.

The definition of the concept determines how we operationalize the construct—that is, what we accept as reasonable operations for measuring the trait. The operations used depend on the conceptual definition of the trait.

In the ability domain, psychologists have been relatively successful in setting up operations that elicit and display the attribute and allow observation under uniform conditions. However, there are many attributes, particularly in the affective domain, which have been less successfully operationalized, including social values, impulsivity, and anger control.

Quantification

The third step involves ascribing units of measurement to the attribute under consideration and expressing the responses elicited in those terms. As a rule, psychological attributes do not have units whose equality can be demonstrated by direct comparisons; even our best psychological units of measurement leave something to be desired. Consequently, we fall back on agreed-upon relative units of measurement. For example, on the *Values Scale* (Nevill & Super, 1989), which measures work values, responding that it is important to "work hard physically," "use powerful machines," or "use my strength" each counts as three points toward the Physical Prowess scale. This response would add nine points to the scale, even though each item might have slightly different weights in evidencing the concept of physical prowess.

Generally, we tend to regard a task successfully completed or responded to as equal to any other task successfully completed or responded to. The total score is generally obtained by combining an individual's total number of successes or weighted responses across tasks.

In measuring grip for the sumo team selection, we might allow the wrestler three tries on the spring compression. If the spring has a zero to five scale, we might have a score such as "12" that successful sumo wrestlers typically can perform; this would be used as a benchmark when selecting new wrestlers.

MODELS AND CONCEPTIONS OF PSYCHOLOGICAL TESTING

Psychological tests and the testing process are conceptualized in a variety of ways as discussed below.

Testing as Domain Sampling: A Basic Testing Rationale

A common notion of a psychological test is that of a limited but objective and standardized sample of behavior from a broader domain. It is rarely the goal to directly measure the behavior sample (i.e., the test) per se. The basic rationale for testing and obtaining a behavior sample is to be able to generalize from the behavior observed in the test situation to the behavior manifested in the larger domain (i.e., the real world). This view serves as a major justification for using psychological tests to draw inferences and conclusions from tests about people's standing with respect to a given construct.

Let's assume we want to measure verbal reasoning ability. The construct domain would include many behaviors, such as classifying objects into categories, thinking by way of analogy or syllogism, discriminating among similar elements, and so forth. The item domain would include all possible tasks that measure each of the behaviors included in the construct domain. For example, the use of verbal analogy could be assessed by a wide array of items such as "Student is to teacher as Socrates is to...?" or "Shoelace is to shoe as...is to shirt?" or "Light is to day as darkness is to...?" and so on. In most cases, we would choose not to present the entire set of possible items to examinees, as this would be time consuming, costly, inefficient, and highly unfeasible. Instead, we would rather select a few possible items in the domain as representative (say, items 1 and 3), and this would constitute our test sample. These items would be presented to examinees, scored, and conclusions drawn not only with respect to the sample but also with respect to the construct at hand, namely, verbal reasoning ability.

According to this logic, tests are hardly ever capable of measuring all aspects or behaviors in the entire domain of a psychological construct under consideration (e.g., verbal ability, mechanical aptitude, coping mechanisms), particularly when the domain is elusive or not well defined. Consequently, the tester and user have to be satisfied with a uniform but limited number of tasks, formally called items, which are presumed to represent the population or universe of all possible tasks. These tasks can then be generated to measure the behavioral domain of interest. This conceptualization differentiates among three related notions:

- The domain of behaviors associated with the construct under consideration, or the *construct domain*

- The domain of possible items designed to test the various behaviors in the domain, or the *item domain*

- The sample of items from the item domain, or the *behavior sample or test*

Figure 8 lists many of the behaviors, feelings, and ideas that we associate with anxiety. Likewise there are many items that we can phrase to describe all of these behaviors, feelings, and thoughts. Yet we can take only a small sample of items to make up the test.

The logic of sampling items from a behavioral domain is analogous to that of drawing a limited sample of subjects from a population and making conclusions about it. Another example would be to draw a small sample of human blood or tissue and from it make conclusions about a person's overall

FIGURE 8. Behavior Samples From a Specific Domain of Anxiety

Construct Domain	Item Domain	Test
Feel worry	I am worried.	I am worried.
Afraid feeling	I am frightened.	I feel like I am in danger.
Body tense	I am tense.	My heart is pounding.
Hyperventilate	I am breathing quickly.	
Feel frozen in place	I feel like I can't move.	
Can't think	I feel like I can't think.	
Feel loss of control	I feel like I have no control over my body.	
Feel danger	I feel like I am in danger.	
Strange feeling in stomach	I feel "butterflies" in my stomach.	
Sweaty palms	My palms are sweaty.	
Heart pounding	My heart is pounding.	
etc.		

health. In order to be able to generalize from the sample of tasks comprising the test back to the desired domain of behavior, the sample should be representative of the total domain of behaviors. If the sample is incidental or biased, it affects our ability to make valid inferences about a person's level of performance or proficiency. For example, if the test includes a disproportionate amount of very easy or very difficult verbal reasoning items, the results would hardly allow us to generalize to the larger domain of verbal reasoning.

Whether the test adequately covers the behaviors under consideration depends not only on the the nature and degree of coverage and representativeness of the items, but also on the number of behaviors (items) sampled from the domain. Obviously, one or two verbal reasoning items drawn from a very sizable number of possible reasoning tasks would provide an inadequate estimate of verbal reasoning ability. In order to test effectively, the performance should be based on a larger set of tasks. In addition, we assume that the domain of items from which we draw our sample actually measures what it purports to measure and is a valid representation of the domain of behaviors we wish to generalize to.

It is important to remember that inferences or predictions based on test scores can be made only if the assumptions above have been met. If we violate the assumptions of testing, we cannot adequately generalize or make valid inferences from the test results, and decisions based on them may well be wrong. That is, we can place a reasonable amount of confidence on the adequacy of the observed data only if we have administered a test that adequately represents the domain of concern, is relatively free from error, and was accurately administered, scored, and interpreted according to appropriate normative sample groups.

Testing as Experimentation

Another conceptualization views psychological testing as a psychological experiment, in that standard or uniform stimuli are presented to an examinee or subject in clearly specified ways, and responses are systematically elicited, recorded, coded, quantified, and evaluated (Newland, 1973). Ideally, the test developer succeeded in controlling all variations in the stimuli except the one the test measures. Any psychological procedure is standardized when the material, administration, instructions to subjects, and scoring are specified as much as possible so that the test is identical for all persons at all times. Standardization of psychological tests is similar to experimental control, which is the attempt to carefully control the extraneous factors that might influence and contaminate the scores and their interpretation.

Testing conditions need to be carefully controlled so that the test interpreter can be confident that the scores reflect variations on what is being measured rather than something extraneous. Part of these controls are in the form of using identical test materials, specific time limits, uniform instructions, and same scoring formats. Other controls involving objectivity in scoring are designed to permit the tester to conclude that the test reflects variations on the dimension being measured rather than variation caused by scoring error (Kleinmuntz, 1985).

Testing as Communication

Psychological testing has been construed as a process of communication between the tester and the subject, a process of asking and responding to the questions (Guttman, 1965a). Thus, to characterize a particular type of test we need to characterize both the nature of the questions and the responses.

Testing as Information Processing

Another conception looks at testing as information processing in that a test element (such as an item, test, or test battery) gauges a person's ability to interpret the meaning of the stimulus, process the stimulus using some form of cognitive processes or performance components (Sternberg, 1985), and make and evaluate an appropriate response requiring "maximal" or "typical" performance.

Tests as Signs of Nontest or Future Behavior

While conceptually it is simpler to consider all psychological tests as behavior samples, from which inferences regarding other behaviors outside the test situation can be made, different types of tests can be characterized as variants of this pattern. For example, tests used for diagnostic purposes are designed to serve as signs of a particular adjustment problem or pathology. Those used for prediction purposes (e.g., selection or classification) are designed to predict future behaviors (e.g., we predict that a student who performs well on the *Scholastic Aptitude Test* [SAT] will also do well in college).

While the practical value of a test, say, for diagnosis, classification, or prediction, depends on the degree to which it serves as an indicator of a relatively broad and significant area of behavior, the test stimuli or items need not closely parallel or resemble the behavior the test is designed to predict. It is only necessary that each test demonstrate a reasonable degree of empirical correspondence between the test and the broader domain of importance, or the subject's performance in nontest situations that relate to the criteria. Thus, if a test of mechanical aptitude allows us to generalize to performance in a larger domain, such as success in working with mechanical devices on the job, the test is achieving its purpose. A French language proficiency test shown to correspond to future success in using the language in the French cultural setting is serving its purpose.

Some test samples are virtually identical to the future nontest performance one would like to predict (e.g., the task of editing a journal manuscript to predict future job success as a member of the journal's editorial board); some tests show a lesser degree of similarity (a figural analogy test to predict performance in medical school); other test samples are not similar at all to the performance related to the criteria (sociometric ratings in which subjects are asked to select the most popular individuals in a group of cadets to predict success in pilot training).

Basic Assumptions Underlying Psychological Test Use

In this section we discuss some basic philosophical assumptions underlying psychological testing and measurement, along with related practical problems inherent in the nature of measuring psychological attributes. The knowledgeable user of a psychological test should keep in mind that failure to meet these assumptions in testing directly affects the validity of the results obtained and can lead to inaccurate or invalid generalizations from test data.

Measurement Is Performed
on Psychological Attributes, Not on Objects

A basic epistemological assumption is that measurement applies to the properties or attributes of objects rather than to the objects per se (Torgerson, 1956). Since measurement of an attribute concerns establishing the relations among objects in a specific dimension, each measure concerns one distinct attribute. Thus, measurement is a process of abstraction in which we single out certain properties to gauge and study, so that we measure students' learning strategies, motivations, self-concepts, self-efficacy, and so forth, rather than measure the student per se.

Measurement of Psychological Constructs Is Generally Indirect

As discussed earlier, psychological constructs are never really directly observed but are inferred from exemplars or instances of behavior. Given the nature of psychological attributes as abstract hypothetical entities, the direct measurement of psychological constructs through direct observation or ostensible procedures is virtually impossible. For example, in order to measure memory for meaningful words we rely on a variety of indicators, such as the amount of savings in the time needed to relearn the words, recall if given a cue for the word, recognition of the word among others, actively remembering the word, and so on.

Because psychological constructs are intrinsically abstract and nonobservable constructions, their measurement is difficult. Since constructs can only be measured indirectly, test experts are challenged to devise ingenious methods to assess them (Crocker & Algina, 1986). Although some approaches become the standard over time (e.g., the *Wechsler Adult Intelligence Scale* for assessing adult intelligence), no single approach to the measurement of a construct will ever gain universal acceptance. Thus, there is always the possibility that two test developers trying to measure the construct from differing theoretical perspectives will choose quite different behaviors to operationally define their constructs.

For example, one approach may measure intelligence on the basis of a subject's reaction time in a choice experiment; another approach may rely on scores on a nonverbal figures test; in yet another, a composite score of verbal and performance test scores would provide the best indication of a person's intelligence.

Moreover, some measures may not be consistent, leading to different conclusions about the level of the trait being considered. For example, we may obtain different results if we measure anxiety through physiological procedures, as opposed to self-report measures, or observation of an examinee in a true-to-life situation. To take another example, we may reach very different conclusions about intelligence differences in ethnic groups, say Hispanic versus Caucasian in the United States, depending on whether we use a verbal or nonverbal test (Jensen, 1980) with more sizable differences on the verbal measure.

PSYCHOLOGICAL MEASURES ARE SUBJECT TO ERROR

It is commonly assumed that any measurement, whether it is in the physical, biological, or behavioral sciences, is subject to error (Green, 1981). Psychological tests, which are typically based on a limited sample of observations taken at only one point in time, are particularly vulnerable to a variety of sources of error. These errors may creep into any stage of the measurement—from the conceptualization of the attribute to the scoring and interpretation of results.

Three main sources of measurement error are listed below:

- Subject-related error (e.g., illness, fatigue, anxiety, motivation)

- Situation-related error (e.g., the test atmosphere, examiner-examinee rapport, noise, lighting, seating)

- Test-related error (e.g., sampling of content, format, language, instructions)

Thus, if an examinee takes the same test twice, his or her level of test anxiety may change depending on the content of the measure used, the atmosphere or situation, the examiner, and so on. Influences specific to the test sample or situation are considered sources of error. It is crucial to identify and control them, as they may limit the validity of the test and impair the generalizability of the results and interpretation.

Interestingly, the error term is a built-in component of the observed score in the *classical model* of a test score (Crocker & Algina, 1986). The classical model for a test score is $X = T + E$, where X is the observed score on a test (the raw score), T the true score of the examinee on the trait (i.e., the score if it were measured without error), and E the error from various sources. For example, two subjects may have the same *true score*, say 80, but one subject will have obtained an 85 because of a positive error score of +5 (due to pure luck or familiarity with the content of the items), while the other examinee has an observed score of 75 on account of a negative error score of −5 (due to bad luck, fatigue, anxiety, and so on). Thus, the first examinee's observed score of 85 may be composed of respective true and error score of 80 and +5, whereas the second examinee's true score of 75 may be composed of respective true and error scores of 80 and −5.

We are concerned with two basic types of errors in the measurement of psychological constructs (Jensen, 1980). The first is *systematic* or constant errors, which occur, for example, if the content of a mechanical aptitude test is overweighted with verbal items, or if a rater constantly gives lower scores to ethnic minority group members. A test free of systematic error is said to be *unbiased*. The second type is *random* error, which occurs when either the measurement device or examiner gives inconsistent results. With respect to random error, the amount and direction will be random, with equal chances of positive and negative scores in a population of examinees. A test relatively free of random error is said to be *reliable*.

Yet another source of measurement error in psychological tests is the inappropriate use of tests. A case in point would be when examiners select tests that do not yield information related to the behavior they wish to understand or predict, or when a test is basically invalid for a given population, or when the examiner reads unwarranted information into the results.

CULTURAL EXPERIENCE AND TEST TAKING ARE RELATED

Examinees taking a particular test should be similar in cultural, educational, and social environments and experiences to those on whom the test was standardized and the test norms were based. When an examinee or group differ from the standardization sample, the use of the norms as an index for evaluating current performance or prediction may be inappropriate. Furthermore, if a test shows different levels of accuracy in assessing the target construct or in predicting a criterion score as a function of subcultural or gender group membership, then that test may not be appropriate for all cultures or genders.

ONLY PRESENT BEHAVIOR IS OBSERVED; FUTURE BEHAVIOR IS INFERRED

It is assumed that only present behavior can be observed and measured; future behavior must be inferred. Thus, one must distinquish between observation and inference. Observed and evoked behaviors are a function of the testing conditions, the nature of the test used, and the approach employed. For example, to observe that one does not make correct responses to series completion or analogy items is one thing; to infer that one cannot and is therefore of low basic intelligence is another. Indeed, much of testing is analogous to the everyday process of classifying individuals according to past behavior and on that basis estimating the probability that a future nontest behavior will occur (Kleinmuntz, 1985).

Psychological testing includes evaluation of *competence* against *performance*. A person may be competent to answer questions correctly on a test but for various reasons may not perform in the testing situation. Understanding the reasons underlying an individual's performance requires individual assessment, including consideration of sociocultural background, present life circumstances, and motivations (Anastasi, 1988). Remember that a test can never tell us *why* an examinee performs as he or she does.

PSYCHOLOGICAL TESTS SERVE AS A BASIS FOR DECISION MAKING

Psychological testing is based on the assumption that decisions made in educational, vocational, clinical, and other settings involve uncertainty or risk with respect to the outcomes. Thus, decisions should be based on information as reliable and comprehensive as possible. The more accurate the information on which decisions are based, the better the resulting decisions are assumed to be (Mehrens & Lehmann, 1984).

Accordingly, tests are designed to provide a source of objective and reliable information to serve as inputs for decision making. Test results may assist clients and professionals in making decisions and in choosing optimal courses of action. However, a test score does not yield conclusions but provides only the raw material, which must be processed through the judgment and insight of skilled professionals before it can be used in making decisions (Thorndike et al., 1977). Tests should be only one source of evidence, especially in decisions that affect an individual's life, such as selection, placement, diagnostic classification, or educational tracking. It is not the tests that are harmful but the classification of people that changes their lives.

Given that psychological tests are no more (and no less) than a tool for gathering systematic data about human behavior, there is really no point in asking whether a test is good or bad. It can be either good or bad, appropriate or inappropriate, depending on its purpose. A test of aesthetic judgment, while appropriate for selecting beauty pageant judges, would hardly do for selecting skilled machine operators.

Functions and Uses of Psychological Tests

PRACTICAL DECISIONS

Individual Versus Institutional

Test data are used in two basic types of decision making: individual and institutional. The first involves the interest of the individual, especially in making the most satisfactory or optimal choice among a wide range of educational or vocational alternatives. Since the values underlying decisions at the individual level are unique and tend to vary from one person to another, what is appropriate for one person may be inappropriate for another (Cronbach & Gleser, 1965; Thorndike, 1982).

Institutional decision making is designed to help an institution, such as a college, company, or government, optimally utilize its human resources by assigning individuals to the most appropriate available slot in the institution—be it a job opening, training program, instructional sequence, or track. It is noteworthy that from the institution's viewpoint, what is important is maintaining a high average level of success across individuals even if it is at the expense of a particular individual who may be placed into a less than optimal slot from his or her point of view. For example, if the army needs to fortify its tank corps, army personnel would simply assign a recruit to a tank division, even if the recruit had requested the medical corp. This is understandable because an institution can replicate its decisions over many persons, relying on their overall or average correctness. An individual, by contrast, cannot usually replicate a decision across many options or treatments and average outcomes in the same way that a company or university can average its risks over many applicants (Thorndike, 1982).

Guidance and Counseling

The major role of testing in counseling and guidance is to provide the client with an estimate of his or her probability of success in different occupations (Cronbach, 1990). In the course of guidance, test results are used to help make choices that are hoped to be optimal for the client. The goal of testing is to assess both the probability of success on the job by measuring aspects such as aptitude and interest, as well as the expected level of satisfaction with a certain occupation. For example, one person may have exceptional mechanical ability but may dislike working with tools. Another may show keen interest in a vocation, say air-traffic control, but lack the spatial skills or personality traits necessary to handle it.

The counseling process tries to help the client make explicit the values sought in a job and to evaluate the extent to which they will be realized. Both the client's probability of success and job requirements need to be synthesized into a final estimate of the job's desirability (Thorndike, 1982). Thus, one would like to be able to tell the client, "You have one in five chances of completing a graduate psychology degree at Stanford and enjoying your studies there very much, as opposed to eight out of ten chances of completing your degree at Newport Tech, but enjoying it less."

Selection, Placement, and Classification

Psychological tests can help contribute to more efficient use of people in organizations and are frequently used for selection, placement, and classification purposes. Tests help to maximize the utility in decision making. *True utility* refers to the actual value or worth of an individual in a particular position. This concept is often elusive and technically difficult to gauge. How do we judge the long-term value of medical or law school studies to an academic institution—from the mean salary of graduates? scientific publications of alumni? clinical expertise? Therefore, we tend to rely on a substitute measure of *predicted utility*, which is an operational measure of the intended criterion performance (e.g., college grade point average).

Unfortunately, however, criterion measures of performance or predicted utility are not available for an individual prior to acceptance or entry into a program. To deal with that problem, some already available estimate of predicted utility is used, such as a test score. Test scores, therefore, are designed to serve as estimators of predicted validity (i.e., the criterion of the test), which in turn are designed to predict true utility. It is therefore imperative that the criterion score correspond as closely as possible to the true utility, on one hand, and that the test score correspond as closely as possible to the predicted utility estimates, on the other.

Test scores $\rightarrow$ predicted utility $\rightarrow$ true utility

The best strategy on the part of an institution for filling its vacancies would be to choose individuals with the highest predicted utility based on test scores. Thus, the student with a GPA of 4.0 should be more valuable than a student with a G.P.A. of 3.2.

Selection tests are designed to provide information on which to help base selection decisions, which are typically dichotomous in nature (i.e., to accept vs. to reject). A minimum quality score on the test, or cut score, is established that can be applied as soon as test and other data are gathered. The cut score

FIGURE 9. Decision-making Errors

| | *Criterion Cutoff* | |
	Candidate Not Successful ↓	Candidate Successful
Test says accept *Test Score Cutoff* →	False positive	True positive
Test says reject	True negative	False negative

is typically set as high as possible while still qualifying enough applicants to meet the needs of the institution doing the hiring. Since selection decisions are usually based on the assumption that those admitted will be successful while those rejected will not, selection decisions are greatly improved when a close correspondence exists between the test results and skills, abilities, and attitudes required for success in the institution. For example, applicants to nursing school may complete an application blank containing biographical information, the SAT, a series of personality tests, and partake in a leaderless group discussion rated by trained observers. These measures are designed to identify candidates for admission with higher chances of succeeding in nursing school than those rejected.

Unfortunately, instruments are fallible predictors, and all selection decisions involve risk. There are two types of risks in using a test (or any other selection device) for decision purposes:

- Admitting an individual into a program who is not eventually successful, *a false positive* error

- Failing to admit an individual who would have been successful if admitted, a *false negative* error

Figure 9 shows the risk variations inherent in hiring based on test results. Note that while no true decision should be based entirely on test results, tests along with other evidence can be valuable in making the decision. Often tests are judged in terms of decisions as if the test alone made the decision. This is useful for evaluating what the test adds to the decision process. In the model shown in Figure 9, you have both the candidate's test scores as a job applicant and subsequent evidence of success or the lack of it. If the test scores were not used in the hiring decision, then you can see how well a test would have predicted success based on a cut score, at which you decide whether to hire or not.

If we separate the people we hire at the cut score, we can see how many above the cut score were successful (*true positives*) and how many were not (*false positives*). Likewise, of the individuals below the cut score (where the test would reject the candidate), we can see how many were successful (*false negatives*) and how many were not (*true negatives*).

Placement tests are designed to optimally assign an individual to different levels or categories in an institution after acceptance. The objective is to determine which possible placement will optimize an individual's value to the organization and best utilize that person's abilities and talents. Examples of placement decisions include: Should a candidate for a banking position be given a job as a teller or immediately placed in a managerial position? Should stressed subjects be given short-term counseling or long-term therapy?

Some global measurement instruments may be useful for selection but not for placement (e.g., SAT scores). These global measures may help predict overall success in any of the categories but not in placement at the most suitable level. What is required ideally is a test that is related positively to success under one situation and negatively under another (Cronbach, 1990).

Classification decisions are basically concerned with assigning people to one of several categories, jobs, treatments, or programs (Cronbach & Gleser, 1965). Once an individual is admitted into a particular institution, placement decisions need to be made about optimal curriculum or job placement. Classification is a broader concept than either selection or placement (Thorndike, 1982). In placement decisions, the grouping of available programs or treatments is vertical (ordered) and the major decision concerns the level most suitable for an individual. In classification decisions, the categories are unordered and the decision is basically about the kind of program an individual will be assigned to. For instance, once accepted into college, a student needs to choose a major course of study; classification tests can be used to assist in that choice. Furthermore, in classification decisions, we are interested in multiple alternatives for each individual, which eventually lead to qualitatively different goals, such as whether someone will be more valuable, from an institutional point of view, as a chemical engineer or as a computer scientist. Placement, by contrast, is concerned with alternative routes to a common goal, such as completion of a language course sequence (Anastasi, 1988).

DIAGNOSIS AND SCREENING

Diagnostic Tests

Diagnostic tests are designed to assess a person's problems, needs, expectations, frustrations, strengths, and weaknesses to help improve overall psychological well-being and performance. Test-based psychodiagnosis in educational and clinical fields may help in accurately identifying people with specific learning and adjustment problems.

Test data facilitates communication among clinicians by suggesting standard diagnostic labels that are helpful in prescribing appropriate treatments. Thus, tests provide part of the information needed to make diagnostic decisions about the environmental experiences, psychological services, treatments, programs, interventions, or learning activities most congenial to an examinee's needs and requirements. This information may help maximize that person's opportunity to attain institutional or personal goals.

Screening Tests

In addition, tests may be used for psychological *screening* purposes, identifying individuals who are sufficiently different from their peer group in either positive or negative ways that they require special attention. Screening tests are typically briefer than diagnostic tests and are given to many more people. The idea is to screen those who could benefit from further testing and a deeper evaluation.

INSTRUCTIONAL USE

Tests may serve important instructional and motivational purposes in a variety of educational settings, especially tests of scholastic achievement. Their many uses for instructional purposes include enhancing student motivation, evaluating learning outcomes, diagnosing strengths and weaknesses of participants in an instructional program, and grading and course evaluation.

Unfortunately, the very announcement of an upcoming test can have a positive or negative effect on students. A test perceived as a realistic challenge can arouse motivation and facilitate success behavior. Viewed more as a threat than a challenge, it can evoke anxiety and fear of failure. To some degree, standardized achievement and ability tests determine what high school students study (as well as what teachers teach!) and what material college applicants prepare for. Furthermore, tests may influence study strategies. Students often gear their studies to the type of test they expect to take. Even the format of the test (multiple choice vs. essay, for example) may determine to what degree students concentrate on specific course material or study in a more global or integrative manner. Prompt feedback provided by tests helps students and instructors set realistic academic goals and judge the effectiveness of instructional procedures.

PROGRAM EVALUATION

Tests can provide important information concerning the workings and impact of psychologically oriented programs. They can be used in program evaluation and in monitoring the progress of psychological or psychoeducational intervention programs. Tests are often used to help administrators plan individual or group educational or psychological intervention programs, including assignment to compensatory or special education programs. Evaluators examine the extent to which test scores (achievement, ability, personality) change as a result of such interventions or programs.

Typically, tests would be administered at the beginning and end of a program so that progress could be measured and a comparison made among various programs under study (Salvia & Ysseldyke, 1991). The use of tests generally assumes some kind of cost-benefit ratio in implementing a program, with benefits measured, among other ways, by student performance on tests. Costs may include program materials, salaries, staff, and time required to meet objectives. Tests may be instrumental in helping the evaluator choose among competing programs, the most effective being the one with the lowest cost per unit for each participant (Rossi & Freeman, 1985).

Classification of Psychological Tests

Psychological tests may be characterized in a variety ways, by their intended uses, content area, strategy for item construction, type of stimuli or responses, method of test administration, degree of procedural standardization, criteria for scoring or test interpretation, and so on. We will highlight some of the major criteria used to classify and differentiate among psychological tests.

ATTRIBUTES MEASURED BY TESTS

It is intuitively appealing to classify tests by content or by the attributes they measure—scholastic aptitude, mechanical ability, school readiness, personality traits, vocational interests, general interests, values, attitudes, and others. Broadly speaking, psychology is currently interested in two classes of human behavior: affective and cognitive (Thorndike et al., 1991). The distinction between the affective and the cognitive in relation to human performance coincides with the distinction between "typical" and "maximal" performance, respectively (Cronbach, 1990). In a maximal performance test, for example, intelligence, aptitude, and achievement tests, examinees are instructed to do their best and put forth maximum effort. By contrast, tests requiring typical performance, as in personality, interest, or attitude inventories, are designed to obtain a sample representative of a person's daily behavior. Thus, examinees are asked to report how they typically feel and what they typically do; they are usually not asked how they could or should feel.

Affective Behaviors

Affective responses cover a wide variety of personal reactions—attitudes, preferences, interests, personality traits, and values—that do not require a judgment of their correctness nor a comparison to some objective criterion (Nunnally, 1978). Instead, affective behaviors are generally perceived as reflecting true reactions or behaviors and are concerned with one's typical response in a given situation. For example, does one express a certain attitude toward the elimination of nuclear weapons; become depressed, anxious, or hostile when frustrated; act submissive or domineering in a group situation; prefer a salary raise over the opportunity to attend an advanced computer training course, and so on.

In measuring affect, emphasis is on obtaining as frank and as truthful a response as possible. The examinee's personal reaction to a stimulus is judged by its direction (positive vs. negative, in favor of or against, relaxed vs. anxious) and intensity (extremely high to extremely low), rather than by an external standard of accuracy. Among the various categories of behavior considered to be relevant to affective measures (Nunnally, 1978) are the following.

Personality tests are designed to gauge a unique and relatively stable constellation of traits, that is, dispositions to react in a way to a given situation. Most personality tests require affective responses more than judgments or cognitive responses.

Attitude scales are aimed at assessing a person's predisposition to think, feel, perceive, and behave in a particular way toward a referent or social object or category of objects. Whereas a personality trait is self-oriented, an attitude usually has an outside object as referent, and concerns the enduring structure of belief that predisposes an individual to behave in a certain manner toward the outside referent object.

Temperament scales are designed to assess conspicuous differences among individuals in energy level, prevailing mood, and general lifestyle.

Interest inventories measure an individual's choices as well as preferences and aversions toward present or future activities. Test takers typically indicate types of activities they like or dislike, such as their preferences for certain vocations in occupational interest inventories.

Character measures are concerned with assessing certain traits to which a definite social value has been attached, for example, bravery, honesty, resilience, loyalty, or sincerity. These social virtues are of prime interest to educational and religious institutions.

Adjustment scales measure behavior patterns instrumental in helping a person enjoy and lead a happy and productive life. Particular emphasis is placed on patterns that help one get along in one's immediate environment.

Cognitive Measures

In contrast to affective behaviors, cognitive behaviors or judgments attempt to measure individual abilities at a particular time (such as the number of digits that can be recalled when stressed, the number of vocabulary words that can be defined, the types of mechanical problems one can solve, and so on). Examinees are encouraged to give the test their maximum effort.

Among the major types of tests in this category are those for achievement, aptitude, and ability. Responses to cognitive test items are interpreted against a criterion of what is correct, ranging from perfectly true to not true at all (Nunnally, 1978). The objective rule by which a subject's response can be judged is either logical ("2 x 7 = ?"), empirical ("What U.S. holiday is celebrated on the 4th of July?"), semantic ("How do you say 'good morning' in Spanish?"), or normative ("What do you do if you find a lost and unsent stamped envelope on the street?").

Since maximal performance is assessed according to an objective or to an estimate of true criterion or rule, an examinee should be given the opportunity to give his or her best single response to the tasks presented. Furthermore, the ability continuum is typically thought to extend in a single direction from "little" or "no" ability to much of it (Thorndike, 1982). Figure 10 shows this progression in the cognitive domain from little ability to a lot of ability; in the affective domain the continuum is expressed as "like" versus "dislike" (or "warm" vs. "cold") and so on. Thus, cognitive measures given in schools assess what a learner knows and can do; affective measures assess how the learner feels.

FIGURE 10. Differences Between Cognitive and Affective Orientations

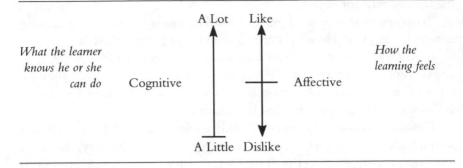

Aptitude Versus Achievement

Both aptitude and achievement tests concern judgment and therefore fall under the rubric of cognitive measures. Although the distinction between the two is by no means clear, a number of dimensions have been suggested for differentiating among them.

One important distinction concerns the proposed temporal direction in using the measure. Whereas in standardized achievement testing our interest is in measuring what has already been learned—with an emphasis on past learning—aptitude tests focus on future behavior. That is, achievement tests measure development and learning to date and aptitude tests predict capability of future learning.

A second important distinction suggested by Guttman (1965b) involves the degree of complexity of the mental operation an examinee must perform. Accordingly, in ability test items the examinee deduces an objective rule embodied in relationships among the test elements and applies it to another element to solve a given task (e.g., kitten:cat :: puppy:?). A correct response is evidence that the examinee has deduced and used the rule appropriately. By contrast, achievement test items assume that the examinee knows the rule, so the question under consideration is whether he or she is able to operate correctly according to that rule (e.g., "2 x 16 =?"; "Who was the third president of the United States?").

A third important distinction is that achievement tests are designed to measure the direct results of schooling or a course of instruction, with their content tied to a particular instructional framework. Aptitude tests, by contrast, assess cumulative achievement over time with the content generally not tied to specific instruction or schooling (Anastasi, 1988). Figure 11 illustrates the distinctions between achievement and aptitude tests.

FIGURE 11. Temporal Directions of Achievement Versus Aptitude

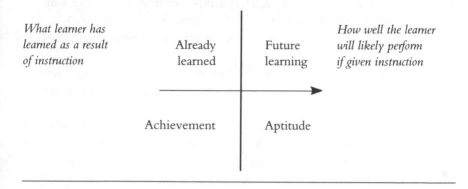

What learner has learned as a result of instruction — Already learned | Future learning — *How well the learner will likely perform if given instruction*

Achievement | Aptitude

STRATEGIES FOR CONSTRUCTING TESTS

The basic strategy underlying test construction may serve as yet another criterion for classification purposes. The major approaches are globally characterized as either *rational* or *empirical*, with the variations proposed by experts subsumed under these two broad categories. A rationally derived scale has items selected by a logical procedure. For instance, a test developer might select the item, "I usually voice my opinions in meetings" for a Dominance scale. In an empirically derived scale, items are selected on the basis of statistical relationships to what the scale is to measure. For example, alcoholics tend to answer true to "I like to cook" so that would be one item (hopefully among many) on a scale for Alcoholism. See Gough and Bradley in this volume for an excellent description of these two test construction methods.

STRUCTURE OF TEST ITEMS

Tests are often characterized in terms of how structured their items are. Both the test stimuli (questions, tasks, problems) and the responses vary along this dimension (Kleinmuntz, 1985). Since each item format has its own strengths and weaknesses, it must be carefully considered in view of the target behaviors to be measured and the intended clientele.

With respect to test stimuli presented to the examinee, some items are uniform and structured, intended to convey standard meanings to respondents ("What is the definition of a triangle?", "2 x 5 = ?"), while other items are less structured, more amorphous, and therefore subject to various interpretations by different people (My father...). Projective personality tests typically present examinees with relatively unstructured, ambiguous stimuli, such as inkblots, pictures, incomplete sentences, and association tasks. Instructions are minimal and the degree of freedom in responding is almost infinite.

By the same token, tests may also be differentiated by how much structure is required or expected in the responses. Some types of responses are relatively open while others are relatively closed. Open items require examinees to supply their own responses, with variable restrictions on scope or length. For example, completion items require examinees to finish an incomplete sentence with a word or short phrase that they supply. By contrast, closed items are highly structured response sets and typically require selection of the most appropriate responses from among a number of given alternatives: for example, "The 1988 Olympic games were held in: (a) New York (b) Munich (c) Seoul (d) Tokyo (e) Los Angeles."

Although there is no one-to-one relationship between the degree of structure of the item stimulus and that of the response, items with structured stimuli tend to elicit more structured responses, while those containing ambiguous stimuli tend to elicit ambiguous, unstructured responses.

STANDARDIZATION OF TEST ADMINISTRATION PROCEDURES

Psychological tests may also be differentiated by their degree of standardization. To be able to compare test scores across contexts and times of measurement, you need fixed observational and administrative procedures, equipment, materials, and scoring rules. These must be standardized, so that exactly the same procedures occur at different places and times. If, for example, 20 minutes are allowed to complete a vocabulary subtest in one group and 25 minutes are allowed for the same subtest in another group, the resulting scores are not comparable since the latter group has a definite advantage.

Standardized tests are typically constructed by experts, such as applied psychometricians, and are associated with a number of features, including uniform materials, uniform directions for administration and scoring, administration of the test to a representative sample of the target population for norming purposes, use of assembled norms (average performance of the target group) to interpret raw scores on the test, use of derived scores or measures such as T-scores or percentiles, and satisfactory psychometric properties of test scores.

It is important to realize that even uniform test stimuli, instructions, and scoring procedures do not necessarily guarantee that all the examinees will similarly perceive and interpret the test and test situation, or that the meanings attributed to various stimuli in the test context are fixed across examinees. Some experts such a Cole and Bruner (1971) have warned that factors in the test situation, including atmosphere and examiner-examinee rapport, may be differently interpreted according to an examinee's sociocultural group, and may affect motivation, cooperation, and performance. Furthermore, it should be remembered that even under the most rigid and controlled circumstances, no two test situations are really identical.

ADMINISTRATIVE CONDITIONS

Psychological tests may be distinguished by the mode in which they are administered: group or individual. A group test is designed to measure many examinees at once; an individual test is designed to measure one examinee at a time and is administered on a one-to-one basis (Salvia & Ysseldyke, 1991). Although it may seem that the difference between group and individual tests is mainly one of economy, the distinction is more subtle than it appears (Salvia & Ysseldyke, 1991).

Individual Tests

To begin with, individual test situations allow a considerable degree of freedom concerning type of test materials—for example, picture arrangement, block design, match arrangement, and so forth. Individual testing can accommodate more complex tasks and more subtle test directions. Also, testing on a one-to-one basis allows evaluation of both the final product and the dynamics of the testing process.

Furthermore, individual tests are usually without severe time constraints and consequently the examiner can adjust the pace, can rephrase or clarify questions, and can probe or reinforce responses to elicit maximal performance. Since the test is administered to one person at a time, it allows maximum interaction between examiner and examinee. Hence, an examiner can observe and gather important qualitative data bearing on the examinee's motivational dispositions, affective orientations, anxieties, and overall strategic approach to the task. The individual test situation, therefore, may enable the examiner to draw important conclusions about strengths and weaknesses in the examinee's performance and uncover possible reasons for poor or erratic test performance. A sample of an individually administered item from the *Embedded Figures Test* is shown in Figure 12.

FIGURE 12. Directions and Stimulus for Individual Adminstration Item From the *Embedded Figures Test*

Directions to Subject

The Subject should be seated on the side of the table next to the Examiner so that the Examiner can present the cards and observe the Subject's tracing easily. He then says:

"I am going to show you a series of colored designs. Each time I show you one, I want you to describe it in any way you wish. I will then show you a Simple Form which is contained in that larger design. You will then be given the larger design again, and your job will be to locate the Simple Form in it. Let us go through a practice trial to show you how it is done."

The Examiner shows the Practice Complex Figure (P–X) for 15 seconds. He then covers it by placing the Practice Simple Form (P) over it. After 10 seconds he says:

"I will now show you the colored design again and you are to find the Simple Form in it. As soon as you have found the Simple Form let me know, and start tracing the Simple Form with this stylus. When you are tracing, do not let the stylus touch the surface of the card."

The Examiner then exposes the Complex Figure again by removing the Simple Form and turning it over. The Examiner now starts timing from zero. As soon as the Subject says he sees the Simple Form, the Examiner notes the time; if the Subject traces the Form correctly, this time is recorded on the data sheet as the solution time for the Practice Item.

Subjects usually have no difficulty finding the Simple Form in the Practice Complex Figure. If a Subject does have trouble, the Examiner may expose the Simple Form again and show the Subject where it is located in the Complex Figure.

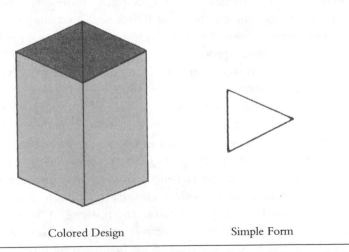

Colored Design   Simple Form

From *Manual for the Embedded Figures Tests* by H. A. Witkin, 1971, Palo Alto, CA: Consulting Psychologists Press. Copyright 1971 by Consulting Psychologists Press. Reprinted by permission.

Group Testing

Tests administered to groups are typically presented in booklet form and examinees respond by selecting from response options under timed testing conditions. Since the examiner needs to monitor the progress of several test takers simultaneously, it is not usually possible to rephrase, probe, or prompt responses. Also, qualitative information about the examinee's overall approach to testing is difficult to obtain. In addition, group tests typically require reading and writing capabilities beyond those of children or foreigners.

A major consideration in group testing is its efficiency when compared to individual testing, including the reduced cost, relatively shorter testing time, and the greater number of individuals who can be accommodated at the same time. The tradeoff is that a group test situation may sacrifice examiner-examinee rapport, personalized test conditions, and ability to gain qualitative information about the examinee. A sample of a group administered item from the *Group Embedded Figures Test* is shown in Figure 13.

Verbal Versus Nonverbal Tests

Test stimuli may be classified according to the language used for communicating the task. Verbal test stimuli are obviously verbal and require comprehension of oral or written instructions to understand what is required and to respond, such as with vocabulary or sentence completion items. These tasks are generally inappropriate for young children, illiterates, or new immigrants. Nonverbal tests, on the other hand, de-emphasize the role of verbal communication by using mainly such nonverbal material as mazes, puzzles, pictures, and so on. This category includes figures and numbers both to communicate the task and as test items. Some tests are purely verbal, others purely nonverbal, and many are a mix of both. A sample verbal versus nonverbal test item from the *Schaie-Thurston Adult Mental Abilities Test* is shown in Figure 14.

Method of Responding

Tests can also be classified according to the method of expressing the response. Some oral tests require just an oral response, no writing or manipulation of materials. Others, known as paper-and-pencil tests, require answers to questions printed in a test booklet. Performance tests require manipulation of test material while the tester observes the examinee's behavior—for example, building blocks according to design, arranging matches, arranging pictures in logical sequence, or arranging pegs on form-board.

FIGURE 13. Directions and Stimulus From the
Group Adminstration Booklet of the *Group Embedded Figures Test*

Instructions: This is a test of your ability to find a simple form when it is hidden within a complex pattern.

Here is a simple form which we have labeled "X":

This simple form, named "X," is hidden within the more complex figure below:

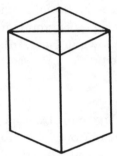

Try to find the simple form in the complex figure and trace it *in pencil* directly over the lines of the complex figure. It is the SAME SIZE, in the SAME PROPORTIONS, and FACES IN THE SAME DIRECTION within the complex figure as when it appeared alone.

From *Group Embedded Figures Test* by P. K. Oltman, E. Raskin, and H. Witkin, 1971, Palo Alto, CA: Consulting Psychologists Press. Copyright 1971 by Consulting Psychologists Press. Reprinted by permission.

EMPHASIS ON TIME

Tests differ in flexibility of their time limits. *Speed tests* are designed so that performance differs not because of the average difficulty of the items but because of how many can be completed in the time allowed. They typically contain relatively easy questions or tasks so that errors are not on account of difficulty but because of stringent time limits, with few examinees able to finish in the allotted time. In fact, it is sometimes not the content of responses that is of interest but the speed with which examinees perform. Clerical aptitude tests, for example, emphasize how rapidly examinees perform routine tasks.

FIGURE 14. Verbal and Non-verbal Test Items
From the *Schaie-Thurston Adult Mental Abilities Test* (STAMAT)

In each of the following exercises, circle the word that means the same as the first word. If you wish to change an answer, cross out your first answer. Then circle the new answer.

c. QUIET	Blue	Still	Tense	Watery
d. SAFE	Secure	Loyal	Passive	Young

Verbal test item from the STAMAT

In the row of objects below, circle EVERY object that is LIKE the first object. Do NOT circle the objects that are made backward.

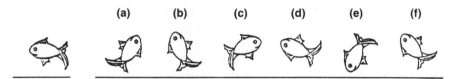

    (a)   (b)   (c)   (d)   (e)   (f)

Non-verbal test item from the STAMAT

From *Schaie-Thurston Adult Mental Abilities Test* by K. W. Schaie, 1985, Palo Alto, CA: Consulting Psychologists Press. Copyright 1985 by Consulting Psychologists Press. Reprinted by permission.

Power tests are less concerned with speed and more with assessing comprehension or understanding. The time limits on power tests are generous and sometimes unlimited—enough so that about 90 percent of the examinees feel they have ample opportunity to finish. Since most examinees are able to attempt every item, differences among individuals are assumed to be more a function of ability to deal with the complexity than with speed of response. In practice, however, even when the intention is to develop a power test, most ability and achievement tests tend to be a mixture of both speed and power.

OBJECTIVITY IN SCORING THE RESPONSES

Tests can also be characterized by the degree of objectivity in scoring. This has little to do with the question of objective content or fair scoring, but rather with the availability of predetermined criteria and standardized scoring procedures and their use in the process. The objective scoring criteria allow independent scorers to agree on the number of points to give a response, which minimizes subjective errors such as the personal attitudes, stereotypes, and biases of the examiner. A subjective test may have predetermined scoring criteria, but they are difficult to apply and involve judgment; hence, different examiners may not assign the same scores to a given response.

Multiple choice tests are said to be objective because the scoring key is set in advance and should produce uniform scores if the test is scored correctly. By contrast, essay tests and some projective measures are notorious for their lack of scoring objectivity; they have a history of being scored differently by various people or differently by the same scorer on different occasions.

A truly objective test is one that has no scorer variance (other than clerical). There would always be perfect agreement between different scorers if the test is objective. The *Wechsler Intelligence Scales* are not objective tests because there is not perfect agreement among scorers (Wechsler, 1974). All multiple-choice questions are completely objective.

Major Criticisms of Psychological Testing

Despite the enormous advances made in psychological testing since the turn of the century, their phenomenal growth in number, variety, and functions and increased usage in decision making have brought them under scrutiny and attack. Several factors may be responsible. On one hand, misapplication and general misuse of test results have raised questions. On the other hand, misconceptions about tests and the testing process by laypeople and professionals may have led to some criticisms and actions which in retrospect may seem as inappropriate or unjust (Cronbach, 1990). Indeed, the recent controversies surrounding ability, personality, and vocational tests recall debates from the beginnings of modern testing, with the same misconceptions and the same value conflicts continually resurfacing (Cronbach, 1990; Jensen, 1980).

We will briefly survey some of the dominant, recurring criticisms of psychological tests, though not necessarily in their order of importance.

Overuse of Psychological Tests in Applied Settings

Psychological testing, it is claimed, is conducted too frequently and often without sufficient justification. Students are required to take a bewildering array of aptitude, achievement, occupational, and personality tests throughout the school years, when time might be spent more usefully on other activities. Furthermore, testing is often carried out without any clear purpose in mind or where better measures of the criteria of interest are easily available.

A case in point would be a school psychologist who administers scholastic aptitude tests to eighth-grade students to predict their academic performance in ninth grade, despite having their cumulative grade point averages through grade eight to refer to.

INVASION OF PRIVACY

Psychological tests are often claimed to be an unwarranted invasion of privacy because they may be used to delve into personal matters of illegitimate concern to the test user. In the past, tests were administered with insufficient regard for such ethical principles as obtaining informed consent or explaining the purpose of testing, the nature of the test items, and how the test data will be interpreted or used. In tests used for selection or placement, examinees have sometimes been required to divulge personal, often intimate information (e.g., hostile feelings, physical symptoms, anxieties, etc.) deemed to be irrelevant to such performance criterion as success on the job. Also, ethical concerns have been raised surrounding psychological tests used in basic research. These involve the invasion of privacy, deceptive ploys (such as informing subjects that the maze test they are taking is an ability test when it in fact measures impulsiveness), and causing psychological harm through aversive test instructions (e.g., creating a highly competitive or threatening test environment to test its effects on performance) or potentially harmful test content. Thus, society's interest in knowledge is often in conflict with an individual's right to privacy (Sax, 1989).

For further information about test ethics, see Eyde in this volume and the ethical standards of the American Psychological Association (1989) and the American Association of Counseling and Development (1988), the *Standards for Educational and Psychological Testing* (American Educational Research Association, American Psychological Association, and National Council on Measurement in Education, 1985) and *Guidelines for Computer-based Tests and Interpretations* (Committee on Professional Standards and Committee on Psychological Tests and Assessments, 1986).

TEST ANXIETY

Psychological tests, particularly maximal performance tests, tend to evoke anxiety. Although what is considered test anxiety varies, there is general agreement that both emotional arousal and cognitive concerns are part of it (Morris, Davis, & Hutchings, 1981). Although small amounts of test anxiety may actually have a facilitating effect, higher levels may impede performance, especially when the task requires abstract and flexible thinking.

The worry component of anxiety has repeatedly been found to be more closely related to academic performance than the emotionality component (Zeidner, Klingman, & Papko, 1988). This supports the notion that in situations where the individual will be judged, highly test-anxious individuals direct their attention away from the task at hand to self-related cognitions, which hinder their performance. To the extent that anxiety is inversely associated with test performance, some examinees perform below their indicated ability, so that if anxiety confounds measurement of ability, it is difficult to obtain a valid picture of true performance level.

CULTURAL BIAS

Bias has become a key villain in the drama surrounding the use of psychological tests (Anastasi, 1988; Jensen, 1980). One of the most prevalent and serious criticisms raised by critics against conventional psychometric testing is that standardized tests are biased in content, procedure, and use in relation to minority groups in the population. Therefore, it is claimed that traditional tests hold questionable validity for assessing the cognitive performance of minority groups or predicting their criterion performance.

More specifically, it has been contended that the sizable, repeatedly observed group differences in favor of majority group examinees in aptitude and achievement test performance are partly due to systematic bias in test content and procedures. Standardized ability tests are said to be constructed by psychologists from middle class majority background who sample test items from western middle–class culture and assume that minority examinees are conversant with the rules of the testing game (answering speed-test items quickly, trying to do one's best with power tests, and in general taking on a competitive attitude). Those non–middle-class students who are said to have had minimal exposure to western middle-class culture, a slow behavioral tempo, poor test motivation, situational anxiety, and low perceived self-efficacy (Zeidner, 1988) may find themselves at a disadvantage in a conventional test situation, with serious negative effects on their ability scores. Psychological measurement literature over the past few years reflects research on an array of situational variables in standardized test administration and content, such as time limits, test attitudes, examiner-examinee rapport, motivation, and anxiety, thought to be detrimental to the test performance of disadvantaged minority groups (Block & Dworkin, 1976). This research finds that the relatively low mean test scores of disadvantaged examinees may reflect negative affect toward the test and test situation no less than actual level of academic ability.

There has also been mounting concern with the fairness of selection tests used among groups that differ in a major way from the norm group on which they were standardized. Moreover, it has also been claimed that standardized tests are predictors of minority group criterion performance, leading to unfair social consequences, inappropriate labeling and classification, and adverse impact for cultural minority groups. This is clearly attested in the severe overrepresentation of disadvantaged children in special education programs and low status tracks.

Interestingly enough, recent reviews of the test bias literature examining properly constructed standardized aptitude tests against various internal and external test bias criteria generally fail to support the cultural bias hypothesis (Zeidner, 1988). The literature also shows a great deal of evidence that for well-constructed tests minority group performance is predicted to be higher than they actually perform in the situation (see Hartigan & Wigdor, 1989). This depends on whether the prediction is based on the performance of the majority group for selecting applicants.

ADDITIONAL ARGUMENTS

In addition to the arguments presented above, which are by no means exhaustive, critics also contended that:

- Standardized multiple-choice test items are often ambiguous or vague and have more than one justifiable answer

- Tests reward students with partial knowledge, penalize bright and creative examinees, and are insensitive to atypical but defensible responses

- Tests measure only limited and superficial aspects of behavior and are unable to measure truly important traits and criteria. Thus, test users make decisions based on relatively unimportant and superficial criteria

- Test usage leads to undemocratic attitudes, since many believe that psychological measurements are infallible and test performance can't be modified. Thus, teachers and parents regard aptitude scores as accurate, unmodifiable measures and treat children according to tested expectation levels, disregarding other evidence

In using tests one should try to remember that psychological tests are not without problems, pitfalls, and hazards. Our present state of practice leaves much to be desired; modern testing is vulnerable to a wide array of criticisms.

To Test or Not to Test

Properly constructed psychological tests are highly cost-effective and generally produce more objective and reliable information than many alternatives. It stands to reason that where test situations can be reliably constructed, administered, and scored—all else being equal—tests should be given priority over other data-gathering techniques since they tend to yield more precise results. However, psychological tests should never be administered indiscriminately or routinely; there should always be underlying justification for their use. Sometimes, it may be more efficient and even wiser not to use a psychological test than to use one without purpose.

Under what conditions should we think twice before administering a test? Some useful guidelines appear below for helping one decide when to test or not.

First, it is important to remember that testing, much as any social program or transaction, grows out of a specific demand or explicitly stated need for certain information (Rossi & Freeman, 1985). Consequently, it makes no sense to administer a test without a clear and specific purpose in mind. When available information indicates that all is well (employees, students, soldiers, etc. are doing just fine and are making normal progress), then there would be no need for administering tests. Why give a scholastic aptitude test to sixth graders if aptitude scores are not used in their school district for any practical purpose, such as for tracking, streaming, and class formation? One can always try to justify the use of a test retrospectively, but that hardly justifies testing in the first place.

Second, before using a test for a particular purpose in a given population, make sure that the test is not only appropriate for the testing goals, but also suitable for the individuals you want to test. In addition, the test should be readily administered and scored and have adequate psychometric properties considering the intended uses and populations. For example, it would make little sense to use a test when the norms are outdated or inappropriate for the target group, when the test has a reading level that is too difficult for the age testing group, or when the test adds little to the prediction of a given criterion.

Third, one can hardly justify the use of tests to gather readily available information. When information essential for research or practical purposes already exists and is accessible (or can be reconstructed or retrieved within reasonable time and budget constraints), administering tests would be futile and not cost-effective. The information may be available in public records or documents, official statistics, school files, college admission office forms, or company computer files. For instance, assuming we need information about the scholastic aptitude of a student sample as part of a research study comparing the coping resources of bright and less bright students, if scores from a recent standardized aptitude test are on record and available, it would hardly make sense to administer an additional test. One must always ask whether the expenditure of resources warrants testing in any given situation.

Fourth, testing may not be a reasonable or viable alternative in gathering data to assess aspects of human behavior. One should remember that a variety of human behaviors and attributes are not readily reduced to standardized test tasks or items, but are more effectively analyzed as real life behaviors. There may be no adequate test substitutes for observations in natural settings for assessing the sociability level of an infant, a student's classroom motivation, a camp counselor's leadership ability, the degree of employee cooperation with peers or management, a child's aggressiveness during play, and so on.

Fifth, giving a test to collect data or information can be futile when the implications, practical guidelines, or decisions that emanate from test results and interpretation cannot be implemented or carried out in the manner needed. It makes no sense for a school counselor or psychologist to administer a diagnostic test in basic mathematic skills designed to extract suggestions for mathematic remediation if the school soliciting the test can not make provisions for remedial math or special treatments indicated by the test results.

In sum, when used intelligently and knowledgeably, psychological and educational tests can have great benefit for understanding and helping people. Tests are a tool, and like any tool, they have power when used appropriately and can be harmful when used or interpreted inappropriately.

We hope that this chapter and subsequent chapters help teach appropriate test use and a perspective of what tests can and cannot do.

References

American Association for Counseling and Development. (1988). *Ethical standards*. Washington, DC: Author.

American Educational Research Association, American Psychological Association, and National Council on Measurement in Education. (1985). *Standards for educational and psychological testing*. Washington, DC: American Psychological Association.

American Psychological Association. (1990). Ethical principles of psychologists (Amended June 2, 1989). *American Psychologist, 45*, 390–395.

Anastasi, A. (1988). *Psychological testing* (6th ed.). New York: Macmillan.

Anastasi, A. (1985). Some emerging trends in psychological measurement: A fifty-year perspective. *Applied Psychological Measurement, 9*, 121–138.

Berk, R. A. (1980). *Criterion-referenced measurement: The state of the art*. Baltimore: John Hopkins Press.

Block, N. J., & Dworkin, G. (1976). IQ, heritability, and inequality. In N. J. Block & G. Dworkin (Eds.), *The IQ controversy* (pp. 410–540). New York: Pantheon Books.

Canter, D. (Ed.).(1985). *Facet theory: Approaches to social research*. New York: Springer-Verlag.

Cole, M., & Bruner, J. S. (1971). Cultural differences and inferences about psychological processes. *American Psychologist, 26*, 867–876.

Committee on Professional Standards and Committee on Psychological Tests and Assessments. (1986). *Guidelines for computer-based tests and interpretations* . Washington, DC: American Psychological Association.

Coombs, C. H., Dawes, R. M., & Tversky, A. (1970). *Mathematical psychology: An elementary introduction*. Englewood Cliffs, NJ: Prentice-Hall.

Crocker, L., & Algina, J. (1986). *Introduction to classical and modern test theory*. New York: Holt, Rinehart & Winston.

Cronbach, L. J. (1990). *Essentials of psychological testing* (5th ed.). New York: HarperCollins.

Cronbach, L. J., & Gleser, G. C. (1965). *Psychological tests and personnel decisions* (2nd ed.). Urbana, IL: University of Chicago Press.

Green, B. (1981). A primer of testing. *American Psychologist, 36*, 1000–1011.

Guttman, L. (1965a). The structure of interrelations among intelligence tests. In *Proceedings of the 1964 Invitational Conference on Testing Problems*. Princeton, NJ: Educational Testing Service.

Guttman, L. (1965b). A faceted definition of intelligence. In R. Eiferman (Ed.), *Studies in psychology: Scripta hierosolymitana* (Vol. 14, pp. 166–81). Jerusalem: Hebrew University Press.

Hartigan, J. A., & Wigdor, A. K. (1989). *Fairness in employment testing: Validity generalization, minority issues and the General Aptitude Test Battery*. Washington, DC: National Academy Press.

Jensen, A. (1980). *Bias in mental testing*. New York: Free Press.

Kerlinger, F. N. (1986). *Foundations of behavioral research* (3rd ed.). New York: Holt, Rinehart, & Winston.

Kleinmuntz, B. (1985). *Personality and psychological assessment*. Malabar, FL: Krieger Publishing.

Mehrens, W. A., & Lehmann, I. J. (1984). *Measurement and evaluation in education and psychology* (3rd ed.). New York: Holt, Rinehart, & Winston.

Morris, L. W, Davis, M. A, & Hutchings, C. H. (1981). Cognitive and emotional components of anxiety: Literature review and a revised Worry-Emotionality Scale. *Journal of Educational Psychology, 73,* 541–555.

Nevill, D. D., & Super, D. E. (1989). *The values scale: Theory, applications, and research.* Palo Alto, CA: Consulting Psychologists Press.

Newland, T. E. (1973). Assumptions underlying psychological testing. *Journal of School Psychology, 11,* 316–322.

Nitko, A. J. (1983). *Educational tests and measurement: An introduction.* New York: Harcourt, Brace, Jovanovich.

Nunnally, J. C. (1978). *Psychometric theory* (2nd ed.). New York: McGraw-Hill.

Rossi, P. H., & Freeman, H. E. (1985). *Evaluation: A systematic approach* (3rd ed.). London: Sage.

Salvia, J., & Ysseldyke, J. E. (1991). *Assessment in special and remedial education* (5th ed.). Boston: Houghton Mifflin.

Sax, G. (1989). *Principles of educational and psychological measurement and evaluation.* Belmont, CA: Wadsworth.

Spielberger, C. D., Gonzales, H. P., Taylor, C. J., Algaze, B., & Anton, W. D. (1978). Examination stress and test anxiety. In C. D. Spielberger & I. G. Sarason (Eds.), *Stress and anxiety* (Vol. 5, pp. 167-191). New York: Wiley.

Sternberg, R. J. (1985). *Beyond IQ: A triarchic theory of human intelligence.* New York: Cambridge University Press.

Stevens, S. (1946). On the theory of scales of measurement. *Science, 103,* 677–680.

Thorndike, R. L. (1982). *Applied psychometrics.* Boston: Houghton Mifflin.

Thorndike, R. M., Cunningham, G. K., Thorndike, R. L., & Hagen, E. P. (1991). *Measurement and evaluation in psychology and education* (5th ed.). New York: Macmillan.

Torgerson, W. S. (1956). *Theory and methods of scaling.* New York: Wiley.

Wechsler, D. (1974). *Manual for the Wechsler Intelligence Scale for Children— Revised.* New York: Psychological Corporation.

Zeidner, M. (1988). Sociocultural differences in examinees' attitudes towards scholastic ability exams. *Journal of Educational Measurement, 2*5, 67–76.

Zeidner, M., Klingman, A., & Papko, O. (1988). Enhancing students' test coping skills: Report of a psychological health education program. *Journal of Educational Psychology, 19,* 114–124.

CHAPTER 2

TEST EVALUATION AND QUALITY

Allen L. Hammer

Introduction

The purpose of this chapter is to suggest a basis for evaluating the quality of a psychological or educational test. First, however, let's consider what is meant by *quality*. Garvin (1987) gives eight definitions of the term, ranging from philosophical ("It can't be defined, but I'll know it when I see it") to standards-based, which refers to conformance to predetermined technical specifications. In fact, evaluating a psychological or educational test requires the simultaneous use of two definitions of quality: a standards-based definition and a user-based definition in which one considers whether the test is right for the particular problem. A set of technical standards has been published against which any test can be evaluated, but they are relevant only when applied to the use of a test in a given situation for a specific purpose. The standards themselves recognize this limitation and explicitly discuss the responsibilities of both test users and developers.

The material in this chapter is organized around three features of psychological and educational tests. In the first section, the meaning of the construct measured by the test is addressed. The second section deals with the psychometric properties of tests, their reliability and validity. The third section addresses practical issues in testing, such as administration and scoring. The final section describes sources of information about tests that are useful

TABLE 1. Evaluating the Quality of a Psychological or Educational Test

---

Identify the construct you wish to measure.

What are your expectations about the construct?
What are the authors' definitions of the construct?

Search for evidence that a particular test measures the construct.

How consistent are the scores?
What do the scores mean?

Evaluate the practical features of the instrument.

Are the administrative and scoring procedures clear?
What are the costs and benefits of testing or not testing?

Consult additional sources about the instrument.

How complete is the test manual?
What do the reviews and published research indicate about the
    quality of the instrument?

---

to consult when evaluating a test. Table 1 gives a summary of the test evaluation process.

DEFINITION OF TERMS

Testing is used in a generic sense in this chapter to mean the measurement of any psychological or educational construct, such as dominance, verbal aptitude, problem-solving ability, or career interests. *Measurement* implies a summation or accrual of observations, which are usually the responses of the test takers to written items, but it could also be the responses of raters based on their observations. In this context, responses to single items, although perhaps interesting, do not constitute testing. Rather, the focus is on a score derived from a number of responses: Test scores are summaries of statements that clients have made about themselves or about their behavior (Tinsley & Bradley, 1986).

Tyler (1984) refers to test scores as clues to follow and combine with clues from other sources in order to understand the client. Even after evaluating a test to determine what the scores mean and how much they can be trusted, the test user still has only a *hypothesis* of what that score indicates about the client (Anastasi, 1988). As Messick (1989) points out in discussing the psychometric issues of testing, "Tests do not have reliabilities and validities, only test responses do." Focusing on responses helps remind users that test scores represent the responses of a single person to a given set of items in a particular context within a circumscribed time frame. With so many variables influencing the meaning of a score, it is easy to see what the limits of measurement might be.

Another basic term in this chapter is *construct,* which refers to the "thing" we are measuring. A construct is a word or label for an abstract human attribute. We think of attributes as being present in people in different amounts or degrees. For example, we may say that a person has more or less verbal ability. Constructs may also represent qualitative distinctions between people, such as saying that one person prefers introversion over extraversion.

Test user refers to the professionals who administer and interpret the test—counselors, psychologists, educators, speech pathologists, and others. Using the test involves more than just administering and scoring it. The essence of the testing process is in drawing inferences about the meaning of the test scores for an individual. These inferences lead to a description, prediction, or decision about, or by, a person. The terms *client, respondent,* and *examinee* are used interchangeably to refer to test takers, who could be students, people in counseling, job applicants, and many others.

Further explanation of the meaning of *standards* is also in order. Published standards exist in the area of testing, with criteria directed at the kind of evidence test developers must collect and present to enable test users to exercise professional judgment about how appropriate a test is for its intended purpose. Evaluating the quality of a test in relation to these standards involves asking questions about what the test scores mean and then searching for evidence (which is rarely either all positive or all negative) to answer those questions. Applying the standards requires test users to judge whether or not the inferences that they wish to draw from the scores are supported by evidence. Test users must also decide whether the standards are relevant and appropriate to the purpose of testing, given the clients to be tested and the context in which testing will be done.

The Meaning of the Construct

Evaluating the quality of a test requires first judging the meaning and relevance of the construct it measures and then the meaning of the scores that measure that construct. Separating these two judgments (Loevinger, 1957) makes it clear that the test score itself is *not* the construct, but rather an approximation of it, or, more precisely, an approximation of the amount of the construct the respondent possesses. This distinction between the construct and the score that represents it lies at the heart of measurement. No score is a perfect representation; it always misses the mark to some degree. In other words, test evaluation poses two questions—(a) What does the construct mean, and (b) to what extent does the test score succeed in measuring the construct (Hogan & Nicholson, 1988). In addition, these questions must be answered from the perspective of how the scores will be used, with whom, and in what setting.

Part of understanding what a construct means is in specifying how the test user expects the construct to behave. More precisely, how do people who have different amounts, levels, or degrees of the attributes named by the construct behave? For example, assume that you are interested in the construct of "frustration tolerance," which you expect people to have in varying degrees. These expectations are formed by your own experience, by explicit or implicit theories of the construct, by definitions of the construct in everyday language, as well as by common sense (Nunnally, 1978).

The differences are illustrated by the example of people driving in rush hour traffic: One person might be extremely frustrated, while another remains calm. To measure frustration tolerance, you could ride with each member of your sample in various traffic conditions and observe them in other situations where you might expect to see differences. Or, you could administer a paper-and-pencil test of frustration tolerance with the expectation that the responses of the two people, and ultimately, their scores on the test, would be different. The point is that with this variable, as with any other, your evaluation of the test is determined in part by your expectations about the concept or behaviors that are being measured.

The first step in evaluating a test, therefore, is to clarify as explicitly as possible the construct you are interested in and how you expect it to manifest itself in different people in different situations. You must then determine if your definition and understanding of the construct matches the test developer's. If you know little about the construct, you should do some preliminary research before evaluating the test.

What you ask yourself about the construct should be guided by how you intend to use the scores and what you want to be able to say to, or about, the individuals or groups being tested. You need to know how the construct might manifest itself in the test takers' responses and in the context in which they will be tested. Table 2 contains some general questions to ask about the construct. The list is not exhaustive, since particular questions may arise only in relation to specific constructs.

TABLE 2. Questions to Ask About a Construct

Is the construct broadly or narrowly defined?

What kinds of responses would be evidence for the construct?

How would you expect individuals with different levels of the construct to behave over time?

What other concepts would you expect the construct to be related to?

What concepts would you expect the construct not to be related to?

Would you expect age or sex differences to be relevant to the construct?

How will the context or situation in which the test is administered affect the scores?

How can the scores be combined with other information about the person?

Are the explicit and implicit definitions of the construct congruent?

To illustrate, assume you are interested in testing the ability of a group of high school students to solve mathematical problems. Start by asking yourself questions about what kind of items you think would measure mathematical ability and how you expect this ability to vary with the kinds of problems selected. You might also expect this ability to be fairly stable over a short time period under similar conditions, that it might be related to general intelligence but not to, say, extraversion, and that there might be age differences in performance, especially on problems with time limits. You may also remember having read that female high school students tend to be more anxious about math, which may lower their scores on an ability test. If your preliminary research on high school students' mathematical ability shows that these expectations are reasonable, then the answers to the questions you posed can help you evaluate a test that claims to measure mathematical problem-solving ability.

After answering the questions you've asked yourself and perhaps reading about the construct, the next step is to compare your understanding of the construct to the author's. To do this, you need the documentation for the test.

DEFINITIONS OF THE CONSTRUCT IN THE TEST MANUAL

Ask yourself whether the definition stated in the manual is broader or narrower than you expected and how it will affect your interpretion of the scores. Note that there are two kinds of definitions to consider: those that are explicitly stated in the test manual and those that are implicit. Implicit definitions must be inferred from items selected by the authors to measure the construct, from the scale names, from the way the items are scored, and from the type of evidence selected to support the scores as a measure of the construct. You need to determine whether or not the explicit and implicit definitions are congruent with each other, with your own understanding of the construct, and with how you want to use the scores. For example, although one version of the *Omnibus Personality Inventory* (Heist, McConnell, Webster, & Yonge, 1968) has a scale labeled Religious Orientation, an examination of the items and scoring procedures reveals that a high score indicates skepticism and rejection of orthodoxy.

STATED PURPOSE OF THE TEST IN THE TEST MANUAL

Related to the definition of the construct is the stated purpose of the test. In evaluating the quality of a test, consider what claims are made for its purposes and uses. A distinction should be made between uses that are supported by evidence and those that are only potential. Listing potential uses is acceptable as long as they are identified with appropriate cautions included. For instance, a test of perceived psychological stress may have been designed primarily as a research instrument, and all of the data reported in the manual are for that specific use. Applications of the scores may have clear clinical utility, however, and this could be discussed if accompanied by a caution that data on the interpretation of scores in clinical contexts is not available. Even for supportable uses, problems that may result from improper use of the test or its scores should also be mentioned in the manual.

SUMMARY

The first step in evaluating a test is to make your expectations about the construct that you wish to measure explicit. You should ask yourself a number of questions designed to lead to a precise set of expectations. For example, do you see the construct as broad or narrow, and how do you expect people with different levels of the construct to behave under different conditions or at different times? The test manual should clearly state the definition of the construct and delineate the test's purposes. Mention of how the test scores can be misused should also be made.

Psychometric Properties of Tests

The second feature to consider when evaluating test quality is its *psychometric properties*. This requires searching for evidence to support the claim that the test is indeed a measure of the construct. To do this you must determine the meaning of the scores; their meaning is evidence for the *validity* of the instrument. Before evaluating validity, though, you must first determine whether or not the scores from the test are repeatable, which is the issue of *reliability*. In other words, to decide whether a score is valid (what it means, and whether it is relevant to your purpose), you must know whether the test can consistently produce that score.

RELIABILITY

It is difficult, if not impossible, to pin down the meaning of a person's score when it changes dramatically and unexpectedly with each testing. This is also the case when there are great differences between the scores of individuals assumed to be the same on the construct. For this reason reliability is said to be a necessary, but not a sufficient condition for, validity. Reliability is necessary because inconsistent scores cannot have meaning, but it is insufficient because an instrument can measure something consistently yet still yield meaningless results. Consider a test that claims to measure perceived stress. It consists of 50 items, each asking for the respondent's view of how much stress he or she generally experiences. If the items are all similar, the stress score could be consistent, yet tell you little or nothing about the sources of stress; therefore, the test would be meaningless or invalid for your purpose. Reliability, then, is the extent to which scores on the test are repeatable.

One way to think about reliability is to ask what factors could cause variations among test scores—that is, differences in the scores of the same person over time, or between two different people at the same time (Aiken, 1985). There are two primary hypotheses about this. One is that the two people really do have different levels of the attribute named by the construct. If it is one person's scores that fluctuate, this hypothesis states that he or she really does exhibit variable levels of the construct at different times. If this is so, then the test may have accurately captured this true difference, leading to the conclusion that one person has more (or less) knowledge, achievement, dominance, or whatever the construct is, than another person does. (Note that it is impossible to ever know how much of a construct a person has; this is always an inference based on some observable behavior—in this case, the test score.)

A second hypothesis for the difference in test scores is that the individuals are not really different, but that errors in measuring the construct make them appear different. These measurement errors might be inherent in the test, or they may be a result of factors in the testing process. For example, two individuals applying for a job as a drill press operator each have the same level of physical ability required to perform the job successfully and are required to take an ability test as part of the selection process. Although the test measures physical ability, the instructions for the test are written, so if one applicant has a reading disability, he or she will score lower on the test. The "error" in this case is that the test measures reading ability in addition to physical ability and test scores will differ accordingly.

The measurement problem is that it is *not* possible to determine which of these two hypotheses is more plausible. Any score obtained from a test will accurately reflect real differences between individuals to some degree, but it will also mask these differences (or similarities) because an error has affected the score. *All* measurement has a degree of associated uncertainty because it is impossible to know for sure the "real" amount of the construct a person has. What is the cause of this uncertainty?

Sources of Error

Some uncertainty results from *systematic* error that has intruded into the testing process. For example, if the test is scored by computer, a programming error could result in one point being consistently added to the scores of males or some other group. Although this type of error is important for practical reasons, once it has been identified, its effect on the score can be determined or corrected. Of more interest are the nonsystematic, or *random,* sources of error.

Innumerable factors can influence an individual's test score. Error can result from characteristics of the person, the situation, or the test itself. Characteristics of the individual that may affect test scores include mood, emotional state, motivation, intelligence, personality, and understanding of the purpose of testing. Situational factors include explicit or implicit demands on the test taker to score a certain way, or distractions in the environment. Test-related factors include the clarity of the items, nonsystematic scoring errors, and the readability of the instructions.

The error caused by these factors is referred to as *random* because it is unpredictable. We cannot know the degree to which these variables influence an individual's responses to the given items on a given day. All we know is that each factor may affect individuals differently and that, therefore, some scores will be overestimated relative to the "true" score, and others will be underestimated. The amount of over- or underestimation is the *error;* the more random error present in the test score, the less consistent it is. The important question is whether the size of this error can be estimated so that we know to what extent the scores are consistent. Fortunately, this is possible. For groups, the estimate is the *reliability coefficient;* for individuals, it is the standard error of measurement. Before describing these estimates of error, however, we need to define the concept of true score introduced above.

True Score

In classical measurement theory, the relationship between true scores and observed (or obtained) scores is expressed in the following equation,

$$\text{Observed score} = \text{true score} + \text{error}$$

The *observed score* is the actual score obtained from the test. The *true score* is a hypothetical entity—the theoretical amount of the trait, attribute, or construct that we expect a person to have. If we could create a test composed of all possible items that measured the construct, the person's score on this hypothetical test would be his or her *true score* (Nunnally, 1978). But this is not possible for two reasons. First, someone could always write a slightly different item to measure the construct. Second, it implies that an exact definition of the construct exists. If we could decide on a set of items to measure the construct, however, and test a person an infinite number of times, his or her average score from the infinite tests would be the true score. This is so because averaging across infinity would average out the random error of single tests.

Remember that we are concerned with the consistency of scores and that all we have to work with is the observed score, which is a function of the true score and the errors of measurement. If we had a way to determine the person's true score there would be no problem because we would know that any differences between the scores of two people, or between the score of the same person at different times, would be real differences. But since it is impossible either to administer a test to one person an infinite number of times or to test using all items that measure the construct, a practical way had to be found to estimate error and determine the consistency of the observed score. One solution is to test a group of people and use the means and standard deviations of the group to derive reliability estimates.

Types of Reliability

CONSISTENCY OVER TIME. Consider an aptitude test administered twice to a group of students, one month apart. Theoretically, it should be possible to rank a group of students on their true aptitude. Aptitude theories, as well as common sense, would lead us to expect that neither an individual's rank nor test score would change dramatically in a month. If the test used to measure aptitude is reliable, we would expect the score to be *repeatable* over a period of time. Thus, a student whose score places her at the top of the class by a wide margin at the beginning of the month should score near the top at the end of the month, other things being equal.

The repeatability of test scores over time is called *test-retest reliability*. It is an estimate of how the score is affected by errors that may result from the passage of time. These may include changes in the client's mood that affect response to the items, or different testing conditions. The greater the test-retest reliability, the more stable or repeatable the scores and the less affected by errors over time. In some circumstances we would expect test-retest reliability to be low. For instance, in evaluating a test designed to measure state anxiety (i.e., anxiety related to a particular situation), you would expect a score from before final exams to differ from one taken afterwards. If the test manual reported a high degree of stability across two conditions presumed to elicit very different degrees of anxiety, then you would rightly question its validity. This would also apply to a test of the ability to make good decisions, an attribute that could be expected to mature or develop. You might expect moderate reliabilities if you were measuring such a developmental variable.

Very high test-retest reliability over a long time period on a developmental variable would suggest (as one hypothesis) that the test was insufficiently sensitive to the developmental changes. Another possible hypothesis is that the variable doesn't change as much as expected. Thus, as with other evidence related to the nature and interpretability of scores, your evaluation of the test-retest reliability coefficients depends on your understanding of the construct you want to measure and how you expect it to behave over time.

In practice, there are a number of ways to get actual estimates of test-retest reliability. The most common is to correlate all the test takers' scores from the first test with all of their scores from the second test; the greater the correlation coefficient, the more reliable the scores. For some tests, such as those that categorize individuals or measure whether or not they have achieved a particular level of the attribute (e.g., achievement mastery tests), an estimate of test-retest reliability can be obtained by comparing the percentage of people who are categorized in the same way at two different times.

INTERNAL CONSISTENCY. Another kind of reliability provides an estimate of how consistent the responses are across the different items of the test. This is an estimate of the test's internal consistency, that is, to what extent the items that comprise the score seem to be measuring the same thing, referred to as *item homogeneity*. In an instrument designed to measure empathy, for example, a low estimate of internal consistency reliability might lead you to conclude that some of the empathy items are really measuring another construct, such as extraversion, that is not necessarily associated with empathy. The same person might score high on empathy, but low on extraversion, which means that the internal consistency of a score compiled by adding the empathy-item responses to those of the extraversion items would probably be low. While it may seem obvious that items that measure different constructs should not be added together into one score if we were interested in high internal consistency, it is not always easy to tell exactly which construct an item is measuring.

High internal consistency is expected for tests designed to tap relatively narrow domains. For example, higher item homogeneity might be expected on a test of simple addition skills than on a test of mathematical problem solving (Messick, 1989, p. 38), since the latter may require both higher level reasoning and higher levels of reading ability. On the other hand, a very high internal consistency coefficient might signal trouble on a test claiming to measure a broad and complex domain. Such a test should be composed of items that measure different facets of that domain.

Internal consistency reliability is usually expressed as a correlation coefficient computed by correlating one subset of items with another subset. For example, a *split-half reliability coefficient* is calculated by randomly selecting half of the items and correlating the responses with those in the remaining half. Another method is to correlate each item with all of the remaining items. Because this yields as many correlations as there are items, the results are often reported as the median or average of all correlations. The most commonly used manner of estimating internal consistency, however, is with *coefficient alpha*. Alpha is, in effect, the average of all of the correlations among all of the items. For example, suppose you have written five items that you want to use to measure depression. Three of the items correlate about .70 with each other, while the other two correlate .05 with the first three and with each other. The average correlation among these five items will be low compared to another test of depression for which all five items correlated about .70 with each other. We would say that the first test has lower internal consistency than the second. In fact, in this situation, the two maverick items in the first test may actually be measuring constructs other than depression.

So, the higher the correlation among the items, the greater the internal consistency reliability coefficient. That is, individuals who respond one way to one item tend to respond the same way to other items. When this is the case, the scale is said to be *homogeneous*.

Test length is another factor that affects reliability. Other things being equal, longer tests are more reliable. With shorter tests there is a greater chance of random error in an individual's responses, resulting in either too high or too low an estimate of the true score. The longer the test, the greater the chance that random errors will cancel each other, with some items overestimating the amount of the construct and others underestimating it. When the responses are added together for the score, the net effect of the errors will be closer to zero. This indicates higher reliability because the observed score for the individual will be closer to the true score.

CONSISTENCY ACROSS DIFFERENT FORMS. Another relevant consistency in testing arises when parallel forms of a test are given to the same people at the same or at different times. Parallel test forms are used when two or more measures of the same construct are desired. This is the case with achievement tests administered at the end of two consecutive school years, or with a test of attitudes toward an issue administered before and after an intervention designed to change those attitudes. Another reason why equivalent test forms might be developed, is to maintain the security of test items. This is so when scores are used to make important decisions about the test takers, such as college admissions. Keep in mind that errors may result from testing twice if the respondent remembers answers to the items on the first test and wants to appear consistent. Errors may also occur because of increased sensitivity to topics measured by the items. A test of attitudes toward death could cause people to ponder a topic they hadn't thought much about before, which could affect their response to test items the second time around. Another hypothesis to consider when evaluating reliability across different forms of a test is that the two forms are really not parallel. Appropriate arguments and evidence to support or disclaim these various hypotheses should be reported in the test manual.

Although each kind of reliability has been discussed separately above, it is also possible to conduct research that provides estimates of the different sources of error at once so that they can be directly compared. This analytical procedure comes from *generalizability theory* and yields coefficients that can be interpreted similarly to the classical reliability coefficients discussed above.

Although beyond the scope of this chapter, such procedures are discussed by Webb, Rowley, and Shavelson (1988). You are not likely to find the results of this procedure offered as evidence for reliability in many test manuals yet, although some journal articles on particular tests are beginning to report such studies.

STANDARD ERROR OF MEASUREMENT. The reliability estimates discussed above—test–retest, internal consistency, and parallel forms—all apply to the scores of a group of people. This is because it is not feasible to give the same test to one person over and over again to determine the true score.[*] Data from a group of test takers are needed to compute the correlation coefficients that provide numerical estimates of reliability. It is possible, however, to use a group's reliability coefficients to estimate how reliable a score is for an individual. This is called the *standard error of measurement* (*SEM*). The relationship between the *SEM* and the reliability coefficients is shown in the following equation:

$$SEM = SD \sqrt{1-r_{xx}}$$

SD is the standard deviation of the scores in the group, and r_{xx} is a reliability coefficient. This formula makes it clear that the *SEM* for an individual's score is always less than or equal to the standard deviation of the group from which it is calculated, since r is always a value between 0 and 1. The standard deviation is an estimate of how much natural variation there is for the construct among members of the group. From the earlier discussion of error, we know that error also contributes to variation: Some of the differences between scores will be the result of error. So, for a perfectly reliable test, $r = 1$, and the *SEM* is zero: By definition, there is no measurement error if an attribute is measured perfectly. For a completely unreliable test, $r = 0$, and the standard error of measurement is the same as the standard deviation of the group. In this case, the estimate of how much error might affect the score can be no better than the estimate of the amount of variation reflected in the scores of the group. There is then no way to determine how much of this variation is due to real differences among individuals and how much is a function of random error.

Once you have computed the *SEM*, you can use it to construct a *confidence band* around a score that enables you to state how likely it is that the band will contain the person's true score. Confidence bands are constructed by

---

[*] Note, however, that there are procedures for estimating true scores. They are not discussed here because they are generally of theoretical interest and do not appear in test manuals.

multiplying the *SEM* by a number that cuts off a certain percentage of the normal curve. For a 95 percent confidence band, this value is 1.96; for a 99 percent confidence band, the value is 2.54. Confidence bands put your interpretation of a score on safer ground. It is more realistic to claim that a given range or band is likely to contain the person's true score than it is to say that a particular observed score is the actual amount of the construct that the person exhibits.

So, although we cannot determine a true score precisely, we can say how probable it is that we have "surrounded" it—established a range within which the true score is likely to fall. This tells the test user how confident he or she can be when using the score to describe or make a decision about an individual. These probability statements are based on the assumption that the scores have a normal distribution and that certain scores will occur with probabilities that can be precisely determined. For example, with a 95 percent confidence band, the range of scores that define the band are said to have captured the person's true score about 95 percent of the time, if the person had been tested an infinite number of times.

Suppose that an aptitude test has been administered for the purpose of deciding which students to admit into an advanced class where aptitude will likely contribute to success. The criterion for admission is a score of 40 or better. If a student scores 38 and, if no further information is considered (always a poor strategy), then the student will not be admitted to the class. If, however, the test manual reports that the standard error of measurement for this particular aptitude score is 2.3 points for a group of students similar to those you are testing, then it can be used to construct a 95 percent confidence band around the score of 38 by multiplying the *SEM* by 1.96 and then adding and subtracting this value (4.5 points), leaving a range of 33.5 to 42.5. Because this range surrounds the cutoff score of 40, the decision about whether to accept this student might differ from the decision made without this information.

Although computing the *SEM* is useful for determining how much trust to place in an individual's scores, certain characteristics of the *SEM* must be noted to ensure its proper use. The *SEM* differs depending on which group is used as the basis of the computation, and it yields different values along the continuum of scores for the scale. The *SEM* varies with which group's statistics are used in its calculation, because the scores of different groups do not have the same standard deviations or reliabilities. For instance, if a test measuring achievement of a particular skill was administered to a group that had just undergone extensive training in the skill, we would expect the variability in scores to be much less than the scores from a mixed group, composed of both people who had and had not received the training. The group in which all the individuals received the training would exhibit a lower standard deviation, which would in turn mean a smaller *SEM*. To illustrate, let's assume that the standard deviation of the training group was 1.5 and that of the mixed group was 4.5. If the reliability of the two groups was the same at .80, then the *SEM* for an individual from the trained group is .67 and for someone from the mixed group is 2.01. Thus, when using the *SEM,* it is important to identify the group on which the computation is based and also how likely it is that the individual whose *SEM* you wish to compute would be a member of that population.

The value of the *SEM* will also vary at different points along the continuum of scores on the scale. Individuals at the extreme ends of a distribution are there in part because their scores have been more affected by errors than have those of people near the middle of the scale. This means that the scores at the extremes are less reliable and that their standard errors of measurement will be greater. Some test manuals reflect this fact by reporting different standard errors for different score intervals. Such information is particularly important for tests used in making important decisions about individuals.

Test users often ask whether objective standards exist for reliability coefficients against which a test can be evaluated. Nunnally (1978) offers some general guidelines suggesting that for exploratory research, reliability coefficients above .70 are probably acceptable, but that in applied settings, where important decisions are being made about individuals, .90 should be a minimum, with .95 the desirable standard. As should be evident from our earlier discussion, though, this presumes that high coefficients are desirable and expected, given the nature of the construct and of the group on which the coefficients are estimated. However, the usefulness of such guidelines is limited by the fact that high reliability coefficients can be achieved fairly easily for many tests. High internal consistency reliability can result from using many very similarly worded items. High test-retest reliability can be accompanied by teaching to the test, or by administering the same test twice with little time in between. Although the coefficients in each of these cases would be high, these procedures do not provide a rigorous estimate of score reliability. Obviously, there can be a tradeoff between efforts to achieve high reliability for its own sake or to meet some arbitrary standard and the meaningfulness and usefulness of the scores. It may be more helpful, therefore, when evaluating reliability estimates, to determine the effect of the test's reliability on the *SEM*. Table 3 shows values of the *SEM* at different reliabilities and standard deviations.

TABLE 3. *SEM* at Different Reliabilities and Standard Deviations

	Standard Deviation					
Reliability	.5	1.0	1.5	2.0	2.5	3.0
0	.5	1.0	1.5	2.0	2.5	3.0
.20	.45	.89	1.34	1.79	2.24	2.68
.40	.39	.78	1.16	1.55	1.94	2.32
.60	.32	.63	.95	1.26	1.58	1.90
.80	.22	.45	.67	.89	1.11	1.34
1.00	0	0	0	0	0	0

To further illustrate the effect of reliability on the *SEM,* we can use the values in this table to construct confidence bands around a score. Assume that a person scored 20 points on a test whose standard deviation is five points and whose reliability is $r = .60$. The 95 percent confidence band for that score ranges from 13.80 to 26.20. If instead, the reliability of the score were r = .95, the band would be 17.80 to 22.19. The range of the confidence band is 12.40 for the less reliable test, compared to 4.38 for the more reliable one. This could be a meaningful difference in making an important decision about an individual. The recognition of the *SEM's* importance is evidenced by the fact that the College Board reports scores to test takers in the form of a band or range and provides an explanation in brochures to counselors (Anastasi, 1985) about how to interpret it.

RELIABILITY IN CONTEXT. When interpreting reliability coefficients for the purpose of evaluating a test, you must take into account the characteristics of the individuals on whom the coefficient was computed. Characteristics such as age, education, gender, and so on may be related to the construct being measured and thus may affect reliability. If, for some reason, the construct-related behavior of the individuals is naturally inconsistent, then this will limit how high a reliability coefficient can be. An obvious example is the effect of education on test scores. Tests with items requiring an advanced vocabulary will have lower reliabilities when administered to a less educated group than to one whose education level matches that required by the test. Consider also the effect of age. Although the internal consistency reliability estimates of the preference scores of the *Myers-Briggs Type Indicator* (MBTI; Myers & McCaulley, 1985) are quite good for adults (.89 for Sensing-Intuition continuous scores), the estimates tend to be lower for adolescents (.73 for the same scale).

Better test manuals often provide reliability estimates for different populations. This enables you to determine whether any of the populations listed are similar to the ones you will be testing. If such information is not provided and the characteristics of your clients differ from those reported in the manual, you should use caution in interpreting their scores. In this case you may have to research the test in journals and form your own hypotheses about how the characteristics of your group might affect the consistency of their response to the items.

Summary

As Nunnally (1978) states, "To the extent to which measurement error is slight, a measure is said to be reliable" (p. 191). In general, the better quality tests have the following characteristics:

- Reliability estimates are reported for different populations.

- Different types of reliability estimates (internal consistency, test-retest) are reported if they are relevant to the proposed uses of the test.

- The reliability estimates are congruent with the theoretical expectations about the construct.

- The *SEM* is reported (or at least can be calculated because the reliability and the standard deviations are reported); the manual should also make clear which sample's statistics were used to compute the *SEM*.

- The *SEM* is reported for different groups and for different intervals along the continuum of scores, if relevant.

- The *SEM* has been used to construct a confidence band around a score.

VALIDATION

Only after it is established that a score can be replicated to some degree does it make sense to raise questions about its meaning. These questions, and the evidence given in answer to them, concern the *validity* of the scores. Suppose, for example, that you wish to use an interest inventory to help a college student make a decision about careers to explore or pursue. You need to know what inferences drawn from that student's scores are relevant to your assessment. Can you conclude that a high score on a scale designed to measure interest in mathematics indicates possible success as a mathematician? If not, what does it mean to have a high score on this scale?

Validity, then, refers to the appropriateness, relevance, and the meaning of inferences about tests scores. It is not an inherent property of a test itself but rather an ongoing process by which to accumulate and judge evidence about the meaning of scores (Landy, 1986; Lawshe, 1985). Because it concerns an unending accumulation of evidence and a human judgment about its quality, it is obvious that "validity is a matter of degree, not all or none" (Messick, 1989, p. 13). Validating a test is a process of inquiry, which means asking questions, forming hypotheses, and evaluating evidence (Cronbach, 1988, 1984; Messick, 1989). This process is conducted by test authors whenever they develop a test and conduct the research reported in the manual.

It is also a process by which users evaluate the validity evidence of the test scores. In the test manual, the author presents arguments about what the scores mean and how they should be interpreted. The test user must also evaluate scores for their meaning and must determine how to interpret them. As stated earlier, any interpretation is based on a theory, explicit or implicit, about what a construct means (Loevinger, 1957) and about what a set of responses means. This process orientation to validation, and to the entire testing enterprise, is reflected in the title of the latest edition of the *Standards*. While previous editions refer to standards for tests, the 1985 edition refers to standards for *testing*.

Cronbach (1988) urges us to think about validation as a persuasive argument, which must be evaluated both for its internal structure and for how the scores will be used in a particular setting. The internal structure of the argument refers to the need to consider each of the possible different explanations of what a score means. The test user must search for evidence to confirm or disprove each argument and then determine which is the most credible.

Validation is thus a process of hypothesis testing (Landy, 1986; Messick, 1989), which means that as it proceeds, research may rule out an alternative hypothesis about what a score means. When we discussed reliability, for example, we saw that there are at least two hypotheses about what a score means: It accurately reflects the person's attributes, or it primarily represents various kinds of error. Evidence in the manual should help you decide which interpretation is more likely, or to what extent each might be true for a given population. This example also points out the vital connection between reliability and validity: even reliability data provide information about the meaning of a score and, thus, about validity.

To take another example, consider a test designed to measure ability to solve mathematical problems whose questions include long paragraphs describing the problem. Two obvious hypotheses about the meaning of the scores are that (a) the scores indeed measure mathematical problem solving or (b) the test scores reflect reading comprehension or vocabulary as much as, or even more than, mathematical problem-solving ability. Research should be presented to discount this hypothesis.

For personality tests, two frequently proposed rival hypotheses are that the test actually measures (a) general aptitude or intelligence, or else (b) the desire of the respondents to describe themselves in socially acceptable ways. To discount these hypotheses, Campbell (1960) suggested that most new tests should have low correlations with measures of intelligence and social desirability. High correlations would suggest problems in interpreting the scores solely as measures of the original personality constructs. Discounting plausible rival hypotheses has been described as the "hallmark of construct validation" (Messick, 1989, p. 24).

The argument for the use of a given score must also be evaluated in terms of context. A score may be valid for one purpose but not for another. Or, it may be valid in a number of contexts, but not uniformly valid across a variety of circumstances or populations. For instance, evidence may exist that the score of a test measuring persistence is valid for the purpose of selecting employees for certain positions in a company. Scores from this test may not be valid, however, for admitting students to college, even though it may appear that persistence would be a valuable attribute in both instances.

Realizing that validity evidence is related to the context of testing makes it clear that responsibility for valid use of a test depends as much on the test user as it does on the author or developer. The test manual's author is responsible for presenting accrued evidence with which the scores of a population can be appropriately interpreted and also for describing the populations in sufficient detail to engage the responsibility of the test user. The user must judge how closely the population described in the manual resembles the user's own population and determine the meaning of the score with the clients at hand, taking into account other information known about the clients. Anastasi (1985) points to this increasing recognition of the test user's role as a positive trend in measurement, since it puts the decision-making responsibility in the hands of professionals and not in the test score.

Validation Evidence

An alternate hypothesis about what a score means leads to the search for evidence to support or refute different claims. If you evaluate a test or a test score that claims to measure leadership, but which on examination appears to measure dominance instead, you would check the manual or research reports for evidence to help you decide which hypothesis is more reasonable. In researching, you might look for correlations of the scores with tests that measure dominance, or submissiveness, or with other tests that purport to measure leadership. But what you search for, and even perhaps whether or not you search, depends on your understanding of the construct. In this example, if you and the test author both define leadership primarily as a tendency to exercise dominance over others, and your examination of the items indicates that this was a large component of the leadership score, then your search would focus on the evidence that supports this interpretation.

There is probably no one best way to categorize the validation process. Traditionally, validity has been thought of as a property of a test and as falling into categories, such as *content, predictive,* or *construct* validity. This is the view reflected in many test manuals. Current conceptions of validity, however, emphasize that it is unitary and that all questions about the meaning of scores are really concerned with *construct* validity (American Educational Research Association et al., 1985; Landy, 1986; Messick, 1989). This is a label that applies to the issue addressed all along in this chapter: What does a score mean? The approach that follows focuses on questions the test user might ask in evaluating a test. Many of these questions, which are listed in Table 4, can be reworded as alternative or rival hypotheses about what a score means. Although the list presents different questions and different kinds of evidence addressed to them, understand that this breakdown is for discussion purposes only. The questions and the evidence required to answer them are not mutually exclusive. Don't be misled into thinking that only one question applies when you evaluate a test or that only one kind of evidence is necessary for a test used in a certain context (Messick, 1989).

■   *Do the items adequately represent the construct and do they cover all the elements that comprise it?*

The first question in the table asks for evidence for the *content representation* of the test. A foreign language achievement test used as an outcome measure for an introductory class should have items that accurately reflect the topics taught in the course. Suppose that the instructor's objectives were to teach basic vocabulary, grammar, and conversational ability, with an emphasis on

TABLE 4. Validity Questions to Ask When Evaluating a Test

Do the items adequately represent the construct, and do they cover all the elements comprising it?

Can the score be used to predict future behaviors? Does the score on this test suggest anything about the person's likely behavior at some future time?

Is the test score related to other test scores or to nontest behaviors in the manner that would be expected? Are the scores related to the scores of other measures of the same construct?

Are the scores unrelated to measures of different constructs?

What do high and low scores mean?

If the test has more than one scale, what do the different scores mean and how are they related?

---

vocabulary, and that these objectives were basically met in the topics covered and in the time spent on each. When evaluating the achievement test, look for evidence of how well the test construct (foreign language achievement) is represented by the test items. Do the test items represent the instructor's objectives, and do they emphasize vocabulary, either by including more items to measure it, or by giving more weight to those items in computing the score? Content representation is especially important in training or educational settings when you want to be sure that the test reflects the important material. If the score measures only one of many facets of the training deemed important, then the validity of the score interpretation is questionable.

This example also illustrates that a test can have different content representation depending on its use (Messick, 1989). If this same achievement test were given as an outcome measure for a course that emphasized grammar instead of vocabulary, the content representation would be different. To determine how well a test covers the construct, a specification table is sometimes prepared in advance. This is a listing of the different elements of the construct and may also reflect the relative importance of each. The test items can then be compared against this table. For example, Table 5 shows a two-way table of specifications for a test designed to measure achievement in a counseling theories section of a psychology course. In this case, the teacher has determined her objectives (recall, understanding, and application) in her course plan and has entered the percentage of items reflecting each objective that she wishes to test for. If she can write items to fit her table of

TABLE 5. Table of Specifications for the Counseling Theories Section of a Psychology Course

Section Content	Course Objectives			
	Recall	Understanding	Application	Total %
Behavioral	5	10	15	30
Cognitive	10	25	15	50
Psychoanalytic	5	15	0	20
Total %	20	50	30	100

Note: Numbers in the table are percentages of items in each category.

specifications exactly, her test will have perfect content representation, but only for those objectives and theories she has specified.

Content representation is also important in areas other than educational testing. If you are evaluating a test designed to measure a complex or multifaceted construct, the items included should reflect this complexity. Note that if such a test does have adequate content representation, it may be earned at the expense of internal consistency reliability. The broader the construct, and the better the test items represent its multiple facets, the more difficult it is to achieve high internal consistency reliability, since the items will not correlate as highly with each other as on a test where all the items measure the same narrow variable. This tradeoff should be kept in mind when evaluating the test.

- *Can the score be used to predict future behaviors? Does the score on this test, at this time, suggest anything about the person's behavior at some future time?*

Often you are interested in predictions in order to make a decision about a person, such as whether or not to hire him or her for a clerical position in your company, or to help the person make a decision, such as helping him or her decide which job to apply for. For example, when evaluating an interest inventory designed for use with college students, you might ask how well a student's high score on an occupational scale predicts entry into that occupation or satisfaction with it. For aptitude tests, you want to know how well test scores predict job performance. The behavior you are trying to predict is called the *criterion*. In these examples, the criterion is occupational choice, job satisfaction, and performance, respectively. Evidence of predictive success can be the number or percentage of "hits." A hit can be defined as an on-target prediction. It can also be represented by the correlation between the test score and the criterion, or by the results of a regression analysis. For instance, the manual for the *Strong Interest Inventory* (Hansen & Campbell, 1985) indicates that the accuracy of the Occupational Scales in predicting occupational choice is around 65 percent for hits rated as moderate and excellent.

There are three questions to consider when searching for evidence to support the use of the test score as a predictor: (a) what is the criterion? (b) how much error is involved in the prediction and what kind of error is most likely? and (c) what would the prediction be without the test score?

A major problem in prediction is that in order to interpret evidence about how well a test score predicts behavior, you must know the meaning of the criterion and how reliable it is (Landy, 1986). In other words, you must be as careful evaluating the appropriateness of the criterion as you are in judging the evidence for the validity of the predictor, which is the score of the test you are evaluating. Consider a test that purports to predict successful performance for telephone operators and that will be used to select them. Meaningful criteria might be the number of calls answered in a given time, the percentage of calls directed to the correct person, or consistently pleasant response to customers. Assume that the test manual reports validity evidence for how well the test predicts pleasantness and claims the attribute is important in measuring the success potential of operators. At this point you should ask how pleasantness was measured. Further reading tells you that five supervisors in one company were asked to rate the pleasantness of their operators on a three-point scale, from "treats customers like dirt" to "is sweet." The results of this "measure" were then correlated with the test scores.

It is clear from this example that in evaluating the predictive validity of the test, you must ask (a) whether pleasantness is a meaningful criterion and (b) what evidence exists that it was measured reliably. The meaningfulness of the criterion is a judgment call on your part and depends partly on how you intend to use the test. Furthermore, its reliability is doubtful because of the small sample and the fact that it is based on a one-item "test." Based on what we have already learned about the many sources of error in measurement, you should suspect that a one-item scale such as this might produce random and, therefore, useless scores.

Another question to ask when examining the evidence of the value of the test as a predictor or a decision-making aid is: What would be the decision without the test? Does using the test actually improve the decision or prediction to a significant degree? (Nunnally, 1978). To answer this, you

72 BASIC CONCEPTS IN PSYCHOLOGICAL TESTING

need to know the *base rate* of the behavior that you want to predict, the rate at which it naturally occurs. The importance of base rates can be illustrated by attempts to predict violent behavior in individuals with little or no past evidence of such behavior. Sensationalist headlines notwithstanding, such behavior is rare—the base rate for it is very low. If such behavior is exhibited by only 1 percent of the population, then for any given individual the statistically best prediction is that the behavior will not occur. It would be very difficult to design a test that will improve on this prediction. Thus, when evaluating a test that claims to predict behavior, look for evidence that using it improves the prediction over what would be expected naturally by chance. Also, you should identify the base rate of the behavior to be predicted in the population you are testing.

■ *Is the test score related to other test scores or to nontest behaviors in the manner that would be expected? Are the scores related to the scores of other measures of the same construct?*

This question asks for *convergent evidence*. Test scores that are related to other test or nontest behaviors measured at the same time (as opposed to criteria measured at a later time) have been traditionally referred to as having *concurrent validity*. If a test is designed to measure introversion, then scores on this test should be related to those of other tests that measure introversion; the correlation coefficient between the two scores should be moderate to high (say, .40 to .70). If the correlation is low, one of the following plausible hypotheses might apply: (a) although the scales have the same name, they may be measuring different constructs (note that this is similar to the criterion problem mentioned earlier; you need to understand the standard against which you are comparing the original test); (b) introversion is a broad and complex construct and each test has succeeded in measuring different aspects of the construct; (c) the reliability of one or both of the tests is low—the low correlation occurred by chance because of a fluctuation in one or both scores due to error. To determine which hypothesis is most plausible, you need to inspect carefully your test items (and perhaps those on the other test as well) and examine the overall pattern of correlations presented in the manual or elsewhere.

Note that in this example, and in general, you also need to consider whether correlations might be too high. If the test score you are evaluating correlates very highly with the score from another similarly named test, one hypothesis is that the two tests measure the same construct; you must then choose between them on other grounds, such as cost or length. In general, it is the pattern of correlations between the test scores you are evaluating, and with important nontest behaviors (job choice or other observable behavior) or the scores of other tests, that must be used to understand the meaning of the scores. For example, in a sample of 854 adults, each scale of the *California Psychological Inventory* (Gough, 1987) was correlated with behavioral ratings of each participant by his or her peers and spouse, and by professional assessment staff, each using three different rating instruments. The overall pattern of findings for each scale was then examined to understand the meaning of the CPI scores.

Some test manuals present page after page of correlations with test scores from whatever study was available. As Messick (1989) argues, such miscellaneous correlations with other instruments are at best weak evidence for validity. Strong evidence is that which is provided on the basis of rational or theoretical expectations about the construct. In this case, the scores correlated with the test you are evaluating have been chosen precisely because their relationship with the construct helps to support or discredit alternative hypotheses about the meaning of the score. For example, correlating a reading comprehension test with a general intelligence test may help rule out the hypothesis that the reading test is just a test of intelligence.

When examining correlations or validity coefficients between the test scores you are evaluating and a criterion, you must keep in mind the relationship between reliability and validity. Low correlations may be evidence that the two scores, which are expected to converge, really measure different things. Another hypothesis is that the true correlation between the two constructs has been understated because of the unreliability of one or both of the measures. Remember, that reliability limits validity. To deal with this problem, some manuals will report coefficients that have been *corrected for attenuation*. Using rather simple formulas, it is possible to compute what the correlation between the two measures would be if either or both of them were perfectly reliable.

If corrected correlations are presented in test manuals, it is important to determine which score has been corrected. Since you are most likely evaluating the test so that you can use the score in an applied setting, you are interested in the meaning of the score. The reliability of the score will not be perfect and therefore a correction that assumes perfect reliability will not be useful. It may, however, be interesting to examine corrected correlations when the criterion is assumed to be perfectly reliable, especially if you believe that you do have a meaningful criterion but know that your measure has some problems. This might be the case when the criterion is job performance measured by supervisors ratings. For practical reasons it may not have been feasible to develop a good rating scale or to get enough supervisors to complete it to increase the probability of getting reliable ratings.

■ *Are the scores unrelated to measures of different constructs?*

This type of evidence, which is called *divergent* or *discriminant evidence,* is concerned with how the test scores are related to other criteria, except that now we are searching for evidence that the test is *not* related to other tests or to nontest behaviors in expected ways. In other words, divergent evidence is that which shows how well the construct diverges from, or can be discriminated from, other constructs. This evidence usually takes the form of low correlations between the scores of the test you are evaluating and the scores of another test or some measure of nontest behavior. In some ways this kind of evidence is even more important than convergent evidence in eliminating rival hypotheses about the meaning of the scores (Messick, 1989).

As discussed earlier, a common rival hypothesis for personality tests is that the score measures the tendency of people to respond in ways they believe are socially acceptable, instead of, or in addition, to whatever the test is supposed to measure. Following Campbell's suggestion (1960) then, some test manuals will report correlations between the test scores and some other measure presumed to measure socially desirable response sets. For other evidence helpful in evaluating the social desirability hypothesis, researchers have asked respondents to answer the items as they think they "should," in a manner they believe will put them in the best possible light.

For tests related to education, a common rival hypothesis is that the score is really a reflection of intelligence and not of some narrower construct such as vocabulary or mathematical problem solving. Although there are numerous other hypotheses about what a score could mean, the test manual should give evidence that helps you decide just how plausible some of these other hypotheses are.

One type of rival hypothesis is troublesome because it may be difficult to discount. This is a question of how much a score really reflects the amount of the attribute and how much is contamination due to the way the construct has been measured. The answer to this question is found by correlating two constructs that have been measured by different methods. The score of a paper-and-pencil test designed to measure manipulation of objects in space may be correlated with performance on an actual manipulation task. Both scores are supposed to represent the same construct. If there is a high correlation between the two, use the score of the paper-and-pencil test which is easier to administer and less costly. If the correlation is low, then it is not clear what the score of the paper-and-pencil test means.

- *What do high and low scores mean?*

One way to determine the meaning of a score is to contrast those who score high on the test with those who score low. Using the *method of contrasted groups,* you identify two groups with known characteristics who are presumed to differ on the scale. For example, when developing a measure of coping resources, Hammer and Marting (1988) contrasted groups believed to have high levels of resources with those predicted to have low or only average resources. One such contrast involved asking college students to rate their health on a ten-point scale and on the basis of this putting them in two groups, labeled healthy and ill. The healthy students had significantly higher resources on four of the five coping scales than those labeled as ill.

- *If the test has more than one scale, what do the different scores mean and how are they related?*

Thus far, we have discussed the meaning of one score only. Many tests, however, yield scores from more than one scale. All of the questions and forms of evidence discussed above apply to the case of multiple scores, but with the additional requirement that evidence must be presented to determine how the scores from the different scales are related. This becomes important when the scores are presented on a profile with an implicit or explicit suggestion that not only the elevations of the scores are important but also the overall pattern and relationship among them.

Questions about the relationships among the scales are usually answered by examining the correlations among the scales for patterns of convergence and divergence. For example, if the test has 100 items that comprise 5 different scales, and all of the correlations among scales are above .80, then a reasonable hypothesis for the meaning of the scores is that they all measure basically the same construct. Therefore, differentiating the construct into 5 parts may not be meaningful or provide much information beyond what any one of the scores would, or beyond what some composite scores would. In some cases, however, even with fairly high correlations (say, .50 or above), examination of the items that make up the scales or other evidence presented for the validity of each scale might lead to the conclusion that there are meaningful differences among the scales.

Even when there is sufficient evidence for interpreting each scale separately, a question may still arise from attempts by authors or test users to interpret the difference between two scores as meaningful. For example, say that a measure of aptitude has scales for verbal and quantitative ability. It is often tempting to directly compare the two scores and to conclude, for example, that on the basis of a ten-point difference in the scores, Sally is better in the verbal area than in the quantitative. From the earlier discussion of reliability we know that each of these scale scores is subject to error; therefore, trying to assert that the *difference* between two scores, both of which are subject to error in different and unknown degrees, is meaningful is obviously a problem. The solution is to construct a confidence band around each scale score based on the standard error of measurement. If there is no overlap between the bands, it is likely that the differences between the scores can meaningfully be interpreted. When evaluating a test for which differences among scale scores are important, the manual should discuss the overlap problem and provide confidence bands or the information that can be used to construct them.

Some tests with multiple scales also have a *total score* derived by combining scores from the scales in some way. You cannot assume that this composite score is meaningful, even if convincing evidence is presented for the meaning of the separate scales that comprise it. Separate evidence must be available for use of the total score, and this evidence must be evaluated in the ways discussed above. In some cases, the opposite condition will be found: The only evidence presented is for the total score. Even if the division of the scales is intuitively correct to both the author and user, evidence must still be presented and evaluated that each scale score is valid.

THE NORMATIVE SAMPLE

Often the individual's score is meaningless without reference to how it compares to the scores of others on the same test. You cannot infer meaning about a person's behavior from a score of 32 on a measure of shyness without knowing how a "typical" person scores on the measure or the average score of a group of people similar to the person in other ways. With a normative group that provides a basis for comparison, we might be able to say that a score of 32 is higher than 90 percent of the people in the norm group. Before trusting your inferences from such comparisons, however, you must find out what the characteristics of the normative group are, how the samples were selected, how large the samples were, and how recently the normative sample was tested.

A sound test provides sufficient information about the normative groups to let you determine how similar the norm group is to the individuals you will test. The more similar on relevant characteristics, the more likely it is that the comparison will be meaningful and relevant. It is not crucial that your group and the normative sample are alike on all possible variables, only that they are similar on variables related to the construct being tested. For example, if you are interested in measuring ability for visual spatialization and know that men and women tend to differ in their relative abilities to perform such tasks, you should find a test that provides separate norms for men and women. The geographic location of the normative sample may not be as important as it would be for other variables, such as attitudes about food or about farming.

To evaluate the adequacy of the norms, you must also know how the samples were selected for testing, since the selection method will influence how representative the sample is of the population. If a normative sample was selected randomly, then every individual in the population had an equal chance of being selected. Samples selected by other means—a favorite is college sophomores because they are readily available to most test authors— may not be typical of the population and therefore limits the utility of the comparison. Achieving the ideal of a random representative sample is difficult and time consuming and may only be practical for nationally administered achievement or aptitude tests. Most personality tests do not have the advantage of such norms.

The size of the normative sample relative to the population is also important, especially if the sampling method was not random. The smaller the sample, the more likely it is that the individual scores in the normative group will not be representative. How recent the normative sample is may also be important. Obviously, what was typical or representative of college students in 1960 might not apply to students in 1992.

Note that if the test scores are reported as percentile ranks, stanines, z-scores, or another kind of standard score, with or without plotting them on a profile, the above questions apply. This is so because the mean and standard deviation of a group are needed to compute any of these scores. If a test is hand scored by the user and the resulting raw scores plotted on a profile with standard score divisions, then a norm group has been used. The manual should make clear which group's statistics are being used to convert the scores and should describe this group in detail.

TEST ITEMS

The way a score is interpreted also depends on the nature of the test items. In general there are three minimal criteria for an item. First, its vocabulary and content should be free of bias toward any group. Second, the item should be simple or one dimensional; that is, it should tap only one concept or behavior. An item that asks people how much they agree with the statement "I like to make decisions and get others to implement them" should probably be separated into two items, since an individual could agree strongly with the first part but disagree with the second. Third, the item should be in a format that fits the construct being measured, such as the items of the MBTI that were written in a forced-choice format to reflect Jung's theory of opposition between the preferences. Or another example, a test designed to hire machine operators that was based on paper-and-pencil self-report items would be less relevant to the specified construct than a test involving hands-on manipulation.

If items do not meet these minimal criteria, both validity and reliability could be affected. Items that ask about the life experiences of everyone but only use male pronouns may introduce error into the responses of women, make the meaning of the scores difficult to establish, and may actually bias the scores against women. Items with inappropriate vocabulary may also lower the reliability of the score. In some situations, it may be important that the items appear to measure the construct named by the scale. In a selection test, for example, if the items do not seem to measure anything related to the job description, respondents may become distrustful or resentful, which may affect their score. On the other hand, if the items are too transparent, then the possibility of faking arises; some instruments provide separate scales or indexes to identify when a score may be invalid for this reason. When evaluating a test, you might want to balance these two factors in the context of your own testing situation.

SUMMARY

Evaluating a test involves asking questions and forming hypotheses about what the scores mean. Questions lead you to search for evidence to use in answering the questions or in deciding that certain hypotheses are implausible. Hypotheses are formed relevent to (a) convergent evidence or divergent evidence; (b) the meaning of high and low scores; (c) the success with which the scores can be used to predict behavior; and (d) the extent to which the scores represent the construct. The meaning of the scores is also determined by what groups the scores are compared to and by the exact nature of the items to which the individuals respond.

Practical Issues in Testing

The third aspect of tests to consider in evaluating them for use in a certain setting includes (a) how the test is administered and scored; (b) the cost of testing; and (c) the availability and quality of support and interpretive materials. Although these aspects of testing are referred to as *practical,* they also can be viewed from the perspective of score meaning. How a test is administered and scored has obvious implications for what the score means. Also, the cost of testing relative to its benefits requires consideration of the utility and social value of testing, which are relevant to the meaning of the scores and the way they will be used in specific settings.

ADMINISTRATION

Instructions for administering the test should mention any special directions needed to insure interpretability of scores. For example, a projective test such as the Rorschach inkblots may be very sensitive to any deviation from the administration instructions; changes in standard procedure could seriously affect the interpretability of the results. Other tests, however, may be more valid for special populations if the instructions are altered to accommodate the special needs of the group (Messick, 1989).

Directions should specify a time limit for administration, if appropriate, or an approximate time range for completing the instrument. Guidelines for handling omitted items are also useful, as are those for dealing with respondents' questions about the tests. Information about the group for whom the test is intended, including recommended age range and lowest required reading level, should be provided. Special training or qualifications needed by the test administrator should also be specified.

SCORING

The primary models for scoring tests are the cumulative, class, and ipsative models. *Cumulative models* are based on the assumption that the number of items endorsed or responded to in the direction specified by the keys represents the amount of the construct or trait the test measures. The higher the score, the more the construct is presumed to be present. This model also includes the option of differentially weighting the items before summing them. The cumulative model is the basis of most educational and personality tests. A *class model* test seeks a score that allows the individual to be placed in a class or category for the purpose of description or prediction. Responses, weighted or unweighted, can be added, but the resulting score is only used to determine the most appropriate category. A mastery achievement test is an example of this type. When using an *ipsative model* to score a test, the concern is with how the individual has performed differentially on a set of variables or scales. When evaluating a test, you must identify how the test is scored. Also, is the method consistent with the definition of the construct and with the way scores will be used in a specific situation?

Mechanically, scoring can be accomplished by (a) mailing a computer scannable answer sheet to the publisher or scoring service; (b) using templates or keys provided by the publisher or described in the manual to hand score the test; (c) using on-site computer software purchased from the publisher; (d) transferring the scores via computer modem directly to the scoring agency; or (e) having the test-taker self-score the instrument, usually with the help of keys or instructions printed on the answer sheet. A high-quality test will make the scoring options clear and will provide detailed directions for each alternative.

An important issue to consider when evaluating a test that requires mail-in scoring is the time that elapses between mailing the tests and their return. It is possible to send by express mail and to request the publisher to return them the same way, although you must usually pay for this service. You can also speed the process by inspecting the answer sheets for marking errors before sending them in for scoring. Another important consideration is the customer service support available should there be problems or questions.

If software is available for on-site computer scoring, the test manual or a software user's guide should explain clearly how to install and use the program. Also, ask what kind of technical support is offered during what hours, and at whose expense. The cost of the phone call may seem trivial until you receive a phone bill for the hours spent discussing your problem. Also, are software updates available when the test items, norms, or scoring keys are revised and at what cost?

If the test is scored by hand, the scoring templates or keys should be easy to use and understand. Some tests have self-scorable versions that allow respondents to score their own tests, usually under professional supervision. If this version is not identical to the standard version of the test, equivalence data should be available. Look in the manual for evidence that the mean and standard deviations of the two tests are similar and that the correlation between them is high, preferably above .90. Also, the self-scoring procedures should be constructed to minimize scoring errors by those unfamiliar with tests.

Cost

The monetary cost of a test should be carefully evaluated with reference to all the quality considerations addressed in this chapter. A low test price may accurately reflect the meager care that has gone into its development. On the other hand, a high price may indicate only the developer's belief in what the market will bear and not the quality of the materials or the care taken in creating the test. Ultimately, cost must be weighed against value received in the particular situation.

Software for computer administration and scoring is generally more expensive than paper-and-pencil materials, since software development requires a considerably greater investment by the publisher. When comparing the relative cost of computer versus hand scoring, however, consider the cost of staff time spent scoring the instrument. Computer scoring services are popular because many test users have decided that the cost of the time spent hand scoring more than outweighs the additional cost of computer scoring.

In addition to monetary costs, the social costs of testing (Messick, 1989) must also be considered. These are clearest when test scores are used for selection, whether in employment, treatment, or educational settings. In this context, monetary cost must be evaluated against the social cost of making a wrong decision, both with and without the test. Some potential costs of using a test for selection are summarized in Table 6.

There are four possibilities to consider. If the test score suggests selecting the person and the decision turns out to be correct, then the costs involved are primarily monetary. In this case, the monetary benefit of selecting an appropriate employee who will be a productive asset to the organization most likely outweighs the monetary cost of testing. If the test score suggests not selecting the person and this is a correct decision, again the cost is primarily monetary, but should be weighed against the money saved in hiring and training an unqualified or inappropriate individual for the job. The two possibilities in the decision correct column summarize the rationale for using tests in selection.

On the other hand, if the test score suggests selecting the person and it turns out to be the wrong decision because the person does not perform as expected, then there is a cost to both the individual and the organization. The individual has wasted time at an inappropriate job or school and may even suffer the consequences of experiencing failure. The organization must bear the cost of rehiring and retraining another applicant. Or, in suggesting against selecting a person, there is the possibility of the test scores rejecting a qualified applicant. This has a cost to both the individual and the organization, although the cost of a missed opportunity for both is very difficult to quantify.

When evaluating the cost of testing, you must also consider the cost of not testing. The potential cost of not using well-validated tests to aid in your

TABLE 6. Potential Costs of Using a Test in a Selection Decision

		Decision Correct?	
		Yes	*No*
Test Suggests	Select	Dollar cost of testing: increased productivity for organization	Dollar cost of testing + cost to individual of wasted time and sense of failure + cost of rehiring and retraining for organization
	Reject	Dollar cost of testing: dollars saved in hiring and training	Dollar cost of testing + cost to individual and organization of missed opportunity

decision are in hiring a person who fails to perform or failing to hire a person who could perform well. Obviously, as a test user, you want to improve the possibilities of making the correct decision. To do this you must carefully evaluate the available evidence on the relationship between test scores and performance.

SUPPORT AND INTERPRETIVE MATERIALS

Unless a test is administered solely for research purposes, you should evaluate the availability and quality of support and interpretive materials along with the other testing materials. Often there are interpretive materials for both the professional who administers and interprets the test and for the respondent. Materials intended for the respondent should report results in nontechnical language and should clearly delineate the limits to which interpretation of the scores are subject.

Interpretive materials for the professional should include sample cases, with descriptions of respondents and how their scores should be interpreted in given contexts. Profiles or results that may present special difficulties for interpretation are especially helpful, along with guidelines for how to proceed in such instances. Since a test manual cannot cover all possible interpretations of a score, however, training programs in the intricacies of interpretation should be explored.

Sources of Information About Tests

The evidence you need to evaluate a test can be found in a variety of sources: manuals of professional standards, test manuals and critical reviews, and published research on the instrument or the construct.

THE *STANDARDS FOR EDUCATIONAL AND PSYCHOLOGICAL TESTING*

Before studying the test manual, familiarize yourself with the *Standards for Educational and Psychological Testing,* the guidelines developed jointly by the American Educational Research Association, the American Psychological Association, and the National Council on Measurement in Education (1985). The *Standards* is comprised of four parts that address technical standards for test construction and evaluation, professional standards for test use, standards for particular applications, and standards for administrative procedures. It is highly recommended that professional test users have a copy of this available as they evaluate a test.

The part of the guidelines concerned with technical standards for test construction and evaluation contains a section on what should be in a test manual. The first standard in this section states that a test manual must be made available when a test is published. This may seem obvious until one stops to consider the number of "tests" available in books, magazines, dissertations, training materials, research journals, and from commercial publishers for which no documentation exists, or when the information provided is not sufficient to evaluate the test. Desk top publishing has made it possible to produce instruments and manuals that look professional but contain no evidence to support the interpretation of the scores. A collection of items that does not provide evidence for the meaning of the scores does not meet the minimum criteria for considering it a test in the sense used here, let alone a quality test. Additional criteria adapted from the *Standards,* along with other material to consider when reviewing a test manual, are included in Table 7.

TEST MANUALS

Promotional information from publishers of commercially available tests should say what the tests purport to measure, the appropriate settings and intended respondents, and where to obtain additional information. If these descriptions suggest that the test may meet your needs, inquire about the

TABLE 7. Information That Should Be Included in a Test Manual

---

Rationale
  Why was the test developed? What makes it unique?

Audience
  For whom is the test intended? Are there age or education standards?

Development
  How was the test developed? How were items chosen, and on what samples were items tested on?

Recommended Uses
  What uses can be recommended? What evidence demonstrates the appropriateness of each?

Possible Misuse
  How might the test be misused? What precautions can be taken?

Reliability and Consistency
  Is there any evidence to support the test's reliability and consistency?

Interpretation
  How are scores interpreted? What factors influence their meaning? Is there a discussion of how to identify invalid results, and are examples provided?

Research
  Are research studies or other available data useful in evaluating the test cited?

Qualifications
  What are the necessary qualifications for users, including any certifications, degrees, or special training required?

Scoring
  Are scoring procedures clear and supportive of the intended uses?

---

possibility of purchasing a specimen set, which often contains a manual and at least one test booklet and answer sheet, and possibly a sample report.

How well you can evaluate a test manual—even a good one—depends on your own level of training and experience with testing and the usability of the manual. Manuals for psychological and educational tests should be clearly written and well organized, but some manuals contain so much technical jargon that only the author, and perhaps some graduate students, can understand them. A review of one test manual concluded that although the chapters on administration, scoring, and interpretation were readable and likely to be useful to the practitioner, the chapter on psychometric issues was "written in the jargon that earns respect from psychometricians, awe from the general public, and snickers from lovers of English" (Fredman & Sherman, 1987).

Even with a well-prepared test manual, your ability to evaluate it depends on your knowledge of the construct and your training in tests and measurement. We have already discussed the importance of understanding the construct. If, in addition, you have a working knowledge of tests and measurement and a familiarity with basic psychometric concepts, you should be able to evaluate most tests. In the case of a manual that reports highly technical information or complicated interpretation procedures, you must honestly assess your own level of competence with the test. You may have to forego its use unless you have been properly trained or have access to a trained supervisor. An ethical professional does not operate beyond his or her level of competence.

CRITICAL REVIEWS AND PUBLISHED RESEARCH

While the *Standards* provides the criteria and the test manual the evidence, other resources are important in evaluating a test. Every test user should be familiar with the *Mental Measurements Yearbooks* (Conoley & Kramer, 1989), which provide critical reviews and lists of published references for almost all commercially available tests, along with the names and addresses of test publishers. Each new volume in the series covers tests published since the last edition, as well as additional and updated reviews of important tests previously covered. Another source is *Test Critiques* (Keyser & Sweetland, 1986), which provides an introduction to a test, discusses practical applications and technical information, and also critiques the test. These reviews, and the research articles they refer to, address the development, validity, reliability, or usefulness of the test. Another resource is *Tests in Print* (Mitchell, 1983), which contains descriptive information and bibliographies for most published tests. These essential references are available in the libraries or in testing or counseling centers of most colleges and universities.

A number of professional journals also contain research reports on the reliability and validity of tests as well as critical reviews. These include *Educational and Psychological Measurement, Journal of Personality Assessment, Journal of Counseling Psychology, Journal of Counseling and Development,* and *Journal of Applied Psychology.* For tests that offer computer-generated reporting services, a useful volume is *Psychware Sourcebook* (Krug, 1988), which is a compendium of information on tests and computer reports.

When reading reviews or research reports, keep in mind that there is often a time lag between completion of a research study and its publication. Compare the date of the manual cited in the review or research article with the date of the latest test manual available from the publisher. Some will have been updated since the published review, often in direct response to earlier reviews. It is also advisable to read more than one review of a test, as reviewers have their own biases about test development that may differ from those of the test authors. In addition to reading reviews and research reports, the user should also examine the testing materials closely, including the test booklet, the items, and any material available for reporting scores or aiding interpretation. Finally, it is often helpful to the potential user to actually take the test.

Conclusion

In summary, when evaluating the quality of a test, you should consider the following questions:

- What is the construct you want to measure and how do you expect it to behave?

- What is your testing goal: interpretation, description, or decision?

- Who are your respondents; what are their special characteristics?

- Is there understandable, comprehensive documentation available that enables you to evaluate how well the test measures the construct?

- Does the test measure the construct consistently over time, or at least as consistently as you would expect it to?

- Is the scale internally consistent; do the items seem to "go together" as much as you would expect, given how broadly or narrowly the construct is defined?

- What factors, other than different degrees of the construct, could explain the test scores; what evidence is provided to support the proposed meaning of the construct?

- Is there a bias in the items, reading level discrepancy, or unclear instructions that might make the test unsuitable for your group?

- Can you score the test accurately?

- Are good interpretive materials available and are you competent to use them?

- What are the monetary and social costs of testing or not testing?

References

Aiken, L. R. (1985). *Psychological testing and assessment.* Newton, MA: Allyn and Bacon.

American Educational Research Association, American Psychological Association, & National Council on Measurement in Education. (1985). *Standards for educational and psychological testing.* Washington, DC: American Psychological Association.

Anastasi, A. (1985). Mental measurement: Some emerging trends. In J. V. Mitchell (Ed.), *The ninth mental measurements yearbook* (pp. xxiii-xxix). Lincoln, NE: The Buros Institute of Mental Measurements.

Anastasi, A. (1988). *Psychological testing* (6th ed.). New York: Macmillan.

Campbell, D. T. (1960). Recommendations for APA test standards regarding construct, trait, or discriminant validity. *American Psychologist, 15,* 546–553.

Conoley, J. C., & Kramer, J. J. (Eds.). (1989). *The tenth mental measurements yearbook.* Lincoln, NE: The Buros Institute of Mental Measurements.

Cronbach, L. J. (1984). *Essentials of psychological testing* (4th ed.). New York: Harper & Row.

Cronbach, L. J. (1988). Five perspectives on the validation argument. In H. Wainer & H. Braun (Eds.), *Test validity* (pp. 3–17). Hillsdale, NJ: Erlbaum.

Fredman, N., & Sherman, R. (1987). *Handbook of measurements for marriage and family therapy.* New York: Bruner/Mazel.

Garvin, D. A. (1987). What does "product quality" really mean? In A.C. Hax (Ed.), *Planning strategies that work.* New York: Oxford University Press.

Gough, H. G. (1987). *California Psychological Inventory: Administrator's guide.* Palo Alto, CA: Consulting Psychologists Press.

Hammer, A. L., & Marting, M. S. (1988). *Manual for the Coping Resources Inventory,* Research Edition. Palo Alto, CA: Consulting Psychologists Press.

Hansen, J. C., & Campbell, D. P. (1985). *Manual for the SVIB-SCII.* Palo Alto, CA: Consulting Psychologists Press.

Heist, P. A., McConnell, T. R., Webster, H., & Yonge, G. D. (1968). *Omnibus Personality Inventory.* New York: The Psychological Corporation.

Hogan, R., & Nicholson, R. A. (1988). The meaning of personality test scores. *American Psychologist, 43*, 621–626.

Keyser, D. J., & Sweetland, R. C. (1986). *Test critiques* (Vol. 5). Kansas City, MO: Test Corporation of America.

Krug, S. E. (Ed.). (1988). *Psychware sourcebook* (3rd ed.). Kansas City, MO: Test Corporation of America.

Landy, F. J. (1986). Stamp collecting versus science. Validation as hypothesis testing. *American Psychologist, 41*, 1183–1192.

Lawshe, C. L. (1985). Inferences from personnel tests and their validities. *Journal of Applied Psychology, 70*, 237–238.

Loevinger, J. (1957). Objective tests as instruments of psychological theory. *Psychological Reports, 3*(Suppl. 9), 635–694.

Messick, S. (1989). Validity. In R. L. Linn (Ed.), *Educational measurement* (3rd ed.). New York: Macmillan.

Mitchell, J. V. (1983). *Tests in print III*. Lincoln, NE: The Buros Institute of Mental Measurements.

Myers, I. B., & McCaulley, M. H. (1985). *Manual: A Guide to the development and use of the Myers-Briggs Type Indicator*. Palo Alto, CA: Consulting Psychologists Press.

Nunnally, S. (1978). *Psychometric theory* (2nd ed.). New York: McGraw-Hill.

Tinsley, H. E., & Bradley, R. W. (1986). Test interpretation. *Journal of Counseling and Development, 64*, 462–466.

Tyler, L. E. (1984). What tests don't measure. *Journal of Counseling and Development, 63*, 48–50.

Webb, N. M., Rowley, G. L., & Shavelson, R. J. (1988). Using generalizability theory in counseling and development. *Measurement and Evaluation in Counseling and Development, 21*, 81–90.

CHAPTER 3

INFLUENCES ON TESTING
AND TEST RESULTS

D. H. Saklofske & V. L. Schwean Kowalchuk

Introduction

Tests are one of the assessment methods most often used by psychologists employed in human service settings to obtain information about individuals or groups for the purpose of making decisions. While tests and their uses are not new or unique to psychology, the possibilities for measuring human characteristics with paper-and-pencil tasks, questionnaires, and even such ambiguous stimuli as inkblots have been embraced by psychologists in this century. Tests are used to measure intelligence and cognitive processes, personality and affect, and a wide range of human performance factors. These tests reflect the best information about human behavior available from theories and research, placed within a framework that further exemplifies the sound psychometric properties of reliability and validity.

An examination of the *Ninth Mental Measurements Yearbook* (1985) reveals that more than 1,400 tests are described across 16 different categories. The *Tenth Mental Measurements Yearbook* (1989) reviews 396 tests, ranging from measures of achievement to vocational preference that are new or have been revised since the previous publication. In addition, there are many more tests that are brief (e.g., the 4–item *Brief Screen for Depression,* Hakstian & McLean, 1989), more experimental in nature, or less well known (e.g., developed by local hospitals, clinics, or school boards).

The proliferation and widespread use of tests requires test consumers to be informed. It is axiomatic in conventional measurement theory that there can be no measurement without error (Berger, 1986). As such, the informed test consumer must know the nature of the errors, the contaminants in the test and test situation, that in either random or systematic ways jeopardize the meaning of test scores. Luftig (1989) points out that test consumers who do not know and report on the degree of inexactness and error in a test abrogate their rights as clinicians. The assumption that error is present in all forms of assessment should influence practice by mandating that psychologists be aware of and try to minimize factors that might contribute to inaccurate test scores and that cautious explanatory hypotheses be advanced in interpreting test data (Witt, Elliott, Gresham, & Kramer, 1988). To this extent, standards have been developed that focus on the technical aspects and also the professional use of tests and test results (e.g., *Standards for Educational and Psychological Testing*, American Psychological Association, 1985).

While personality and attitudinal measures assess typical performance, Messick (1984) reminds us that the intent of achievement and ability testing is to assess the examinee's competence, that is, his or her knowledge under ideal circumstances. However, it is performance or what is actually done under existing circumstances that is assessed. Whereas competence embraces the structure of knowledge and abilities, the processes of accessing and utilizing those structures and a host of affective, motivational, attentional, and stylistic factors also affect performance (p. 217). Messick argues that

> these adulterating influences include a variety of other
> psychological and situational factors that technically constitute
> either construct-irrelevant test difficulty or construct-irrelevant
> contamination in score interpretation, or both. In jeopardy in the
> first instance are the accuracy and meaning of the test scores and,
> in the second instance, the appropriateness of implications for
> action. (p. 216)

The inexact nature of psychological measurement underscores the importance of assessment rather than merely administering and scoring of tests. Taylor (1989) and others (e.g., Matarazzo, 1990) point out that although assessment is considered synonymous with testing, the former is much more exhaustive. Assessment "includes the careful analysis of the information provided by various instruments and techniques (including tests), which should result in functional, relevant, appropriate decisions" (Taylor, 1989, p. 2). Sattler's (1988) discussion of the "four pillars of assessment" clearly points to the importance of integrating test data with information that can be obtained via other methods or sources (e.g., observations, interviews, and informal assessment procedures).

There are few psychologists who do not use tests or value the information that can be inferred from them. However, these same psychologists recognize the limitations of tests and that it is unwise to rely exclusively on test results to assist in making decisions that will have an impact on an individual. Our knowledge of human behavior is incomplete and our tests are imperfect. Psychologists can only attempt to measure those processes and products that we already know about and can capture with the aid of a psychometrically sound test while remaining aware of the numerous factors that can affect test scores. It is some of these personal and contextual factors that we will now focus on.

Sources of Error and Poor Test Performance

[A] child's performance in a standard test situation may not reflect how the child would perform if he or she were more comfortable, stimulated or inspired, healthier, or less upset by family anxieties.... The child's cumulative achievement reflects the outcome of complex interactions involving ability, motivational dispositions... task requirements, incentives, opportunities, in the immediate environment, and other factors that influence the child to engage in various activities.... Unfortunately, there is no simple way to separate out the influence of each component on the final test score. (Sattler, 1988, pp. 535-536)

Sattler (1988) and others, including Cronbach (1984), Goslin (1963), Korchin (1976), and Lyman (1978) have provided insightful descriptions of the various factors that can influence test performance and that should be considered in interpreting the meaning of any score. Sattler (1988), for example, contends that no single factor is sufficient to explain an individual's test performance; rather, failure results from the interaction of both individual (neuropsychological, physical, experiential, temperamental) and environmental (school, home, peer, group) factors. Sattler's framework is schematically represented in Figure 1.

Goslin (1963), in a somewhat different representation of contaminating influences on test scores, identified input (innate factors, background, and environment) and intervening (personality, situation, test demands, random variation) variables. Cronbach (1984) provides a succinct summary, pre-

FIGURE 1. Major Factors That May Account for Failures on Tests or in School

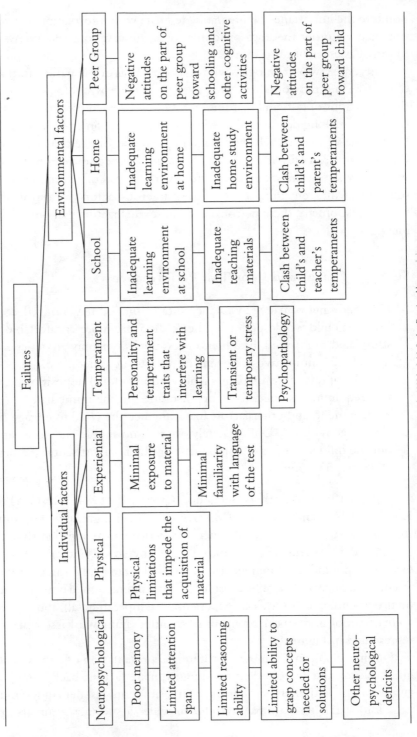

From *Assessment of Children* (3rd ed., p. 535) by J. M. Sattler, 1988, San Diego, CA: Sattler. Copyright 1988 by J. M. Sattler. Reprinted by permission.

TABLE 1. What Error Means Under Several Procedures

	Sources of Variation That Increase the Reported SEM When the Analytic Procedure Is			
	Internal-consistency	*Correlation of Test Forms Given on Same Day*	*Correlation of Test Forms Given on Different Days*	*Correlation of Test and Retest (Same Form, Different Days)*
Momentary inattention, luck in guessing	X	X	X	X
Choosing a particular set of items to represent the universe	X	X	X	
Health, mood, or other temporary state of the test taker			X	X
Shift in motivation from occasion to occasion			X	X
Opportunities for learning that change pupil standings as time passes			X	X

From *Essentials of Psychological Testing* (5th ed.) by L. J. Cronbach, 1990, New York: HarperCollins. Copyright 1984 by L. J. Cronbach. Reprinted by permission.

sented in Table 1, of the various sources of measurement error and how they can affect test scores. Of course, it must be remembered that as the standard error of measurement within a test increases, the test becomes less reliable and therefore also less valid. Lyman's (1978) description identifies the test content, the situation, the examiner, temporal consistency, and the person as potential sources of error. Korchin (1976) points to four rival sources of poor performance: the test and test content, the examiner, person factors, and situational factors. We will adapt the description of Korchin (1976) and Lyman (1978) to more fully explore the psychological and contextual factors that may influence test performance in either facilitative or debilitative ways.

THE TESTS AND TEST CONTENT

Anastasi (1988) defines a psychological test as "an objective and standardized measure of a sample of behavior" (p. 23). Such tests are commercially available instruments that are both standardized and norm-referenced; however, criterion-referenced tests, tests that compare performance to a criterion rather than to a reference group, are increasingly used. By norm-referenced, we mean that the test allows for a comparison of the examinee's performance with that of a normative group. A standardized instrument is one for which a standard format is adopted for administration, scoring, and interpretation. To use the test norms with confidence, the examinee's characteristics must be consistent with those of the normative group on which the test was standardized, and the instrument must be administered and scored in accordance with the standard conditions under which the test was normed. The technical adequacy (i.e., reliability, validity) of formal tests must also be demonstrated; poorly constructed instruments may contribute to inconsistent variation (Tindal & Marston, 1990).

In addition to the standardized instruments Anastasi (1988) refers to, informal tests, such as many observational formats and interviews, can be tailored to meet the specific needs of the examinee. Informal measures are neither norm-referenced nor standardized. As a consequence, administration, scoring, and interpretation are subject to the idiosyncrasies of the examiner. Moreover, because informal measures do not usually have demonstrated technical adequacy, the appropriateness of inferences based on informal test scores remains questionable.

Tests can also be differentiated as group or individual measures. While group tests are given to several people simultaneously, individual measures involve a one-on-one exchange between examiner and examinee. By enabling the examiner to be more readily responsive to the physiological and psychological states of the examinee, individual tests are more likely than group measures to elicit optimal levels of performance. The need to use individual measures, for instance, is particularly apparent when assessing young children, where sustained compliance with examiner and test directives in a group situation is unlikely due to limited attention span and reading skills.

The material or content being assessed is another factor that must be taken into account in test interpretation. Tests can vary widely in terms of content; some assess global competencies and characteristics, as in tests of general mental ability; others probe more specific traits or abilities, as in tests of nonverbal reasoning ability or information processing style. For example, two children may earn average IQ scores of 100 but while one child earns similar scores on both verbal and performance scales (Verbal IQ = 102, Performance IQ = 96), the other child manifests a significant difference in favor of the verbal scale (Verbal IQ = 112, Performance IQ = 86). Thus, the interpretation and hypothesis that may be generated to explain these two profiles will be very different. As a further example, a significant difference between an average score on the Picture Completion subtest of the *Wechsler Intelligence Scale for Children - Revised* (WISC-R; Wechsler, 1974) contrasted with a high or low score on the Arithmetic subtest will certainly result in various different interpretations about a child's abilities related to concentration for auditory versus visual stimuli. To further illustrate this point, high scores on the Pd (Psychopathic Deviate) scale of the *Minnesota Multiphasic Personality Inventory* (MMPI) may signal a passive-aggressive personality when high scores are also observed on the Hy (Conversion Hysteria) scale; when high Pd scores occur together with an elevated Ma (Hypomania) scale, this is more suggestive of an antisocial personality.

Furthermore, marked variations in scores can occur depending on how the construct under measurement was operationalized and whether it was assessed in a global or specific fashion. Although two tests purport to assess the same construct, an examinee may earn quite different scores because the two instruments define and measure a construct differently. Thus, a theory-driven intelligence test such as the *Stanford-Binet Intelligence Scale: Fourth Edition* (SB:FE; Thorndike, Hagen, & Sattler, 1986), containing 15 subtests that yield four area scores and a composite score of general mental ability, may be expected to provide a different estimate of intelligence than very brief tests such as the *Matrix Analogies Test–Short Form* (MAT-SF; Naglieri, 1985) or the *Draw-A-Person Test: A Quantitative Scoring System* (DAP-QSS; Naglieri, 1988). This point is reflected in two studies of elementary schoolchildren in which the short form (four subtests) of the SB:FE was moderately and significantly positively correlated with MAT-SF but not with the DAP-QSS; the latter two tests showed a small but significant correlation (Saklofske & Braun, 1989; Saklofske, Yackulic, Edwards, & Naglieri, in press). The same phenomena can be observed on measures claiming to assess similar traits: A recent study suggested that children identified as depressed varied according to the measuring instruments used (Saklofske, Janzen, & Pannanan, 1987).

How the test content is presented and the mode in which the examinee is expected to respond may also affect test performance. For example, assessment of some competencies is conducted by verbally presenting instructions and then requiring the examinee to select, within a timed interval, the correct response from among a series of choices. In other cases, a written presentation model is used to assess the same competencies, with the expectation that the examinee take all the time needed to self-produce the appropriate written response. A number of permutations involving different presentation models and response demands are also possible. Different outcomes may result from each of these variations, depending on the examinee's strengths and weaknesses. The adult, for instance, who has only a rudimentary grasp of spoken and written English will be at a considerable disadvantage on intelligence tests that are heavily weighted in verbal content/ responses or in reading and understanding the items on a personality test.

The amount of content is also an important consideration. While tests only sample behavior, inferences about the examinee's competence will be made on the basis of task performance. In general, the more exhaustively the test items probe the construct under measurement, the more likely the test score will reflect the examinee's competence. Conversely, if the item pool is inadequate, the amount of information that is available is reduced while the possible interpretation errors are increased.

Scoring errors are a final contaminating content factor to be considered in test interpretation. We have already seen that because formalized tests provide a standardized format for coding and scoring responses, they are not as likely as informal measures to lead to scoring variance. However, even in the case of formal instruments, scoring errors remain relatively common (Sherrets, Gard, & Langner, 1979), and considerable disagreement arises when examiners are asked to score ambiguous responses (Sattler, Andres, Squire, Wisely, & Maloy, 1978).

THE EXAMINER

The test administration skills and interpersonal style of an examiner are critical influences on the test performance of an individual (Witt et al., 1988). Optimal levels of examinee performance are not likely to be forthcoming when an examiner is inadequately trained or lacks the interpersonal competence needed to build a dynamic working relationship with the examinee.

Regardless of the nature of the test, the examiner must have adequate training. In the case of informal measures, adequate training implies knowledge of the content area under measurement, knowledge of test construction and implementation, awareness of measurement concepts, and knowledge of good assessment practices. Formal measures require that the examiner have additional knowledge of the standardization procedures as they pertain to the administration, scoring, and interpretation of each test. To acquire this knowledge, aspiring examiners are usually required to undergo formal training and in some cases, such as with most intelligence tests, will have to demonstrate their competence before being licensed to administer that instrument.

The influence of the examiner on examinee performance has been considered from such perspectives as rapport or interpersonal relationship, race, sex, expectancy effects, and reinforcement practices. Establishing rapport refers to the psychological preparation of the examinee and the construction of an atmosphere of trust and security. According to Anastasi (1988), this involves motivating examinees and encouraging their ongoing cooperation and responsiveness. Most clinicians suggest that examiner sensitivity to the physiological needs of the examinee (e.g., hunger, thirst, fatigue), to scheduling concerns (e.g., ensuring that testing doesn't conflict with other important activities or that the sessions are too lengthy), to his or her emotional needs (e.g., presenting opportunities for an active person to move about), and to the examinee's needs for information (e.g., explaining the purpose of the test) all contribute to establishing positive rapport. Research has shown that a warm interpersonal relationship during testing may have a facilitative effect for some individuals (Anastasi, 1988; Sattler, 1988).

Variations in examiners' interactional patterns can also effect testing outcomes. A number of studies have examined the effects of reinforcing particular or correct responses (e.g., Saigh, 1981). Findings indicate that while reinforcement in general seems to improve performance on intelligence tests, the results vary as a function of sex, socioeconomic status, culture, and type of reinforcer (e.g., Bradley-Johnson, Graham, & Johnson, 1986).

Examiner beliefs and attitudes are also likely to influence interpersonal relations and data interpretation. A number of studies have reported that examiner knowledge of an examinee's race, sex, socioeconomic class, and cultural and educational background can significantly affect assessment outcomes. Fuchs and Fuchs (1986), for instance, reported that intelligence test scores were slightly higher for children who were familiar to the examiner, and this effect was somewhat greater when the children were of lower socioeconomic status. Expectancy effects such as those studied by Rosenthal (1966) and communicated verbally or nonverbally during testing may also influence the administration and scoring of a test. Moreover, the theoretical orientation of the examiner may lead to bias; assessment practices and interpretation may be narrowly framed within one orientation and consequently fail to examine and incorporate pertinent information. Anastasi (1988) summarizes much of the current research findings:

> Many other, more subtle testing conditions have been shown to
> affect performance on ability as well as personality tests. Whether
> the examiner is a stranger or someone familiar to the test takers may
> make a significant difference in test scores....[The] general manner
> and behavior of the examiner as illustrated by smiling, nodding, and
> making such comments as "good" or "fine" were shown to have a
> decided effect on test results....In a projective test requiring the

respondent to write stories to fit given pictures, the presence of the examiner in the room tended to inhibit the inclusion of a strongly emotional content.... Job applicants typed at a significantly faster rate when tested alone than when tested in groups of two or more. (p. 35)

To illustrate psychologists' recognition of the importance of examiner characteristics as they affect test performance, the *Standards for Educational and Psychological Testing* (American Psychological Association, 1981) was created to provide a clear outline for the best practices of test use, with five of the nine standards relating to the issue of fairness. It is the intention of these standards and of the ethical guidelines governing the practice of psychology to promote an acceptable pattern of practice (Jacobs, 1983). Furthermore, test manuals, such as that for the *Kaufman Assessment Battery for Children* (Kaufman & Kaufman, 1983), give considerable attention to the importance of establishing rapport in the test situation: "Any profile of scores obtained within a poor psychological environment is suspect and should be treated as either invalid or of questionable validity, depending on the nature and degree of the rapport problem" (p. 11).

Recent advances in computer technology and the availability of computers in settings ranging from schools to hospitals has encouraged the use of computerized testing. Publications directed to psychologists and other professions advertise software for testing intelligence, personality, interests, vocational preferences, and achievement. The test content is presented on a screen as programmed on disk, and the subject is required to press keys or use some sensitive marker to indicate the response. Although this approach may be less suitable for individuals who need assistance in understanding the nature of the task or the required response or who have reading problems or are less motivated to perform in a person-machine interaction, there is little doubt that the computer will play an increasing role in routine assessment procedures.

Person Factors

While the nomothetic approach to understanding human behavior is important and useful, the idiographic approach is especially relevant in clinical work. A dual approach encourages psychologists to search for and apply general and robust laws of human behavior, while being alert to the possibility that the consistency, accuracy, and meaningfulness of the data samples obtained from tests may vary considerably for individuals. The importance of individual differences variables in human behavior descriptions has received increasing attention in journals such as *Personality and Individual Differences* and in recent books (e.g., Ackerman, Sternberg, & Glaser, 1989; Eysenck & Eysenck, 1985; Saklofske & Eysenck, 1988).

Although it may seem contradictory that the person being tested can also be a source of error, we must remember that human behavior reflects a complex interaction of biological, psychological, and social factors. Each test, however, samples only a small behavior domain; all other person factors that enter into the measure may be considered a source of error. For example, Benson and Weinberg (1990) describe eleven sources of phenotypic variation that must be recognized in the measurement of human behavior.

Such "other" factors can never be totally eliminated. The task of the psychologist is to recognize how a test score is being influenced by other factors and take this into consideration in the process of assessment. For expository purposes, let us look at several of these person factors in more detail.

Heredity
Goslin's (1963) analysis of influences on test scores includes heredity factors. The debate on the heritability of intelligence and personality, as well as such human conditions as depression, has continued unabated during this century. However, the evidence clearly points to the role of genetics in offering a partial explanation of general intelligence (e.g., Bouchard & McGee, 1981; Jensen, 1980); for specific abilities reflected, for example, in the subtests of the Wechsler scales (e.g., Segal, 1985); for various personality traits (e.g., Goldsmith, 1983); and for conditions ranging from learning disability to schizophrenia.

Personality
Individual differences in personality are not only important in a description of human behavior but must also examined in terms of their relationship and interaction with each other and with other behaviors. For example, Robinson (1985) has reported that adult extraverts and introverts show differential performance on verbal and performance intelligence test scales, although these findings are less clear with children (Saklofske, 1985; Saklofske & Kostura, 1990). Wakefield (1979) has suggested that rewards and punishments presented by teachers differentially affect the achievement of introverts and extraverts. Hoeppel (1990) reported that children's test responses vary as a function of both personality (introversion versus extraversion) and time of day. Brebner and Cooper (1986) have also pointed to the importance of

personality factors such as introversion and extraversion in inspection time research (i.e., a measure of differences in the speed or efficiency of low-level cognitive processes), which has been suggested as a measure of intelligence.

Anxiety

Anxiety is one of the most studied affective variables in psychology, spanning the writings of Freud to present descriptions of anxiety disorders contained in DSM-III-R. Examinations have been conducted on the interaction between anxiety and ability as it relates to student achievement under various conditions of rewards and direct or indirect teaching. For example, Eysenck (1985) reported that anxiety has an adverse effect on the performance of complex letter transformation tasks by impairing the rehearsal and storage of task-relevant information. Furthermore, monetary incentives improved the performance of low-anxiety subjects but had no effect on those with high levels of anxiety.

Anxiety has received particular attention because it has been recognized that beyond an optimal level, it may negatively affect performance in everything from sports (Hanin, 1988) to intelligence tests and school achievement (Sarason, 1980). In particular, test-anxious students have been shown to have more negative thoughts and higher arousal during an exam in contrast to unanxious peers and this is consistent across time (Minor & Gold, 1986). In addition, high test-anxious subjects appear to experience greater cognitive interference and task-irrelevant thinking (Hammermaster, 1989). As Zeidner and Most point out in their introductory chapter to this book, it is the worry component (cognitive) that is consistently found to be more strongly related to test anxiety relative to the emotionality component (bodily arousal and tension). Edelmann and Hardwick (1986) reported that distraction and relaxation were related to lower levels of test anxiety in comparison to seeking social support and catharsis; performance and anxiety were uncorrelated, suggesting that not all test-anxious individuals perform poorly on exams but that the experience is an unpleasant one. Various scales have been developed to assess test anxiety (e.g., Alpert & Haber, 1960; Mandler & S. Sarason, 1982; I. Sarason, 1958; Liebert & Morris, 1967; Spielberger, Anton, & Bedell, 1976); and different treatments have been successfully employed (e.g., Hembree, 1988; Meichenbaum & Butler, 1980; Wolpe, 1969).

Motivation

Motivation, much like anxiety, is an important variable in the assessment process. Cronbach (1984) states that likewise, in weighing a person, when we put him on the scale, we get a good measure no matter how he feels about the operation. In a psychological test the subject places himself on the scale, and unless he cares about the result, he cannot be measured. (p. 69)

Motivation and related variables such as self-efficacy (Bandura, 1986) and attributions (e.g., locus of control, learned helplessness) have been carefully studied in relation to learning and performance. Achievement motivation (Atkinson & Raynor, 1974; McClelland, 1985) has also received considerable attention. *Motivation* is a term frequently used in psychological reports to account for the performance of clients. Thus, a clinician's report may read, "Bill was highly motivated during the administration of the intelligence tests …. He persisted with more difficult items, gave detailed answers to verbal questions…verbalized the enjoyment and challenge he felt during testing." Alternatively, a report that describes the intelligence test performance of a schizophrenic patient may note the patient's "unmotivated and apathetic behavior, disorganized approach and confusion in solving problems and the frequent off-task verbalizations." From another perspective, individuals who are motivated to present a particular picture of themselves during a job interview may respond to items on a self-report questionnaire so as to appear "energetic, honest, cooperative, hard-working, and sociable."

One example of a motivational variable that has been examined in the personality measurement area is generally referred to as *faking*. Although it may not be as serious a problem as once thought, it is not uncommon to see recently published articles with titles such as "Usefulness of the K Correction in MMPI Profiles of Patients and Nonpatients" (Colby, 1989), "Faking on the Mississippi Scale for Combat-Related Postraumatic Stress Disorder" (Dalton, Tom, Rosenblum, Garte, & Aubuchon, 1989) or "Dimensions of Deceptive Responding in Criminal Offenders" (Lanyon et al., 1989). Since the most common method of personality assessment involves the use of self-report questionnaires, clinicians need to be aware that these measures are susceptible to both conscious and unconscious distortion (Murphy & Davidshofer, 1988). Aiken (1989) states:

> Outright malingering (faking bad) and faking good are not the
> only response tendencies that affect the validity of personality test
> scores: acquiescence, social desirability, overcautiousness, extremeness,
> oppositionalism, and other response sets or response styles also con-
> tribute to a distorted picture of personality. All of these response sets
> are tendencies to respond to an item in a particular way, regardless of
> its content. (pp. 195–196)

A number of different procedures that can be embedded within a personality test to detect faking have been developed. For example, the *Eysenck Personality Questionnaire* (Eysenck & Eysenck, 1975) contains a single Lie scale to detect dissimulation, while the MMPI includes the Cannot Say (uncooperativeness or defensiveness), Lie (fake-good or present a favorable self-image), Frequency (fake-bad, confusion, severely disturbed), and the defensiveness scales. Some scales such as the Dy (desirability) scale of the *Jackson Personality Research Form* (Jackson, 1974) are based on the assumption that deliberate deception can be detected by single dimension scales reflecting faking bad at one extreme and faking good at the other end. Alternatively, other personality tests such as the *California Psychological Inventory* (Gough, 1987) do not view faking as a bipolar dimension but rather include separate scales to tap faking (Wb or fake bad, Gi or fake good, and Cm or random responding), which can be further combined into equations to detect invalidity. While these scales may provide important information in themselves, their use as a corrective factor in the interpretation of other personality measures included in the same instrument may not be quite so straightforward. Hogan and Nicholson (1988) reviewed studies suggesting that the factor structure of the MMPI is not changed by controlling for social desirability but rather that validity coefficients are reduced: "People primarily respond to the content of items, regardless of their rated desirability.... The social desirability response set hypothesis is most usefully seen as an early theory of item responses rather than an indictment of personality assessment" (p. 624). A more in-depth discussion of response bias and test taking attitudes in the assessment of personality may be found in Aiken (1989), Anastasi (1988), and Murphy and Davidshofer (1988).

Examinee Sophistication

Test wiseness, test experience, and test taking practice have been examined for their possible influence on test scores. Anastasi (1988) states that a "test score is invalidated only when a particular experience raises the score without appreciably affecting the behavior domain that the test is designed to measure" (p. 43). It is common practice to employ a different intelligence test if a second testing is required in a short time period because of so-called practice effects. Anastasi (1988) has argued that individuals tend to perform better on a retest or alternate form of the same test, and many teachers would confirm that students who have taken a pretest prior to instruction tend to perform better on the post-test than students who have not done so. Somewhat improved test performance may be the result of practice and increased familiarity with the item content and test situation; debilitating anxiety levels may be reduced or eliminated because of this familiarity. While the individual should be prepared or ready for the test, this is quite different from coaching a child to improve performance on an intelligence test by teaching the test (see Cronbach, 1990, pp. 82-86).

A thorny issue in assessment relates to the impact of informal and formal training on ability test performance. At one time, it was held that exposing an examinee to items and subtests on the test to be used was necessary for optimal performance. Most clinicians would now argue that this strategy is untenable: If the chosen intelligence test is likely to provide a biased measurement, then another instrument should be used rather than confounding the results by altering the administrative procedures. Another well-established practice used to compensate for inequities in experience involves compensatory preschool programs. While the evidence for IQ gains following such intervention is relatively well established, there is less convincing evidence for the long-term effects on IQ scores and achievement (Ramey, Bryant, & Suarez, 1985). However, these group data often obscure the rather large IQ score changes for individuals. The preparation provided by the home is also a matter for consideration. The data are quite consistent in reporting moderate to high correlations between children's intelligence and family background (e.g., parent education, income occupation) and home environment factors that encourage, for example, independence, achievement motivation, and language development (see Sattler, 1988, for a discussion of environmental influences on intellectual functioning).

Temporal Consistency

Psychologists have long recognized that human behavior is not static or unchangeable, but rather, dynamic. Certainly, this is the main point of any of the various developmental stage theories of human behavior, such as Piaget's (1970) stages of cognitive development, Erickson's (1963) stages of psychosocial development, or Kohlberg's (1981, 1984) stages of moral development.

A consideration of trait theory informs us that because some human behaviors are relatively more or less stable than others, considerable caution must be exercised in test interpretation. Trait theorists differentiate between *states*, which are transitory mood conditions such as anger, fear, and sadness, and *traits*, which are more enduring characteristics such as intelligence or self-confidence. The situational pervasiveness of a trait is also at issue; for instance, although an individual may score very high on a measure assessing a particular trait (e.g., introversion or extroversion), that does not imply that the behavior will be displayed consistently at a particular level by the person across all situations and at all times. Similarly, it is recognized that various psychological disorders (e.g., seasonal affective disorder, bipolar depression) can be variable in symptom pattern and duration. These features of human behavior complicate efforts at classification and diagnosis. While some studies (Helson & Moane, 1987) have reported that personality does change over time, a number of other longitudinal investigations spanning 20 or more years suggest that personality remains relatively stable over the adult years (McCrae & Costa, 1984; Stevens & Truss, 1985).

Finally, it is worth noting that temporary body states can also produce both short- and long-term changes in behavior. Chemically altered states of consciousness such as those produced by stimulants, depressants, and hallucinogens (e.g., LSD) can have the immediate effect of altering reaction time and judgment. In some cases (e.g., alcohol), this effect may become chronic if abuse continues over an extended time period. In the treatment of various mood and anxiety disorders, positive short- and long-term effects can occur from the use of prescribed medications (Hyman & Arana, 1987). For example, the use of monoamine oxydase inhibitors or tricyclic antidepressants in the treatment of a major depressive disorder produces changes in self-reported mood. Stimulant medications such as methylphenidate (i.e., ritalin) can reduce motor activity and impulsivity as well as improve attention in both hyperactive and normal children (Zahn, Rapoport, & Thompson, 1980). However, short-term administration of ritalin does not appear to significantly alter the performance of ADHD children on such general mental ability tests as the new WISC-III (Saklofske & Kowalchuk, 1991).

A loss of sleep can negatively affect attention, concentration, mood, and motivation; longer sleep deprivation can cause the person to become quite disoriented and confused. Fortunately, these effects are often only temporary and without lasting consequences (Dement, 1976). Self-reported mood states are sensitive to various internal and external conditions. Even a brief ten-minute brisk walk has been shown to affect feelings of tension and energy for up to two hours (Saklofske, Blomme, & Kelly, 1991; Thayer, 1989). Further, Thayer (1989) has discussed the complex interaction of such factors as biopsychological cycles, personality, health, and cognitive processes on mood and arousal. Psychologists continue to study the effects on human performance of such other variables as circadian rhythms, hypnosis, meditation, and such conditions as premenstrual syndrome.

Other Person Factors

Finally, it is important to note that a host of other person factors can influence test performance. For example, the psychologist must remain alert to the impact on test performance of the adult who has chronic pain and severe activity-restricting respiratory and cardiovascular health problems, an adolescent with an undiagnosed hearing impairment, or the person with cerebral palsy. Furthermore, gender, linguistic, and cultural issues are important considerations. There is an increasing recognition of the biological basis of human behavior noted in writings spanning research on personality (Eysenck & Eysenck, 1985) to the recent interest by psychologists in neuropsychological assessment. An even greater recognition of the interaction of personal and contextual factors in assessment has grown out of the clinical and research work by psychologists.

SITUATION FACTORS

Mischel (1977) argued that a description of human behavior requires not only a consideration of the person but also the situation. The dynamic nature of human behavior suggests that it is not completely predictable across time or situations. For example, the individual who experiences extreme and debilitating test anxiety may be seen as quite relaxed and easygoing in various other contexts, such as sport activities or social interactions.

We also know that behavior is influenced by the physical environment. For example, studies show that the amount of classroom floor space available to students has an impact on their disruptive and aggressive behaviors (Hood-Smith & Leffingwell, 1984; McAfee, 1987). In the same way, situational factors can influence test performance, potentially jeopardizing the meaning of scores. Anyone who has written an examination in an unbearably hot and crowded lecture room can attest to the physical environment's debilitative effect.

A plethora of environmental stimuli may impinge on performance. McLoughlin and Lewis (1990) outlined situational contaminants that relate to the test room, seating arrangements, and test equipment, summarized in Table 2.

Interaction of Factors

We have argued that personal and contextual variables effect change in test behavior. However, by imposing parameters around each of the influences, our analysis has been a simplistic one. Bandura's (1978, p. 344) discussion of causal processes from a social learning approach reminds us that "psychological functioning involves a continuous reciprocal interaction between behavioral, cognitive, and environmental influences." In a testing situation, this analysis suggests that contextual factors do not change behavior in a

TABLE 2. Situational Contaminants

Test Room	Seating Arrangements	Test Equipment
Room either too large or too small for test	Inadequate seating (e.g., chairs too large or uncomfortable)	Not readily available to the examiner
Inadequate lighting	Inappropriately sized work surface	Disorganized
Extremes of temperature	Too close/far away from test materials and examiner	Not functional
Poor ventilation		Poorly maintained
Visual and auditory distractions and disruptions		Examiner lack of familiarity

mechanistic way; rather, stimuli are filtered through cognitions, perception, and other internal states before a determination about behavioral change is made. This kind of interaction has been recognized in aptitude-treatment interaction research (Cronbach & Snow, 1977), including process–oriented variables, and is not dissimilar from the way that medical doctors approach the diagnosis of various physical conditions. Thus, it is commonplace to see descriptions such as Spiel's (1981) recommendation that child neuropsychiatric diagnosis include an examination of somatic, psychological, and social/ interpersonal factors, with particular attention given to basic endowment, developmental processes, and various acute events.

An interactive analysis of this sort is fundamental to the assessment of most psychological conditions. The facilitative or debilitative effect of a particular factor may change qualitatively when considered in relationship to other factors. Consider, for example, the assessment of attention deficit hyperactivity disorder (AD-HD), a developmental disability affecting anywhere from 3 percent to 12 percent of school-age children and characterized by core deficits in sustained attention, impulsivity, arousal modulation, and inclination to seek immediate reinforcement (Douglas, 1983). While an examiner's use of a particular reinforcement schedule may serve to enhance the performance of most children on a given measure, that same schedule may degrade the performance of an AD–HD child. Douglas and Peters (1979) comment that for the hyperactive child "the reinforcers become a highly salient aspect of the learning situation.... More attention [is paid] to the reinforcers themselves (or the reinforcing person) than to the particular behavior being reinforced, or to the specific stimuli associated with it" (p. 209). In a performance situation, the AD–HD child may miss out on important instructions or on learning the task because of attention directed toward the reinforcer.

Moreover, because an individual constitutes a complicated system of interdependencies, the clinician must anticipate that certain factors will influence or interfere with the assessment of other factors (Messick, 1984). For instance, lowered self-esteem, poor performance on some cognitive tasks, lowered social competence, and a depressive attributional style appear to be associated with depression in children and adults (Fauber, Forehand, Long, Burke, & Faust, 1987; Kaslow, Rehm, & Siegel, 1984). These particular characteristics are likely to degrade the depressed examinee's scores on such performance measures as school achievement and possibly intelligence. At the same time that intelligence scores may be lower for the clinically depressed client, by the very nature of this disorder, the scores may not serve as a valid predictor of future ability and achievement after successful therapy. Similarly, the tendency for aggressive children to respond impulsively to stimuli (Dodge & Frame, 1982; Dodge & Newman, 1981) might lower various test scores. Alternatively, an argument with one's spouse prior to testing could well result in a low score on a test of marital satisfaction!

Depression can be used to illustrate how the dynamic and interactive nature of human behavior influences the selection of assessment methods and instruments. The diathesis stress model of depression (Akiskal & McKinney, 1975) recognizes the role of genetic and developmental predispositions and physiological and psychosocial stressors that may alter the level and production of particular neurotransmitters, which, in turn, produces a malfunction of the central nervous system reward systems, culminating in clinical depression. Also, the DSM-III-R lists a number of different symptoms ranging from dysphoric mood to feelings of worthlessness and difficulty in thinking that must be demonstrated before a diagnosis of major depression can be made. Thus, self-concept and guilt scales, intelligence tests, mood checklists, and various depression inventories may all be employed along with other medical and social assessment techniques in this diagnostic process.

Testing of Special Populations

A particularly intractable issue in assessment concerns the use of tests with culturally diverse individuals. The differential treatment of ethnic and cultural minorities as a result of testing (e.g., overrepresentation of minority children in all types of special education programs), together with findings that indicate performance differences for culturally diverse individuals on even such brief scales as Naglieri's (1985) group administered *Matrix Analogies Test–Short Form* (e.g., Bardos, 1990; Saklofske & de Lacey, 1990) or on such measures as the *Eysenck Personality Questionnaire* (Eysenck & Eysenck, 1975) for both children and adults have led to heated debate over whether discriminatory testing practices or inherent group differences account for the disparities. Although the battle over whether cultural bias in standardized testing exists has been waged in the research literature (Jensen, 1980), as well as in the courts (*Larry P. vs. Wilson Riles*, 1979) and legislatures, an accord has not been reached. It is still common to hear critics of the testing movement assert that "current tests purporting to measure intelligence, aptitude, or achievement are biased against certain ethnic/racial groups" (Williams, 1985, p. 192), while proponents claim that "psychological tests, especially aptitude tests, function in essentially the same manner across race and sex" (Reynolds, 1983, p. 249).

Given the current uncertainty regarding test bias, psychologists are directed to provide a "thorough discussion of the limitations of their data, especially where their work touches on social policy or might be construed to the detriment of persons in specific age, sex, ethnic, socioeconomic, or other social groups" (American Psychological Association, 1981, p. 633). With regard to cultural and racial minorities, a number of potential biasing factors could be identified. Johnson (1979) states that

> many factors operate to attenuate or lower test scores.... These include factors which affect the actual performance of individuals on the test, such as socioeconomic status, differences in educational opportunity, motivation, narrowness of content of the test, atmosphere of the testing situation, and the perceived relevance of the test to success. They also include factors that affect the test score more directly such as the composition of the group used for item tryouts and item selection and analysis which precede the actual standardization, composition of the standardization or normative group, and the techniques and procedures employed in item construction. Also the validity or appropriateness of tests often differ for [different cultural minorities], in relation to the same future performance or criterion. (p. 3)

A variety of suggestions has been advanced for reducing error when testing cultural and racial minorities (e.g., Massey, 1988). Ideas include imposing a moratorium on testing, multifactored assessment, use of nonverbally based measures, use of tests with norms especially adapted to minority populations, improving test-taking skills, ethnicity matching, translation, and pluralistic assessment (Fradd & Hallman, 1983; Lewis & Samuda, 1989; Mick, 1984/85).

Over the past decade, considerable concern has also been expressed over potential bias in testing exceptional individuals. Exceptional individuals include the visually and hearing impaired, the physically handicapped, persons with learning and developmental disabilities, the mentally handicapped, and individuals with communication and behavior disorders. Such persons typically possess a variety of characteristics that increase errors of test administration and interpretation when standardized tests are used (Luftig, 1989). "A failure to take these characteristics into account results in faulty and erroneous conclusions based on invalid test scores" (Luftig, 1989, p. 217).

Testing of limits (Sattler, 1988) or modification of administration procedures is generally recommended practice when evaluating exceptional individuals to ensure a valid and comprehensive assessment. For example, when assessing a hearing-impaired child, communication can be facilitated through sign language or pantomime. Large-print materials might be used with a visually impaired adult. McLoughlin and Lewis (1990) note that although modifications can provide useful information, results of tests administered under altered conditions must be interpreted with great caution. Other recommendations concerning the assessment of exceptional individuals include the use of tests designed for and standardized on handicapped populations (Salvia & Ysseldyke, 1988) and multisource assessment (Witt et al., 1988). A checklist for minimizing bias associated with the selection, administration, scoring, and interpretation of tests is presented in Figure 2. Although intended for use in the clinical assessment of children, it is also applicable to adults. Sattler's (1988) text is rich in suggestions for testing special populations.

Conclusion

There is little argument that while tests are an important tool in psychological measurement, they are also imperfect. As such, caution must be exercised when selecting, using, and interpreting tests.

FIGURE 2. Checklist for Minimizing Bias
During Interpretation of Results

Name _____ School _____

Examiner _____ Date _____

Examine Child's Score *A check (✓) indicates potential bias*

___ Compare them to the adaptive behavior information
___ Look for characteristics of the child which might bias or influence the
results such as:
   ___ native language
   ___ age, health, nutrition
   ___ handicapping conditions
   ___ mode of communication
   ___ sensory and performance modalities
___ Look for characteristics of the tests and techniques which might bias or
influence the results, such as
   ___ purpose
   ___ communication modalities (a) child-test (b) child-examiner
   ___ norms
   ___ reliability and validity
   ___ type of measure
   ___ relevance of items
   ___ scoring criteria
   ___ type of scores
___ Look for characteristics of the examiner which might bias or influence
the results, such as
   ___ appropriate training
   ___ communication mode and language
   ___ previous experience
   ___ attitudes
   ___ skills
   ___ knowledge
___ Look for conditions within the assessment situation which might bias the
performance, such as
   ___ time of day
   ___ distractions
   ___ testing materials
   ___ inappropriate use of cues
   ___ length of session
   ___ comfort and accessibility of materials
   ___ order of assessment activities

FIGURE 2. Checklist for Minimizing Bias
During Interpretation of Results (continued)

___ Look for conditions between the examiner and child which might bias
the performance
    ___ rapport
    ___ attending behavior
    ___ initial success or failure
    ___ maintaining responding behavior
    ___ communication
    ___ dress and/or mannerisms
___ Try to determine if the child's performance is representative and/or
approximates his/her potential
___ Compare the results of multiple measures

Testing errors stem from problems in the test itself, situational and interactional factors that occur during administration of the test, and variables associated with the examinee. "Best practice" dictates that psychologists continue to develop and use tests that exemplify sound psychometric properties and that result in reliable and valid data for purposes of decision making. Furthermore, psychologists recognize and take into account the wide range of contextual and personal factors that can contaminate test interpretation. It is all of these reasons that led Kaufman (1979) in his description of intelligence testing to state that "the burden is on the test users to be 'better' than the tests they use."

We have identified a number of personal and contextual factors that may influence an individual's test responses. Whether these factors positively or negatively influence behavior can vary across individuals and situations. For example, optimal levels of anxiety are generally recognized to enhance performance, while extremes such as those exhibited by the test-anxious person can he debilitating. Similarly, high levels of motivation on an achievement test may lead to persistence and task-oriented behaviors resulting in effective problem solving. In contrast, high levels of motivation when taking a personality test may underlie the selection of socially desirable responses. A mildly distracting environment may have little or no observable affect on one individual's performance but may be sufficient to cause attention and concentration difficulties in another person. Thus, performance-enhancing or debilitating factors need to be assessed along a continuum that takes into account individual differences.

The complex nature of human behavior, together with inexact measurement techniques, requires the psychologist to collect and interpret multisource data, that is, to engage in assessment rather than just testing. It is only through the process of assessment that human behavior can best be understood in the promotion of psychological well-being.

References

Ackerman, P. L., Sternberg, R.J., & Glaser, R. (Eds.). (1989). *Learning and individual differences: Advances in theory and research.* New York: Freidman.

Aiken, L. R. (1989). *Assessment of personality.* Boston: Allyn & Bacon.

Akiskal, H. D., & McKinney, W. T. (1975). Overview of recent research in depression: Integration of ten conceptual models into a comprehensive clinical frame. *Archives of General Psychiatry, 32,* 285–305.

Alpert, R., & Haber, R. N. (1960). Anxiety in academic achievement situations. *Journal of Abnormal and Social Psychology, 61,* 207–215.

American Psychological Association. (1981). Ethical principles of psychologists. *American Psychologist, 36,* 633–638.

American Psychological Association. (1985). *Standards for educational and psychological testing.* Washington, DC: Author.

Anastasi, A. (1988). *Psychological testing* (6th ed.). New York: Macmillan.

Atkinson, J. W., & Raynor, J. V. (Eds.). (1974). *Motivation and achievement.* Washington, DC: Winston.

Bandura, A. (1978). The self system in reciprocal determinism. *American Psychologist, 33,* 344–358.

Bardos, A. N. (1990). *Multicultural assessment using the Matrix Analogies Tests.* Paper presented at the annual meeting of the National Association of School Psychologists, San Francisco.

Benson, M. J., & Weinberg, R. A. (1990). Contributions of the psychology of individual differences to school psychology: Different drummers—one beat. In T. B. Gutkin & C. R. Reynolds (Eds.), *The handbook of school psychology* (2nd ed., pp. 218–243). New York: Wiley.

Bouchard, T. J., & McGee, M. (1981). Familial studies of intelligence: A review. *Science, 212,* 1055–1059.

Bradley-Johnson, S., Graham, D., & Johnson, C. (1986). Token reinforcement on WISC-R performance for white low socio-economic upper and lower elementary school aged students. *Journal of School Psychology, 24,* 73–79.

Brebner, J., & Cooper, C. (1986). Personality factors and inspection time. *Personality and Individual Differences, 7,* 709–714.

Colby, F. (1989). Usefulness of the K Correction in MMPI profiles of patients and nonpatients. *Psychological Assessment, 1,* 142–145.

Cronbach, L. J. (1990). *Essentials of psychological testing* (5th ed.). New York: HarperCollins.

Cronbach, L. S., & Snow, R. G. (1977). *Aptitudes and instructional methods: A handbook for research on interactions.* New York: Irvington/Naiburg.

Dalton, J. E. , Tom, A. , Rosenblum, M. L. , Garte, S. H. , & Aubuchon, I. N. (1989). Faking on the Mississippi Scale for Combat-related Posttraumatic Stress Disorder. *Psychological Assessment, 1,* 56–57.

Dement, W. C. (1976). *Some must watch while some must sleep.* New York: Norton.

Dodge, K. A., & Frame, C. L. (1982). Social cognitive biases and deficits in aggressive boys. *Child Development, 63,* 620–635.

Dodge, K. A., & Newman, J. P. (1981). Biased decision-making processes in aggressive boys. *Journal of Abnormal Psychology, 90,* 375–379.

Douglas, V. I. (1983). Attentional and cognitive problems. In M. Rutter (Ed.), *Developmental neuropsychiatry* (pp. 280–329). New York: The Guilford Press.

Douglas, V. I., & Peters, K. G. (1979). Toward a clearer definition of the attentional deficit of hyperactive children. In G. A. Hale & M. Lewis (Eds.), *Attention and the development of cognitive skills* (pp. 173–247). New York: Plenum Press.

Edelmann, R. J., & Hardwick, S. (1986). Test anxiety, past performance and coping strategies. *Personality and Individual Differences, 7,* 255–258.

Erickson, E. (1963). *Childhood and society* (2nd ed.). New York: Norton.

Eysenck, M. (1985). Anxiety and cognitive-task performance. *Personality and Individual Differences, 6,* 579–586.

Eysenck, H. J., & Eysenck, S. B. G. (1975). *Manual of the Eysenck Personality Questionnaire.* San Diego: Education and Industrial Testing Service.

Eysenck, H. J., & Eysenck, M. (1985). *Personality and individual differences: A natural science approach.* New York: Plenum Press.

Fauber, R., Forehand, R., Long, N., Burke, M., & Faust, J. (1987). The relationship of young adolescent Children's Depression Inventory (CDI) scores to their social and cognitive functioning. *Journal of Psychopathology and Behavioral Assessment, 9,* 161–172.

Fradd, S., & Hallman, C. L. (1983). Implications of psychological and educational research for assessment and instruction of culturally and linguistically different students. *Learning Disability Quarterly, 6,* 468–478.

Fuchs, D., & Fuchs, L. S. (1986). Test procedure bias: A meta-analysis of examiner familiarity effects. *Review of Educational Research, 56*, 243–262.

Goldsmith, H. H. (1983). Genetic influences in personality from infancy to adulthood. *Child Development, 54*, 331–355.

Goslin, D. A. (1963). *The search for ability: Standardized testing in social perspective*. New York: Sage.

Gough, H. G. (1987). *California Psychological Inventory: Administrator's guide*. Palo Alto, CA: Consulting Psychologists Press.

Hakstian, A. R., & McLean, P. D. (1989). Brief screen for depression. *Psychological Assessment, 1*, 139–141.

Hammermaster, C. S. (1989). Levels of performance and cognitive interference in text-anxious subjects. *The Alberta Journal of Educational Research, 35*, 164–170.

Hanin, Y. L. (1988). Cross-cultural perspectives in the assessment of individual differences: Methodological and conceptual issues. In D. H. Saklofske & S. B. G. Eysenck (Eds.), *Individual differences in children and adolescents: International perspectives* (pp. 313–320). London: Hodder & Stoughton.

Helson, R., & Moane, G. (1987). Personality change in women from college to midlife. *Journal of Personality and Social Psychology, 53*, 176–186.

Hembree, R. (1988). Correlates, causes, effects, and treatment of test anxiety. *Review of Educational Research, 58*, 47–77.

Hogan, R., & Nicholson, R. A. (1988). The meaning of personality test scores. *American Psychologist, 43*, 621–626.

Hood-Smith, N. E., & Leffingwell, R. J. (1984). The impact of physical space alteration on disruptive classroom behavior: A case study. *Education, 104*, 224–230.

Hoeppel, R. (1990). Temporal variability: Effects of extraversion and time of day upon children's test responses. *Personality and Individual Differences, 11*, 1271–1281.

Hyman, S. E., & Arana, G. W. (1987). *Handbook of psychiatric drug therapy*. Boston: Little, Brown.

Jackson, D. N. (1974). *Personality Research Form: Manual* (rev. ed.). Port Huron, MI: Research Psychologists Press.

Jacobs, D. F. (1983). The development and application of standards of practice for professional psychologists. In B. D. Sales (Ed.), *The professional psychologist's handbook* (pp. 19–75). New York: Plenum.

Jensen, A. R. (1980). *Bias in mental testing*. New York: Free Press.

Johnson, S. T. (1979). *The measurement mystique*. Washington, DC: Institute for the Study of Educational Policy.

Kaslow, N. J., Rehm, L. P., & Siegel, A. W. (1984). Social-cognitive and cognitive correlates of depression in children. *Journal of Abnormal Child Psychology, 12,* 605–620.

Kaufman, A. S. (1979). *Intelligent testing with the WISC-R.* New York: Wiley.

Kaufman, A. S., & Kaufman, N. L. (1983). *K-ABC: Kaufman Assessment Battery for Children.* Circle Pines, MN: American Guidance Service.

Kohlberg, L. (1981). *Essays on moral development: Vol. 1. The philosophy of moral development: Moral stages and the idea of justice.* San Francisco: Harper & Row.

Kohlberg, L. (1984). *Essays on moral development: Vol. 2. The psychology of moral development: The nature and validity of moral stages.* San Francisco: Harper & Row.

Korchin, S. J. (1976). *Modern clinical psychology.* New York: Basic Books.

Lanyon, R. I., Dannenbaum, S. E., Wolf, L. L., & Brown, A. (1989). Dimensions of deceptive responding in criminal offenders. *Psychological Assessment, 1,* 300–304.

Larry P. v. Wilson Riles. (1979). Opinion, U.S. District Court for Northern District of California (No. C-712270 RFP).

Lewis, J., & Samuda, R. J. (1989). Non-discriminatory assessment of culturally different students. *McGill Journal of Education, 24,* 253–266.

Liebert, R. M., & Morris, L. W. (1967). Cognitive and emotional components of test anxiety: A distinction and some initial data. *Psychological Reports, 20,* 975–978.

Luftig, R. L. (1989). *Assessment of learners with special needs.* Boston: Allyn and Bacon

Lyman, H. B. (1978). *Test scores and what they mean* (3rd ed.). Englewood Cliffs, NJ: Prentice-Hall.

Mandler, G., & Sarason, S. B. (1982). A study of anxiety and learning. *Journal of Abnormal and Social Psychology, 47,* 166–173.

Massey, D. S. (1988). Cross-cultural psychological assessment: A clinical model of service delivery. *Canadian Journal of School Psychology, 4,* 21–37.

Matarazzo, J. D. (1990). Psychological assessment versus psychological testing. *American Psychologist, 45,* 999–1017.

McAfee, J. K. (1987). Classroom density and the aggressive behavior of handicapped children. *Education and Treatment of Children, 10,* 134–145.

McClelland, D. C. (1985). *Human motivation.* Glenview, IL: Scott, Foresman.

McCrae, R. R., & Costa, P. T. (1984). *Emerging lives, enduring dispositions: Personality in adulthood.* Boston: Little Brown.

McLoughlin, J. A., & Lewis, R. B. (1990). *Assessing special students* (3rd ed.). Columbus, OH: Merrill.

Meichenbaum, D., & Butler, L. (1980). Toward a conceptual model for the treatment of test anxiety: Implications for research and treatment. In I. G. Sarason (Ed.), *Test anxiety: Theory, research, and applications*. Hillsdale, NJ: Erlbaum.

Messick, S. (1984). The psychology of educational measurement. *Journal of Educational Measurement, 21,* 215–237.

Mick, L. B. (1984-85). Assessment procedures as related to enrollment patterns of Hispanic students in special education. *Educational Research Quarterly, 9,* 29–35.

Minor, S. W., & Gold, S. R. (1986). Behavior of test anxious students across time. *Personality and Individual Differences, 7,* 241–242.

Mischel, W. (1977). On the future of personality measurement. *American Psychologist, 32,* 246–254.

Murphy, K. R., & Davidshofer, C. D. (1988). *Psychological testing: Principles and applications.* Englewood Cliffs, NJ: Prentice Hall.

Naglieri, J. A. (1985). *Matrix Analogies Test–Short Form.* Columbus, OH: Merrill.

Naglieri, J. A. (1988). *Draw A Person: A quantitative scoring system.* San Antonio, TX: The Psychological Corporation.

Piaget, J. (1970). Piaget's theory. In P. H. Mussen (Ed.), *Carmichael's manual of child psychology* (Vol. 1, 3rd ed., pp. 703–732). New York: Norton.

Ramey, C. T., Bryant, D. M., & Suarez, T. M. (1985). Preschool compensatory education and the modifiability of intelligence: A critical review. In D. K. Detterman (Ed.), *Current topics in human intelligence (Vol. 1)– Research Methodology* (pp. 247–296). Norwood, NJ: Ablex.

Reynolds, C. R. (1983). Test bias: In God we trust: All others must have data. *The Journal of Special Education, 17,* 241–260.

Robinson, D. L. (1985). How personality relates to intelligence test performance: Implications for a theory of intelligence, aging research and personality assessment. *Personality and Individual Differences, 6,* 203–216.

Robinson, D. L. (1986). The Wechsler Adult Intelligence Scale and personality assessment: Toward a biologically based theory of intelligence and cogni-tion. *Personality and Individual Differences, 7,* 153–159.

Rosenthal, R. (1966). *Experimenter effects in behavioral research.* New York: Appleton-Century-Crofts.

Saigh, P. (1981). The effects of positive examiner verbal comments on the total WISC-R performance of institutionalized EMR students. *Journal of School Psychology, 19,* 86–91.

Saklofske, D. H. (1985). The relationship between Eysenck's major person-ality dimensions and simultaneous and sequential processing in children. *Personality and Individual Differences, 6,* 429–433.

Saklofske, D. H., & Braun, S. (1989). *A psychometric investigation of the D-A-P: A Quantitative scoring system utilizing a Canadian sample.* Paper presented at the annual meeting of the Canadian Association of School Psycholo-gists, Edmonton.

Saklofske, D. H., Blomme, G., & Kelly, I. W. (1991). *Introversion-extraversion, exercise and arousal.* Paper presented at the 5th Biennial Conference of the International Society for the Study of Individual Differences, Oxford, England.

Saklofske, D. H., & de Lacey, P. R. (1990). *Non-verbal cognitive functioning: A comparative study of draw-a-person and matrix analogies performance.* Paper presented at the annual meeting of the International Association of Cross-cultural Psychology, Japan.

Saklofske, D. H., & Eysenck, S. B. G. (Eds.). (1988). *Individual differences in children and adolescents: International perspectives.* London: Hodder & Stoughton.

Saklofske, D. H., Janzen, H. L., & Pannanan, N. (1987). Predictors of childhood depression: Literature review and empirical findings. *Canadian Journal of Special Education, 3,* 1–14.

Saklofske, D. H., & Kostura, D. D. (1990). Extraversion-introversion and intelligence. *Personality and Individual Differences, 11,* 547–551.

Saklofske, D. H., & Schwean Kowalchuk, V. L. (1991). *Cognitive and intel-lectual performance of ADHD children.* Paper presented at the annual meeting of the American Psychological Association, San Francisco.

Saklofske, D. H., Yackulic, R. A., Edwards, W., & Naglieri, J. A. (in press). Canadian children's performance on the Matrix Analogies Test–Short Form. *Canadian Journal of School Psychology.*

Salvia, J., & Ysseldyke, J. E. (1988). *Assessment in special and remedial education* (4th ed.). Boston: Houghton Mifflin.

Sarason, I. G. (1958). Effects on verbal learning of anxiety, reassurance and meaningfulness of material. *Journal of Experimental Psychology, 56,* 472–477.

Sarason, I. G. (Ed.). (1980). *Text anxiety: Theory, research and applications.* Hillsdale, NJ: Erlbaum.

Sattler, J. M. (1988). *Assessment of children* (3rd ed.). San Diego: Sattler.

Sattler, J., Andres, J., Squire, L., Wisely, R., & Maloy, C. (1978). Examiner scoring of ambiguous WISC-R responses. *Psychology in the Schools, 15,* 486–488.

Segal, N. L. T. (1985). Monozygotic and dizygotic twins: A comparative analysis of mental ability profiles. *Child Development, 52,* 1051–1052.

Sherrets, S., Gard, G., & Langner, H. (1979). Frequency of clerical errors on WISC protocols. *Psychology in the Schools, 16,* 495–496.

Spiel, W. (1981). Some critical comments on a systematic approach to diagnosis: Contributions to a documentation and classification system in child neuropsychiatry. *Acta Paedopsychiatrica, 47,* 269–278.

Spielberger, C. D., Anton, W. D., & Bedell, J. (1976). The nature and treatment of text anxiety. In M. Zucherman & C. D. Spielberger (Eds.), *Emotions and anxiety: New concepts, methods and applications* (pp. 317–345). New York: Wiley.

Stevens, D. P., & Truss, C. V. (1985). Stability and change in adult personality over 12 and 20 years. *Developmental Psychology, 21,* 548–568.

Taylor, R. L. (1989). *Assessment of exceptional students: Educational and psychological procedures.* Englewood Cliffs, NJ: Prentice-Hall.

Thayer, R. E. (1989). *The biopsychology of mood and arousal.* Oxford: Oxford University Press.

Thorndike, R. L., Hagen, E. P., & Sattler, J. M. (1986). *Technical manual, Stanford-Binet Intelligence Scale: Fourth Edition.* Chicago: Riverside.

Tindal, G. A., & Marston, D. B. (1990). *Classroom-based assessment: Evaluating instructional outcomes.* Columbus, OH: Merrill.

Turnbull, A. P., Strickland, B. B., & Brantley, J. C. (1982). *Developing and implementing individualized education programs* (2nd ed.). Columbus, OH: Merrill.

Wakefield, J. A., Jr. (1979). *Using personality to individualize instruction.* San Diego: Educational and Industrial Testing Service.

Wechsler, D. (1974). *Manual for the Wechsler Intelligence Scale for Children-Revised.* San Antonio, TX: The Psychological Corporation.

Williams, T. S. (1985). Some issues in the standardized testing of minority students. *Journal of Education, 10,* 192–208.

Witt, J. C., Elliott, S. N., Gresham, F. M., & Kramer, J. J. (1988). *Assessment of special children: Tests and the problem-solving process.* Glenview, IL: Scott, Foresman.

Wolpe, J. (1969). *The practice of behavior therapy.* New York: Pergamon.

Zahn, T. P., Rapoport, J. L., & Thompson, C. L. (1980). Autonomic and behavioural effects of dextroamphetamine and placebo in normal and hyperactive prepubertal boys. *Journal of Abnormal Child Psychology, 8,* 145–160.

CHAPTER 4

THE INTERPRETATION OF TESTS

Bruce A. Bracken

This chapter addresses procedures and rationale for test interpretation, including norm-referenced, ipsative, criterion-referenced, and curriculum-based approaches. The chapter also discusses use of combined interpretation styles within the same test, the integration of test scores with other assessment information, the importance of clinical observation and judgment in interpretation of test performance, and psychometric reasons for similar tests producing dissimilar results.

Approaches to Test Interpretation

NORM-REFERENCED TEST INTERPRETATION

Norm-referenced assessment is the process of measuring an individual's level of skill or ability and comparing it to the performance of a designated reference group. Norm-referenced assessment allows comparisons among the performances of individuals within the norm-based reference group, and between the performance of an individual outside the reference group and those individuals within it. Essentially, the purpose of norm-referenced assessment is to rank individuals by their performance on a measure, allowing judgments to be made about examinees' abilities relative to all other members of the reference group; hence, an individual test score is *referenced* against a *normative sample*.

As generally acknowledged, raw scores in and of themselves provide limited information for evaluating examinee performance. A raw score cannot be fully appreciated or adequately interpreted until one knows such basic information as the number of items on the test and how well the average examinee performed. Once the examinees' raw scores are combined and rank ordered by level of performance, the mean and standard deviation of the score distribution determined, and each raw score in the distribution converted to a percentile rank and/or a standard score (e.g., z-score), individual raw scores become more meaningful and valuable.

A raw score of 65 on a measure of perceptual speed, for example, acquires meaning only when the mean and standard deviation of the perceptual speed test are also known. For illustration, let's say the mean of this hypothetical perceptual speed distribution is 50 and the standard deviation is 5. With these numbers and a table depicting "area under the normal curve," we can determine that a perceptual speed raw score of 65 is exactly three standard deviations above the average score (i.e., equal to a z-score of +3). Further, we can see that the examinee's level of perceptual speed is as good or better than 99.87 percent of all the examinees in the reference group. Thus, the valueless raw score of 65 yields considerable meaning and information when interpreted against a norm.

While raw scores reflect absolute measures of ability (i.e., how many items the examinee passed or failed), they reveal little information about performance relative to the examinee's peer group. Norm-referenced standard scores (e.g., z, T, IQ), on the other hand, depict relative performance but do not provide knowledge about absolute performance or competence in a given skill area.

Norm-referenced test interpretation is used primarily to help make decisions about which examinees might be best suited for a limited number of available positions or opportunities, such as scholarships or placement in special programs, for example. Also, in highly competitive educational programs, such as graduate programs in psychology, medicine, or law where only a few candidates can be selected from a large pool of highly qualified applicants, the selection process typically gives much weight to norm-referenced performance on aptitude tests such as the *Graduate Record Exam* (GRE) or the *Miller Analogies Test* (MAT). In selection processes like this, a minimum GRE standard score might be used as a cut score, or minimal criterion score, to reduce the large initial applicant pool to a more manageable data aggregate. Once the applicant pool is sufficiently reduced by eliminating all those below the cut score, then other important characteristics and criteria can be considered.

One major benefit of norm-referenced assessment is that it provides an objective rank ordering of examinees on a variable that is chosen because of its importance in the selection process (e.g., aptitude, achievement). While considerable controversy prevails over the relative value of specific entrance exams like the GRE, MAT, and LSAT, it is undeniable that in the relatively subjective process of applicant selection, test scores provide an objective source of data (Anastasi, 1988; Salvia & Ysseldyke, 1981). Without the objective information derived from norm-referenced assessment, important placement and selection decisions would be made largely on subjective criteria, a situation that very few would find acceptable.

A major consideration in norm-referenced assessment is that the majority of scores (approximately 68%) are distributed within one standard deviation of the mean; that is $, +/- 1$ z. With the majority of examinees scoring within the average range of abilities (i.e., $+/- 1$ z), there might be little value in norm-referenced assessment, unless normalcy is the condition one seeks to affirm. Norm-referenced assessment offers little meaningful discrimination among the performances of the vast majority of those tested because the majority of scores are comparable and within the average range.

It is those at the opposite ends of the score distribution, those whose scores deviate significantly from average, who typically are targeted for norm-referenced assessments. For example, examinees who score two or more standard deviations *below* the mean on measures of intelligence are identified as functioning in the mentally retarded range of intellectual abilities. Comparably, those who score two or more standard deviations *above* the mean are identified as functioning in the intellectually gifted range. Because schools have special programs for retarded and gifted students, and significant deviation from average intelligence is one prerequisite for admission into the special programs, those children who are suspected by their teachers or parents as being either gifted or retarded would most likely be referred for an individually administered norm-referenced intelligence test. Children who are commonly accepted by their teachers or parents as intellectually "average" or "normal" are rarely referred for such assessments.

National Norms Versus Local Norms
An important issue related to norm-referenced assessment is whether the normative reference group is the most appropriate comparison standard.

Typically, on commercially produced norm-referenced tests, the normative sample is selected on a stratified basis to reflect the characteristics of the national population. For example, a normative sample would typically include representative proportions of examinees from different minority and majority groups, socioeconomic strata, geographic locations, gender groups, and so on, according to the most recent U. S. census count. A nationally normed test has appeal because its "representative" norms can be used throughout the country, and an individual's test score can be compared to the "average" person of that same chronological age in the nation as a whole.

Representativeness of norms is an important consideration when deciding whether to use existing published norms or to create local norms. National norms are sometimes inappropriate. For example, if all kindergarten-age children within a single community are assessed to identify those "at risk" for early school failure, then national norms might shed little light on the likelihood of success or failure in that isolated community school system. In a community where the majority of children score below the national average and achieve in school at the same delayed pace relative to the national average, local norms would provide a more appropriate standard for comparison. While the majority of the children in this school system would be identified as at risk for school failure if national norms were used, fewer children would be truly at risk for failure in that particular school system if local norms were used.

Because local residents do not always reflect the national population on important demographic characteristics, local norms are often the best and most appropriate reference standard available. The use of local norms allows for a standard of comparison and prediction that is more sensitive to the local criterion standard (i.e., academic success or failure in that particular school system). Local norms are developed in a fashion similar to national norms, except local norms are much more likely to include the entire population of the community (e.g., all public school kindergarten children in the community) rather than a stratified sample of the population. When an entire population is included in the norming process, examiners can be confident in the meaningfulness of the norms because there is no sampling error; that is, every child in the population is included in the norming procedure.

As a second example, in some high socioeconomic, professional communities, it is common for the "average" student to function intellectually in the average to high range of abilities, with a mean IQ in excess of 120 (national norm is an IQ of 100). In an affluent community of this sort, a child with low to average intellectual ability (e.g., IQ of 90) would be two standard deviations below the local school norm and functioning at a "retarded" level relative to his or her same-age classmates in that school system. While this child would be considered neither intellectually nor academically retarded when compared to the national average, this performance would be ranked at less than the third percentile when compared to local school classmates. This child very well might suffer the same frustrations, diminished self-concept, and social difficulties that mentally retarded children experience when their intellectual and academic progress is gauged against the progress of other nonretarded children.

In these two examples, a different interpretation of the child's ability is made when compared to local rather than national norms. It can be argued that both local and national norms provide interpretative value and should be considered when important decisions are made about individuals. Fortunately, the majority of U.S. school systems "fit" the national characteristics sufficiently well that the use of local norms would not alter decision outcomes. Where local norms seem to have the most value (and national norms are most limited) are in communities where the residents differ radically from the national norm on variables known to be correlated with the assessed construct. Socioeconomic status, parental education levels, and geographic region have all been found to be related to the construct of intelligence.

Other Norms

Norm samples are usually selected on a stratified basis from the larger population on a set of characteristics common among individuals in the reference group. Because many abilities and skills are developmental and improve with age, age is usually the most important stratification variable used in the selection of individuals in norm development. Some skills, however, are influenced more by the environment or experience with specific opportunities. For example, academic achievement is related more to children's grade placement than chronological age. Academic achievement does not increase directly as a function of age, but as a function of exposure to academic experiences germane to the content taught in each grade.

Because achievement is grade dependent, most achievement tests develop grade norms, and some present both grade and age norms. Because ages and grades are closely related (e.g., most six-year-olds are in first grade and ten-year-olds in fifth grade), the use of age or grade norms makes little difference for the typical child. However, the relationship between age and grade placement is less than perfect, especially in the case of children kept back or promoted beyond their expected grade placement, and the wise use of the appropriate norm (age or grade) is important when making decisions about atypical children's test performance.

Meaningful Deviations in Norm-referenced Assessment

Norm-referenced test interpretation facilitates decision making by allowing individuals to be identified as "meaningfully different" from others in the normative sample based on test performance. The degree of deviation considered important or meaningful might vary considerably, depending on the decisions to be made, the nature and size of the examinee pool, and the inclusion of additional criteria in the decision-making process. Further, deviant scores may be viewed as positive or negative, depending on the characteristic assessed and the decisions that must be made; they might be considered meaningful if they differ in only one direction, such as significantly above the average test score, or in both, that is, above or below the average score range.

In a situation where a personnel psychologist must select the top five individuals from a pool of 100 applicants and test scores alone are to be used to make the hiring decisions, applicants ranked in the top five percent (95th percentile rank and above) will automatically be chosen to fill the positions available. All who score below are considered unsuitable. Someone whose score is at the 94th percentile is treated no differently from an applicant ranked at the 1st percentile. In this case, "meaningful deviation" is defined arbitrarily as the 95th percentile rank and above.

Whether a score is considered meaningfully different is usually determined in a fairly arbitrary manner by the dictates of the number of available positions to be filled (e.g., 100 applicants and only 5 available positions), by an empirical finding related to the nature of the trait or construct assessed (e.g., the majority of individuals who score above a given level succeed in law school), or by an accepted operational definition (e.g., retarded functioning is defined as two or more standard deviations below the national mean). In general, scores of a magnitude that have practical or theoretical import are identified as meaningfully different from average.

Frequently, what is determined to be meaningfully different is a score that is statistically rare, based on probability theory. For example, scores that occur in the normal population at a rate of less than 5 times in 100 or once in 100 (alpha levels of .05 and .01, respectively) are often considered meaningful because they are statistically rare at a predetermined criterion rate (i.e., 1 or 5 times in 100 cases). Likewise, scores that are a given number of standard deviations from the mean are frequently considered meaningful. While in both cases meaningful deviation is determined statistically, the criterion level for meaningful deviation is still relatively arbitrarily set, with little rationale for why a given alpha level or z-score is more important than another, other than relative rarity.

As an example of empirical determination of meaningful deviance, consider the situation where it has been found previously that persons who handle heavy machinery perform safely on the job only if they demonstrate an "average" level of manifest anxiety. Those machine operators who score more than one standard deviation *above* average on a trait anxiety scale tend to make impulsive decisions that result in work site accidents. Those machine operators who score one standard deviation or more *below* average on the scale tend to be insufficiently alert to make important decisions quickly, again resulting in work site accidents. In this example, the employment of a norm-referenced manifest anxiety scale in the selection of potential employees could help identify those individuals meaningfully different from average (i.e., $> +/-1\ z$) on this empirically demonstrated important trait. An assessment of potential employees' level of manifest anxiety would allow the employer to hire employees who would likely, as a result, have reduced risk of causing serious accidents, and the employer would avoid hiring those machine operators who pose the greatest danger to themselves and their co-workers on the work site.

In sum, norm-referenced tests are intentionally designed to discriminate a full range of examinee abilities. Test scores in a norm-referenced distribution are ordered, and test interpretation stems from determining whether a particular score is either sufficiently rare or average relative to the norm to warrant inclusion or exclusion in further considerations or selection. Norm-referenced interpretation does not reflect an examinee's absolute performance on the test, but an examinee's performance relative to the performance of the norm-based peer group. At times, it may be more meaningful to use local rather than national norms, especially when local conditions deviate greatly from the national norm. Whether a score is considered meaningfully or statistically different from average is decided in a relatively arbitrary fashion, but is typically linked to practical, empirical, and theoretical determinants.

IPSATIVE PROFILE INTERPRETATION

At times it is desirable to learn where an individual ranks relative to peers on a given variable, but there are also times when the question of interest is not related to level of performance as compared to the norm group. There are also times when the concern is oriented more toward the rate of development of one skill or ability relative to all other skills or abilities. In multidimensional, multiple-skill assessment, an examiner might be interested in whether these various skills are developing uniformly. That is, is there a developmental lag in some skill areas, and quicker progress in others. This sort of intra-examinee test comparison is referred to as *ipsative profile interpretation* (Cattell, 1944).

In ipsative profile interpretation, an examinee's development rate or performance level on subsets or portions of a test (e.g., subtests, scales, specific skill areas) is compared with overall level of functioning on the entire test. While norm-referenced assessment identifies areas in which examinees progress at faster or slower rates relative to their peer group, ipsative profile interpretation focuses on variation in performance on specific subtests or scales relative to their own overall level of performance. Ipsative interpretation allows the individual's strengths and weaknesses to be identified relative to his or her overall test performance.

Cattell (1944) appears to have coined the term "ipsative" interpretation; Davis (1959) is noted for having developed the working formula for its implementation; Kaufman (1979a, 1979b) made ipsative profile interpretation popular with the Wechsler intelligence scales; Silverstein (1982) refined the procedure and pointed out the need to correct for the loss of accuracy when making multiple score comparisons; McDermott (e.g., McDermott, Fantuzzo, & Glutting, in press) has been among the strongest critics of the practice; and Bracken et al. (1990) and Roffe and Bryant (1979) have revealed the instability of ipsatively derived subtest profiles. Given a history of nearly 50 years, few tests employ this intra-individual interpretive approach. The tests that do allow for ipsative profile analysis are almost uniformly measures of intellectual or cognitive abilities, such as the fourth edition of the *Stanford-Binet Intelligence Scale*, the *Matrix Analogies Test,* or the *Wechsler Intelligence Scales*. While the practice of ipsative interpretation continues to gain popularity among practitioners, there are good reasons to question its utility (Bracken et al., 1991; McDermott, Fantuzzo, & Glutting, in press).

Ipsative profile analysis is accomplished by (a) summing the standard scores for all relevant subtests (S_s); (b) determining the examinee's average subtest score (M_s); (c) calculating the difference between each subtest score $(s_1 - n)$ and (M_s) to obtain a difference score for each subtest $(ds_1 - n)$ [i.e., $(M_s) - (s_1) = (ds_1)$, and so on for each subtest through n]; (d) comparing d_s with a table of predetermined figures that indicates the standard error of difference between the average subtest score and any one of the scores entered into the computation of that average; and (e) if d_s exceeds the tabled critical value for the subtest at whatever alpha level is desired (e.g., .05, .01), then the subtest is identified as being significantly different from average, and either a relative strength or weakness.

TABLE 1. Ipsative Subtest Interpretation of the WISC-R Verbal Scale

Subtest	Standard Score	d	Ability Designation
Vocabulary	11	0	Average
Similarities	6	−5	Weakness
Arithmetic	9	−2	Average
Vocabulary	10	−1	Average
Comprehension	17	+6	Strength
(Digit span)	13	+2	Average

Sum of subtest scores = 66
Sum of *d* = 0
Average subtest score = 11

Note: *d* = the difference between the obtained subtest score and the average subtest score.

As a working example, consider a profile from the Verbal scale of the *Wechsler Intelligence Scale for Children* as shown in Table 1. The examinee's subtest scores totaled 66, and the resulting average subtest score was 11. By subtracting each subtest score from the average score, we obtain the difference score and find that the range of difference scores extends from −5 points (Similarities) to +6 points (Comprehension). The question of importance now is whether either of these two subtests (or any of the others) differs significantly from this child's average subtest score. Based on calculations of the standard error of the difference provided by Kaufman (1979a, 1979b), it is the recommended rule of thumb that any differences equal to or larger than +/− 3 points from the average Verbal scale score should be considered a significant deviation at the .05 alpha level. That is, such a difference would not occur by chance more than five times in a hundred.

Using Kaufman's calculations, the Similarities subtest would be considered a significant weakness and Comprehension a significant strength relative to the child's overall verbal abilities. It should also be noted than none of the remaining four subtests deviates significantly from the average subtest score and all are therefore considered to reflect skills that are evenly developed at a level commensurate with the child's overall verbal abilities.

The primary proposed benefit of ipsative profile interpretation is that an examinee's pattern of subtest scores acquires additional interpretative meaning beyond that available from norm-referenced interpretation. Ipsative interpretation offers another vantage from which to consider an examinee's skill and ability development; the scores can be compared to a peer group standard via norm-referenced interpretation *and* to the examinee's own overall level of functioning through ipsative interpretation. Regardless of how the examinee compares to the normal population, the examiner can explore the examinee's personal strengths and weaknesses to develop a remediation plan tailored to that child's ability pattern. For example, suppose the assessment was conducted on a retarded child. Compared to his or her normal peer group, the child evidences below average functioning in all skill areas assessed by the test; however, when the child's individual skills are compared to his or her own overall retarded level of functioning, it becomes apparent that the child has intellectual strengths in some skill areas and weaknesses in others. Once the examinee's ipsative strengths and weaknesses are identified, a remedial instructional plan for the student can be developed in an aptitude-by-treatment interaction (Cronbach, 1957, 1975)—that is, using the student's strengths to help remediate his or her weaknesses. Note that while aptitude-by-treatment remedial efforts seem to make sense intuitively, historically they have proved to be largely unsuccessful (Arter & Jenkins, 1979). Notice that in this example the child would only have had weaknesses identified if the comparison had been made only against the normal peer group. Instead, by using the ipsative interpretation procedure, both intellectual strengths and weaknesses were identified.

CRITERION-REFERENCED INTERPRETATION

Norm-referenced test interpretation compares a student's performance to that of the "typical" individual in the reference group, and ipsative profile interpretation permits intra-individual test interpretation, but neither approach yields information about the examinee's *absolute* ability or competence in specific areas assessed. When information is needed concerning a student's competeny or absolute performance, test interpretation takes a different orientation (Popham & Husek, 1971). Lemke and Wiersma (1976) conclude that "norm-referencing and criterion-referencing can be viewed as the extremes of a purpose continuum on which maximum variance and zero variance, respectively, are desired" (p. 261). That is, in norm-referenced assessment, difference among individuals is desired; in criterion-referenced assessment, *no* difference is desired.

Educational goals and objectives frequently become operationally defined criteria for students' grade retention or promotion, and assessment takes on the task of determining the extent to which the criteria have been met by the student. To determine whether the examinee is making sufficient progress toward the predetermined goals and objectives, the student's achievement can be monitored through multiple, on-going criterion-referenced assessments. Criterion-referenced assessment and interpretation is oriented toward making comparisons between the examinee's test performance and the operationally defined criterion level of competence or skill attainment.

The following scenario illustrates when criterion-referenced assessment might be an appropriate approach to interpretation. An employer with a shortage of typists might want to hire a limited number of highly competent clerk typists and sets out to develop a means of distinguishing skill levels among candidates. Typing competency criteria could be determined by the personr¹ ...ager (personnel psychologist), and only job candidates who pass the criteria would be considered sufficiently competent to be hired. To meet the typing proficiency criteria, management might require that all successful candidates type at least 80 words per minute with no more than 5 errors in a 400-word passage. In this instance, the criteria are both speed and accuracy. Any candidate who fails to meet these criteria would be deemed unqualified for the position, while these who do meet it would be deemed equally qualified and suitable for employment.

An obvious benefit of such criterion-referenced test interpretation is that it does not force a comparison between an examinee and his or her peers, but rather compares the examinee's performance to a previously determined standard or with one's own past performance (i.e., one "criterion" might be merely the demonstration of improvement or gain in proficiency since the last assessment).

In norm-referenced interpretation, examinees who score below the norm might find it frustrating to be continually compared with a norm group that always performs at a higher level. For students who are below average and have virtually no chance of performing at a normal level, any demonstrable improvement and progress toward the goal can be especially encouraging and can foster continued student effort. Thus, criterion-referenced assessment can encourage students to work toward goals. Also, with norm-referenced assessment, the examinee has no way of judging beforehand what the standard of comparison will be, but with criterion-referenced assessment the examinee can know in advance what the expected criterion is. This allows test takers to realistically gauge the likelihood of meeting the standard before initiating the assessment. In the clerk typist example, candidates who apply for the typist position and know what the job criteria are would likely take the typing test only if they believed there was a reasonable likelihood of success.

The orientation of criterion-referenced interpretation is to determine students' progress toward the mastery of goals or objectives. Observable gains and progress typically become the focus of criterion-referenced assessment, and with it students are able to gauge firsthand their progress toward the goal. Additionally, the speed with which the norm group progresses toward the goal is not a central issue in criterion-referenced assessment. The important issue is the absolute level of performance demonstrated by individual students and whether they have met the minimal criterion established. With objective criteria set from the onset of instruction, students know what content or skills they must master, and the assessment indicates in specific terms the extent to which they have met the criteria.

Because retarded and delayed children develop and learn at a slower pace than their normally developing peers, criterion-referenced assessment is often preferred with this population. By definition, retarded individuals fall behind their normative peer group, but realistic instructional or behavioral objectives (i.e., criteria) can be set for them, and follow-up evaluations can be conducted to determine their progress toward achieving the specified goals.

Setting Criteria

In criterion-referenced assessment, there must be a method of determining what is a suitable or reasonable criterion. Both practical and theoretical rationale are used in criterion setting, and one approach is not necessarily better than the other. Using a practical rationale, one might argue that the clerk typists discussed previously who cannot type at least 80 words per minute with fewer than 5 errors per 400 words are too limited in ability to keep up with a company's typing demands. Given the company's high productivity requirement, typists must be able to type at least at this level to perform at a minimum the amounts of work typically assigned to clerk typists. In this example, the practical demands of the company's secretarial work load create the practical dictates that determine the criterion for a successful typist. Those dictates and criteria would change from business to business or setting to setting.

A theoretical determination of criteria is more likely to be based on what is known about normal development or rate of learning within a population. As an example, "typical" children entering first grade can print their names and recite their addresses and phone numbers. These three basic skills represent the modal or typical behavior of entering first-grade students. Also, these skills are important for the protection of children who might find themselves separated from their parents while in public. While being able to perform these skills is not necessary for success in first grade, the skills are possessed by the typical five- and six-year-old child. Because the skills are functionally important and accomplished by the typical child of this age, they might be designated as three of the criterion behaviors for kindergarten completion. Thus, children assessed at the end of kindergarten for first-grade readiness might be expected to perform these specific tasks in addition to meeting a variety of other academic and social criteria.

It is obvious that in some instances criterion-referenced tests are also norm-referenced. The normal or typical behavior for a group of children of a given age helps define the criterion behavior for individual children of the same age. The differences between norm-referenced and criterion-referenced test interpretation tend to be related more to the content assessed than to whether norms are used. To illustrate the principal difference between the two testing approaches, consider the difference between two constructs, intelligence and achievement.

Intelligence tests are norm-referenced because an individual's performance is compared to that of peers in the norm-based reference group. Because intelligence, as a construct, is global and not readily amenable to change, it is highly unlikely that anyone would set criterion-related goals to improve intellectual functioning (e.g., the child will increase in intelligence to an assessed IQ of 110), though general intellectual improvement might be desired over a substantial time period. The construct of intelligence is too general and global in nature for realistic goals to be developed to systematically teach a person to become more intelligent.

Achievement, a more specific construct than intelligence, is considerably more readily assessed in a criterion-referenced way. Also, achievement is more amenable to change, thus making criterion setting more appropriate. Regardless of the rate at which children typically progress toward mastery of a specific skill, a competency criterion can be set for all individuals.

Mastery of multiplication tables, for example, is an important skill; the content is specific and is known to be "teachable"; the expected outcome is clearly defined (e.g., 100 percent mastery of the multiplication of numerals 0 through 9); and the rate at which the typical child acquires the skill doesn't matter. An older child (or even adult) who is deficient in his or her knowledge can be taught the skill, and after sufficient instruction and practice, the individual can be assessed to determine his or her level of mastery in this skill area.

CURRICULUM-BASED INTERPRETATION

Related to criterion-referenced interpretation, curriculum-based assessment (CBA) is an approach oriented toward assessing an examinee's progress within a specific educational curriculum. While criterion-related assessment tends to focus on specific abilities and their absolute level of development, those abilities might or might not be linked to a specific educational curriculum. Curriculum-based assessment is linked directly to the assessment of skills and abilities taught specifically in an instructional curriculum. This sort of assessment is designed to more directly enhance the treatment utility of assessment (Hayes, Nelson, & Jarrett, 1987). The movement toward curriculum-based assessment is described as more "edumetric" than "psychometric" because of its focus on matching an educational curriculum to the assessment process (Carver, 1974; Shinn, Rosenfield, & Knutson, 1989).

While Shinn, Rosenfield, and Knutson (1989) identify at least four models of curriculum-based assessment, Frisby (1987) believes all CBA models share four common principles, including: (a) student assessment in curricular content, (b) brief and (c) multiple assessments, and (d) systematic plotting of student progress. The heart and soul of CBA rests in the belief that whatever is important enough to teach is important enough to assess, and if it is worth assessing, it should be worth teaching. Within this basic philosophy, the procedures and practices of CBA vary somewhat across models, but there is considerable consistency across all approaches (see Shinn, Rosenfield, & Knutson, 1989, for elaboration).

Just as good instruction begins with sound goals, CBA is founded on the same premise. If a teacher, school system, or national advisory council believes it is an important goal to have students identify each of the 50 states and their capitals, for example, then the social studies curriculum would need to be designed to include the appropriate lessons, materials, readings, and activities to reach this goal. Given the goal, each student's progress could be monitored by assessing how many states and capitals each student could accurately identify.

The teacher could assess the students' knowledge after all 50 states and capitals had been covered instructionally, but assessment at the end of the instructional unit would not provide timely information about any student who was lagging behind. Ideally, remedial instruction would be implemented *during* the general instructional unit, not after it was completed. Rather than wait until all the material had been covered, the teacher could effectively rate the students' progress with multiple, brief assessments in the form of daily quizzes, worksheets, individual or group recitation, tests related to regions of the country, and so on. With these frequent, brief assessments, the teacher and the students could effectively plot the number of state and capital pairs successfully learned by each student, identifying also those that individual students had failed to label correctly. Remediation efforts could then follow directly as needed.

CBA test items are selected uniquely from the curricular content. Curriculum-based assessment should produce results that indicate the degree to which specific curricular goals have been achieved and identify which have not been achieved. After each brief assessment, future instructional efforts would be founded on the results of the previous assessment. Hence, in the CBA paradigm, instruction guides assessment, which in turn guides instruction. A teach–test–teach instructional assessment model of this sort leads directly to educational accountability through the constant evaluation of instructional efficacy and remedial efforts.

The principal benefit of CBA is direct linkage between instruction and assessment. Assessment becomes a functional activity, one in which test results have obvious and explicit value to the student and teacher. In contrast, norm-referenced and ipsative assessment approaches yield results that tend to be less specific and less directly beneficial in the instructional realm. For example, in a typical norm-referenced achievement test, the results will indicate how well the student performed relative to peers or to his or her own overall level of functioning, but will not identify specific areas of learning difficulties, nor will they indicate specific curricular mastery, such as which mathematical subroutines have been mastered or which scientific principles are understood.

Combining Interpretation Styles Within the Same Test

While each of the four procedures of test interpretation has been dealt with separately in this chapter, there are some tests designed to be interpreted in more than one fashion, including some in all four ways. One such example is the *Bracken Basic Concept Scale* (BBCS; Bracken, 1984), a measure of basic concept acquisition for children between the ages of 2 1/2 and 8 years. The BBCS assesses 258 specific concepts in 11 content domains and has an accompanying curriculum, the *Bracken Concept Development Program* (BCDP; Bracken, 1986). In developing the BBCS, over 300 basic readiness concepts were identified through the investigation of several preschool curricular programs. The BCDP was then developed to teach children these same concepts.

NORM-REFERENCED INTERPRETATION OF THE BBCS

When the comparison of a child with peers is the desired focus of interpretation, the examiner can compare the child's performance on the BBCS to his or her age peers in the nationally representative standardization sample by focusing on the range of available standard scores, percentile ranks, and concept age equivalents (i.e., test age equivalents). In Figure 1, subtest and total test raw scores are reported in the first column, standard scores in the second column, and percentile ranks and concept age equivalents in the third and fourth columns, respectively. The data depicted in the first four columns provide the information necessary for norm-referenced interpretation.

Examination of the raw scores in column one provides the only source of information about this student's absolute test performance: She earned a raw score of 44 on the School Readiness Composite (SRC), with the remaining subtest scores listed below the SRC raw score. As mentioned previously, raw scores are of little value by themselves, other than to indicate the actual number of concepts over which the child evidenced mastery. Until one knows the number of items that comprise the SRC (i.e., 61) and how many SRC items the typical child of this age answers correctly (i.e., 33 to 35), Becky's SRC raw score means very little. However, given the answers to these two questions, Becky's performance can be considered more meaningfully by comparing it to that of her peers in the standardization sample.

The subtest standard scores presented in the second column are age adjusted, with means of 10 and standard deviations of 3; the BBCS Total Test Score has a mean of 100 and standard deviation of 15. The subtest and Total Test raw scores are converted to standard scores by entering an age-based norm table in the BBCS Examiner's Manual. With the conversion of BBCS raw scores to standard scores, it now becomes apparent that Becky's SRC concept mastery was two-thirds of a standard deviation above her age peers (i.e., $(12 - 10) / 3 = +.67\ SD$). Further, it is learned that performance at this level is as good or better than that of 75 percent of her age peers (column 3), and developmentally is much like that of the typical child 4 years 10 months old. The remaining subtests and total test scores can also be examined in this fashion. Becky's total test performance earned a standard score of 104, which is slightly above average and is ranked at the 61st percentile. Also, her total test performance earned an age equivalency of 4 years 5 months, just three months beyond her chronological age of 4 years 2 months.

By examining the standard scores and percentile ranks presented in Figure 1, this child's performance on the BBCS is much more clearly understood. Her conceptual knowledge varies across subtest domains, with a low subtest score of 6 ($-1.33\ SD$ and a percentile rank of 9) on the Texture/Material subtest to a high subtest score of 13 ($+1.0\ SD$ and percentile rank of 84) on the Direction/Position subtest. Her concept age equivalencies range from 2 years 6 months to 5 years 2 months, evidencing considerable variation in the

FIGURE 1. Sample Record Form for the BBCS

Record Form

Name/ID No. _Becky D._

Address _3419 Maple Drive_
Cedar Bluff, MA

Parents' Name _Mr. and Mrs. Edward D._

School/Agency _Happy Hills Preschool_

Referred by _Teacher_

Place of testing _Preschool_

Tested by _Hank Ancel_

Race   B   (W)   Other   Spanish Origin   Yes   (No)

	Year	Month	Day	
Date Tested	90	6	18	Age _4-2_
Date of Birth	86	4	8	Sex _F_
Chronological Age	4	2	10	Grade _PreK_

Bracken Basic Concept Scale
by Bruce A. Bracken, Ph.D.

Subtests	Raw Score	Standard Score	P'tile Rank	Concept Age	Strength/ Weakness
I-V SRC	44	12	75	4-10	S
VI Direction/ Position	43	13	84	5-2	S
VII Social/ Emotional	13	9	37	3-10	A
VIII Size	8	10	50	4-2	A
IX Texture/ Material	4	6	9	2-6	W
X Quantity	18	10	50	4-2	A
XI Time/ Sequence	17	11	63	4-6	A
Total Test Score	147	104	61	4-5	

$\bar{x} = 10$

Additional Tests	Date	Raw Score	Standard Score	P'tile Rank	Concept Age
Screening Test A					
Screening Test B					
Other					

Subtest Profile

Diagnosticians who desire to plot a conceptual profile should enter subtest standard scores below and connect subtest entries with a line.

	I-V	VI	VII	VIII	IX	X	XI	
Standard Score	12	13	9	10	6	10	11	Standard Score

+3SD	19	.	.	.	.	.	.	.	19 +3SD
	18	.	.	.	.	.	.	.	18
	17	.	.	.	.	.	.	.	17
+2SD	16	.	.	.	.	.	.	.	16 +2SD
	15	.	.	.	.	.	.	.	15
	14	.	.	.	.	.	.	.	14
+1SD	13	.	.	.	.	.	.	.	13 +1SD
	12	.	.	.	.	.	.	.	12
	11	.	.	.	.	.	.	.	11
Mean	10	.	.	.	.	.	.	.	10 Mean
	9	.	.	.	.	.	.	.	9
	8	.	.	.	.	.	.	.	8
−1SD	7	.	.	.	.	.	.	.	7 −1SD
	6	.	.	.	.	.	.	.	6
	5	.	.	.	.	.	.	.	5
−2SD	4	.	.	.	.	.	.	.	4 −2SD
	3	.	.	.	.	.	.	.	3
	2	.	.	.	.	.	.	.	2
−3SD	1	.	.	.	.	.	.	.	1 −3SD

From *Bracken Basic Concept Scale* (p. 1) by B. Bracken, 1984, San Antonio, TX: The Psychological Corporation. Copyright 1984 by The Psychological Corporation. Reprinted by permission. All rights reserved.

rate at which she has acquired conceptual knowledge across the various BBCS subtest areas.

Norm-referenced test interpretation of this sort yields a fairly clear normative picture of Becky's abilities in each of the content areas assessed by the BBCS. The profile plotted to the right of the scores provides a graphic display of the child's norm-based performance and facilitates her parents' and teachers' understanding of her pattern of test performance. By examining Becky's plotted profile it can be seen that she performed in the normal band of variation (i.e., all scores are plotted within the grey band that includes scores between +/− 1 *SD*) on all subtests except Texture/Material.

Ipsative Profile Analysis of the BBCS

While it is now known how Becky performed relative to her age peers, it is important instructionally to determine in which content areas she has strengths and weaknesses relative to her own overall level of functioning. Following the procedures outlined in the BBCS Examiner's Manual (Bracken, 1984), each subtest is contrasted against Becky's average subtest score. By summing the subtest standard scores in the second column and dividing that sum by the number of subtests (i.e., 7), it is learned that this child's average subtest score is 10.14, rounded down to 10 (which, coincidentally, is the average subtest score for her age peers in the standardization sample).

To contrast each subtest score with the average subtest score, a difference score must be computed by subtracting the subtest standard score from the average subtest score. The difference scores for the various subtests are: +2, SRC; +3, Direction/Position; −1, Social/Emotional; 0, Size; −4, Texture/ Material; −1, Quantity; and +1, Time/Sequence. Table 2 presents critical values necessary for a subtest to be considered significantly different from average (ignoring the sign before the difference scores). The table is entered by age level (i.e., ages 3, 4, 5, 6, or 7 years) and alpha level (i.e., .05 or .01) by subtest. The obtained difference scores are contrasted against these tabled critical values to determine whether Becky's various subtest performances represent skills that are relative strengths, weaknesses, or skills that are average relative to her overall level of development.

Given Becky's chronological age (4 years, 2 months) and a desired alpha level of .05, it can be learned that Becky's difference score of +2 for the SRC does differ significantly from her average score of 10 (any difference score greater than the 1.71 critical value is significant at the .05 confidence level)

TABLE 2. Standard Score Differences Required for Significance When Comparing Subtests

Age	Significance Level	I-V School Readiness Composite	VI Direction/ Position	VII Social/ Emotional	VIII Size	IX Texture/ Material	X Quantity	XI Time/ Sequence
3	.05	1.77	1.91	2.80	3.65	2.76	2.42	2.42
	.01	2.09	2.26	3.31	4.32	3.26	2.86	2.87
4	.05	1.71	1.55	2.47	3.73	2.68	2.02	1.97
	.01	2.02	1.84	2.93	4.41	3.17	2.38	2.33
5	.05	2.49	2.27	2.97	4.58	3.22	2.95	2.52
	.01	2.94	2.68	3.51	5.42	3.80	3.48	2.98
6	.05	3.25	3.33	4.47	5.19	4.58	3.09	3.87
	.01	3.84	3.93	5.28	6.14	5.41	3.65	4.57
7	.05	3.19	2.66	3.19	4.55	3.49	2.83	2.97
	.01	3.77	3.14	3.77	5.38	4.12	3.35	3.51

and is considered a strength relative to her overall level of performance. Also, Direction/Position is a strength (+3 difference score is greater than the 1.55 critical value). All the remaining subtests, except Texture/Material, are average relative to Becky's overall performance on the BBCS. That is, none of the respective difference scores exceeded the critical values cited in Table 2. However, Becky's performance on the Texture/Material subtest results in a difference score of −4.0, which is greater than the subtest's critical value of 2.68 at the .05 alpha level. Hence, Becky has ipsatively derived strengths in her comprehension of School Readiness and Direction/Position concepts, but she is significantly weak in her knowledge of Texture/Material concepts. The pattern of Becky's strengths, weaknesses, and average performance is shown in the fifth column of data shown in Figure 1.

When engaged in norm-referenced interpretation, only Becky's performance on the Texture/Material subtest exceeded the normal range of abilities illustrated graphically in Figure 1. Thus, Becky's norm-referenced analysis only depicts a single weakness and no strengths relative to her age peers. When an ipsative profile analysis is conducted, however, it can be seen that Becky has both strengths and weaknesses relative to her own overall developmental level. Her strength in School Readiness concepts suggests that she has benefited greatly from her preschool experiences. Becky's understanding of spatial concepts assessed by the Direction/Position subtest is also an area of relative strength. While SRC and Direction/Position concepts are routinely taught in most preschool curricula, Texture/Material concepts are not. Becky's weak performance on the Texture/Material subtest illustrates a weakness that is likely due to a lack of exposure, and systematic instruction of these concepts might be undertaken to remediate this ipsative and norm-based weakness.

Criterion-referenced Interpretation of the BBCS

Any number of criteria could be set for performance on the BBCS, depending on the goals of the school. It could be determined, for example, that all children should perform at least at age level expectancy. In this case, the performance criterion for Becky would be a concept age equivalent of 4 years 2 months. Through inspection of Figure 1, we see that Becky met this criterion on five of the 7 subtests, but would need additional instruction in the remaining two areas (i.e., Social/Emotional and Texture/Material subtests).

Other criteria might be related to absolute test performance (e.g., Becky will learn all 258 BBCS concepts prior to finishing preschool); standard score performance (e.g., Becky will earn standard scores above 10 on all subtests); percentile rank attainment (e.g., Becky will achieve at or above the 85th percentile on all BBCS subtests); or ipsative performance (e.g., Becky will have no subtests that are identified as relative weaknesses). Each of these criteria is objectively determined, goal oriented, potentially obtainable, and easily assessed and reassessed. Becky's progress toward meeting the criteria can be easily followed, and her progress can be charted or graphed and made available to all parties involved in her instructional endeavor.

Obviously, the criteria set must be reasonably acquired by Becky if they are to have any remedial value. While most children can learn the BBCS concepts by the time they are 8 or 9 years old, gifted children will learn them faster, developmentally delayed children will acquire them more slowly, and some retarded children may never fully comprehend all the concepts. Thus, appropriate criteria would differ for each of these groups of children, especially at different age levels; however, all the BBCS concepts have inherent value for verbal comprehension, and an ultimate and eventual criterion of 100 percent mastery is recommended, regardless of exceptionality.

CURRICULUM-BASED ASSESSMENT OF THE BBCS

Use of a CBA paradigm with the BBCS results in a fine-tuned integration of assessment and instructional activities as presented in the *Bracken Concept Development Program* (BCDP; Bracken, 1986). The BCDP consists of 81 specific lessons within 11 instructional units. The program's lessons integrate regular classroom materials and activities with the program's five full-color posters, forty full-color instructional concept cards, and 153 multiple-item worksheets. The two programs were designed to meet the dictates of curriculum-based assessment. In the preface to the BCDP, Bracken (1986) states that his program is appropriate for children in preschool and the primary grades and jointly offers the school psychologist and the classroom teacher a

> direct link between assessment and remediation. This "direct link" allows for the demonstration of educational accountability.... Whereas in most areas of psychoeducational assessment this direct link is not available...basic concept deficiencies can be identified, and remediated, and progress in conceptual acquisition can be assessed and noted. (p. iv)

In curriculum-based assessment, the examiner becomes an educational diagnostician, seeking to identify specific concepts that Becky does and does not comprehend. The examiner has advance knowledge of the rate and sequence at which children typically acquire basic concepts because the BBCS and BDCP both arrange concepts by content domain (e.g., Direction/ Position concepts, Social/Emotional concepts) and difficulty level. Once the examiner separates the concepts that the child does not understand from those he or she does, instructional recommendations can be made for the teacher as to where to begin regular and remedial instruction. The BCDP also provides a list of 19 instructional psychology principles that serve as general instructional guidelines for the teacher, as well as specific lessons and materials to use for direct instruction. Hence, the BBCS and the BCDP are inextricably linked for assessment and instructional purposes.

Integrating Test Scores With Other Assessment Information

Administering and interpreting tests are only two aspects of psychological assessment. Psychologists must integrate other nontest information and their clinical impressions with test scores and use clinical judgment to make sense of all the formal and informal data collected. Whether test interpretation is norm-based, ipsative, criterion-referenced, or curriculum-based, the data from all the tests should be contrasted across measures to assess the consistency of the results and, ultimately, the reliability of the interpretations and decisions to be made from those results (Barnett, 1988).

The integration of test results across instruments in a battery should flow from the most reliable measures to the least reliable (Kaufman, 1979b) and should always be interpreted in light of clinical observations (Bracken, 1990). In practice, this usually means that global test scores are contrasted first, followed by scale scores, then theoretically grouped clusters of individual subtests, subtests, and finally, individual test items. An example of how such a sequence of test interpretation might work follows. Let's presume that the two tests in comparison include two standard measures of intelligence, the *Wechsler Intelligence Scale for Children* (revised edition) and the *Stanford-Binet Intelligence Scale* (fourth edition) (see Table 3).

GLOBAL SCORE COMPARISON

Because most comprehensive intelligence measures are theoretically and factor analytically multidimensional in design, the tests produce a wide range of scores reflecting examinee performance on subtests, scales, and the total test. The total score comprises, through some combination and weighting of subtests and scales, all of the subordinate scores produced by the test. As such,

TABLE 3. Comparison of Subtest, Scale, and Total Test Scores on the WISC-R and Stanford–Binet IV

WISC-R	Scale Scores	Stanford-Binet IV	Scale Scores
Verbal Scale		Verbal Reasoning Area	
Vocabulary	12	Vocabulary	54
Similarities	10	Comprehension	64
Arithmetic	8	Absurdities	50
Vocabulary	13	Verbal reasoning SAS	**111**
Comprehension	14		
(Digit span)	15	Abstract/Visual Reasoning Area	
Verbal IQ	**107**	Pattern analysis	40
		Copying	46
Performance Scale		Matrices	48
Picture completion	6	Abstract/visual reasoning SAS	**87**
Picture arrangement	5		
Block design	8	Quantitative Reasoning Area	
Object assembly	11	Quantitative	56
Coding	7	Number series	49
Performance IQ	**82**	Quantitative reasoning SAS	**105**
Full-scale IQ	**95**	Short-term Memory Area	
		Bead memory	51
		Memory for sentences	57
		Memory for digits	64
		Memory for objects	45
		Short-term memory SAS	**111**
		Sum of Areas SASs	**104**

the total test score is the most reliable measure and the most important score for decision making. The total test score is the only one that reflects the client's overall performance.

Total test scores for most measures of intelligence typically have been demonstrated, through concurrent validity studies, to be highly intercorrelated; hence, the various measures of intelligence are judged to be interchangeable for clinical practice. Because the various total test scores tend to be highly intercorrelated, they also tend to produce comparable scores when the same individual is administered more than one intelligence test. A rule-of-thumb index of comparable performance is plus or minus one standard deviation (Sattler, 1982, 1988).

In the example illustrated in Table 3, it is seen that the two tests have total scores that are nine points apart. While the WISC-R has a mean of 100 and standard deviation of 15, the Stanford-Binet has a mean of 100 and a standard deviation of 16. Regardless of which standard deviation is used in the application of Sattler's (1982, 1988) rule-of-thumb (i.e., 15 or 16), the nine-point difference between total test scores is not significant or meaningful. In this case, it is judged to be due to measurement error rather than to real differences in abilities as assessed by the two instruments.

SCALE COMPARISONS

The WISC-R is comprised of only two scales, the Verbal and Performance scales; the Stanford-Binet consists of four scales. For comparison of scales across instruments, one should contrast those that purport to assess the same general construct or domain. In this example, it is clear that the WISC-R Verbal scale should be contrasted with the Stanford-Binet Verbal Reasoning scale because both purport to assess verbal comprehension and reasoning and both possess similar subtests across the scales. One exception to the similarity in subtest structure across the two scales is that the WISC-R includes an arithmetic subtest on its Verbal scale, while the Stanford-Binet does not. There are other nuances between the scales that are typically considered by experienced clinicians, but for illustration purposes our example will disregard them. It is apparent from the structure of the scales and the compilation of subtests that the WISC-R Performance scale should be contrasted with the Stanford-Binet Abstract Visual/Reasoning scale.

As with the total test scores, the two instruments have dissimilar standard deviations for the scales (i.e., 15, WISC-R; 16, Stanford-Binet). We can choose to use either standard deviation for our comparison with little loss of accuracy, especially since ours is only a rule-of-thumb criterion and not empirically determined. Also as with the total test scores, we see that the verbal scales across the two instruments are commensurate. The WISC-R Verbal IQ of 107 is only 4 points less than the Stanford-Binet Verbal Reasoning area score of 111. Again, this minor difference is attributed to random error and is not viewed as an interpretatively meaningful difference. The five-point difference between the WISC-R Performance IQ and the Stanford-Binet Abstract/Visual Reasoning area score is also nonsignificant and suggests a comparable level of nonverbal, visuospatial performance across the two instruments.

SUBTEST CLUSTER COMPARISONS

Test and book authors have proposed many schemes for interpreting collections of subtests. Basic to this practice is the identification of underlying skills and abilities presumed to be assessed by the individual subtests and then the collapse of those subtests into subsets that appear to assess the same unique abilities. It should be recognized that the unique abilities presumed to be assessed by individual subtests are based on clinical acumen and conjecture (Bracken & Fagan, 1988; Chattin & Bracken, 1989). Very little research has been conducted on empirical determination of abilities shared by various subsets of subtests.

Several authors have conjectured subtest clusters on the WISC-R, but Kaufman's (1979b) list is the most inclusive. Likewise, Delaney and Hopkins (1987) and Sattler's (1988) description of Stanford-Binet subtest shared abilities are probably the most complete lists for measurement of intelligence. An example of a subtest cluster believed to share a common element is the group of three WISC-R subtests—Information, Vocabulary, and Arithmetic—which are believed to be related to knowledge acquired through school learning or prior academic preparation. Comparably, the Vocabulary and Qualitative subtests of the Stanford-Binet would be expected to be similarly related to prior academic exposure.

While it makes intuitive sense that the task demands of these subtests are very much related to academic preparation, there is little more than subjective task analysis to support this supposition. However, accepting the premise that previously identified clusters of subtests share some common underlying ability, then those clusters of scores might contribute meaningfully to a more complete understanding of the client's cognitive abilities. Continuing with the example depicted in Table 2, we see that this cluster of five "academically" oriented subtests all fall within plus or minus one standard deviation of their normative mean scores of 10 and 50 for the WISC-R and the Stanford-Binet subtests, respectively. Hence, the subtests in this academic cluster all are fairly evenly developed at an average level. Other such clinically derived clusters should be investigated systematically to identify any areas of cognitive weakness or strength. The interested reader might wish to consult Kaufman (1979b), Kaufman and Kaufman (1977), Delaney and Hopkins (1987), and Sattler (1988) for a thorough list of shared abilities clusters identified for common measures of intelligence. For a discussion on the limited degree to which practicing psychologists agree with the conjecture-based shared abilities clusters suggested by test authors, refer to Bracken and Fagan (1988).

SUBTEST INTERPRETATIONS

As with subtest cluster analysis, clinicians should compare the examinee's performance on individual subtests that appear to assess similar constructs across a battery. Again, a rule-of-thumb discrepancy criterion of one standard deviation would be appropriate. Comparing subtests across the two instruments in our example requires that the subtest scores be first reduced to a common metric. The WISC-R subtests have means of 10 and standard deviations of 3, while the Stanford-Binet subtests have means of 50 and standard deviations of 8 (not to be confused with T-scores with a mean of 50 and standard deviations of 10). The reduction of scores to a common metric can be accomplished by reducing both sets of scores to z-scores or by converting one set of scores to the parameters of the other through the implementation of the standard score conversion formula.

The WISC-R–Stanford-Binet subtest pairs that should be contrasted as measures of the same construct include: Vocabulary-Vocabulary, Arithmetic-Quantitative, Comprehension-Comprehension, and Digit Span-Memory for Digits. Using a one standard deviation discrepancy criterion, it can be seen that this child's performance on the WISC-R Vocabulary subtest ($+1$ z) is comparable to his performance on the Stanford-Binet Vocabulary subtest ($+1/2$ z), with a discrepancy of only $1/2$ z between the two. Similarly, the child's performance on the two Comprehension subtests and the two measures of memory for digits are comparable across the two instruments. However, the two measures of arithmetic ability are discrepant. The WISC-R Arithmetic subtest score of 8 is equal to a z-score of $-.67$, whereas the Stanford-Binet Qualitative subtest score of 56 is equal to a z-score of $+.75$. As such, the two scores are nearly one and one-half z-scores discrepant.

If a significant discrepancy between measures of the same construct occurs, the clinician must work to resolve it. A discrepancy of this magnitude did not likely occur due to chance fluctuations in scores. The explanation of significant differences might be attributed to differences within the individual (e.g., he or she was too fatigued at the time of taking the second measure, and consequently did not do as well as on the first test); differences in the environment (e.g., disruptive noise outside the examining room at the time of the second administration reduced the client's concentration); or differences in the tests (e.g., difference between oral and visual presentation of mathematical problems). Later in this chapter, the most common psychometric reasons for differences in test performance will be further elaborated upon.

Item Comparisons

In an analysis of subtest performances, it is important that the clinician conduct an examination of specific items passed and failed and consider the trend in performance across measures. For example, if both tests assess the child's understanding of a basic concept such as *before*, the clinician should determine whether the child passed the item on both instruments. If the child demonstrated comprehension of the concept on one test but not the other, there might be a variety of important diagnostic or developmental reasons for this lack of consistency.

Clark (1973) and Johnson (1975) have shown that the demonstration of conceptual knowledge is affected by the complexity of the sentence in which the concept is embedded. For example, it is easier for young children to comprehend the sentence, "Drink your milk *before* you go outside" than to comprehend "*Before* you go outside, drink your milk." Children comprehend concepts in the context of the entire phrase, and the latter sentence is more complex because the order of the activities mentioned is the reverse of the expected behavior (i.e., go outside, drink your milk).

Developmental or edumetric task analysis of specific test items within a subtest and across subtests in a battery frequently yields specific diagnostic information that contributes to meaningful interpretation and recommendations. For example, it might be learned that a child recognizes uppercase letters, but not lowercase; a child might have mastered addition and subtraction, but not multiplication and division; a child might be able to describe similarities in words when the words represent concrete objects (e.g., how are cars and trucks alike?), but not abstract concepts (e.g., how are labor and love alike?); or the child might be able to repeat digits successfully when they are to be repeated in the same order as presented, but not in reverse. In these instances, performance on single items yields information about the child's level of development in each of these separate perceptual, academic, verbal reasoning, and memory areas.

Clinical Observation and Judgment in Interpretation of Test Performance

Examiners must do more than merely administer tests and look up scores in a test manual if they are to be effective psychologists. A psychologist's role is to gather information through any medium to make accurate diagnostic and prognostic statements and to suggest meaningful interventions. To interpret tests in the most comprehensive fashion, the psychologist must integrate behavioral observations and clinical judgments into the interpretation process (Bracken, 1990).

Careful observation of the client who is completing test items might yield valuable information that will help understand the person's test performance and ultimately the "true" level of ability. It is not sufficient for a psychologist to note that a client failed a test item without also attempting to determine why. There are as many reasons for this as there are examinees, and comprehending the reason for failure is as important as noting it. For example, if someone fails to successfully complete mazes on the Mazes subtest of the *Wechsler Adult Intelligence Scale* (Wechsler, 1981), what does it imply? The observed performance might be more important in the determining implications and level of cognitive functioning than the actual failure.

The individual might have failed because he or she drew a line straight from the starting point to the maze exit, without following any of the pathways. The reason for this response might be profound retardation, a serious mental disorder, or any other condition associated with inability to comprehend even the very basic nature of the task—to follow the pathways from the starting point to the exit without crossing through any borders. Another person might have successfully exited the maze, but accumulated too many errors while completing it to receive credit as a passed item. The level of task comprehension shown is greater than the first person's and demonstrates greater cognitive ability, but the result is still failure on the Maze item. Finally, a third examinee might have successfully completed the maze without any errors, but failed to do so within the required time limit. In this last example, the examinee demonstrated the cognitive ability to comprehend and successfully perform the task, but required more time than allowed. All three people failed the same item, but for different reasons. Their actual performance on the task, when observed and clinically interpreted, provides considerably more information about the level of cognitive development and ability than the mere fact of failure on the same item.

Psychometric Reasons for Similar Tests Producing Dissimilar Results

Bracken (1988) cites ten common psychometric reasons why tests purporting to measure the same construct sometimes produce significantly different scores. As mentioned previously, an examinee might attain significantly different scores on similar tests because of intraindividual, environmental, interpersonal, and psychometric reasons. Sound testing practices and procedures can all but eliminate most nonpsychometric reasons for differential test performance, but even the best instruments available have limitations that affect how an examinee performs. A summary follows of ten psychometric aspects that should be considered when interpreting tests individually and collectively.

FLOOR EFFECTS

The floor of a test represents the extent to which an individual can earn low test scores. Obviously, if a test is to be used for the identification of retarded individuals (those individuals who by definition perform at least two standard deviations below the mean), then the test must produce standard scores that extend at least two standard deviations below average. Even when tests extend to at least $-2z$, two similar tests can still produce dissimilar scores as a result of floor effects. Standard scores on one test might extend to $-4z$, while on another test only to $-3z$. If the examinee is profoundly retarded and is actually functioning at a cognitive level $-4z$, then the second instrument will artifactually make it appear that he or she is functioning at a higher level than in reality because it limits level of performance to $-3z$.

While retardation at a level 3 to 4 standard deviations below average is profound, there is still a qualitative and quantitative difference between the two levels of functioning. If one test will report IQs as low as 40 ($-4z$) and another only to 55 ($-3z$), then the 15-point discrepancy earned on the two tests is not meaningful; it is merely artifactually related to the limitations of the latter test. That is, the difference in scores is a result of the tests' inability to distinguish different levels of profound retardation, not differing levels of examinee performance on the two measures.

CEILING EFFECTS

A test's ceiling refers to the extent to which the test can distinguish between varying levels of high ability. As with floors, some instruments have limited ceilings and do not produce standard scores that extend into the gifted range of abilities. Obviously, an examiner should not select such an instrument if the purpose of the assessment is to identify children for school-based gifted programs. Two tests can easily produce significant differences in their total test scores if one has a truncated ceiling and the other does not. In such a case, the test that has the truncated ceiling will produce artifactually low standard scores and may result in a gifted child being passed over in the selection process.

Item Gradients

The item gradient of a test refers to how steeply items are arranged by difficulty level and the distance that exists between resulting standard scores. For example, some tests have a sufficient number of items arranged across the ability range to result in minor changes in standard scores as a function of minor changes in raw scores. However, some tests have item gradients so steep that a single raw score variation can change the standard score by as much as one half a standard deviation or more. This level of item insensitivity only provides gross estimates of examinee ability and is not sufficiently refined for making important decisions. For example, on the *Battelle Developmental Inventory* (Newborg, Stock, Wnek, Guidubaldi, & Svinicki, 1984) the raw score item gradient on the Memory subtest (ages 1 1/2 years to 2 years) is so steep that a raw score of 7 is ranked at the first percentile, but a raw score of 8 leaps to a percentile rank of 74. Distinction of ability from the 1st to 74th percentiles should not rest on a single item. Such a steep gradient makes no meaningful distinction between retarded and above average functioning. Some of the other Battelle subtests are similarly affected by small changes in raw scores.

Differences in Norm Tables

Some tests have norm tables that are grouped by four-month age levels, while others are grouped by three-month intervals. While this appears on the surface to be a minor problem, the rapid rate with which young children develop sometimes results in differences that can be quite dramatic. Smaller age intervals in norm tables would help control for the rapid changes in preschool children's growth and development, but no current preschool tests have norms that are sufficiently sensitive developmentally (e.g., norm tables set at one-month intervals rather than three). A child who is 2 years 7 months and 16 days old who earns raw scores on the *McCarthy Scales of Children's Abilities* (McCarthy, 1972) that are identical to those earned by a child only one day younger will earn standard scores on all scales of the McCarthy that are approximately one-half a standard deviation less than the second child. Because the McCarthy norm tables are insufficiently sensitive to developmental growth, a one-day difference in age can result in a one-half standard deviation in standard scores when there was *no* concomitant difference in obtained raw scores.

AGE OR GRADE EQUIVALENTS USED FOR COMPARISON

Reynolds (1981) pointed out that age and grade equivalents should not be used for making important decisions about the examinee. Age and grade equivalents are not standard scores and do not possess the psychometric characteristics of standard scores; they are overly sensitive to minor changes in raw scores; they do not represent equal units of measurement; they often do not uniformly correspond to comparable changes in standard scores (e.g., a single grade equivalent does not necessarily correspond to the same standard score on any of the subtests within an instrument). As such, age and grade equivalents are too error prone to provide accurate data for meaningful interpretation and often reflect nonmeaningful differences in performance across measures. Despite such admonitions, educators and psychologists frequently interpret mental ages and test age equivalents as though they possess the characteristics of standard scores.

DIFFERENCES IN RELIABILITY

As tests decrease in reliability, they should subsequently decrease the confidence one has in their resulting scores. Obviously, if two tests have low reliabilities, they can easily produce disparate scores merely as a result of the increased measurement error associated with the lower reliabilities. That is, score variance can be partialed into reliable variance and error variance. Reliability coefficients constitute the proportion of the score variance that is error free (i.e., .80 reliability means 80% reliable variance and 20% error variance).

Two tests that have internal consistency (reliability) coefficients of .60 have scores that are comprised of 60 percent reliable or true variance and 40 percent error variance. With each test comprised of this much error (i.e., 60%), it is easy to understand why the two tests might produce scores that are not comparable, even though they purport to assess the same construct. Given a reliability coefficient of .60 and an IQ equivalent standard score (i.e., $M = 100$, $Sd = 15$), scores obtained on two comparable tests could be 19 points apart and still be within one standard error of measurement of each other. Said differently, the two scores could be considered equivalent. While no test is error free, it is the responsibility of examiners to be ethical in their selection and use of tests and ensure that instruments are sufficiently reliable for their intended purposes.

Skill Differences Across Tests

It should be recognized that all tests possessing the same or similar titles (e.g., Arithmetic, Vocabulary, Comprehension) do not necessarily assess the same skills. Two tests that purport to assess vocabulary, for example, might assess different underlying elements of the construct. Some "vocabulary" tests assess receptive vocabulary (e.g., *The Peabody Picture Vocabulary Test*), others assess one-word vocabulary labeling (e.g., The *One-Word Expressive Vocabulary Test*), others assess expressive vocabulary (e.g., the Vocabulary subtest on the WISC-R), and still others combine receptive and expressive vocabulary assessment within the same measure (e.g., the Vocabulary subtest on the Stanford-Binet). An examinee with expressive language difficulties might do very well on a measure of receptive vocabulary, slightly less well on a measure of one-word labeling, still less well on a measure that assesses both receptive and expressive vocabulary, and the least well on a comprehensive measure of expressive vocabulary. While each of these measures assesses vocabulary development, it would be common for some examinees to obtain different scores on each of the four previously mentioned scales, depending on their receptive as opposed to expressive language abilities.

Content Differences Across Tests

Similarly, differences might occur on separate measures of the same construct because some tests sample the universe of relevant item content in differing degrees. For example, of several tests that assess arithmetic ability, one test might assess numerical concepts in a story or verbal problem format (e.g., more-less, first-second-third, denominator-numerator, tangent-arc); another might focus largely on the four basic mathematical operations, using whole numbers in either verbal problems or with paper and pencil (e.g., addition, subtraction, multiplication, division); another might assess to a larger extent such operations as decimals, fractions, and percentages; and yet another test might emphasize basic algebra or geometry. Each of these could assess important aspects of arithmetic ability, but the various test authors would determine during the construction of the tests which aspects of the content universe to assess and with what emphasis. Examinees might very well obtain different scores on any of these arithmetic tests as a function of the degree to which the tests differentially weight the mathematics content included or excluded in the test.

DIFFERENCES IN PUBLICATION DATES

It is well known, but often forgotten, that tests more recently published result in lower scores than tests with older publication dates (Bracken, 1981; Flynn, 1984; Kaufman, 1979b; Sattler, 1982, 1988). As a society, we are gaining in intelligence as the years pass; our current generation evidences higher levels of assessed intelligence than past generations. This gradual increase in intelligence results in differences in test scores as a function of standardization dates of the tests.

Subjects who were administered the *Stanford-Binet Intelligence Scale,* Form LM (1960 norms) earned higher scores than when they were compared to the 1972 Stanford-Binet norms, though the test did not change any of its content. The sole reason for higher scores on the 1960 version is that the subjects included in its standardization sample did not constitute as high a standard of comparison as the more contemporary 1972 sample. When compared to the "less intelligent" 1960 cohort group, a given performance level ranks higher than when compared to the more competitive and "brighter" 1972 cohort group. This has been referred to as *norm softening* (Flynn, 1984) and appears to be a worldwide phenomenon.

The implication of norm softening is that psychologists should strive to use the most recently normed instruments and set aside older versions of tests as soon as newer editions are published. Also, it is important that differences between test scores be considered in light of the differences in the tests' publication dates. Flynn (1984, 1987) estimates that intelligence test scores decrease at a rate of three points per decade—meaning that societal intelligence increases at the same rate. Thus, a test published in 1974 (e.g., WISC-R) would be expected to produce scores about 3 to 5 points higher than a test published in 1990 (e.g., the *Differential Abilities Scale;* Elliott, 1990).

Of even greater concern for psychologists are tests that go several decades without having been revised or renormed. For example, the 50-year span between the publication of the *Vineland Social Maturity Scale* (Doll, 1935) and its revised *Vineland Adaptive Behavior Scales* (Sparrow, Balla, & Cicchetti, 1984) resulted in average score differences between the two scales of more than one standard deviation. Differences of such a magnitude can seriously affect the diagnostic interpretation of client performance. Unawareness of norm softening can add a major source of error to psychologists' interpretation of examinee performance. Psychologists should be wary of using instruments that are more than 15 years old and should always consider the age of a test's norms when interpreting the instrument.

REPRESENTATIVENESS OF THE NORMATIVE SAMPLE

Earlier in this chapter I discussed the relative benefits of using local or national norms. Whether norms are derived locally or nationally, the normative sample should be representative of the population with whom the test will be used. There are important demographic variables related to test performance, such as urban versus rural residence, gender, ethnic group status, region of the country, socioeconomic status, and educational level. Failure to include representative portions of the population in the standardization sample can adversely effect the quality of the norms. For example, in the standardization of the *Kaufman Assessment Battery for Children* (Kaufman & Kaufman, 1983), the test publisher systematically overrepresented more highly educated minorities and underrepresented less well-educated minorities. This resulted in artifactually higher test scores for minorities and led the authors to conclude erroneously that the K-ABC is a more culturally fair instrument for minority individuals. Unfortunately, what occurred in this sort of nonrepresentative sampling was that the minority norms were inflated by about two points, thus resulting in a more difficult norm for minority children rather than an easier or fairer norm (Bracken, 1984).

Summary

Psychological tests are designed for many purposes; the test's intended use dictates how it is best interpreted. When examinees' test scores are rank ordered for the purpose of making judgments based on relative performance, then norm-referenced assessment is the most meaningful approach to interpretation. When decisions are made about an examinee's performance in one skill or ability area relative to the examinee's overall level of development, then ipsative interpretation is appropriate. The comparison of examinee performance against a predetermined criterion requires criterion-referenced interpretation; yet when the criterion is defined within a specific educational curriculum, then curriculum-based assessment makes sense. Regardless of the interpretive approach used, examiners must go beyond the test scores and consider clinical issues related to the examinee's level of motivation, extraindividual conditions present during the assessment, and psychometric considerations of the various instruments and procedures used during the assessment. Anastasi (1988) makes clear the distinction between testing and assessment. Assessment is an ongoing evaluative process that may or may not include tests; testing is merely the administration of tests. Sound psychological assessment requires the astute combination of test administration, clinical observation and judgment, consideration of historical information, and reflection on the reason for the assessment. In combination, these aspects of test administration and interpretation will yield more accurate diagnostic and prognostic statements, better intervention strategies, and a fuller understanding of the psychological functioning of the client.

References

Anastasi, A. (1988). *Psychological testing* (6th ed.). New York: Macmillan.

Arter, J. A., & Jenkins, J. R. (1979). Differential diagnosis—prescriptive teaching: A critical appraisal. *Review of Educational Research, 49*, 517–555.

Barnett, D. W. (1988). Professional judgment: A critical appraisal. *School Psychology Review, 17*, 658–672.

Bracken, B. A. (1981). McCarthy Scales as a learning disability diagnostic aid: A closer look. *Journal of Learning Disabilities, 14*, 128–130.

Bracken, B. A. (1984). *Bracken Basic Concept Scale*. San Antonio, TX: The Psychological Corporation.

Bracken, B. A. (1985). Critical review of the Kaufman Assessment Battery for Children (K-ABC). *School Psychology Review, 14*, 21–36.

Bracken, B. A. (1986). *Bracken Concept Development Program*. San Antonio, TX: The Psychological Corporation.

Bracken, B. A. (1987). Limitations of preschool instruments and standards for minimal levels of technical adequacy. *The Journal of Psychoeducational Assessment, 4*, 313–326.

Bracken, B. A. (1988). Ten psychometric reasons why similar tests produce dissimilar results. *The Journal of School Psychology, 26*, 155–166.

Bracken, B. A. (1990). The assessment of preschool children with the McCarthy Scales of Children's Abilities. In B. Bracken (Ed.), *The psychoeducational assessment of preschool children* (2nd ed.). San Antonio, TX: The Psychological Corporation.

Bracken, B. A., & Fagan, T. K. (1988). Abilities assessed by the K-ABC mental processing subtests: The perceptions of practitioners with varying degrees of experience. *Psychology in the Schools, 25*, 22–34.

Bracken, B. A., Howell, K. K., Harrison, T., Stanford, L. D., & Zahn, B. H. (1991). Ipsative subtest pattern stability of the Bracken Basic Concept Scale and the Kaufman Assessment Battery for Children in a preschool sample. *School Psychology Review, 20,* 315–330.

Carver, R. P. (1974). Two dimensions of tests: Psychometric and edumetric. *American Psychologist, 29,* 512–518.

Cattell, R. B. (1944). Psychological measurement: Normative, ipsative, and interactive. *Psychological Bulletin, 51,* 91–97.

Chattin, S. H., & Bracken, B. A. (1989). School psychologists' evaluation of the K-ABC, McCarthy Scales, Stanford-Binet IV, and WISC-R. *Journal of Psychoeducational Assessment, 7,* 112–130.

Clark, E. V. (1973). Non-linguistic strategies and the acquisition of word meanings. *Cognition, 2,* 161–182.

Cronbach, L. J. (1957). The two disciplines of scientific psychology. *The American Psychologist, 12,* 671–684.

Cronbach, L. J. (1975). Beyond the two disciplines of scientific psychology. *The American Psychologist, 30,* 116–125.

Davis, F. B. (1959). Interpretation of differences among averages and individual test scores. *Journal of Educational Psychology, 50,* 162–170.

Delaney, E. A., & Hopkins, T. F. (1987). *Examiner's handbook: An expanded guide for fourth edition users.* Chicago: Riverside.

Doll, E. A. (1935). *Vineland Social Maturity Scale.* Circle Pines, MN: American Guidance Service.

Elliott, C. D. (1990). *The Differential Ability Scales.* San Antonio, TX: The Psychological Corporation.

Flynn, J. R. (1984). The mean IQ of Americans: Massive gains 1932 to 1978. *Psychological Bulletin, 95,* 29–51.

Flynn, J. R. (1987). Massive IQ gains in 14 nations: What IQ tests really measure. *Psychological Bulletin, 101,* 171–191.

Frisby, C. (1987). Alternative assessment committee report: Curriculum-based assessment. *CASP Today, 36,* 15–26.

Hayes, S. C., Nelson, R. O., & Jarrett, R. B. (1987). The treatment utility of assessment: A functional approach to evaluating assessment quality. *American Psychologist, 42,* 963–974.

Johnson, H. L. (1975). The meaning of before and after for preschool children. *Journal of Experimental Child Psychology, 19,* 88–89.

Kaufman, A. S. (1979a). WISC-R research: Implications for interpretation. *School Psychology Digest, 8,* 5–27.

Kaufman, A. S. (1979b). *Intelligent testing with the WISC-R.* New York: Wiley.

Kaufman, A. S., & Kaufman, N. L. (1977). *Clinical evaluation of young children with the McCarthy Scales.* Orlando, FL: Grune & Stratton.

Kaufman, A. S., & Kaufman, N. L. (1983). *Kaufman assessment battery for children.* Circle Pines, MN: American Guidance Service.

Lemke, E., & Wiersma, W. (1976). *Principles of psychological measurement.* Chicago: Rand McNally.

McCarthy, D. (1972). *The McCarthy scales of children's abilities.* San Antonio, TX: The Psychological Corporation.

McDermott, P. A., Fantuzzo, J. W., & Glutting, J. J. (in press). Just say no to subtest analysis: A critique of the Wechsler theory and practice. *Journal of Psychoeducational Assessment.*

Newborg, J., Stock, J. R., Wnek, L., Guidubaldi, J., & Svinicki, J. (1984). *Battelle Developmental Inventory,* Allen, TX: DLM/Teaching Resources.

Popham, W., & Husek, T. (1971). Implications of criterion-referenced measurement. In W. Popham (Ed.), *Criterion-referenced measurement.* Englewood Cliffs, NJ: Educational Technology Publications.

Reynolds, C. R. (1981). The fallacy of "two years below grade level for age" as a diagnostic criterion for reading disorders. *Journal of School Psychology, 19,* 350–358.

Roffe, M. W., & Bryant, C. K. (1979). How reliable are MSCA profile interpretations? *Psychology in the Schools, 16,* 14–18.

Sattler, J. M. (1982). *Assessment of children's intelligence and special abilities* (2nd ed.). Boston: Allyn & Bacon.

Sattler, J. M. (1988). *Assessment of children.* San Diego: Author.

Salvia, J., & Ysseldyke, J. E. (1981). *Assessment in special and remedial education.* Boston: Houghton Mifflin.

Shinn, M.R., Rosenfield, S., & Knutson, N. (1989). Curriculum-based assessment: A comparison of models. *School Psychology Review, 18,* 299–316.

Silverstein, A. B. (1982). Pattern analysis as simultaneous statistical inference. *Journal of Counseling and Clinical Psychology, 50,* 234–240.

Smith, D. K., Bolin, J. A., & Stovall, D. L. (1988). K-ABC stability in a preschool sample: A longitudinal sample. *Journal of Psychoeducational Assessment, 6,* 396–403.

Sparrow, S. S., Balla, D. A., & Cicchetti, D. V. (1984). *Vineland Adaptive Behavior Scales.* Circle Pines, MN: American Guidance Service.

Thorndike, R. L., Hagen, E. P., & Sattler, J. M. (1986a). *The Stanford-Binet Intelligence Scale* (4th ed). Chicago: Riverside.

Thorndike, R. L., Hagen, E. P., & Sattler, J. M. (1986b). *Technical manual,*

Stanford-Binet Intelligence Scale (4th ed.). Chicago: Riverside.

Wechsler, D. (1974). *Wechsler Intelligence Scale for Children*. San Antonio, TX: The Psychological Corporation.

Wechsler, D. (1981). *Wechsler Adult Intelligence Scale* (Rev. ed.). San Antonio, TX: The Psychological Corporation.

PART II

TEST DEVELOPMENT

CHAPTER 5

PSYCHOLOGICAL TESTS: DEVELOPMENT, PUBLICATION, AND DISTRIBUTION

Gary J. Robertson

Introduction

The development, publication, and distribution of psychological tests in the United States has occurred within the context of a free enterprise economic system. Publication of psychological tests for economic gain has occurred for about 70 years, although no single publisher has survived for the entire period untouched by acquisitions, mergers, and competitive market forces. Today there are more than 200 publishers listed in the files of the American Psychological Association; however, the bulk of test sales in the United States is accounted for by fewer than 20 of these publishers. Moreover, their influence on the quality, dissemination, and use of their test publications has been and continues to be profound.

It is essential that users of psychological tests understand the role of the commercial test publisher in the development and dissemination of test products in use daily in myriad settings throughout the nation and abroad. This chapter describes the processes used by test publishers to develop, publish, and distribute test publications. The specialized knowledge and skill needed to use most psychological tests places a special responsibility on test publishers: Test publications should be sold only to qualified users. The problems related to determining test purchaser qualifications form a major part of the discussion on test distribution practices.

For convenience, this chapter is divided into three major sections. The first section is devoted to a discussion of the test development process within an entrepreneurial context, although the steps in test development outlined apply to the construction of any test, regardless of the setting. The second section outlines the process leading to the publication of a test, again from a commercial perspective. The third section explores some basic issues in assessing the qualifications of test purchasers and offers some new perspectives based on the work of the Test User Qualifications Working Group (TUQWoG). The chapter concludes with some guidelines for the proper use of tests by again drawing on the findings from the research conducted by TUQWoG.

Test Development

Successful test development requires at least two essential ingredients: adequate financial resources and professional technical expertise. Many test publications require heavy "front end" expenditures because the time required for their development is often 3 to 5 years, during which time research costs and staff salaries must be paid. Thus, the availability of adequate financial resources is an important consideration in the decision to develop a test publication. The major test publishers employ a highly trained technical staff that includes psychometric experts, editors, artists and designers, and publications production personnel. Successful test publishing requires that all of these individuals work as a team.

The most responsible technical positions in test publishing firms are held by persons with doctoral level training in a variety of specialties: measurement, statistics, psychometrics, and research methodology, as well as specialized knowledge in a particular discipline or content specialty. In the past 30 years, computers and optical scanners have done much to lighten the workload where data processing operations are concerned; however, test publishing still remains highly labor-intensive. A competent, efficiently functioning staff is essential for effective test publication.

The material presented in this section is based on the following major steps of test development and publication:

- Publication selection
- Content preparation
- Content tryout
- Standardization

These major activities of test development are described within the context of commercial test publishing, where tests are developed and sold to various types of purchasers—school districts, private practitioners, government agencies, industrial concerns, university training programs, psychological clinics, and numerous others. The discussion also focuses on norm-referenced ability and achievement tests developed for educational use; however, the steps of the test development process can be applied, with some modification, to the development of almost any type of test in any setting, commercial or otherwise. The development process is described for both group and individually administered tests because there are major differences in procedural details necessitated by test format.

Both professional standards and market forces influence the quality of test publications. Although there are no uniform standards of quality imposed on test publishers at present, professional organizations such as the American Psychological Association, the American Educational Research Association, and the National Council on Measurement in Education have published joint technical standards periodically since 1954. The most recent version of these is the 1985 *Standards for Educational and Psychological Testing* (AERA, APA, & NCME). The various issues of the technical standards have influenced test publishers as well as test users by outlining recommended procedures for various aspects of test development, such as test standardization and validation. Dissemination of the technical standards to a wide audience has influenced the demand for higher quality test publications. Publication of test reviews, such as those in the various editions of the Buros *Mental Measurement Yearbook,* has also contributed to the quality of commercial test publications.

PUBLICATION SELECTION

The selection of publications is obviously one of a test publisher's most important activities for two reasons. First, the publications selected and the manner in which they are developed will greatly influence the publisher's professional image. Second, the success of the publications determines the financial success of the company. The process by which publication ideas are refined and shaped is obviously vital to the company's long-term success.

Generating Ideas for Test Publications

Test publishing begins with ideas for test publications that come both from within the publisher's staff and from outside individuals such as college and university faculty members, school personnel, psychologists in private practice, and others whose training and experience enable them to perceive unmet needs in areas where instrumentation is entirely lacking or technically inadequate and to generate appropriate publication ideas to meet such needs. Publishers are now beginning to use more sophisticated market research tools to identify unmet needs and new product opportunities in the markets they serve.

The submission of ideas for new test publications shows wide variability: Some may take the form of brief letters of inquiry, while others may have extensive documentation in the form of research data or a master's or doctoral dissertation. In an attempt to standardize and improve the publications selection process, most major test publishers have developed guidelines that outline the type of information prospective test authors should submit with a publication proposal in order for it to be evaluated properly. Table 1 provides an example of the type of information requested by American Guidance Service when publication proposals are submitted for review. Although all of the information in Table 1 may not be available at the time of submission, the information outlined represents the ideal situation in which reaching a decision would be greatly facilitated by having at hand most of the required information.

Considerable refinement is usually required to shape an idea into an acceptable publication; thus, publications often change markedly during the course of development. Such change is often a natural evolution of the development of a good idea that is further refined and shaped by the publisher's development and marketing staff responsible for working with the original author to achieve the final publishable product. No amount of shaping and refinement, however, will guarantee the success of a publication, unless it meets market acceptance. In evaluating possible publications it thus becomes extremely important to identify the factors needed for success and to determine the extent to which a proposed publication contains these essential elements.

Evaluating Publication Submissions

Test publishers typically evaluate proposed publications in stages, each of which is characterized by differing degrees of thoroughness. The first scrutiny of a proposed publication is usually made to determine whether it fits the market the publisher serves. Specialization has occurred within the test publishing industry, with different publishers serving different market segments. For example, a publisher specializing in individually administered achievement tests would probably not be interested in publishing an objective personality test. Prospective test authors are well advised to identify carefully the publisher most appropriate for the particular type of test being

TABLE 1. American Guidance Service's Publication
Proposal Submission Requirements

The publisher requests that as much of the following information as is available
be submitted with the publication proposal:

I. Statement of the purpose and rationale for the test
II. Description of the test
   a. Measurement properties
   b. Age/grade range
   c. Structure/subtests
   d. Administration time
   e. Method of administration
   f. Type of scoring/time
III. Components
   a. Nonconsumable items
   b. Consumable items
IV. Primary markets
   a. Users
   b. Qualifications needed for administration and interpretation
V. Competition
   a. Availability of similar tests
   b. Need for new test
   c. Advantages over competitors
VI. Research summary
   a. Pilot studies
   b. Special research studies
   c. Additional research planned
VII. Review
   a. Results of expert review
   b. Results of submission to other publishers
VIII. Author credentials (vita)

Reprinted by permission of American Guidance Service, Inc.

proposed before submitting a proposal to any test publisher. Such a strategy
saves time and increases the likelihood of generating interest on the part of
the prospective publisher.

Once a proposed publication has survived the first screening, the next
phase of evaluation typically consists of more rigorous and formal scrutiny.
It is important, for example, to investigate the soundness of the theoretical
assumptions on which the publication is based as well as its uniqueness,
practical utility, and market demand. Because a publisher's financial resources

are limited, it becomes important to obtain an index of the financial contribution the proposed publication is expected to make to the publisher's revenues and profits. If a consistent procedure is used to evaluate proposed publications, then it becomes possible to rank proposed publications and select those with the highest return, based on theoretical, practical, and financial considerations. Such an evaluation system can assist greatly in the proper use of a company's investment in new products.

Such a system is used by American Guidance Service to evaluate all of its proposed publications. There are two parts to the evaluation process. First, the proposal is rated on the intangible factors shown in Table 2: product integrity, marketability, research and development capability, and production capability. Each of these factors is weighted differently to arrive at a total score ranging from 10 to 100. (This rating system is based on one proposed by O'Meara [1961] to evaluate consumer products.) Next, those proposals that survive the initial screening are subjected to financial analysis to forecast their revenue and profit contributions. Publications that meet the criteria for both the intangible and financial evaluations are placed on the list of approved new products; work begins as soon as the financial resources become available.

Various approaches to selecting new publications are possible. Some publishers may use only advisory boards composed of development, marketing, and finance executives to make final publication decisions. Others may place more reliance on a formal rating process such as that described above for AGS. Still others may use a combination of formal ratings and executive consensus. It is important that whatever method is used be applied consistently in the evaluation of new publication proposals in order to accumulate the experience needed to use the system effectively and to modify it as needed.

Formalizing Publication Arrangements

Once a decision to accept or reject a proposed publication is made, the prospective author is notified. If a decision to reject was made, the author may submit it to another publisher. If accepted, then the publisher negotiates such terms as royalty rates, sharing and recovery of development costs, advances, and manuscript delivery dates. These terms are then formally recorded in a contract, a binding legal document that specifies the responsibilities of both author and publisher. Most contracts cover in detail the arrangements for one edition of a test but provide for revisions only in rather general terms. As soon as the contract has been negotiated and signed, the publisher and author are ready to begin collaborative work on the publication. The next step in the development process is the preparation of test content.

TABLE 2. Factors and Subfactors Comprising American Guidance Service's Proposed New Product Rating System

---

I. Product integrity
   a. Theoretical soundness
   b. Ease of use
   c. Originality
   d. Authorial credentials
   e. Proof of effectiveness
   f. Product longevity
II. Marketability
   a. Size of market
   b. Market needs/wants
   c. Nature of competition
   d. Importance of consumables/services
   e. Prime/value relationship
   f. Relation to present customer/promotion mix
   g. Effects on sales of present products
   h. Order fulfillment demands
III. Research and development capability
   a. Staff knowledge
   b. Staff experience
   c. Outside consultation required
   d. Managerial complexity
   e. Magnitude of project
   f. Time needed for development
   g. Access to outside resources
   h. Authorial compatibility
IV. Production capability
   a. Staff knowledge/experience
   b. Inventory complexity
   c. Assembly requirements
   d. Existing vendor capability
   e. Outside design requirements

Reprinted by permission of American Guidance Service, Inc.

CONTENT PREPARATION

If a test is to function as intended, the test items must be well conceived, clearly presented, and appropriate for measuring the desired behavior. This section addresses the preparation of test content for achievement and ability tests, which represent the most common types of tests for which content is developed.

Content preparation begins with the development of a set of specifications for the test. The specifications define the scope of the content to be measured by the test by providing a listing of content categories and the relative weight each is to have in the content sampling. In addition, this test *blueprint* will also specify the number of items to be prepared, the item format, targeted difficulty level of the items, and related details that will facilitate item development. Once the items are written, they must be reviewed thoroughly by both content and editorial experts for errors or ambiguities. When the desired number of items has been prepared, critiqued, revised, and edited, the items are tried out under conditions similar to those of their final use. The statistical item data obtained from this process is subsequently used to select the final set of items for publication.

Preparing Specifications for an Achievement Test

Achievement tests measure the outcomes of instruction in a particular area of knowledge. For example, physics, American literature, and woodworking all represent content areas in which achievement tests could be used to assess the degree to which students had achieved the goals or outcomes of instruction. Sometimes the source of content is a single textbook, as is the case of teacher-made tests. For broader achievement tests applicable to many schools, the scope of the content must be distilled from diverse curricula drawn from numerous sources. It is the responsibility of the test constructor either to prepare the outline of test content or guide its preparation by curricular experts.

In addition to an outline of test content, the specifications for achievement tests also frequently include so-called process objectives. Learning in a particular content area is seen to occur as a result of the interaction of the learner's mental processes with the content in that knowledge domain. Such mental processes as recalling, recognizing, defining, identifying, applying, analyzing, synthesizing, evaluating, generalizing, and predicting are examples of process objectives (Thorndike & Hagen, 1977). Such terms attempt to describe learning in objectively verifiable behaviors that provide evidence of the occurrence of such learning. Content specifications for achievement tests are often expressed in terms of a two-way grid, with the content dimensions along one axis and process objectives along the other axis. Such a framework provides a systemic means for assessing various combinations of content-process objectives.

A major influence on the development of process objectives was Bloom's (1956) *Taxonomy of Educational Objectives, Handbook I: Cognitive Domain.* Bloom envisioned a hierarchical structure of knowledge organized in six areas: knowledge, comprehension, application, analysis, synthesis, and evaluation. Knowledge, defined as recall or recognition of facts, was seen as the essential element required for application of the other five higher-order mental processes (see Tinkelman, 1971, for a more complete discussion). Bloom's work called the attention of test developers and educators to the desirability of including the higher mental processes in education and in tests designed to measure educational outcomes. Bloom's work revealed that much of school learning and testing dealt with facts, with little attention given to such higher-order thinking skills as application, analysis, synthesis, and evaluation.

An example will serve to illustrate how the test specifications were prepared for a nationally normed mathematics achievement test. Table 3 shows the partial content structure of *KeyMath-Revised: A Diagnostic Inventory of Essential Mathematics* (Connolly, 1988), an individually administered test of basic mathematical skills for pupils in grades 1 through 8.

The content of *KeyMath-R* is pyramidal in nature, beginning with three broad content groupings—basic concepts, operations, and applications. These are subdivided into 43 content domains, each with six items. Thus, the test contains a total of 258 items, of which only a relatively small number are administered to any one pupil. The content of *KeyMath-R* was based on an extensive analysis of mathematics instructional materials and curriculum guides as well as opinions of a panel of nationally recognized experts in the teaching of mathematics (Connolly, 1988). The behavioral objectives for the items within a content domain illustrate the interaction of content and process in defining the learning outcomes to be assessed.

Writing Items for an Achievement Test

Item writing can begin as soon as the content specifications have been completed. Items of high quality are essential if a test is to perform its intended function well. Considerable training and practice are required to prepare acceptable items, especially multiple-choice items. Although a number of writers have provided excellent sets of rules for item writing (Ebel & Frisbie, 1991; Mehrens & Lehmann, 1984; Thorndike & Hagen, 1977), more than just knowledge of such rules is required if items are to function well. Good writing skills are essential, as are critiques from experienced item writers. Knowledge of content and flexibility in thinking are also contributors to effective item development. No matter how good the item writer, all items must be subjected to rigorous editorial scrutiny prior to tryout to identify those items with flaws of one sort or another.

TABLE 3. Partial Content Structure for *KeyMath—Revised: A Diagnostic Inventory of Essential Mathematics*

Content Area	Content Strand (Subtest)	Domains	Item Objectives*
Basic concepts 66 items; 11 domains	Numeration (24 times)	A. Numbers 0–9 B. Numbers 0–99 C. Numbers 0–999 D. Multidigit numbers	The student can A-1 Count objects (1–5) in a set A-2 Form a set A-3 Read one-digit numerals (0–9) A-4 Order a set A-5 Count objects (1–9) in a set A-6 Name the ordinal position
	Rational numbers (18 items)	A. Fractions B. Decimals C. Percents	B-1 Determine decimal tenths B-2 Determine decimal hundredths B-3 Give the next number in a sequence of decimal values B-4 Express decimal hundredths as a fraction B-5 Order a set of decimal values from smallest to largest B-6 Identify which decimal value in a set is closest to a given common fraction
	Geometry (24 times)	A. Spatial/attribute relations B. Two-dimensional shapes C. Coordinate...geometry D. Three-dimensional shapes	

TABLE 3. Partial Content Structure for *KeyMath—Revised: A Diagnostic Inventory of Essential Mathematics* (continued)

Content Area	Content Strand (Subtest)	Domains	Item Objectives[*]
Operations (90 items: 15 domains)	Addition (18 items)	A. Modes and basic facts B. Algorithm to add C. Adding rational numbers	A-1 Determine the total A-2 Determine the total A-3 Identify the multiplication A-4 Complete multiplication A-5 Complete multiplication fact A-6 Complete multiplication facts
	Subtraction (18 items)	A. Models and basic facts B. Algorithm to subtract C. Subtracting rational numbers	
	Multiplication (18 items)	A. Models and basic facts B. Algorithm to multiply C. Multiplying rational numbers	
	Division (18 items)	A. Models and basic facts B. Algorithms to multiply C. Dividing rational numbers	
	Mental computations (18 items)	A. Comparisons B. Whole numbers C. Rational numbers	

TABLE 3. Partial Content Structure for *KeyMath—Revised: A Diagnostic Inventory of Essential Mathematics* (continued)

Content Area	Content Strand (Subtest)	Domains	Item Objectives[*]
Applications (102 items; 17 domains)	Measurement (24 items)	A. Comparisons B. Using nonstandard units C. Using standard units—length D. Using standard units—weight	A-1 Identify a season of the year A-2 Sequence a set of events in chronological order A-3 Identify yesterday, today, and tomorrow A-4 Read a monthly calendar to identify date of a given day A-5 Read a monthly calendar to identify the date at the end of a given interval A-6 Read a date presented in short form
	Time and money (24 items)	A. Identifying passage of time B. Using clocks C. Monetary amounts D. Monetary amounts	
	Estimation (18 items)	A. Whole and rational numbers B. Measurement C. Computation	
	Interpreting data (18 items)	A. Charts B. Graphs C. Probability statistics	
	Problem solving (18 items)	A. Solving routine problems B. Understanding nonroutine problems C. Solving nonroutine problems	

[*] Each domain contains six item objectives; only selected item objectives are shown as examples.

Preparing Specifications for an Ability Test

Aptitude and ability tests are not tied to a particular curriculum or course of study as are achievement tests, but relate directly to the test developer's theoretical stance on the important components of a particular ability or trait. The statistical tools of correlation, regression, and factor analysis frequently play a key role in the definition and structuring of aptitude and ability tests. Consider a psychologist who is constructing a new intelligence test. If the psychologist adheres to a theory of g, or general intelligence, the test will be quite different from one based on a multiple factor theoretical orientation. Frequently, aptitude and ability tests require considerable refinement and reshaping as data from item analysis and standardization become available.

Writing Items for an Ability Test

Taxonomies of the types of items used in ability tests have been prepared by both French (1951) and Guilford (1967), using different approaches. French (1951) surveyed a wide array of factor-analytic studies, systematized the results, and published a *Kit of Tests for Reference Factors,* which contained recommended tests for each of the factors identified. Guilford and his colleagues, on the other hand, conducted a large-scale aptitudes research project that provided a basis for Guilford's (1967) *structure-of-intellect model* (SIM). The SIM is shown as a three-dimensional solid defined by *contents, operations,* and *products.* Each of the 120 cells formed by the content-operation-product dimensions of Guilford's model represents a separate ability and thus results in a highly splintered and rather controversial view of human abilities; a number of the cells are still unconfirmed. A vast array of tests was created to identify the separate cells in Guilford's model.

The most frequently encountered types of items found in ability tests are shown in Table 4. Items are classified according to three common types of content: verbal, symbolic, and figural. *Verbal content* is that encountered in items using words and sentences; *symbolic content* employs letters and numerals; and *figural content* uses pictorial, geometric, or abstract figures and designs. Ability tests often assess the ability to reason or solve problems by framing items using these various types of content. Space limitations preclude giving examples of the common types of content frequently used to measure the types of items shown in Table 4. Readers unfamiliar with them should consult Thorndike (1982) for examples.

There are no sets of guidelines for preparing ability items as there are for achievement test items. Much depends on the ingenuity of the item writer in devising unusual or novel problem situations and in developing good foils,

TABLE 4. Types of Items Commonly Used in Ability Tests

Item Type	Content Dimension		
	Verbal /Semantic (Words /Sentences)	Symbolic (Letters /Numerals)	Figural/Pictorial (Geometric /Abstract)
Analogies	X	X	X
Classification	X	X	X
Series completion	X	X	X
Matrices	X	X	X
Synonym/antonym	X		
Sentence completion	X		
Reasoning problems	X	X	
Disarranged stimuli	X	X	
Synthesis	X	X	X
Immediate/delayed recall	X	X	X
Visualization: two dimensions			X
Visualization: three dimensions			X

From *Handbook of Psychological & Educational Assessment of Children–Intelligence & Achievement* (p. 72) by C. R. Reynolds and R. W. Kamphaus (Eds.), 1990, New York: The Guilford Press. Copyright 1990 by Guilford Press. Reprinted by permission.

or misleads, for multiple-choice items. Just as with achievement test items, it is important for ability items to be critiqued and edited carefully prior to tryout.

Number of Items Needed for Tryout

The number of items that need to be prepared for tryout is always of concern to test developers. Unfortunately, there is no simple answer to the question of how many items are needed. Judgment and experience ultimately dictate the answer. Factors that need to be considered in reaching a decision are (a) the age or grade range covered by the test, (b) the number of test forms needed and test length, (c) the novelty of the item type(s), (d) the skill of the item writer(s), and (e) the funds available for the enterprise. These factors must be weighed carefully in arriving at a final decision. Cost factors are certainly important and probably should be one of the first items considered. If a test relies on expensive artwork or illustrations, then fewer items would be possible than would be true if the test relied on words, letters, or numerals. If verbal analogy items were being written for ages 9 through 18, for example, more items would be needed than if the test spanned only one or two age levels. Inexperienced or novice item writers will most likely have to produce more items to meet the required target number for tryout than will experienced item writers. As a general rule of thumb, it is recommended that 25 percent to 50 percent more items than needed be prepared, with the exact number determined after consideration of the factors mentioned.

CONTENT TRYOUT

When the test items have been written, reviewed, revised, and edited, they are ready for tryout with a sample of individuals as similar as possible to those with whom the test will be used in its final form. Among the factors that will directly influence the scope of the tryout program are financial resources, age or grade levels for which information about item functioning is needed, size of the tryout sample, and related practical considerations such as the time available for testing, time of year, and administrative arrangements needed. These influences are discussed below.

Financial Resources

The scope of the item tryout program is directly related to the funds allocated by the publisher to this enterprise. The type of test greatly influences the type of item tryout that will be needed. Novel item types generally require a larger tryout program than more conventional items. Test format also influences cost, with individually administered tests typically using smaller tryout samples due to cost factors that relate to finding suitable subjects and testing each one individually. For example, a comprehensive, individually administered intelligence test may require payments of $25 to $35 or more per examinee to the test administrators. Group tests usually permit much larger samples for tryout because the individuals can be tested in groups.

The tryout costs for an individually administered general achievement battery are shown in Table 5. It was assumed that test items in the areas of reading comprehension, word recognition, mathematics, spelling, and writing would be tried out on a sample of 1,000 pupils in grades 1 through 12. It can be seen that the total tryout program is estimated to cost $45,000, excluding the publisher's permanent staff salaries; moreover, the high cost expense items are test administration payments to examiners (57.8%), consultants who critique the test items (10.0%), and payments to clerical workers employed on a temporary basis to assist with the statistical analysis of the tryout data (14.4%).

TABLE 5. Item Tryout Budget for a General Achievement Battery

Type of Expenditure	Explanation	Budgeted Amount (In Dollars)	Percentage of Total Budget
Inducements	Materials for participating school	500	1.1
Clerical services	Payment to hourly clerical worker	6,500	14.4
Item writing	Preparation of additional items	1,000	2.2
Testing	Examiner payments for test administration (to 1,000 students)	26,000	57.8
Consulting	Payments to subject matter experts	4,500	10.0
Shipping	Shipment of tryout material to coordinators	1,000	2.2
Printing and binding	Preparation of tryout materials	2,000	4.4
Travel	Travel to authorial meeting	2,500	5.6
Misellaneous	Uncategorized expenditures	1,000	2.2
	Project total	45,000	99.9

From *Handbook of Psychological & Educational Assessment of Children–Intelligence & Achievement* (p. 73) by C. R. Reynolds and R. W. Kamphau (Eds.), 1990, New York: The Guilford Press. Copyright 1990 by Guilford Press. Reprinted by permission.

Age or Grade Levels

Careful planning is needed to ensure that test items are tried out at appropriate age or grade levels. If sufficient resources are available, it is advisable to conduct the tryout program in two phases. As soon as item writing, review, and editing are completed, it is recommended that the items be tried out on a small sample to obtain a rough approximation of their difficulty level. This is especially important for novel types of items or items where no previous data exist to permit estimates of their difficulty. This first tryout on a small sample of convenience can obviously be omitted if data for other similar types of items are available or if the experience of the test author or item writer is such that a reliable estimate of difficulty can be made. The procedure is especially recommended for individually administered tests where smaller numbers of items are tried out than is the case with group tests. For group tests, items may easily be repeated at several age or grade levels to obtain information about item functioning over a broad developmental span. Preliminary information about item functioning greatly facilitates item placement for the second phase of item tryout, in which the items are tested on a larger cross-section of individuals than was true of the first preliminary item tryout. Occasionally additional item tryouts are necessary if there is unusually high item attrition due to undetected item flaws or misjudged difficulty level.

Size of the Tryout Sample

Judgment usually dictates the size of the tryout sample because the decision must be based on both practical and theoretical considerations. Authorities agree that reasonably stable estimates of item difficulty and discrimination indices are possible with tryout sample sizes of 200 to 500 individuals (Henrysson, 1971; Thorndike, 1982). Beyond the sheer number of individuals, however, it is important to consider the composition of the tryout sample. The more closely the tryout sample is representative of the final individuals for whom the test is designed, the more valuable the item data are. Thus, it is important that the tryout sample match the final population of test takers on relevant demographic factors to the extent possible. If special subsamples are needed for any special item analyses, such as minorities for studies of differential item functioning, then care must be taken in the planning to oversample these individuals to insure enough cases to permit the needed analyses.

Practical Considerations

Several practical considerations merit attention if the item analysis data are to be maximally useful. First, it is important that the length of the tryout tests fit into the amount of time available for testing. If too many items are included in one test form, examinees may not finish the items near the end of the test and, as a result, there will be little dependable information about these items. A good rule of thumb is to construct tryout test forms of a length such that about 90 percent of examinees have time to attempt all of the items. The desired number of final test forms is a major factor in determining tryout test length. If several final test forms are needed, multiple tryout test forms will be required. For individually administered tests, multiple tryout test forms will be needed if the total testing time exceeds one to one and a half hours, depending on the age of the examinee. Examinee fatigue is obviously an undesirable influence on test performance and should be avoided by tailoring test forms to the age level of the examinees as well as the time available for testing.

Another important consideration, mainly for achievement tests, is the time of year of item tryout. Obviously, the item tryout should occur at the same time of the school year as the anticipated final test use. If a particular test will be administered largely in the fall, then the item tryout program should occur in the fall. If an achievement battery will be used in both fall and spring, for example, then item analysis data will probably be needed for both times of the school year. This is especially important where differential growth rates occur for school subjects between the fall and spring of the school year.

Finally, it is important that administrative arrangements and details be carefully thought out in advance of testing. Directions for administering the test must be clear; test books and answer sheets must be carefully designed and printed. It is important that the tryout testing occur under uniform conditions so that item analysis data will be truly meaningful.

Item Analysis

The term *item analysis* refers to the statistical examination of examinee responses to test items. The end result of item analysis is the identification of essentially three classes of items: (a) those satisfactory for operational use without further work, (b) those with marginal item statistics that may be salvageable after revision, and (c) those whose item statistics warrant their being discarded. The final test forms can be assembled only when there are sufficient numbers of acceptable items either from class 1 or from class 2 after revision and, if necessary, additional tryout.

There are essentially two main classes of item analysis procedures: classical and item response theory (IRT). Both methodologies provide useful information about items, and most major publishers of achievement and ability tests use both methods to study item responses. *Classical* item analysis refers to the standard item statistics used over the past 60 to 70 years, such as item difficulty (percent of examinees responding correctly to an item) and item discrimination (an index of the item's ability to discriminate those having more from those having less of a particular ability, skill, or trait). *Item response theory* (IRT), also known as *latent trait,* is a form of item-test regression analysis and refers to procedures that have evolved over the last 25 years, including several latent-trait models that have proved useful in calibrating individual test items. Both types of item analysis are discussed below.

CLASSICAL ITEM ANALYSIS. Classical item analysis is based on two types of information—item difficulty and item discrimination. *Item difficulty* is measured by the percentage of examinees answering an item correctly; *item discrimination,* by the correlation of an item with total test score. For multiple choice tests, the percentage of examinees choosing each *distractor,* or foil, is also frequently determined as well as the item-total correlation of each of the distractors. Applications of classical item analysis are essentially of two types: (a) within groups and (b) between groups.

Within-group Item Analysis. Within-group applications of classical item analysis base item statistics on a single reference group. The group may consist of any collection of individuals with a common defining characteristic of interest; for example, first-year Spanish students, college-bound high school seniors, and machine-shop students all constitute single reference groups that might be of interest to test developers. Assuming that a test appropriate to each group was under development, items would be selected by considering item analysis data based on the performance of that single reference group. In this case, there is no interest in the performance of items across multiple reference groups.

Between-group Item Analysis. Between–group applications are item analyses based on multiple reference groups. This type of information is important for studying item functioning across several ages or grades. Important reference groups might be successive age or grade groups. In achievement and ability tests designed to function over a range of ages or grades, items are needed that perform well in several age or grade groups for which a test is designed, not just a single age or grade reference group. Items in intelligence tests, for example, must show an increase in the percentage of examinees passing an item across successive age levels for the item to be retained in the final test. Such analyses as these are really a form of item regression on age, where the slope of the regression line defined by the percentage of examinees passing at each age is the main criterion for determining item acceptance. Terman and Merrill (1937) used this form of item analysis in their revision of the *Stanford-Binet Intelligence Scale*. From the percentage passing graph, or curve, for each item, the age where 50 percent of the individuals passed the item was determined. In this way, an *item age* was obtained for each item and could be used to arrange items in order of difficulty across a broad age span.

ITEM RESPONSE THEORY. Item response theory, or IRT, also known as latent trait analysis, item characteristic curve theory, and item calibration, became feasible with the availability of high-speed electronic computers. IRT is basically a type of item–test score regression that permits single test items to be calibrated or referenced against the underlying, or latent, trait measured by a test (Lord, 1980). Two significant advantages result from such capability. First, item difficulty and person ability can be referenced to the same scale. This permits individual test items to be referenced directly to the underlying ability scale and provides significant advantages in test construction. Classical item analysis methods do not provide such a convenient and directly accessible reference to the underlying ability measured by the test. Second, because IRT is a type of regression methodology, estimates of item characteristics remain invariant across groups of different ability (Lord, 1980). Unlike classical item analysis, in which item indices change in direct relation to changes in the group on which they are based, IRT estimates remain relatively unaffected by the group of individuals on which they are based. Both of these advantages constitute persuasive arguments for the use of IRT methods in test construction. There are, at present, three main types, or models, of IRT in use.

Both classical and IRT methods provide useful and rather different types of information helpful in test construction. Most test development efforts benefit from having both types of information available, often at different stages in the test development process. Specific needs and conditions will dictate the exact type of information most appropriate for a given type of test. Research on the many different applications of IRT is still underway; new developments and applications will undoubtedly result from present and future research efforts.

STANDARDIZATION

Standardization refers to the process used to achieve uniformity and objectivity in test administration, scoring, and interpretation. In order for test results to be meaningful, the directions for administering need to be worked out carefully so that different examiners in different settings will obtain comparable results if the directions are followed carefully. Scoring of examinee responses must also be as objective as possible to minimize scoring errors and enhance comparability of the resulting scores. Both uniform directions for administration and objectivity of scoring are necessary preconditions for the normative interpretation of performance on a test (Anastasi, 1988).

This section is organized around the following elements of test standardization: assembly of the final operational test, including the directions for administering and scoring; the selection of a standardization sample, including the norming of group and individually administered tests; supplementary research studies; and development of test norms.

Final Test Assembly

Items from the tryout versions of a test are placed in final versions of the test by means of a test blueprint. The blueprint specifies the types and numbers of items comprising the final test forms. Information obtained from the item analysis program is used to determine the acceptability of each item. On the basis of the item analysis information, items are usually sorted into groups such as *acceptable, acceptable with modifications,* and *unacceptable.* Items from the "acceptable" and the "acceptable with modifications" categories are used to assemble the final test forms. If a test requires more items than are available from these categories, either the test blueprint must be modified or new items must be written and tried out. To avoid costly delays, it is recommended that a sufficient surplus of items be tried out to allow for attrition caused by poorly performing items.

If multiple parallel test forms are being developed, then items from the "acceptable" and "acceptable with modifications" categories of the item pool are used by test developers to construct the final test forms matched on content coverage, item difficulty and discrimination, and item intercorrelations. Careful balancing of the test forms is needed in order to meet the requirements for parallel forms: equal means, equal variances, and equal intercorrelations (Gulliksen, 1950). In actual practice, the construction of multiple parallel test forms by exact balancing of item statistics rarely occurs and thus represents an ideal rarely, if ever, achieved.

After the final test forms are assembled for use in the standardization program, other materials needed, such as directions for test administration and answer sheets, can be developed. In addition, a variety of special control forms will be needed. For some individually administered tests, manipulatives may need to be manufactured. Such items must be manufactured to the same rigorous specifications as those contained in the final test.

Special care must be taken to ensure that the directions for administering the test receive a thorough editing before they are finalized for standardization because the normative data must be gathered using the final directions to be published with the test. Answer sheets and record forms need not be in their final form, but they should be in a format that is functional and easy to use by students and examiners.

Selection of the Standardization Sample

Standardization sample selection procedures vary markedly for group and individually administered tests, despite the fact that the end result is similar— to describe the performance of a representative sample of the population on a measure of a particular attribute, trait, or skill. The first step in a standardization effort, group or individual, is the development of a carefully designed plan for obtaining the types of individuals needed in the standardization program. A discussion of the characteristics desired in a comprehensive standardization program plan will be presented, followed by separate discussions for group and individual test standardization efforts.

THE NEED FOR CAREFUL PLANNING. A test standardization, or norming, program yields meaningful results only if a detailed, comprehensive plan was used to guide the effort. Representativeness is a desired attribute in all test standardization programs because the test results are typically used to generalize about the national population of interest, usually by grade level or age level. Detailed, careful planning is required in order to exercise control over as many factors as possible to minimize the introduction of various undesired biases that will distort the test results.

Test standardization programs always represent a compromise between what is optimally desirable from a theoretical perspective and what is feasible from a practical standpoint. Standardization testing represents the single largest expenditure in most test development efforts, so cost considerations play a significant role in delimiting the scope of the standardization program. The goal of all norming efforts should be to obtain the best standardization sample possible within the imposed cost constraints. A carefully developed, systematic norming plan will greatly facilitate obtaining a standardization sample that is both scientifically defensible and practically feasible.

Various elements are included in a test standardization plan. Of paramount importance is the particular reference group. Educational and psychological tests are usually referenced to national grade or age groups. Educational achievement tests designed to measure specific curricular outcomes are most often grade-referenced, while aptitude and ability tests are more often age-referenced. The same sample may be appropriately age- or grade-referenced, depending on the types of norms that are appropriate. Reference groups for most published tests are national, but local norms may be appropriate for meeting the needs of local school districts. National norming programs typically require highly complex multistage sampling methods to identify the sample of individuals to be tested, while local norms demand less elaborate designs. A well-developed plan for obtaining the norms is essential in either type of norming operation.

Besides the reference group, the standardization sampling plan should indicate the role of various demographic factors in sample selection, such as socioeconomic level, gender, geographic region, urban-rural residence, and race or ethnic group. A test that purports to offer national norms will have the success of its standardization effort judged by the extent to which its sample matches national census data for the relevant demographic factors. Prudent test developers will, therefore, work out the details of the sampling plan carefully in order to replicate national demographic statistics to the fullest extent possible in the test norming sample.

An additional element of the norming plan is the method to be used to select the sample from the population. Although norming samples were once largely samples of convenience, their quality has improved greatly during the past 25 to 30 years. The introduction of probability sampling methods by test publishers has improved the precision of their norms. Although probability sampling methods are desirable because they permit the estimation of the amount of error present in the norms (Angoff, 1971), they represent an ideal methodology that can at best be only approximated in practice. True random samples, though highly desirable, are usually not feasible, due to a variety of practical constraints. These practical realities of norming are well illustrated by comparing the methods used to standardize group and individually administered tests. Although both types of tests share the same desired result of obtaining representative national norms, format and cost factors necessitate the use of quite different norming procedures. The norming procedures for group and individual tests are discussed separately in the following sections.

GROUP TEST NORMING PROCEDURES. Group test standardization procedures contrast rather markedly with individual test standardization procedures in several respects. The salient features of group test standardization efforts are outlined below in terms of ease of execution, precision, and cost.

Ease of Execution. Group administered test norming programs are much easier to conduct than individually administered test norming programs. First, the examiners administering the tests do not typically require specialized training. Directions for administering the tests are relatively straightforward and easily understood. The main requirement of examiners is that they follow the printed directions exactly, especially if there are prescribed time limits. Individuals with little or no specialized training in testing can easily administer most group tests. Next, test materials usually consist of printed matter such as test question booklets, answer sheets, and directions for test administration. Such materials are easily prepared and easy for examiners to handle. Finally, group test samples are more accessible than those for individual tests. Participants in group test norming programs are tested in naturally occurring groups such as classes or grades. Access to these groups usually occurs through school districts that are easily identified by means of state education directories or other comprehensive listings. Each school district that agrees to participate will contribute a number of individuals to the norming program. No effort will be required to recruit and test individual examinees apart from the groups in which they exist within the school system. This feature of group test standardization programs renders them relatively easy to conduct.

Precision. Ideally, test norms should be based on a random sample of the relevant population because it is not possible to test every individual member of that population. For example, if national U.S. fifth-grade norms are being prepared for a reading test, it will be feasible to test only a sample of the U.S. population of fifth graders, not all of them. In practice, it is never possible to obtain a strict random sample of examinees for either group or individual tests. It is, however, possible to come closer to such an ideal random sample for group tests than for individual tests. When participants are selected by naturally occurring units such as schools or classes, it becomes possible to use a type of probability sampling known as *multistage stratified random cluster sampling.* The advantages of this type of sampling are several: (a) The process of selecting the elements (schools or classes) to be tested is objective and automatic and not determined by idiosyncratic judgment or mere availability, (b) each element (school or class) in the sample has a known probability of being selected, and (c) known selection probabilities can be used to develop weights to correct for over- and underrepresentation within the sample when the norms are developed (Angoff, 1971). The term *multistage* means that the sample of individuals to be tested is selected in stages, beginning with assembling an exhaustive list of all elements (schools or classes) comprising a particular population. To increase the ease and efficiency of sampling, the complete listing of population elements may be arranged in certain groups, for example, size, socioeconomic status, and geographic region, among others. Once these subunits, or *strata,* are formed, it then becomes possible to sample randomly within strata. Thus, the selection process for a group test standardization sample proceeds in a systematic fashion from school districts to individual schools and, finally, to classes within schools. Once a certain class is selected for participation, then all individual student members of that class become sample participants. It should be pointed out, however, that the ideal of random samples of participants is never actually realized in group test norming because the final sample is composed of school districts that voluntarily participate. At present, there is no way a test developer can compel or require a school district to participate in a norming program. Thus, while it is difficult to determine exactly the precision of the norms, it is safe to conclude that group test norms based on a carefully developed multistage sampling procedure where 10,000 or more students are tested at each grade level are more accurate than those from an individual test where 100 or so students are tested at each grade or age level. A direct result of the larger group test samples is increased precision of the norms. Although size per se does not guarantee greater accuracy of test norms, well-designed group test standardization programs that base norms on several thousand students per grade or age level do permit more precise estimates of norms in the population than is the case where only 100 or so students are tested at each age or grade level.

Cost. In general, the administrative unit cost per examinee is less in a group test norming program than for an individual test. The fact that group tests can be administered by teachers or others with little specialized training in testing, together with the greater ease of identifying and testing examinees, makes group tests much cheaper to administer than individual tests. For this reason, group test standardization programs usually include much larger samples of participants than is true for individual tests. Thus, a group achievement test for use in grades 1 through 8 might be normed on a sample of 80,000 to 150,000 individuals, while an individually administered achievement test for the same grade range might be normed on a sample of 800 to 1,000 students. As stated in the previous discussion, a direct benefit of the decreased administrative cost per examinee is the increased precision resulting from the feasibility of using larger samples for determining group test norms.

INDIVIDUAL TEST NORMING PROCEDURES. Individual test norming programs, as stated in the discussion above, differ rather markedly from group test norming programs. Again, as with group tests, the salient features of individual test norming programs are discussed below in terms of their ease of execution, precision, and cost.

Ease of Execution. Most individually administered test standardization programs require examiners with special qualifications and training. Individual tests are usually much more complex and demanding in their administration and scoring than are group tests. For this reason, considerable care must be exercised in the recruitment of examiners for tests which require such a high degree of expertise. Examinees are usually more difficult to locate, especially if the test is designed for preschoolers or adults who cannot be contacted through schools. Examinees must be located on a case-by-case basis, and parental consent is required before an examinee below age 18 can be tested. Individual test norming programs are usually not administered by a school district, as is true of group test norming programs; therefore, publishers must set up test centers throughout the country to obtain a national sample. Test center coordinators must also be located, hired, and trained before any recruitment of examiners or training of examiners can begin. Thus, individual test norming programs require considerably more effort in their organization and staffing than is true of group tests that rely largely on school district personnel already in place. The time required to locate and test individual examinees means that the total time required to complete an individual test norming program will greatly exceed that for a group test. The only exception might occur where a group achievement test is to be administered in both the fall and spring of the school year in order to measure growth during the school year more accurately. The more complex individually administered tests, however, typically require a year or more for the norming to be completed.

Precision. Samples for individually administered tests are usually obtained by *quota sampling* methods, because probability sampling methods cannot be used. The need to obtain parental consent for preschool and school-age examinees and the need to locate each examinee to match a number of demographic characteristics are constraints that dictate quota samples. Thus, all individual test norming samples are quota samples based on voluntary examinee participation that, in turn, precludes the estimation of the precision of the resulting norms (Angoff, 1971). There are, however, procedures that can be used to minimize sources of bias in the sample. A carefully worked out plan is essential if individual test norming programs are to be conducted efficiently. Usually, there is a detailed specification similar to the one shown in Figure 1 for each examinee that must be located and tested.

    In addition to having a carefully developed specification for each examinee, one additional source of error and bias can be eliminated if standardization site coordinators do not have to find an examinee to match a specification but are simply told which of the examinees available to them locally must be tested. American Guidance Service has used this strategy successfully during the past decade in its conduct of a number of large-scale individual test norming programs. Sites must first be canvassed to locate a pool of examinees for testing. Demographic data are collected for these individuals and forwarded to the publisher where the data are entered into a computer database from which individuals can be randomly selected according to specifications similar to that for Examinee No. 93 in Figure 1. Although the use of this strategy requires a considerable amount of lead time to assemble the computerized database, the increased efficiency and accuracy in conducting the actual testing program more than compensate for the added initial time. Experience has shown that this strategy is preferable to one where the site coordinators must locate individuals to match specifications similar to the one shown in Figure 1.

FIGURE 1. Example of Detailed Examinee Specifications

Individual Reading Test Standardization Program

Specifications for Examinee No. 93

US Geographic Region: Midwest
Age: Between 11 years 0 months and 11 years 5 months
Ethnic Group: Black
Parental Education: High school graduate
Gender: Female
Community Type: Suburban

Cost. As stated earlier in discussing the cost of group test norming programs, the administrative cost per examinee is considerably higher for individual test norming programs because of the need for specialized personnel and the difficulty in locating appropriate examinees. It is not unusual for publishers to spend $50 to $75 per case when examiner and site coordinator fees are considered. The labor intensive effort required to locate and test suitable examinees, together with time and cost factors, results in much smaller samples of examinees for individual test norming programs. As a general rule of thumb in the testing industry, individually administered tests base their norms on a minimum of 100 individuals per grade or year of age. This is in sharp contrast to group tests that employ several thousand examinees for single grade or age levels. Other things being equal, group tests norms are generally more accurate and stable than norms for individually administered tests.

Supplementary Studies
The need for certain types of data to support the psychometric properties of a test necessitate the conduct of special supplementary studies concurrently with the standardization program. For example, test–retest reliability estimates may be needed. Other examples of supporting data include the equating of old and new editions of a test, the equating of levels of a broad gauge group test, and the validation of a test in relation to various criteria (e.g., course grades, results of other tests, supervisory ratings, etc.). In some cases, the examinees can be drawn from the standardization sample, while in others additional examinees will be needed to fulfill the requirements for the special studies. The types of data needed at the time of publication are outlined in

the *Standards for Educational and Psychological Testing* (AERA, APA, & NCME, 1985).

Development of Test Norms

As soon as the standardization testing has been completed, statistical analysis of the data can begin. Before any analyses are performed, however, it is essential that careful planning of the data analysis be undertaken. Lack of a carefully developed plan invariably results in greater time and cost because analyses must be frequently rerun as unforeseen needs develop. Norms development usually follows these steps: (a) data editing and checking, (b) data entry and scoring, (c) statistical analysis, (d) development of norms tables, and (e) supplementary data. Each of these aspects of norms development is discussed below.

DATA EDITING AND CHECKING. The use of machine-scannable answer forms saves much labor-intensive manual effort. Such answer media are particularly well suited to group tests, where scannable booklets have been used in the primary grades and separate answer sheets at the elementary and secondary levels. With individually administered tests that employ answer forms that cannot be scanned by machine, considerable hand coding and checking may be required before the data are entered into the computer system for further analysis. Such data as date of birth, age, grade, and other information may need to be translated into numeric code before data entry. There may need to be a check of each individual tested to make certain that he or she meets the original quota sample specifications. It is essential that a coding scheme be developed to take account of all the data that will be needed in the various statistical analyses planned.

Answer forms for individually administered tests may also need to be inspected to check for examiner accuracy in adhering to basal and ceiling rules. Also, for some free-response subtests, the responses may need to be scored by hand and then coded in terms of correct-incorrect on a machine-scannable form. Machine-scannable forms can be used with individual tests, but considerable effort may need to be expended to code the item responses onto machine-scannable answer forms. A careful cost-benefit analysis would need to be done to evaluate the financial feasibility of such an action. With multiple-choice individual tests, it is easy to record responses directly onto a scannable sheet.

For group tests using machine-scannable answer forms, little hand scrutiny and checking of the answer forms are required because most checks can be performed by computer if the data have been coded in preassigned grids on the answer booklets. In most instances, answer sheets for group tests have only to be batch-coded by means of a special scannable document known as a *header sheet*. The answer sheets are then ready for transport to the electronic scanning equipment used to scan or read the marks made on the answer forms.

DATA ENTRY AND SCORING. Responses coded on scannable answer forms can be entered onto magnetic tape easily by means of the high-speed electronic processing equipment used to read and transfer the marks from the answer forms. Scanners employ photoelectric reading heads that use either reflected or transmitted light to reproduce a record of responses on magnetic computer tape. Once the answer responses are recorded on the computer tape, certain checks can be performed and responses scored for further analysis. Scanners are essential for high-volume standardization programs because such machines can process several thousand answer forms per hour of operation.

STATISTICAL ANALYSIS. As soon as the scoring has been completed, including a manual edit of responses flagged "questionable," the data analysis can begin according to the plan previously executed. Such analyses often begin with the basic descriptive statistics for each subtest, such as raw-score frequency distributions, cumulative percents, and means and standard deviations. Subtest intercorrelations and various types of item analyses may also be undertaken. Demographic counts are often obtained along with the basic descriptive statistics. Various additional analyses may also be undertaken, depending on the special needs of a particular test. The foregoing operations are all essential to the actual work of norms development described next.

DEVELOPMENT OF NORMS TABLES. Interpretation of performance on norm-referenced tests is accomplished by means of tables of derived scores. These tables of norms usually constitute a major portion of a test manual and represent both the science and art of applied psychometrics. Considerable experience is required to actually construct the various types of tables appropriate for a particular test.

Anastasi (1988) has offered a useful classification scheme for the most common types of derived scores. As shown in Table 6, there are essentially two types of norms: developmental and within-group. *Developmental norms* place an individual along a span or continuum of development. Age and grade equivalents are the most common types of developmental norms. Both scales offer limited information because they match an individual's performance to the average performance of a particular age or grade group. For example, a

TABLE 6. Classification of Some Common Norm-referenced Scores

Type of Comparison	Norm-referenced Scores	Frame of Reference
Developmental	Grade equivalents	Multiple grade groups
	Age eqivalents	Multiple age groups
Within-group	Percentile ranks	Single age groups
	Standard scores	Single grade groups
	Stanines	Single reference groups of any sort
	T-scores	

Reprinted with permission of Macmillan Publishing Company from *Psychological Testing* (5th ed.) by Anne Anastasi. Copyright © 1982 by Anne Anastasi.

grade equivalent of 4.7 means that the individual's performance was equal to the average performance of pupils in the seventh month of the fourth grade. A similar interpretation can be made when test scores are referenced to age equivalents. Test users obviously want more meaningful information than that provided by developmental norms which merely show the age or grade level for which a pupil's score corresponds to the average. Within-group norms provide more refined information and are recommended over developmental norms.

Within-group norms reference an individual's performance to a single reference group of interest. Age and grade are two of the most useful groups; any sort of meaningful reference groups are appropriate. Standard scores, a popular form of within-group norms, can be prepared for many different groups, for example, age groups, grade groups, special groups of job applicants, or groups applying for licensure and certification.

As a general rule, within-group norms yield more precise, psychometrically sound information than do developmental norms because it is possible to place an individual more precisely within a group of peers. Standard scores typify the most desirable type of within-group comparison because they express the extent to which a particular raw score differs from the mean raw score of an age or grade group in terms of standard deviation units. Percentile ranks are another popular form of within-group derived score; they show the rank of the individual within a typical reference group of 100 persons. Within-group norms take account of the full range of talent found in a particular reference group, while developmental norms do not. This is a major limitation of developmental norms.

As stated previously in the discussion under standardization sample selection, individually administered test norms are hampered by their small sample size, which, in turn, makes norms development difficult. Group tests, with their much larger samples (often of 10,000 to 20,000 cases per age or grade group), perform much more consistently with statistical expectation than do the much smaller samples (100 cases) for individual tests. Angoff and Robertson (1987) devised a norming procedure that compensates for small sample sizes and has been successfully used in several norming programs for individual tests.

In the past, norms development was time consuming and costly because most of the work was done by hand. Data were plotted by hand, and smoothed curves were fitted by eye. The norms tables were then developed by reading from the smoothed curve. Recent developments in computer graphics and related analytical methods now permit norms to be developed much more easily and efficiently. It seems likely that future technological developments will streamline the process even more. It must be pointed out, however, that the norms appearing in the final norms tables in a test manual still depend on highly skilled human intervention in smoothing out slight anomalies in computer-generated norms data.

The use of item response theory extends the normative data to all items calibrated on the IRT scale. Thus, if items have been calibrated to a common scale and if the scale has been normed, then any item or any collection of items from the item bank can be referenced to the underlying normative scale. Thus, with a single norming it becomes possible to generate norms for a large number of different test forms constructed from an item bank. Such capability has greatly extended the concept and utility of normative scales.

SUPPLEMENTARY TECHNICAL DATA. In addition to the norms tables, summary tables containing various types of technical data must be developed so that these can be included in the test manual at the time of publication. Reliability statistics for the various derived scores provided in the test must be computed and analyzed carefully before publication. For multilevel group tests, equating of levels and scaling must be analyzed before the norms development operation can be completed. These special analytical procedures must also be described and summarized for publication in the test manual. Validity data available prior to publication must also be analyzed and prepared for publication in the test manual. Readers interested in obtaining a more complete discussion of the various procedures for executing these studies should consult Angoff (1971) and Thorndike (1982).

Test Publication

Because it is often difficult to gauge the amount of time required for completion of the standardization program, especially for individually administered tests, the final publication date cannot be projected accurately until the standardization program, supplementary studies, and norms development work have been completed. Careful planning of the remaining work to be done in producing the final publication components and in marketing the product is essential. Each of these activities will be discussed below.

FINAL PRODUCTION OF PUBLICATION COMPONENTS

The final components of a test usually consist of the following items in one form or another: test question books, answer forms, scoring keys, and manuals. Other support materials may be available, depending on the type of test. There are two phases of work involved in producing the final publication components. The first phase relates to the development and editing of the manuscript copy of each component; the second phase is the actual transformation of the manuscript copy for each component into printed form.

Manuscript Copy Preparation
Manuscript copy must be prepared for each component of a publication. This is the copy that will be set in type, so the final version of the manuscript copy represents the end product that will be seen in the printed version of the component. During the past few years, developments in computerized editing and typesetting have changed the meaning of "final manuscript." At one time, the term referred to actual paper copy created by a typist; however, the term has now been broadened to include the storage of the final version of a component on computer disk. It is, moreover, feasible for the entire editing and certain of the production processes to occur without the creation of a paper manuscript copy of the text of the component.

Either the author or members of the publisher's staff prepare the final manuscript copy for each component. Staff members skilled in content editing then edit the manuscript, after which it is returned to its originator for review and resolution of the content edit. Content edits can be either perfunctory or extensive, depending on the quality of the manuscript received and, hence, can require brief or lengthy amounts of time in direct proportion to such manuscript quality. As soon as the content has been finalized, the manuscript is copyedited by a copyeditor trained to check for consistency of style, mechanics such as grammar, punctuation, capitalization, and spelling, and general clarity and readability. As soon as the copyedit is completed, the final production processes occur, starting with typesetting and culminating in printing of the components.

Production Processes

Production of final components really begins with the development of a final publication schedule following completion of the standardization program. Actually, a tentative schedule is developed at that point, with preparation of the final publication schedule occurring as soon as the content and copyediting have been completed. Once the publication schedule is established, the final production processes begin, and the final publication date can usually be determined quite accurately.

SETTING THE FINAL PUBLICATION SCHEDULE. The publication schedule established after norms development has been completed represents the best estimate of the participating staff members. The unknown factor is the amount of time needed for content editing since this depends on the quality of the manuscript. The established schedule will need to be checked frequently and revised as required. Unforeseen delays in the preparation and editing of final copy are not uncommon in test publishing.

Two basic elements must be present if a publication schedule is to be useful. First, the schedule prepared must be realistic. Past information should be used as much as possible to set dates that accurately reflect the time required for various steps. Establishing completion dates that are impossible frustrates everyone and leads to demoralization of the staff, not to mention the added expenditures incurred by such unrealistic schedules. Postponement of various marketing activities and the inability to meet promised product delivery dates to customers add further complications if schedules are unrealistic.

A second requirement for an effective publication schedule is that it be established jointly by those staff members who must adhere to it. The staff members actually engaged in the day-to-day work activities are those best qualified and informed about the time requirements for various production activities. A publication schedule imposed from above by upper management is almost always doomed to failure if it does not reflect the knowledge and experience of the staff members who must carry it out and if their endorsement is not sought before the schedule is finalized.

An example of a final publication schedule is shown in Table 7 for a hypothetical publication, the *Essential Mathematics Test*. The completion of various steps in final development and publication shown in Table 7 is expressed in terms of weeks prior to publication. For example, norms development is scheduled to be completed 85 weeks prior to publication. It is important to note that scheduling requires that each component be treated separately; however, final publication cannot occur until all components have completed the appropriate processes. The most complex component is usually the test manual, and completion of the manual, in actuality, sets the final release date. The staff responsible for each step in Table 7 is also shown. All steps from typesetting through printing and final warehouse delivery are the responsibility of the production staff, while the steps preceding typesetting are the responsibility of the research and development staff. According to this schedule, the steps required to edit the manual require 22 weeks for completion. At first glance, this amount of time may seem excessive, but experience has proved otherwise, particularly for manuals of the length shown here.

PRODUCING THE FINAL COMPONENTS. Rendering the components of a test publication in printed form is a highly complex, demanding task that requires highly skilled personnel. Designers, artists, typesetters, and printers all bring highly specialized expertise in publishing technologies required for a successful test publication. Production personnel usually begin with a manuscript, either printed or on computer disk, which is then transformed into printed copy. Typesetting is now done by computer, sometimes by the publisher, and at other times by outside staff. As stated above, editors now have the capability of editing directly on CRT displays, with the edited material then being transferred to automated typesetting equipment. In this way, it is possible to avoid typing and retyping the manuscript that was once characteristic of the editing and typesetting process.

Test manuals almost always contain large amounts of tabular material. In the past, the preparation, typesetting, and proofing of this material, especially the norms tables, has required enormous amounts of time at great cost. Computer interfaces, or networks, now permit the development of norms on one computer and the transfer of the final norms tables to a second computer system used for typesetting, thereby eliminating the time-consuming intermediate steps of typing, proofreading, and correcting norms tables manually on paper before entering them again for typesetting.

Careful checking is required at every step in the production of final materials. The complexity of test manuals varies in direct proportion with the numbers of statistical tables and figures used. It is especially important to check the text, figures, and tables carefully before sending them to the printer.

Special expertise is also needed to design answer forms and scoring keys. If machine-scorable answer forms are required, then such forms must conform to the design of the optical scanner used to read marked answer

TABLE 7. A Practical Model for Test Development
Final Publication Schedule for the *Essential Mathematics Test*

Componnent	Activity	Staff Responsible	Completion Time in Weeks*
Manual (150 pages)	Norms development	D	P - 85
	Manuscript development: Chapters 1 & 2: General background administration, scoring	D	P - 79
	Manuscript development: Chapters 3, 4, & 5: Technical and interpretive material	D	P - 59
	Editing steps	D	P - 58 to P - 37
	Final edit, Chapters 1-5	D	P - 36
	Typesetting (galley proofs), Chapters 1-5	P	P - 32
	Proofreading, Chapters 1-5	P	P - 40
	Keylining, Chapters 1-5	P	P - 22
	Silver proofs, Chapters 1-5	P	P - 12
	Printing	P	P - 08
	Binding	P	P - 02
	Warehouse	P	P
Answer sheet (2 sides)	Basic layout, design	D	P - 81
	Typesetting	P	P - 33
	Final proof	P	P - 21
	Printing/packaging	P	P - 09
	Warehouse	P	P
Test booklet (24 pages)	Design cover/pages	P	P - 50
	Final edit of items and directions	D	P - 40
	Typesetting (galley proofs)	P	P - 30
	Proofreading	P	P - 26
	Keylining	P	P - 19
	Silver proofs	P	P - 14
	Printing	P	P - 10
	Binding	P	P - 03
	Warehouse	P	P

*Completion time is in terms of weeks before publication; P - 78, for example, means 78 weeks prior to publication. D = Research/Development staff; P = Production staff.

forms. For individually administered tests that use manipulatives, considerable ingenuity and skill are also required from production personnel.
Developing cost-effective manufacturing processes for manipulatives is
almost always a highly demanding activity, drawing on production, design,
and research and development staff.

The above discussion assumes the final publication will be in printed form.
It is conceivable, however, that the final form of a publication could be on
an information storage and retrieval device such as a microcomputer disk or
a videodisk. If this is the case, the same procedure is required for editing any
copy that appears in stored form. The actual production process would differ,
depending on the nature of the final product.

MARKETING FUNCTIONS

Once final copies of a commercially published test arrive in a publisher's
warehouse, the release of the test for general use occurs. The demand for a
publication at the time it is published is, to some extent, a function of the
marketing activities that preceded its release. Price of the product is also a
factor in determining product demand, particularly for products that have
well-established competitors and thus directly affect the price sensitivity of a
particular product. Where the release of a test publication was at one time
marked by an announcement in a test catalog or an occasional advertisement,
current practices reflect the forces of a competitive marketplace requiring
highly sophisticated marketing strategies.

A variety of activities typically occur to acquaint potential users with a
new product or a revision of an old product. Publishers have recognized the
value in preparing a comprehensive marketing plan prior to the initiation of
any marketing activity. Such a plan provides a comprehensive overview of
the actions the marketing staff see as essential to the position of a product in
the marketplace. Such a plan enables other members of the publisher's staff
to review and question the assumptions made by the marketing staff in
developing the plan. In addition, a comprehensive marketing plan also
permits a realistic assessment of the cost of the marketing program. It is
essential that the marketing plan be prepared well in advance of the actual
release date for a publication.

The elements of the marketing plan usually consist of these activities:
direct mail promotion, space advertising, field sales staff functions, and
advertising/direct sales at professional meetings. One or more of these
channels may be used, depending on the type of test and the ease with which
potential purchasers can be reached. Each of these is discussed briefly below.

Direct Mail Promotion

Direct mail promotion relies on reaching potential customers by mail with informative, attractive brochures that contain carefully selected product information. Such promotion represents a relatively economical means of reaching a large number of potential product purchasers. Mailing lists are available from commercial sources; it is possible to target specific user groups where interest is greatest. For example, if a particular product is one that would be of interest to clinical psychologists, such a listing may be purchased from a supply house that sells mailing lists. A publisher's catalog is another source of product information disseminated by direct mail.

Space Advertising

Space advertising refers to advertisements placed in a variety of periodicals, such as journals, newsletters, professional magazines, and newsletters. Convention programs are also another vehicle where space advertisements may be placed. Creating space advertisements that are accurate is a particularly challenging activity for the publisher's advertising and promotion staff.

Field Sales Staff Functions

The larger test publishers use individual sales consultants who engage in direct selling activity. These individuals have the educational background and experience needed to explain highly specialized technical products to potential purchasers in schools, colleges and universities, and a broad array of practicing professionals in education and psychology. Field sales staff members frequently manage a publisher's materials exhibit at professional conventions and meetings. In addition, members of the sales force frequently provide special workshops for a particular test as well as in-service training in school districts using a publisher's testing materials.

Customer Contacts at Professional Meetings and Conventions

Many test users attend professional meetings and conventions, such as the annual conventions of the American Psychological Association, the International Reading Association, and the National Council of the Teachers of Mathematics, to mention just a few. Test publishers have found that attendance at such professional meetings helps greatly in directly reaching customers and potential customers. Also, the fact that most conventions or professional meetings focus on one particular segment of the test market means that publishers can target appropriate products for maximum exposure.

Competitive market forces have changed the nature of test marketing in the last few years. Whereas test publishers were once content to remain rather passive in announcing and selling products, such firms now take more aggressive action to position and market their publications. The test publishing industry is slowly plodding toward maturity, with its earlier focus largely on sales and selling replaced by a broader marketing orientation that uses modern marketing tools strategically chosen to match the requirements for launching, positioning, and maximizing a product's market acceptance.

Test Distribution

Standardized tests are highly technical tools that must be used appropriately if their results are to be meaningful and trustworthy. The central problem of test distribution is that of correctly matching a particular test with an adequately qualified purchaser (user). For the test publisher, this problem becomes one of making a judgment about the suitability of a particular individual to purchase a particular test. This section is devoted to a consideration of the issues surrounding sale of testing materials to individuals, with a historical perspective on ways that have been used to address this problem. The results of a study undertaken to improve methods of screening test purchasers are reviewed with an eye toward improving present practices and ultimately reducing test misuse.

THE PROBLEM OF TEST MISUSE

There is little disagreement that the misuse of tests occurs frequently and represents a serious problem for both test users and test takers. Horror stories about misuses of test results are familiar to professionals in all disciplines that use tests. Further documentation about the extent of test misuse was provided by the American Psychological Association Committee on Professional Standards (1985), in which a survey of state boards of psychology revealed that of 776 complaints received by state boards in a single 12-month period, 44 (5.7%) involved complaints about test misuse by psychologists. The full extent of the problem is apparent when one notes that this survey was only done for psychologists who presumably have more training in the use of psychological tests than do practitioners in other disciplines using tests. Test misuse concerns lead directly to the question of control over access to tests and to the role of the test publisher in regulating such access.

Anastasi (1988) cites two principal reasons for controlling the use of psychological tests: (a) to ensure that the examiner is qualified to administer, score, and interpret the test and (b) to protect the security of the test content, thereby maintaining the validity of the test. For test results to be useful, one needs to have confidence that the examiner chose a particular test for administration based on its having acceptable technical properties and that the test was administered and scored according to the instructions contained in the test manual. The sound interpretation of test results cannot be done casually by any interested individual, but requires a thorough understanding of such topics as reliability, validity, and the quality and types of norms available. Test security is important to preserve the meaning of the test scores. Exposure to the test items changes the conditions under which a test is taken and invalidates the use of the norms. Under these conditions, the test results are virtually useless. Maintenance of test security need not, however, restrict the communication of information to examinees about the purpose of the test. The actual test items need not be released to achieve this goal.

THE ULTIMATE GOAL: SELF-REGULATION

There is no system of controls, however ingenious and foolproof it may seem, that will prevent test misuse. The diverse groups of test users from many different disciplines precludes the use of a central agency to screen test purchasers; in fact, if such a policing function were feasible, it would be considered to be in restraint of trade and, therefore, illegal. The ideal solution is self-regulation, where the individual test purchaser (and user) makes a decision about appropriate tests to use based on knowledge of the character- istics of the test and the extent to which his or her training and experience match the requirements of the test. Reliance on self-regulation was an underlying principle of the *Standards for Educational and Psychological Testing* (1985), referred to here as *Standards,* developed jointly by the American Educational Research Association, the American Psychological Association, and the National Council on Measurement in Education. The *Standards,* for example, contains one entire section that sets forth thirteen guidelines for test users. The following excerpt shows the level of responsibility placed on the test user:

> The test user, in selecting or interpreting a test, should know the purposes of the testing and the probable consequences. The user should know the procedures necessary to facilitate effectiveness and

to reduce bias in test use. Although the test developer and publisher should provide information on the strengths and weaknesses of the test, the ultimate responsibility for appropriate use lies with the test user. The user should become knowledgeable about the test and its appropriate uses and also communicate this information, as appropriate, to others.[*]

A similar point of view is contained in the Joint Committee on Testing Practice's (1988) *Code of Fair Testing Practices in Education,* which lists the eight responsibilities of test users shown in Figure 2. Note the emphasis placed on the responsibility of the individual test user for proper test selection and use and the statement this makes to the public concerning what they may rightly expect as far as the behavior of persons using tests is concerned. Added support for self-regulation of test users comes from two studies reported below: (a) the research into test user qualifications conducted by the Test User Qualifications Working Group (Eyde, Moreland, & Robertson, 1988) and (b) the survey of British psychological society members by Tyler and Miller (1986). Because the ideal principle of self-regulation in test use relies on the assimilation of requisite knowledge, skills, and moral and ethical codes of conduct, test use cannot be regulated entirely by reliance on an assumption of individual self-regulation. For this reason, test publishers must institute screening procedures to determine those individuals qualified to use a particular test. The historical development of such practices is outlined below.

SCREENING TEST PURCHASERS—AN HISTORICAL PERSPECTIVE

Historically, screening of test purchasers (users) to determine their professional qualifications dates from 1950, when the American Psychological Association released its *Code of Ethical Standards for the Distribution of Psychological Tests.* At that time, testing was viewed as an activity primarily within the purview of the psychologist, and the Code was based on the assumption that there were really only two classes of test users—psychologists and nonpsychologists. The increased use of tests by diverse groups outside the field of psychology that has occurred during the past 40 years makes the Code too narrow to be broadly applicable and useful today. This was a major

---

[*]From *Standards for Educational and Psychological Testing* (p. 41). Copyright 1985 by the American Psychological Association. Reprinted by permission.

FIGURE 2. An Example of the Responsibilities
Test Users Must Assume

Test users should select tests that meet the purpose for which they are to be used
and that are appropriate for the intended test-taking populations.

Test Users Should:

First define the purpose for testing and the population to be tested. Then, select
a test for that purpose and that population based on a thorough review of the
available information.

Investigate potentially useful sources of information, in addition to test scores,
to corroborate the information provided by tests.

Read the materials provided by test developers and avoid using tests for which
unclear or incomplete information is provided.

Become familiar with how and when the test was developed and tried out.

Read independent evaluations of a test and of possible alternative measures.
Look for evidence required to support the claims of test developers.

Examine specimen sets, disclosed tests or samples of questions, directions,
answer sheets, manuals, and score reports before selecting a test.

Ascertain whether the test content and norms group(s) or comparison group(s)
are appropriate for the intended test takers.

Select and use only those tests for which the skills needed to administer the test
and interpret scores correctly are available.

From *Code of Fair Testing Practices in Education* (1988), Washington, DC: Joint Committee on Testing Practices. Reproduced with permission. (Mailing address: Joint Committee on Testing Practices, American Psychological Association, 1200 17th Street, NW, Washington, DC 20036).

impetus for the research into test misuse and the subsequent development of
competency-based test user qualification screening procedures by the Test
User Qualifications Working Group, as described in fuller detail below.

A major contribution of the 1950 Code was a three-tiered system for
classifying tests and relating them to the qualifications of test users. The three
levels were adapted from APA (1950, pp. 620–626) by Eyde et al. (1988,
p. 19).

- *Level A*—Tests that can be adequately administered, scored, and
  interpreted with the aid of the manual and a general orientation
  to the kind of organization in which one is working. Examples
  include educational achievement and vocational proficiency tests.
  Such tests may be given and interpreted by responsible nonpsychologists such as school principals and business executives.

- *Level B*—Tests that require some technical knowledge of test construction and use and of supporting subjects such as statistics, individual differences, and guidance. Examples include general intelligence and special aptitude tests, interest inventories, and personality screening inventories. The tests in Level B can be used by persons who have had suitable psychological training; who are employed and authorized to use them in their employment by an established school, government agency, or business enterprise; or who use them in connection with a course of study of such instruments.

- *Level C*—Tests that require substantial understanding of testing and supporting psychological topics, together with supervised experience in the use of these devices. Examples include clinical tests of intelligence and personality tests. Tests such as those in Level C should be used only by the following persons: (a) those with a master's degree in psychology or above and at least one year of properly supervised experience; (b) with suitable precautions, by psychologists who are using tests for research or self-training; (c) by members of kindred professions with adequate training in clinical psychological testing; or (d) by graduate students and other professionals under the supervision of a qualified psychologist.

The so-called ABC test classification system is still in use by a number of test publishers, despite problems with its limited applicability. One of the reasons for the longevity of the Code was its endorsement in the 1966 *Standards for Educational and Psychological Tests and Manuals* (APA, AERA, & NCME). Another reason the code has persisted is that it was adopted by a number of test publishers who proceeded to assign a code level (A, B, or C) designation to all of their test publications. Publishers also began to state in their catalogs that they adhered to APA standards, referring to the Code and the three-tiered system. The use of tests by nonpsychologists has increased dramatically during the past 25 years. This is, in part, due to a broad expansion in the use of tests. For example, guidance and counseling personnel, school psychologists, and speech-language clinicians all use tests and have developed their own codes of ethical principles that include test use and interpretation. Professionals in these fields and others voiced frustration with the ABC system and its assumption that psychologists were duly qualified to use every test available, while other nonpsychologists who might be trained in another field would not be qualified according to the ABC system. Thus, a dissatisfaction with the ABC system evolved gradually in view of its implicit assumptions and narrowly restrictive viewpoint about who is qualified to give and interpret a test.

The ABC system was challenged at the 1984 conference of psychologists and test publishers called by the American Psychological Association. One outgrowth of this conference was the formation of the Test User Qualifications Working Group (TUQWoG) in the spring of 1985. TUQWoG contained representatives from the test publishing industry as well as representatives from professional associations and had the following as its mission statement: "Consistent with professional standards and ethical principles, to establish a procedure for classifying tests that will lead to a uniform system for assessing user qualifications" (Eyde et al., 1988, p. 22).

In elaborating upon its mission statement, TUQWoG mentioned four basic objectives that would guide its work:

- To facilitate access by qualified users to testing materials

- To facilitate test publishers' procedures for screening

- To protect test takers from those who would administer and/or interpret tests they are not qualified to use

- To use the data to improve the education of those who use tests (Eyde et al., 1988)

In order to maximize their usefulness, it was felt that the work of TUQWoG should be based on scientific methods designed to identify test user competencies that, when applied, would minimize or eliminate various test misuses. Purchaser qualification forms, a desired end product, were to be created through the various types of research conducted by TUQWoG in its studies of test misuse.

TUQWoG Research

There were four separate research studies planned and conducted by TUQWoG. The purpose and results of each of these is summarized below.

Study 1: Identification of Content Domain
In this initial study, critical incidents of observed test misuse were gathered from testing experts such as test reviewers, textbook authors, test authors, trainers, and practitioners. A total of 62 experts submitted critical incidents of test misuse in which 48 commercially available tests were cited. From these critical incidents, Primoff (1975) used his job element methodology to abstract a list of 86 generic subelements that applied to tests in general. These generic subelements, which may be thought of as key behaviors for the correct use of tests in general, were used as a basis for further research in

Studies 2 and 3. An example of a subelement would be "Understanding test norms and their limitations." Additional examples are shown in Table 8, along with the other factors on which these subelements loaded highest in a principal factor analysis, described in the following section.

Study 2: Key Behaviors Evaluated for Tests in General
This study had as its objective the identification of those subelements identified in Study 1 as most relevant for tests in general. In order to obtain data appropriate to make this determination, a panel of 19 experts used the 86 subelements identified in Study 1 to rate tests in general on four dimensions:

- *Trouble likely*—How likely is this subelement to cause trouble if it is not considered in qualifying test purchasers?

- *Barely acceptable behavior*—How frequently does this behavior appear among marginally competent test users?

- *Superior behavior*—How frequently does this behavior appear among expert test users?

- *Practicality*—Is it practically feasible to include this behavior in qualifying test purchasers?

Primoff's (1975) job elements methodology was used to determine the overall importance of each of the 86 subelements, or behaviors, to proper test use; in addition, the importance of each of the behaviors as a minimum requirement for test use was also determined (Eyde et al., 1988, p. 27). As a result of his analyses, Primoff identified two major subelements having the greatest comprehensiveness as suitable organizers for other subelements: (a) knowledge of the test and its limitations and (b) acceptance of responsibility for competent use of the test. In addition, Primoff identified 12 subelements, termed *screenouts,* judged so basic for competent test use that their absence justifies immediate rejection of an individual applying to purchase tests. More will be said in a later section about these behaviors.

Study 3: Taxonomic Research
The third study was designed to obtain ratings on individual tests so that data more specifically useful to test publishers might be obtained. A total of 487 ratings on some 73 tests supplied by approximately 200 raters was used as a basis for the research conducted in Study 3 (Eyde et al., 1988, pp. 27–28). In order to obtain information about the underlying dimensions of test misuse,

TABLE 8. Subelements Loading Highest on Seven Test Misuse Factors

Factor	Subelements (In shortened form)
1. Comprehensive assessment	23. Psychosocial history 35. Considering patient's state 37. Teaching research evidence and test limitations 45. Choice of test to sample relevant behaviors 77. Follow-up with psychosocial history 79. Use of tests to generate hypotheses 82. Proper reporting of clinical observations during testing
2. Proper test use	1. Acceptance of responsibility for competent use of tests 7. Refraining from helping a favored person earn a good score 8. Appropriate training and quality control over operations for all users of tests and test results
3. Psychometric knowledge	20. Considering measurement error in test scores 32. Considering the standard error of measurement 44. Understanding the standard error of measurement
4. Maintaining integrity of test results	39. Limitations of GE & PR for specific situations 49. Cutoff scores questionable due to disregard of the *SEM*
5. Accuracy of scoring	55. Avoid errors in scoring and recording 56. Use checks on scoring accuracy 57. Checking frequently during scoring to catch lapses 58. Following scoring directions
6. Appropriate use of norms	31. Matching person to job on aptitude validities 59. Not assuming norm for one job applies to another
7. Interpretive feedback	71. Willingness to give interpretation and guidance to test takers in counseling situations 72. Able to give interpretation and guidance to test takers in counseling situations 73. Having enough staff to provide counseling

Note: *SEM* = standard error of measurement; GE = grade equivalent; PR = percentile rank.

the 487 ratings on 50 tests having six or more ratings were analyzed by using a principal components (principal-factor) with varimax rotation. The results are shown in Table 8. It can be seen that seven factors of test misuse were extracted from the data. The subelements that best define each factor (those with the highest factor loadings) are also shown in Table 8. A second goal of Study 3 was that of developing a heuristic taxonomy of tests so that a practical way of assessing test purchaser qualifications could be offered to publishers with both narrow and broad test product lines. Ward's minimum variance cluster analysis (Romesburg, 1984) was applied to standardized mean trouble-likely scores for the 50 tests used in the analysis. Results are shown in Table 9. It can be seen that eight clusters of tests were selected based on the various clusterings obtained in the analysis. The two types of information obtained in Study 3—the factors of test misuse and the cluster analysis—were subsequently used in Study 4.

Study 4: Development of Empirically Based Test Purchaser Forms
This study was designed to use the results of the previous studies to construct improved test purchaser screening forms. Primoff's job elements analysis of the test-in-general ratings obtained in Study 2 resulted in the content classification structure in Table 10. These results were subsequently used by the writer to develop the test purchaser qualification form shown in Figure 3. The advantage of this form over previous test purchaser forms is that it is based on more objective information than was previously the case. It also permitted the development of a more systematic way to analyze the results from test purchaser forms. Table 11 shows an evaluation procedure for analyzing responses to the test purchaser form shown in Figure 3 in order to determine whether the applicant is qualified to purchase an individually administered intelligence test. It can be seen that points have been assigned to the possible responses to the questionnaire items. Total points can then be linked to criteria established by the publisher for determining qualification status of the applicant. The results of Study 3 also provide information that publishers may find helpful in developing test purchaser qualification forms. Interested readers are directed to Eyde et al. (1988) for a complete discussion of the procedures for developing such forms.

Several test publishers have now revised their test purchaser forms based on data provided by TUQWoG. It is hoped that the new forms will offer an improved means for determining the qualifications of individual test purchasers and that more individuals with appropriate qualifications will be permitted access to testing materials than was previously the case.

TABLE 9. Eight Clusters of 50 Commercial Tests Using Ward's Minimum Variance Clustering Method, Based on Ratings of Test Misuse

Cluster A: Group Educational Tests	Cluster B: Ability and Preference Tests	Cluster C: Learning Disability/Neuropsychological Tests	Cluster D: Individual Intelligence Tests	Cluster E: Readiness Tests	Cluster F: Objective Personality Tests	Cluster G:	Cluster H: Projective Personality Tests
California Achievement Test	Activity Vector Analysis	Bayley Scales of Infant Development	Full-Range Picture-Vocabulary Test	Boehm Test of Basic Concepts	Bem Sex Role Inventory	Self-Directed Search	Rorschach
Cognitive Abilities Test	Armed Services Vocational Aptitude Battery	Bender-Gestalt Test	Goldman-Fristoe-Woodcock Test of Auditory Discrimination	Metropolitan Readiness Tests	California Psychological Inventory		Rotter Incomplete Sentences Blank
Iowa Tests of Basic Skills	Bennett Mechanical Comprehension Test	Denver Development Screening Test	Illinois Test of Psycholinguistic Abilities	Peabody Individual Achievement Test	MMPI		Thematic Apperception Test
Iowa Tests of Educational Development	Differential Aptitude Tests	Goldman-Fristoe Test of Articulation	Kaufman Assessment Battery for Children	Slosson Oral Reading Test	Rotter Internal-External Locus of Control Scale		
Metropolitan Achievement Tests	Kuder Occupational Interest Survey	Halstead-Reitan Neuropsychological Battery		Stanford Diagnostic Reading Test	State-Trait Anxiety Inventory		

TABLE 9. Eight Clusters of 50 Commercial Tests Using Ward's Minimum Variance Clustering Method, Based on Ratings of Test Misuse (continued)

Cluster A: Group Educational Tests	Cluster B: Ability and Preference Tests	Cluster C: Learning Disability/ Neuropsychological Tests	Cluster D: Individual Intelligence Tests	Cluster E: Readiness Tests	Cluster F: Objective Personality Tests	Cluster G:	Cluster H: Projective Personality Tests
Otis-Lennon School Ability Test	Myers-Briggs Type Indicator	Porch Index of Communicative Ability	Peabody Picture Vocabulary		Sixteen (16) Personality Factor		
	Purdue Pegboard						
School & College Ability Tests	Raven Progressive Matrices	Welchsler Memory Scale	Stanford-Binet Intelligence Test		Strong Interest Inventory		
Stanford Achievement Test	Wesman Personnel Classification Test		Welchsler Adult Intelligence Scale-R				
Tests of Achievement & Proficiency			Welchsler Intelligence Scale for Children-R				
Wide Range Achievement Test							

TABLE 10. Primoff's Content Classification Scheme
Obtained from Ratings for Tests in General

Element 1. Knowledge of the test and its limitations

Subelements: A. Knowledge of basic measurement principles and application
  of principles for sound test interpretation
  B. Knowledge of current practices, research, and trends
  C. Knowledge of the need for multiple sources of information
  about examinees

Element 2. Acceptance of the responsibility for the competent use of tests

Subelements: A. Selection of tests appropriate to purpose and test takers
  B. Use of proper procedures for test administration
  C. Use of controls for proper test scoring and release of test
  results

From *Test User Qualifications: A Data-Based Approach to Promoting Good Test Use* (p. 37) by L. D. Eyde, K. L. Moreland, and G. J. Robertson, 1933, Washington, DC: American Psychological Association. Copyright 1988 by L. D. Eyde, K. L. Moreland, and G. J. Robertson. Reprinted by permission.

THE MOST ESSENTIAL ELEMENTS OF GOOD TEST USE

As mentioned when the results of Study 2 were discussed, Primoff analyzed the tests-in-general ratings to determine the subelements most basic to proper test use. Although 12 subelements were identified by Primoff (Eyde et al., 1988, p. 82), the writer judged five to be so basic to proper test use that test purchasers are required to sign a compliance statement at the time they complete the test purchaser qualification blank shown in Figure 3. Test purchasers who do not practice these behaviors warrant immediate rejection as a test purchaser. The five screenout subelements judged most important are as follows:

- *Avoidance of using tests to coach examinees on individual test items.*
  Coaching examinees on test items prior to testing has probably
  occurred most often in so-called high stakes educational
  achievement testing where test results were being used to hold
  teachers and administrators accountable for pupil achievement.
  Because revealing test items to pupils prior to testing destroys
  the meaning of the test results and is unfair both to the examinee
  and to the end users of the test results, this behavior can never be
  sanctioned.

FIGURE 3. Sample Test User Qualification Form

Test Purchaser Qualification Form

AGS requires all first-time individual test purchasers to furnish evidence of their qualifications to use tests. Test use should be consistent with sound professional practice, particularly those principles outlined in the 1985 APA, AERA, NCME publication *Standards for Educational and Psychological Testing*. Supply the information requested below, read carefully the "Principles of Effective Test Use," and sign the form to indicate acceptance of the responsibility for proper use of tests.

Identification Information (please complete all blanks)

Name	Position	Telephone ( )
Address: Street	City	State Zip
Employer	Supervisor	
Employer's Address: Street	City	State Zip

A. Evidence of Appropriate Training in the Use of Tests

1. Your purpose for using tests (check as many as apply)
☐ Educational diagnosis/remediation ☐ Clinical diagnosis/classification ☐ Counseling ☐ Therapy ☐ Personnel selection ☐ Research
☐ Learning disabilities screening ☐ Other

2. Your level of training (check as many as apply)
☐ Bachelor's Degree: Year   Institution   Major field of study
☐ Master's Degree: Year   Institution   Major field of study
☐ Doctorate: Year   Institution   Major field of study

3. Your professional credentials (check as many as apply)
☐ Licensed in: Area   State   License #
☐ Member of professional organization(s): (AACD, AERA, APA, ASHA, CEC, NASP, etc.)
☐ Formally recognized professional competence (fellow, diplomate, special certificate): ☐ fellow   ☐ diplomate   ☐ other certification
   Organization

4. Your educational background (courses and other study)
   a. Courses (check each course completed and circle level at which course was completed.)
   U = Undergraduate, G = Graduate, O = Other (special course you have completed, workshop, in-service training, etc.)

	(circle)			(circle)	
☐ Basic tests and measurements	U G O	☐ Use of tests in counseling	U G O
☐ Descriptive statistics	U G O	☐ Career assessment	U G O
☐ Intelligence testing	U G O	☐ Neuropsychological assessment	U G O
☐ Speech, hearing, language assessment	U G O	☐ Other (list below)	
☐ Educational diagnostics	U G O		U G O
☐ Assessment course in major field:	U G O		U G O

   b. Other Study (check each type of program completed)
   ☐ Practicum in test administration and interpretation
   ☐ Internship (school psychology, counseling, etc.) type:

5. Your updating of professional knowledge and skills (check activities below and give an example)
☐ Attending workshops, seminars, conferences:
☐ Reading professional publications (journals, test manuals, etc.):

6. Your special competence
(List one test which you use regularly that best illustrates your skill in test administration and interpretation.)

B. Evidence of Acceptance of the Responsibility for Sound Use of Tests

Principles of Effective Test Use

Sound, professional use of educational and psychological tests means that all test users must:
1. maintain the security of testing materials before and after testing.
2. avoid labeling students based on a single test score.
3. adhere strictly to the copyright law and under no circumstances photocopy or otherwise reproduce answer forms, test books, or manuals.
4. administer and score tests exactly as specified in the manual.
5. release results only to authorized persons and in a form in keeping with accepted principles of test interpretation.

Your signature indicates acceptance of and compliance with the above Principles.

142 Signature   Date

Copyright 1990 by American Guidance Service. Reprinted by permission.

TABLE 11. A Sample Crediting Plan for Individual Intelligence Tests

Purpose: To evaluate the ability of applicants who apply to purchase individually administered intelligence tests

Element	Credits
Element 1. Level of Training	
a. Advanced degree (master's, doctorate) in field relevant to individual assessment	4
b. Bachelor's degree only	0
Element 2. Professional Credentials (Credit licensing, membership, and competence separately)	
a. State licensing in area relevant to individual intellectual assessment	2
(no state certification)	0
b. Professional membership in organization relevant to individual intellectual assessment	2
Other organizations	0
c. Professional competence	
Fellow/diplomate in relevant organization	2
Recognition of competence in other organization not relevant to individual intellectual assessment	0
Element 3. Educational Background Courses (Give the highest credit deserved.)	
a. Intelligence testing	5
b. Neuropsychological assessment	4
c. Educational diagnosis	3
d. Basic tests and measurements, descriptive statistics	2
e. Use of tests in counseling; career assessment	1
Other study (Give the highest credit deserved.)	
a. Internship in relevant professional field	5
b. Practicum in test use and interpretation	4
c. Relevant supervised experience	3
Element 4. Updating Professional Knowledge and Skills Workshops, Seminars, Conferences (Give the highest credit deserved.)	
a. Attending a seminar or workshop on an individual intelligence test (WISC-R, K-ABC, Stanford-Binet)	3
b. Attending a workshop on a particular test other than an individual intelligence test	2
c. Attending a general workshop on test use or interpretation or attending the annual convention of a relevant professional association	1
Reading professional publications (Give the highest credit deserved.)	
a. Lists reading manual of individual intelligence test	2
b. Indicates reading of appropriate educational/psychological journal	1

TABLE 11. A Sample Crediting Plan
for Individual Intelligence Tests (continued)

Element	Credits
Element 5. Special Competence (Give the highest credit deserved.)	
a. Lists K–ABC, WISC–R, WAIS, WPPSI, Stanford–Binet	3
b. Lists any group intelligence tests	2
c. Lists any brief individual intelligence tests	1
(Solosson, McCarthy Screening, etc.)	
Maximum total credits:	28

Note: This sample is for illustrative purposes only. A publisher could have an expanded list of criteria based upon its own tryout of the form.

From *Test User Qualifications: A Data-Based Approach to Promoting Good Test Use* (p. 48) by L. D. Eyde. K. L. Moreland, and G. J. Robertson, 1988, Washington, DC: American Psychological Association. Copyright 1988 by L. D. Eyde, K. L. Moreland, and G. J. Robertson. Reprinted by permission.

- *Avoidance of labeling individuals with a single test result.* It is important to use various sources of information when making decisions about individuals. The use of a single test score, without other relevant background information, is to be avoided at all costs. The fact that tests yield results in numeric form tempts users to rely solely on numbers and to ignore other information that may be much more difficult to quantify.

- *Maintaining the security of test items and answer keys.* At first glance, this might seem to overlap with the first subelement concerning avoidance of coaching examinees; however, this subelement refers not to using test items for teaching purposes, but to carelessness in keeping test items and keys secure. Tests and answer keys should be stored in places where unauthorized individuals will not have access to them. This requires special attention and planning by those individuals responsible for the testing program.

- *Avoidance of photocopying or otherwise reproducing test answer forms, test items, and manuals.* Under no circumstances can test users photocopy any of the test materials without first obtaining authorization from the publisher. The copyright law definitely forbids such practice. High-resolution and high-speed photocopiers have been used on occasion to reproduce answer sheets, test booklets, and test record forms for individual tests. Not only is this practice illegal, but also subtle changes occur when these materials are reproduced in this way. Such changes may distort or adversely affect test results because the reproduced forms differ from those that were actually used in standardization. Materials prices charged by test publishers are also based on the assumption that all materials will be purchased from the publisher and not photocopied. Publishers would be forced to charge much higher prices if such practices were to become widespread.

- *Following manual directions exactly for test administration and scoring.* Maintaining standard testing conditions is important if the test results are to be meaningful. This entails adhering exactly to the directions stated in the manual for administering and scoring the test. Although circumstances may sometimes seem to warrant changing procedure, this cannot be recommended without first contacting an experienced examiner, a supervisor, or the test publisher.

Some General Guidelines for Test Use

As stated previously, the factor analysis of ratings for specific tests described in Study 3 resulted in the identification of seven factors of test misuse. Consideration of these factors, along with the subelements having the highest factor loadings on these factors, suggests the following general guidelines for proper test use.

- *Conduct testing and assessment activities within a broad context, avoiding placing undue emphasis on a single test score.* This principle recognizes the fact that while useful under certain circumstances, test results must be interpreted against a broad array of background information about an individual. In the spirit of this guideline is the recognition that tests are most useful in generating hypotheses about individuals, to be verified by a consideration of other relevant personal background information. Test users should exercise care in the selection of a particular test and should be aware of its strengths and limitations; blind use and acceptance of test results is to be avoided.

- *Accept the professional responsibilities that accompany proper test use.* This principle recognizes the fact that proper test use can occur only if test users internalize professional standards of good test use. External controls and guidelines will not, by themselves, achieve the goal of appropriate test use. Among such behaviors in the TUQWoG research were the avoidance of revealing test items and scoring keys under

inappropriate circumstances and obtaining proper training to permit
one to exercise and maintain quality control over all functions of
testing—selection, administration and scoring, and interpretation
and use.

- *Exercise the appropriate psychometric knowledge when interpreting test results.*
  It is important for test users to realize that tests are fallible and that
  no single test result is perfectly accurate, due to imperfections in the
  measurement procedure itself. In addition, human beings fluctuate in
  their day-to-day behavior, and this renders a single test result a less
  than perfect indicator. In technical terms, it becomes important for
  test users to consider measurement error in the interpretation of test
  scores.

- *Exercise care in the selection and use of norm groups and normative scores.*
  This principle recognizes a duality in the use of norms. One aspect
  refers to the selection of an appropriate reference group for score
  interpretation. In most educational and psychological tests of a
  cognitive nature, as stated earlier in the chapter, the two most
  frequently used national reference groups are age and grade level.
  In industrial testing, it is most important that a job applicant, for
  example, be compared to an appropriate reference group and that
  the validity of a test for various jobs be considered when norms are
  used. Another aspect of proper norms use refers to selection of the
  score metric to be used to report scores. Users are best advised to
  recognize the limitations of all score metrics, especially age and grade
  equivalents, for educational and psychological tests. Standard scores
  and percentile ranks, while recommended as the preferred means for
  most types of test interpretation, do nevertheless warrant thoughtful
  consideration in their use.

- *Provide responsible, professional feedback of test results to clients.* If tests
  are used for individual assessment, counseling, and guidance, it is
  important that test users give clients appropriate interpretations of test
  performance and assist with the appropriate integration of test results
  into the broad array of information available about an individual. It is
  important that clients not give undue weight to test results to the
  exclusion of other significant information.

While the above principles are not new and have been stated in count-
less ways in a variety of sources, the TUQWoG research provided another
means for reinforcing their relevance and calling attention to their
importance.

Conclusion

This chapter has given a brief overview of the major aspects of test development, test publication, and test distribution. The goal of the chapter was to give persons unfamiliar with these topics sufficient understanding to gain a broad view of the various facets operative in each of the areas considered. Space limitations precluded the treatment of many interesting and relevant aspects of test development. Readers will need to pursue the topics discussed here in greater depth to acquire a deep understanding of them. The reference list offers a good start for those who wish to engage in additional pursuit of the topics presented here. Readers are urged to reflect upon and, if appropriate in their situation, put into practice the guidelines for good test use adapted from the TUQWoG research. In the final analysis, improved use and understanding of tests will occur only if we practice these guidelines assiduously and use them as a starting point in our quest for a deeper meaning and understanding of tests and of the individuals we are attempting to help.

References

American Educational Research Association (AERA), American Psychological Association (APA), & National Council on Measurement in Education (NCME). (1985). *Standards for educational and psychological testing.* Washington, DC: American Psychological Association.

American Psychological Association, American Educational Research Association, & National Council on Measurement in Education. (1966). *Standards for educational and psychological tests and manuals.* Washington, DC: American Psychological Association.

American Psychological Association Committee on Professional Standards. (1985). *Survey: Reported misuse of tests.* Agenda item no. 19, Committee on Psychological Tests and Assessments.

APA Committee on Ethical Standards for Psychology. (1950). Ethical standards for the distribution of psychological tests and diagnostic aids. *American Psychologist, 5,* 620–626.

Anastasi, A. (Ed.). (1988). *Psychological testing* (6th ed.). New York: Macmillan.

Angoff, W. H. (1971). Scales, norms, and equivalent scores. In R. L. Thorndike (Ed.), *Educational measurement* (2nd ed., pp. 508–600). Washington, DC: American Council on Education.

Angoff, W. H., & Robertson, G. J. (1987). A procedure for standardizing individually administered tests, normed by age or grade level. *Applied Psychological Measurement, 11*(1), 33–46.

Bloom, B. M. (Ed.). (1956). *Taxonomy of educational objectives: Handbook I. Cognitive domain.* New York: McKay.

Connolly, A. J. (1988). *KeyMath–Revised: A diagnostic inventory of essential mathematics.* Circle Pines, MN: American Guidance Service.

Ebel, R. L., & Frisbie, D. A. (1991). *Essentials of educational measurement* (5th ed.). Englewood Cliffs, NJ: Prentice-Hall.

Eyde, L. D., Moreland, K. L., & Robertson, G. J. (1988). *Test user qualifications: A data-based approach to promoting good test use.* Washington, DC: American Psychological Association.

French, J. W. (1951). The description of aptitude and achievement tests in terms of rotated factors. *Psychometric Monographs* (No. 5).

Guilford, J. P. (1967). *The nature of human intelligence.* New York: McGraw-Hill.

Gulliksen, H. (1950). *Theory of mental tests.* New York: Wiley.

Henrysson, S. (1971). Gathering, analyzing, and using data on test items. In R. L. Thorndike (Ed.), *Educational measurement* (2nd ed., pp. 130–159). Washington, DC: American Council on Education.

Joint Committee on Testing Practices. (1988). *Code of fair testing practices in education.*

Lord, F. M. (1980). *Applications of item response theory to practical testing problems.* Hillsdale, NJ: Erlbaum.

Mehrens, W., & Lehmann, I. (1984). *Measurement and evaluation in education and psychology.* New York: Holt, Rinehart, & Winston.

O'Meara, J. T., Jr. (1961, January-February). Selecting profitable products. *Harvard Business Review,* pp. 83–89.

Primoff, E. S. (1975). *How to prepare and conduct job element examinations. Supplement. U.S. Office of Personnel Management, Office of Personnel Research and Development Report 82-3.* Washington, DC (NTIS No. PB 84-148 162).

Romesburg, H. C. (1984). *Cluster analysis for researchers.* Belmont, CA: Lifetime Learning Publications.

Terman, L. M., & Merrill, M. (1937). *Measuring intelligence.* Boston: Houghton-Mifflin.

Thorndike, R. L. (1982). *Applied psychometrics.* Boston: Houghton-Mifflin.

Thorndike, R. L., & Hagen, E. P. (1977). *Measurement and evaluation in psychology and education* (4th ed.). New York: Wiley.

Tinkelman, S. N. (1971). Planning the objective test. In R. L. Thorndike (Ed.), *Educational measurement* (2nd ed., pp. 46–80). Washington, DC: American Council on Education.

Tyler, B., & Miller, K. (1986). The use of tests by psychologists: Report on a survey of BPS members. *Bulletin of the British Psychological Society, 39,* 405–410.

CHAPTER 6

COMPARING TWO STRATEGIES FOR DEVELOPING PERSONALITY SCALES

Harrison G. Gough & Pamela Bradley

Introduction

Two contrasting methods are generally used in developing scales for self-report personality inventories. One name applied to the first is *rational,* which to some extent is a misnomer, insofar as it implies that the other method is nonrational or irrational. Also, the name "rational" does not easily convey the picture of what psychologists do when they use this technique for developing scales. Nonetheless, the descriptive term is widely used and as a sort of shorthand indicator is acceptable.

Another name for this approach is *internal consistency,* which comes closer to indicating what is actually done. That is, in a rational scale, an essential condition is that the items correlate positively with each other and that all of the items correlate appreciably with the total score for the scale. If, in fact, all of the items in a scale covary significantly and to a high degree, the scale may be described as internally consistent, homogeneous, unidimensional, or even monofactorial. The idea of rationality enters the scene in that the central theme or unifying dimension around which the items cluster is one that was conceptually articulated beforehand by the developer of the measure and from which the scoring of each item is determined in a logical and understandable way.

In the realm of self-report personality assessment, there are many examples of scales and complete inventories developed by internal consistency methods. Among the most widely used devices are Cattell's *Sixteen Personality Factor Questionnaire* (Cattell, Eber, & Tatsuoka, 1970), the *Edwards Personal Preference Schedule* (Edwards, 1953), the *Guilford-Zimmerman Temperament Survey* (Guilford, Zimmerman, & Guilford, 1976), and Jackson's *Personality Research Form* (Jackson, 1984).

The other most frequently used method for developing scales is some-times called *empirical*. This name is also something of a misnomer insofar as it implies that the internal consistency method is nonempirical, insensitive to data, or not based on observable evidence. Another name for this method is *criterion-keying,* which is clear in that it refers to an essential component of the technique. That is, in the empirical method of scale development, each item is scored, or *keyed*, according to the magnitude and direction of its correlation with an outside or nontest criterion. Only minimal attention, if any, is paid to the degree to which the items intercorrelate with each other or to the degree to which each item correlates with the total score of the scale.

Although the empirical or criterion-keyed method of scale development is less frequently used by test authors than the rational or internal consistency method, two of the most widely used inventories in the world were constructed by the empirical strategy. One of these, the *Minnesota Multiphasic Personality Inventory* (MMPI; Butcher, Dahlstrom, Graham, Tellegen, & Kaemmer, 1989; Hathaway & McKinley, 1943), is addressed to major psychiatric syndromes such as paranoia and schizophrenia. The other, the *Strong Interest Inventory* (Hansen & Campbell, 1985; Strong, 1943), is scored for occupational and vocational interest scales.

Other examples of tests developed largely by the empirical method are the *California Psychological Inventory* (Gough, 1987) and the *Personality Inventory for Children* (Wirt, Lachar, Klinedinst, & Seat, 1984). The latter test is adminis-tered to a knowledgeable observer of the child, usually the mother. There are even a few tests which used both empirical and rational techniques for constructing their scales, a good example being the *Millon Clinical Multiaxial Inventory* (Millon, 1983).

In regard to the advantages and disadvantages of each strategy, those favoring internal consistency methods usually mention that the items within a scale are aligned with an articulated formulation of the concept or attribute to be assessed and that the scoring of the items is therefore implicitly understandable. Another advantage is that the homogeneity of the items within a rational scale will enhance its reliability. A third is that scales developed in this way tend to have lower correlations with each other than do scales developed according to empirical strategy.

Advantages of the empirical approach, as seen by its advocates, tend to be just the other side of each of the above points. For instance, if items not known or conceptualized to be indicative of a criterion turn out to predict it validly, then the discovery of such items can lead the test author out of the domain of ignorance or partial understanding within which the work originated. High intercorrelations among the items of a scale, although good for the internal reliability of the scale, may well furnish weaker prediction of the criterion for the scale than items individually predictive of that criterion but only modestly correlated with each other. On the third point (independence of the scales within a multivariate inventory), if the criteria to be forecast by each scale are in fact correlated, then a more accurate portrayal of the nontest world will be produced by scales that reflect or map those correlations than by scales that are uncorrelated.

What this comes down to is that the choice of either method tends to be more a matter of personal preference on the part of test developers than of any proved superiority of either method to the other. It should also be noted, as stated above, that excellent and widely accepted scales and tests have been developed by each technique.

How the Two Methods Are Usually Applied

Our discussion thus far has been abstract, dealing with generalities and broad issues. One might well ask how, in fact, a scale would be developed by means of the rational or internal consistency method, or, what is actually done when someone develops a scale by the empirical strategy.

THE RATIONAL APPROACH

Let us consider the rational approach first. Suppose the goal of the test developer was to devise a new self-report scale for leadership or leadership potential. The first step would be to examine past writings on the psychology of leadership to see what personal attributes and views concerning interpersonal relationships have been found important. Among the characteristics often found relevant are self-confidence, resilience in dealing with stress and opposition, good intellectual ability, a knack for understanding others and sensing what they feel and think, forcefulness, competitiveness, and a belief that individual and shared effort can be effective in producing constructive change.

Each of these notions can be translated into self-report items whose relevance to leadership will be obvious. Here are some examples of true-false items that derive from the attributes mentioned (many if not most personality inventories make use of statements to be responded to as true or false):

- I generally feel sure of myself and self-confident. (T)

- When others disagree with me, I usually just keep quiet or else give in. (F)

- I believe that I am distinctly above average in intellectual ability. (T)

- I often feel that I have a poor understanding of how other people will react to things. (F)

- My friends would probably describe me as a strong, forceful person. (T)

- I tend to avoid any situation in which I will be in direct competition with others. (F)

- Once people start working together there is almost no social problem that cannot be solved. (T)

The T and F letters after each statement show how it would be scored according to the concept of leadership underlying the construction of the scale.

The test author would probably prepare something like 75 to 100 such items, each one logically linked to a stated notion about the psychology of leadership. Then the pool of items would be administered to a sample of persons as similar as possible in general characteristics to those with whom the scale is eventually to be used. For instance, if the scale were to be used with managers in business and candidates for managerial training, then research testing should be done with persons in these categories. If the goal of the scale is to assess leadership potential among military personnel, then the research testing should be done with persons in military environments. If the scale is intended for use with both men and women, then (obviously) both men and women should be included in the research sample.

The number of people needed in the research sample is a matter of judgment. The minimum is probably about 100, but larger numbers are better. The issue is generalization, that is, to what extent can the findings in a particular sample furnish valid estimations of what will occur among people in general? The larger the research sample, the more likely generalizations from it will be valid.

Let us say that in our example, 75 questions pertaining to leadership are administered to 200 college students, 100 of each sex. Each student will have a total score on the initial pool of items, ranging from the lowest possible score of 0 to the highest possible score of 75. In practice, one would anticipate scores going from about 20 to 25 up to 65 or 70. The reason for fewer very low scores than those near the upper range of possible scores is that items tend to be answered in accordance with their social desirability (Edwards, 1957), and leadership is viewed by most as a desirable attribute.

The next step in a rational analysis is to examine the relationship of each item to the central concept. One way to do this is to intercorrelate all the items in a 75 x 75 matrix and then carry out a factor analysis to identify the first factor and the items that are primarily aligned with it. In this approach, at least 300 respondents are necessary to give a ratio of at least 4 to 1 for subjects versus items. The leadership scale that would result from this analysis would ordinarily consist of those items with the largest loadings on the first unrotated factor.

The factorial approach, however, is less often used than a simpler strategy that merely correlates each of the preliminary items with the total score. In this more common analysis, the dichotomy formed by the true–false response format is often expressed by a dummy weight of 1 for an answer corresponding to the scoring key and 0 for the other answer. This dichotomy is then correlated with the array of total scores, in what may be conceptualized as a biserial correlation, that is

$$r_{bis} = \frac{M_p - M_q}{SD_t} \; \text{x} \; \frac{pq}{y}$$

where

M_p = the mean score for all respondents giving the correct answer to the item

M_q = the mean score for all respondents giving the wrong answer to the item

SD_t = the standard deviation of the array of scores for all respondents

p = percentage of respondents giving the correct answer

q = percentage of respondents giving the wrong answer

y = the ordinate of the normal curve with surface equal to 1.00 at the point of division between p and q

In practice, even the biserial correlation is seldom computed nowadays. Most researchers simply use the correlational program on file in their local computer, pitting the 1–0 dummy weights for each item against the total score for each respondent. In effect, this usually gives rise to a point biserial correlation between each item and the total score.

Once the set of 75 correlations is available, the researcher scans the list to see if any produced a negative coefficient. This would signify a reversal of function and lead to the item being discarded. Items with very low correlations, even if in the proper direction, would also usually be thrown away. The goal is to end up with from 25 to perhaps 40 items, each having a significant ($p < .05$) relationship to the total. Such a scale, once assembled, is now ready to be tried out as a predictor of leadership where the leadership criterion is defined by ratings or other evaluations deemed valid in the setting.

THE EMPIRICAL APPROACH

A researcher following empirical pathways would begin in the same way—by perusing past work to identify relevant attitudes and dispositions. An initial pool of items would also be drawn up, many quite similar to those formulated by the internal consistency advocate. A difference, however, would occur in that the empiricist would add quite a few other items on the basis of pure hunches or just because they seem to be *ego-syntonic* (an *ego-syntonic* statement is an assertion that respondents like to endorse or reject).

For instance, to the pool of 50 to 75 items clearly relevant to hypotheses about leadership, the empiricist would probably add another 40 to 50 items such as these:

- One way or another, we must solve the overpopulation problem if the world as we know it today is to survive.

- If I had my choice of when to live, I think it would be England in the mid-1800s.

- The old and the young will never really understand each other.

- There are many foods that other people like but that I do not like and do not eat.

Armed with an experimental pool of, say, 125 items, the empirical researcher would now seek samples to which the preliminary inventory could be given and for which nontest criteria of leadership could be gathered. For example, in a military training school, either the students or the supervisors or both could be asked to rate each student on leadership, defined in a way relevant to that setting. In a business firm, the employees could be rated for leadership, again defined in a way pertinent to the demands of that setting. The critical requirement is that a reliable nontest criterion for leadership be obtained.

The next step for the empiricist is to correlate each of the experimental items with the criterion. With true-false items, dummy weights of 1 for a true response and 0 for a false could be used. Each of the 125 items would then have a correlation with the criterion, showing the degree of relationship. Positive coefficients would identify items for which "true" is the reply given by persons rated higher on leadership, and negative coefficients would identify items for which "false" is the indicated reply. Items with statistically significant correlations would be retained, and those with zero or trivial correlations would be deleted. Then the process would be repeated at least once, this time carrying forward only those items that showed promise in the first sample. This cross-validation is essential with the empirical method to guard against purely chance or random correlations that will always occur in any sample. The items that appeared acceptable on statistical grounds in both the first and the validational sample would then constitute the empirical scale for leadership potential.

It can be seen in the above examples that the two approaches are similar in that both appeal to data to decide which items to keep and which to drop from an initial pool. The critical and defining difference is that in the rational approach the scoring of each item is predetermined by the researcher, whereas in the empirical approach the scoring is determined entirely by the direction of the correlation between item and nontest criterion.

Two Scales for Personal Adjustment

We now proceed to a full demonstration of the two methods, where both are applied to a common pool of items administered to the same individuals. We begin with a definition of personal adjustment:

> Absence of serious emotional problems; stability of mood and manner; adaptivity, ability to deal with the new and unexpected; good balance of social conformity and spontaneity

This is a folk view of adjustment, with an emphasis on observables and no mention of internal resolution of psychodynamic conflicts, psychological insight, or other considerations that a clinician might stress. One reason for this is that the people we shall study were seen in interactive settings, not in psychotherapy or psychiatric treatment. Our raters found it easy to work with this common sense definition; the interjudge reliability coefficients within the subsamples of people rated were all above .85, with a median of .91.

The initial sample consisted of 198 college sophomores at Berkeley, 99 of each sex, who took part in one-day assessments at the Institute of Personality Assessment and Research (IPAR). Ordinarily, 10 students participated each day. The assessment staff consisted of from 15 to 20 persons—4 or 5 faculty members and supervisors and the rest doctoral candidates in personality psychology. Each participant was rated by all of the staff members present on that day on a set of 20 or more qualities, including personal adjustment or *soundness*. The ratings for each student were averaged, and then these averages were standardized within the sample of students present on the same day. This was done to equalize averages and standard deviations of the criterion ratings by day of assessment and to allow the compositing of all 198 students into a single sample within which ratings of soundness were comparable.

The students took two published personality tests—the *Minnesota Multiphasic Personality Inventory* (MMPI; Hathaway & McKinley, 1943) and the *California Psychological Inventory* (CPI; Gough, 1987). In addition, they took a 127–item supplemental inventory that had been developed by the IPAR research staff in the early 1950s. These 127 items embodied hypotheses and hunches about self-realization, academic potential, creativity, ego resilience, and coping ability. It is this set of 127 items that will serve as our basic item pool to illustrate the two methods of scale development.

DEVELOPMENT OF THE RATIONAL SCALE

For the rational scaling, the first task was to obtain judgments of the diagnostic relevance of each item for personal adjustment. To do this, we presented the 127 items to 35 male and 22 female students in beginning psychology classes and asked them to rate each item on a five-step scale. These were the specific instructions:

> If you think that a "true" response is strongly indicative of good personal adjustment, rate the item +2. If you think a "true" response is probably indicative of good adjustment, rate the item +1. If a "true" answer is strongly indicative of poor adjustment, rate the item −2. If a "true" answer is probably indicative of poor adjustment, rate the item −1. If the item is neutral, or unrelated to personal adjustment, rate it 0.

When the ratings for one half of the men were compared with those of the other half, the correlation of the two arrays was .81. When the same split-half correlation was computed for women, the correlation was .88. When the ratings by all 35 men were correlated with the ratings by all 22 women, the correlation was .88. These figures show a strong consensual theme running through the ratings, with certain items having an agreed-upon positive diagnostic value for adjustment, and certain others having an agreed-upon negative diagnostic value. The mean rating for all 127 items by the 35 men was .04, and the mean rating by the 22 women was .00.

Because of the congruence of ratings by men and women, their evaluations were combined into a single average rating for each item. The possible range of these means was from −2.00 to +2.00, but the actual range was from −1.68 to +1.52, as shown in the Appendix.

To get enough items for a sufficiently long preliminary scale, we set the cutpoint for inclusion at +.66 and above for items indicative of good adjustment, and at −.60 and below for items contraindicative of this criterion. By use of these cutpoints, 53 items were chosen for the preliminary rational scale, 26 to be scored for a true response and 27 for a false response. The true items all had mean ratings of +.66 or greater, and the false items all had mean ratings of −.60 or lower. Fourteen of the trues had ratings of +1.00 or above, and 13 of the falses had ratings of −1.00 or below. The 53 items are identified in the first column of the Appendix.

Scores were tallied for the 198 students on this 53-item preliminary scale, producing means of 40.42 (SD = 5.97) for men and 41.08 (SD = 5.58) for women. For all 198 students, the mean score was 40.75 (SD = 5.77). These scores were then correlated with all 127 items for men and women alone and for the full sample of 198 students. In the Appendix, only the correlations for the total sample are reported. From this analysis, 40 items were chosen for the rational personal adjustment scale, called PAR. These 40 items are identified in the Appendix.

Fourteen items were scored for true on PAR, with correlations with the 53-item total score ranging from .23 to .54. The most prototypical true item (with a correlation of +.54) was number 104, "In the morning I usually look forward with pleasure to the day's activities."

Twenty-six items were scored for false on PAR, with correlations versus the 53-item scale ranging from −.23 to −.54. Item number 1, "I doubt if I shall ever be a very important person in my work," had the strongest negative coefficient (r = −.53).

Scoring the protocols of the 198 students for this 40-item PAR scale produced means of 30.46 (SD = 5.93) for men, 30.30 (SD = 5.72) for women, and 30.38 (SD = 5.81) for all students. Correlations of PAR with the assessment staff ratings of personal adjustment were .30 for men, .40 for women, and .35 for all students. Later in our discussion, we will compare these coefficients with those found for the empirical scale and for scales from the MMPI and CPI.

DEVELOPMENT OF THE EMPIRICAL SCALE

To develop the empirical scale, called PAE, the IPAR staff ratings of the students for personal adjustment were correlated with the 127 items for men alone, women alone, and all students. These three sets of correlations were computed, as they were for PAR, to check for items that had markedly different values for either sex. Our goal was to choose items that were unisex, that is, that had indicative correlations with the criterion for both sexes.

The PAE findings for the total sample of 198 students are given in the Appendix, in the third column of figures. As typically happens when within-test item coefficients are compared with coefficients for items versus nontest criteria, the correlations for the rational analysis are much higher than those for the empirical. The differences are due to the contrast between within-domain and cross-domain analysis. That is, for the rational scale, self-report items are correlated with a self-report sum, but for the empirical scale, the correlations are between self-report items and observers' ratings.

To preserve commonality between PAE and PAR at this step, 40 items were chosen for the empirical scale, of which 10 were scored for true and 30 for false. The coefficients for the true items ranged from .12 to .19. The item with the largest coefficient ($r = .19$) was number 127, "I am happy most of the time."

The items scored for false had coefficients ranging from −.13 to −.30. The item with the coefficient of −.30 was number 1, "I doubt if I shall ever be a very important person in my work." It is not surprising that item 1 appears in both PAE and PAR, but we did not anticipate that it would be the single strongest item in both scales. Apparently, for college students at this stage of their lives, seeing oneself as having poor prospects for future occupational attainment is a significant sign of current problems in adjustment.

Item 5, "A person who lets himself get tricked has no one but himself to blame," with a correlation of .15 with the outside criterion, was not included on PAE. This was because of contradictory findings by gender. For the 99 men, this item correlated +.29 with the ratings, but for the 99 women its correlation was −.02. We would not want to include an item in PAE that had a reverse correlation for either sex.

Item 9, "There is too much emphasis in college on intellectual and theoretical topics, not enough on practical matters and the homely virtues of living," had a correlation in the total sample of −.15 with the outside criterion. This would make it a good candidate for a false item in the scale. However, there was again too great a difference by gender. For the females, the correlation of item 9 with the observers' ratings was −.29, but for the males, the correlation was only −.04. Because of this minimal correlation for males, the item was not included in PAE. A similar explanation holds for item 41, "Disobedience to the government is never justified." Although its criterion correlation was −.13 in the total sample, its coefficients were +.02 for males and −.27 for females.

Comparison of Selected Items and Scale Content

Perusal of the Appendix will reveal some interesting trends. For instance, PAE and PAR share 24 items, suggesting that in outcome the two methods are not very different if applied to the same items. For PAR, 35 of the 40 items came from the preliminary set of 53, with five new items being, as it were, discovered by the item analysis. A good example is number 90, "Sometimes the world just doesn't seem to make any sense." The raters assigned a mean value of −.04 to this item, whereas its correlation with the preliminary scale was −.23. There were also some items given strong ratings by the raters that failed to correlate with the 53-item preliminary measure. A good example is item 75, "I work best when I have some particular problem which I must finish by a certain time," which had a mean rating of +.91, but a correlation of only .02 with the preliminary scale.

Among the items retained for PAE were several that had only minimal ratings and also only near-zero correlations with the 53-item preliminary rational scale. The best example is number 40, "I don't like modern art." The mean rating by the judges for this item was −.11, and its correlation with the preliminary rational scale was −.05. However, its correlation with the nontest ratings of personal adjustment was −.15.

An example of an item with a strong rating by the judges and also a significant correlation with the preliminary rational scale was number 13, "There are as many opportunities for a good man in my field today as there ever were." The mean rating by judges for this item was 1.09, and its correlation with the preliminary rational scale was .23. However, its correlation with the nontest ratings of personal adjustment was only .02.

The content of each scale should be noted. When the 40 items in PAE were factor analyzed for the combined sample of men and women, four broad themes emerged. Among the prominent items on the first theme were "I am happy most of the time" (true), "I am generally not in doubt as to what will win approval for me" (true), "I am frequently in low spirits" (false), and "I doubt if I shall ever be a very important person in my work" (false). We may call this factor *positive affect*.

Critical items on the second dimension included "Whether you call it fascism, communism, or democracy, every government grabs what it can get away with" (false), "Sometimes the world just doesn't seem to make any sense" (false), "I find discussions of politics boring" (false), and "An invention which takes jobs away from people should be suppressed until new work can be found for them" (false). There were no items in this factor with significant positive loadings, signifying that its main emphasis is on skeptical social and political beliefs. Because it would be scored for good adjustment, if treated as a separate variable, we want the name suggested for it to refer to the favorable pole of the continuum. Something like *optimistic political and social attitudes* would be appropriate.

Four items which stand out for the third theme are "Barring emergencies, I have a pretty good idea what I'll be doing for the next ten years" (true), "Usually I put a great deal of zeal and energy into my work" (true), "Much of my work is far inferior to what I can really do" (false), and "I do not pay much attention to other people" (false). A reasonable description of this factor would be a favorable sense of *occupational and interpersonal effectiveness*.

Four strong items from the fourth factor are "I like to fool around with new ideas, even if they turn out later to be total waste of time" (true), "Many of my friends would probably be considered unconventional by most people" (true), "I would enjoy an experience of living and working in a foreign country" (true), and "I don't like modern art" (false). The name we suggest for this factor is *openness to new experience*.

A similar analysis of 40 items in PAR also gave rise to four major themes. Prominent items for the first were "I am happy most of the time" (true), "Almost everyone is really friendly and kind at heart" (true), "I guess my friends tend to think of me as a cold and unsentimental person" (false), and "I get nervous and upset whenever I have to compete with anyone "(false). Our name for this theme is *positive feelings about self and others*.

For the second PAR factor, these are the best illustrative items: "There are as many opportunities for a good man in my field as there ever were" (true), "In the morning I usually look forward with pleasure to the day's activities" (true), "I get discouraged when I hear about another person's success" (false), and "Sometimes the world just doesn't seem to make any sense" (false). *Optimism* is a name that captures the general flavor of the items.

The third factor for PAR was strongly defined by these items: "I usually put a great deal of zeal and energy into my work" (true), "Barring emergencies, I have a pretty good idea what I'll be doing in the next ten years" (true), "It is hard for me to make quick decisions" (false), and "I am frequently in low spirits" (false). A *good sense of personal competence* appears to underlie this factor.

The fourth factor for PAR had major loadings on these items: "I enjoy the company of strong-willed people" (true), "I like to fool around with new ideas, even if they turn out later to be a total waste of time" (true), "When I sit down to study it is hard to keep my mind on the material" (false), and "It is often hard for me to understand what the questions are driving at in a school test" (false). *Openness to new experience* seems to be a reasonable formulation of this factor.

If we look at the four factors extracted from the two scales, it is apparent that there is considerable similarity. This is not surprising, considering that they have 24 (of 40) items in common. The informally assigned factor names give a good summary of the kinds of feelings and reports about self that are indicative of good personal adjustment, namely, (a) positive affect, (b) optimism, (c) good sense of personal competence, and (d) openness to new experience.

Relations to Criteria

We turn now to relationships of PAE and PAR to other tests, and to the criteria of personal adjustment available for the college students. As would be expected, given the overlapping items, the two scales correlate highly with each other, with coefficients of .88 for the total sample, and .86 and .89 for males and females, respectively.

Means, standard deviations, internal consistency coefficients (alpha), and correlations with the assessment staff ratings of personal adjustment are presented in Table 1.

For both PAE and PAR, means are about the same for males and females. The ·alpha reliability coefficients are in the usual range for personality measures (in the vicinity of .70), with slightly higher values for men than for women. PAE has higher correlations with the nontest criterion than does the PAR (.48 vs. .30 for males, and .50 vs. .40 for females). Because the 40 items in PAE were chosen for their relationships to the staff ratings, this difference is not very meaningful. The empirical scale must be correlated with criteria

TABLE 1. Means, Standard Deviations, Reliabilities, and Correlations With Criteria of the Empirical and Rational Personal Adjustment Scales in the Initial Samples

Samples	N	PAE (Empirical scale)				PAR (Rational scale)			
		M	SD	Alpha	r	M	SD	Alpha	r
Males	99	27.00	5.69	.73	.48	30.46	5.93	.76	.30
Females	99	27.25	5.43	.70	.50	30.30	5.72	.70	.40
Total	198	27.13	5.55	.71	.49	30.38	5.81	.73	.35

of personal adjustment in a new sample before any conclusions can be reached about its validity. On the other hand, because PAR was developed without any attention to the staff ratings, its correlation of .35 in the total sample of 198 students is a finding worth noting.

In Table 2 we give correlations of the staff rating of personal adjustment with the scales of the MMPI and CPI for the total sample only (coefficients for men and women separately were much the same as those reported in Table 2 for the total sample).

The largest single correlation was −.36 with the Depression scale of the MMPI. This makes sense, as the Depression scale was constructed to identify people suffering from discouragement, self-doubt, and feelings of insufficiency (Hathaway & McKinley, 1942). All of the MMPI clinical scales either had negative or, at the minimum, zero correlations with rated adjustment. Two MMPI scales, the K scale for test-taking strategies and the Ego Strength scale (Barron, 1953), had positive and statistically significant ($p < .01$) correlations.

The largest correlation with the staff ratings for the scales of the CPI was for Self-acceptance ($r = .35$), and the next largest was for Intellectual Efficiency ($r = .32$). Nineteen of the 20 CPI scales had positive correlations with the staff ratings. This corresponds to the purposes of the CPI, which are to assess favorable, achievement-oriented facets of personality. The fact that the largest correlations for both the CPI and the MMPI are in the region from .30 to .36 indicates that the .35 coefficient found for PAR is quite comparable to what well-established and widely validated inventories can produce for this same sample.

TABLE 2. Correlations of the CPI and MMPI Scales
With Observers' Ratings of Personal Adjustment

CPI Scales	r	MMPI Scales	r
Dominance	.31**	L (Lie scale)	−.09
Capacity for Status	.31**	F (Unusual responses)	−.25**
Sociability	.32**	K (Minimal self-disclosure)	.24**
Social Presence	.28**	Hs+.5K (Hypochrondriasis)	−.08
Self-acceptance	.35**	D (Depression)	−.36**
Independence	.23**	Hy (Hysteria)	−.04
Empathy	.26**	Pd+.4K (Psychopathy)	−.15*
Responsiblity	.25**	Mf (Femininity)	−.09
Socialization	.23**	Pa (Paranoia)	−.11
Self-control	.08	Pt+K (Psychasthenia)	−.25**
Good Impression	.14*	Sc+K (Schizophrenia)	−.28**
Communality	.27**	Ma+.2K (Hypomania)	.00
Well-being	.31**	Si (Social introversion)	−.35**
Tolerance	.19*	A (Factor 1, anxiety)	−.31**
Achievement via Conformance	.28**	R (Factor 2, repression)	−.10
Achievement via Independence	.27	ES (Ego strength)	.29**
Intellectual Efficiency	.33**		
Psychological-mindedness	.24**		
Flexibility	.06		
Femininity	−.12		

Notes:
*$p < .05$
**$p < .01$
$N = 198$ college students

Cross-validation

As mentioned above, a check of both item and scale validities in a new sample is essential for any measure developed by the empirical method, and it is also a wise step to take for rationally developed scales. For this analysis, we used four other groups assessed at IPAR and rated by staff observers. One consisted of 76 males, residents of the San Francisco Bay area who took part in studies of population psychology and marital relationships. Another was composed of 66 seniors in the School of Engineering at Berkeley. The third included the 76 wives or partners of the Bay Area residents, and the fourth included 40 women assessed during their first year in the University of California Boalt Hall School of Law. This gave a total of 142 men and 127 women.

For a criterion of personal adjustment, we again had IPAR staff ratings, with panels of from 2 to 18 furnishing ratings for each assessee. Interjudge reliability coefficients in the various subsamples (defined by date of assessment) within the total of 258 ranged from .85 to .95, with a median of .90. The ratings by each panel were converted to averages, and then these averages were standardized to means of 50 and standard deviations of 10 within subsamples to allow for combining of all cases in a single sample.

For cross-validation, we also made use of an additional criterion of adjustment, based on Block's (1961) 100-item *California Q-sort*. Each of the 258 individuals had been described on the Q-sort by from two to six observers; then these formulations were pooled and the composite rearrayed into the prescribed Q-sort distribution for each assessee. In his book, Block gives a sorting of the 100 descriptions as a prototypical characterization of the ideally adjusted person. The sorting positions (from 9 to 1) assigned to each of the 100 items in the ideal Q-sort can be correlated with the sorting positions given to the items when used to characterize a person in fact observed. The magnitude of the correlation can be used to index the adequacy of adjustment (specifically, approach to an ideal of adjustment). The higher this correlation the better the adjustment of the person being described by observers, and the lower the correlation the poorer the adjustment.

In this new sample of 258 persons, we looked first at the 40 items in PAE to see if any showed reversals or loss of diagnostic validity. The item versus rating correlations were computed for men alone, women alone, and the total sample, and the same three correlations were computed with the Q-sort criterion. We set up three rules to detect items we would drop. The first was any reversal in the direction of correlation with either criterion (rating or Q-sort) in the total sample. Six items (numbers 51, 56, and 82, scored for true, and numbers 28, 37, and 89, scored for false) were deleted for this reason. An example is the item "I sometimes sleep in the nude," which correlated −.06 with the rating criterion in the cross-validating sample.

The second rule for dropping was a double reversal for either sex. One item (number 2, "I often doze off and let my mind wander during class periods") was dropped for this reason. In the new sample of 142 men, it correlated +.03 with the rating criterion and +.05 with the Q-sort criterion. Because it was initially scored for a false response, confirmatory correlations would have been in the negative direction.

The third rule stated that an item would be dropped if it showed a reversal of direction of magnitude of .10 or greater in any sample. One item was dropped by application of this rule (number 22, "I could cut my moorings—quit my home, my parents, and my friends—without suffering great regrets"). Because it was initially keyed for a false response, the item should have had negative correlations in all cross-validating subsamples. In fact, its correlation with the rating criterion was +.10 for the 142 men.

These deletions left 32 items in the revised PAE scale, which we will term PAE-2. The alpha internal consistency coefficients for PAE-2 were .72 for the 142 men, .70 for the 127 women, and .71 for all 258 subjects. The deletion of the eight items did not lead to any weakening of the internal homogeneity of the measure.

On PAE-2, however, a small difference did appear between the average scores of the 142 men and 127 women. The mean for men was 23.15 (SD = 4.41) and that for women was 22.06 (SD = 4.26). The difference in favor of men (1.09) was just significant at the .05 level of probability, as indicated by a t-test of 2.00.

We also examined anew the items within PAR, correlating them with total score on PAR for men alone, women alone, and all subjects. The rule for deletion was any reversal of direction in correlation from the way in which the item was initially keyed. Five items showed such reversal (numbers 72 and 113 scored for true, and numbers 35, 98, and 101 scored for false). The PAR-2 scale formed by the 35 retained items had alphas of .77 for men, .75 for women, and .76 for all subjects. Means were 28.00 (SD = 4.57) for men and 26.94 (SD = 4.47) for women, giving a difference of 1.06 in favor of men. The t-test for this difference was 1.87, just short of the .05 level of probability (p = .06).

The two refined scales, PAE-2 and PAR-2, and two of the MMPI scales with strong relationships to personal adjustment in the initial sample—

TABLE 3. Correlations in the Cross-validating Sample
Among the Revised Empirical and Rational Scales
for Personal Adjustment, the MMPI Scales for Depression
and Ego Strength, and Two Criteria of Personal Adjustment

	PAR-2	Depression	Ego Strength	Rating	Q-sort
Empirical scale (PAE-2)	.86	−.40	.55	.21	.33
Rational scale (PAR-2)		−.52	.54	.21	.33
MMPI Depression			−.51	−.17	−.29
MMPI Ego Strength				−.26	.30
Staff ratings					.42
Staff Q-sorts					—

$N = 258$
All correlations are significant beyond $p = .01$.

Depression (D) and Ego Strength (Es)—were then correlated with each other
and with both criteria in the cross-validating samples. Because the results for
men and women were almost identical, we report in Table 3 only the matrix
for the full sample of 258 persons.

Perhaps the most striking finding in Table 3 is the exactly equal validities
of PAE-2 and PAR-2 against both the ratings and the Q-sort criterion of
personal adjustment. Against the staff ratings of the 258 assessees, PAE-2 and
PAR-2 both had correlations of .21, and against the Q-sort criterion both had
correlations of .33. These are rather modest values, but it needs to be kept in
mind that personal adjustment is itself a complex, multifaceted phenomenon,
hardly something to be estimated or forecast with precision by short 32-item
or 35-item self-report scales.

The well-validated MMPI Depression scale, it should be noted, had even
lower validates of −.17 and −.29. Barron's MMPI scale for Ego Strength had
correlations with the criteria of .26 and .30. All four of these scales, in other
words, were similar in their relationships to the two criteria. However, it
should be emphatically stressed that the two experimental scales we are using
to show how empirical and rational measures are developed are not considered in any way as the equal of the two MMPI scales. Those scales have
been confirmed and validated in many different settings and in many different

samples. Their value, then, is a matter of record. PAE-2 and PAR-2, on the other hand, are merely provisional measures designed for illustrative purposes.

Something more should also be said about the complexity of the criterion of personal adjustment. Note that the ratings and the Q-sort criterion correlate only .42, even though both are aimed at the same evaluation. All four of the scales reported in Table 3 had stronger validities when the Q-sort criterion was used. The Q-sort criterion may be superior to the rating criterion because of the linkage of ratings to small ten-person subsamples. Recall that the staff ratings for each weekend were ordinarily processed and then standardized for just those persons studied at that time. The Q-sort descriptions furnished by the staff had no such limitations to any subsample or to any time period.

Conclusion

The aim of this chapter has been to illustrate the actual steps taken to develop empirical and rational self-report personality inventory scales. To enhance the meaning of the comparison, both techniques were applied to the same pool of 127 items and were addressed to the same criterion of personal adjustment. In the initial sample of 198 college students (99 of each sex), comparability was furthered by selecting 40 items for each scale.

In the cross-validating sample of 142 males and 127 females, eight of the empirical items washed out, reducing the empirical scale (PAE-2) to 32 items. Five of the items from the initial 40-item rational scale also washed out, making the final version of that scale (PAR-2) 35 items in length.

When PAE-2 and PAR-2 were correlated with ratings of personal adjustment and with a Q-sort formulation of the same criterion, in a cross-validating sample of 258 subjects, identical correlations of .21 against ratings and .33 against the Q-sort formulation of ideal adjustment were obtained. For the empirical scale, this was not a complete cross-validation, as items versus criterion relationships in the sample led to the discarding of eight items. If PAE-2 were to be developed as a scale for use beyond this illustrative exercise, at least one new tryout would be required in which the 32-item scale could be evaluated against a nontest criterion. This kind of successive refinement and improvement of the measure is what one typically finds in the developmental history of the best empirical scales, such as those in the MMPI and the *Strong Interest Inventory*.

Finally, enthusiastic partisans of either rational or empirical methodology will not find much to cheer about in the exactly equivalent results we obtained. In this regard we should recall that an early systematic attempt to compare the yield of the two approaches (Goldberg, 1972) found similar commonality. Effective, or ineffective, scales can be evolved by both methods. A researcher's choice of which pathway to follow will stem more from personal paradigm preferences than from any documented superiority of one method to the other.

References

Barron, F. (1953). An ego strength scale which predicts response to psycho-therapy. *Journal of Consulting Psychology, 17,* 327–333.

Block, J. (1961). *The Q-sort method in personality assessment and psychiatric research.* Springfield, IL: Charles C. Thomas.

Butcher, J. N., Dahlstrom, W. G., Graham, J. R., Tellegen, A., & Kaemmer, B. (1989). *Manual for the restandardized Minnesota Multiphasic Personality Inventory: MMPI-2. An administrative and interpretive guide.* Minneapolis: University of Minnesota Press.

Cattell, R. B., Eber, H. W., & Tatsuoka, M. M. (1970). *Handbook for the Sixteen Personality Factor Questionnaire.* Champaign, IL: Institute for Personality and Ability Testing.

Edwards, A. L. (1953). *Edwards Personal Preference Schedule.* New York: Psychological Corporation.

Edwards, A. L. (1957). *The social desirability variable in personality assessment and research.* New York: Dryden.

Golberg, L. R. (1972). Parameters of personality inventory construction and utilization: A comparison of prediction strategies and tactics. *Multivariate Behavioral Research Monographs, 72* (2).

Gough, H. G. (1987). *California Psychological Inventory administrator's guide.* Palo Alto, CA: Consulting Psychologists Press.

Guilford, J. S., Zimmerman, W. S., & Guilford, J. P. (1976). *The Guilford-Zimmerman Temperament Survey handbook: Twenty-five years of research and application.* San Diego: Educational and Industrial Testing Survey.

Hansen, J. C., & Campbell, D. P. (1985). *Manual for the SVIB-SII* (4th ed.). Stanford, CA: Stanford University Press.

Hathaway, S. R., & McKinley, J. C. (1942). A multiphasic personality schedule (Minnesota): III. The measurement of symptomatic depression. *Journal of Psychology, 14,* 73–84.

Hathaway, S. R., & McKinley, J. C. (1943). *The Minnesota Multiphasic Personality Inventory.* Minneapolis: University of Minnesota Press.

Jackson, D. N. (1984). *Personality Research Form Manual.* Port Huron, MI: Research Psychologists Press.

Millon, T. (1983). *Millon Clinical Multiaxial Inventory manual* (2nd ed.). Minneapolis, MN: National Computer Systems.

Strong, E. K., Jr. (1943). *The vocational interests of men and women.* Stanford, CA: Stanford University Press.

Wirt, R., Lachar, D., Klinedinst, J., & Seat, P. (1984). *Multidimensional description of child personality: A manual for the Personality Inventory for Children—Revised.* Los Angeles: Western Psychological Service.

APPENDIX. Rating of Items for Personal Adjustment, and Correlations of Items with Scores on the Preliminary 53-item Rational Scale, and With Observers' Ratings of Personal Adjustment

Items	Item Ratings	Corrrelations With	
		Preliminary Rational Scale	Observers' Ratings
1. I doubt if I shall ever be a very important person in my work.	−1.68[b]	−.53[d]	−.30[f]
2. I often doze off and let my mind wander during class periods.	−0.11	−.22	−.15[f]
3. I cannot overcome a deep feeling that something is wrong with sex as such.	−0.87[b]	−.27[d]	−.16[f]
4. I am frequently in low spirits.	−1.04[b]	−.50[d]	−.23[f]
5. A person who lets himself get tricked has no one but himself to blame.	−0.42	.00	.15
6. If people knew my inner thoughts, I am sure they would think less of me.	−0.65[b]	−.41[d]	−.11
7. I get nervous and upset whenever I have to compete with anyone.	−0.70[b]	−.33[d]	−.21[f]
8. I tend not to have personally friendly relations with my employers.	−0.70[b]	−.33[d]	−.11
9. There is too much emphasis in college on intellectual and theoretical topics, not enough on practical matters and the homely virtues of living.	0.17	−.16	−.15
10. I am generally not in doubt as to what will win approval for me.	1.11[a]	.28[c]	.13[e]
11. In religious matters, I believe I would have to be called an agnostic.	0.24	−.02	−.08
12. Many of the girls I knew in college went with a fellow only for what they could get out of him.	−0.89[b]	−.24[d]	−.03
13. There are as many opportunities for a good man in my field today as there ever were.	1.09[a]	.23[c]	.02
14. I sometimes used to feel that my parents did not really love me.	−1.24[b]	−.32[d]	−.13[f]

APPENDIX. Rating of Items for Personal Adjustment, and Correlations of Items with Scores on the Preliminary 53–item Rational Scale, and With Observers' Ratings of Personal Adjustment (continued)

Items	Item Ratings	Correlations With	
		Preliminary Rational Scale	Observers' Ratings
15. A person who works hard has a right to be successful in his field.	1.52[a]	.17	−.02
16. A person has to be prepared to rule out most of the pleasures and diversions of life if he wants to become a really illustrious or renowned person in his field of scholarship.	−0.61	−.27[d]	−.19[f]
17. Whether you call it facism, communism, or democracy, every government grabs what it can get away with.	−0.13	−.13	.−18[f]
18. I sometimes like a good hot argument.	0.71[a]	.21	.06
19. The details of a job are as important as the job itself.	0.95[a]	.09	−.10
20. I frequently undertake more than I can accomplish.	−0.27	−.22	−.13[f]
21. The unfinished and the imperfect often have greater appeal for me than the completed and polished.	−0.32	−.09	−.08
22. I could cut my moorings—quit my home, my parents, and my friends—without suffering great regrets.	−1.11[b]	−.24[d]	−.20[f]
23. Politically I am probably something of a radical.	−0.11	.15	.03
24. I think I take primarily an aesthetic view of experience.	0.58	.18	.12
25. I remember that my first day at school was very painful.	−0.52	−.13	−.11
26. I would enjoy the experience of living in a foreign country.	1.00[a]	.33[c]	.13[c]
27. I don't expect to have more than two children.	0.32	−.10	.02

APPENDIX. Rating of Items for Personal Adjustment, and Correlations of Items with Scores on the Preliminary 53-item Rational Scale, and With Observers' Ratings of Personal Adjustment (continued)

		Corrrelations With	
Items	Item Ratings	Preliminary Rational Scale	Observers' Ratings
28. Many of my friends would probably be considered unconventional by other people.	−0.09	−0.07	−.15[f]
29. The way things look now I guess I won't amount to much in the world.	−1.65[b]	−.50[d]	−.23[f]
30. I enjoy discarding the old and accepting the new.	0.69[a]	.29[c]	.13[e]
31. I doubt if anyone will ever be able to predict my every move.	0.88[a]	.16	.07
32. Some of my friends think that my ideas are impractical, if not a bit wild.	−0.07	.01	−.07
33. When someone talks against certain groups or nationalities, I always speak up against such talk, even if it makes me unpopular.	1.00[a]	.17	.01
34. I enjoy the company of strong-willed people.	1.16[a]	.24[c]	.13[e]
35. As a child my home life was not as happy as that of most others.	−0.93[b]	−.37[d]	−.10
36. I have always had goals and ambitions that were beyond anything practical or that seemed capable of being realized.	−0.13	−.18	−.13[f]
37. I often get the feeling that I am not really part of the group I associate with and that I could separate from it with little discomfort or hardship.	−0.54	−.32[d]	−.17[f]
38. People would be happier if sex experience were taken for granted in both men and women.	−0.32	.03	−.03

APPENDIX. Rating of Items for Personal Adjustment, and Correlations of Items with Scores on the Preliminary 53–item Rational Scale, and With Observers' Ratings of Personal Adjustment (continued)

Items	Item Ratings	Correlations With	
		Preliminary Rational Scale	Observers' Ratings
39. I guess my friends tend to think of me as a cold and unsentimental sort of person.	−1.26[b]	−.41[d]	−.10
40. I don't like modern art.	−0.11	−.05	−.15[f]
41. Disobedience to the government is never justified.	−0.94[b]	−.20	−.13
42. Perfect balance is the essence of all good composition.	0.36	.00	−.07
43. It would be better if our professors would give us a clearer idea of what they consider important.	0.61	−.04	−.06
44. Straightforward reasoning appeals to me more than metaphors and the search for analogies.	0.37	.01	.06
45. It is a pretty callous person who does not feel love and gratitude toward his parents.	0.54	.04	−.06
46. Things seem simpler as we learn more about them.	1.07[a]	.22	−.08
47. Every wage earner should be required to save a certain part of his income each month so that he will be able to support himself and his family in later years.	0.44	.03	.01
48. Kindness and generosity are the most important qualities for a wife to have.	0.18	−.13	−.14[f]
49. When a person has a problem or worry it is best for him not to think about it, but to keep busy with more cheerful things.	−0.44	−.11	−.08
50. It is the duty of a citizen to support his country, right or wrong	−0.65[b]	−.12	−.10

APPENDIX. Rating of Items for Personal Adjustment, and Correlations
of Items with Scores on the Preliminary 53-item Rational Scale,
and With Observers' Ratings of Personal Adjustment (continued)

		Corrrelations With	
Items	Item Ratings	Preliminary Rational Scale	Observers' Ratings
51. Barring emergencies, I have a pretty good idea of what I'll be doing for the next ten years.	0.84[a]	.31[c]	.13[e]
52. Army life is a good influence on most young men.	−0.47	−.11	.03
53. I prefer team games to games in which one individual competes against another.	0.41	.06	−.02
54. An invention which takes jobs away from people should be supressed until new work can be found for them.	0.07	−.18	−.14[f]
55. It is easy for me to take orders and do what I am told.	0.39	−.09	−.01
56. I like to fool around with new ideas, even if they turn out later to be a total waste of time.	0.84[a]	.29[c]	.13[e]
57. Human nature being what it is, there will always be war and conflict.	0.36	−.06	.02
58. What this country needs most, more than laws and political programs, is a few courageous, tireless, devoted leaders in whom the people can put their faith.	0.24	.00	−.16[f]
59. I must admit that I would find it hard to have for a close friend a person whose manners or appearance made him somewhat repulsive, no matter how brilliant or kind he might be.	−0.73[b]	−.15	.03
60. What the youth needs most is strict discipline, rugged determination, and the will to work and fight for family and country.	−0.32	−.07	−.11

APPENDIX. Rating of Items for Personal Adjustment, and Correlations of Items with Scores on the Preliminary 53-item Rational Scale, and With Observers' Ratings of Personal Adjustment (continued)

Items	Item Ratings	Correlations With	
		Preliminary Rational Scale	Observers' Ratings
61. I would rather have a few intense friendships than a great many friendly but casual relationships.	1.23[a]	.14	−.03
62. The happy person tends always to be poised, courteous, outgoing, and emotionally controlled.	0.36	.01	.02
63. Science should have as much to say about moral values as religion does.	0.06	.10	−.03
64. Young people sometimes get rebellious ideas, but as they grow up they ought to get over them and settle down.	0.11	−.08	−.08
65. I have seen some things so sad that I almost felt like crying.	1.07[a]	.13	−.10
66. I don't understand how men in some European countries can be so demonstrative to one another.	−0.32	−.06	.02
67. A person should not probe too deeply into his own and other people's feelings, but take things as they are.	−0.56	−.11	−.05
68. I acquired a strong interest in intellectual and aesthetic matters from my mother.	0.46	.07	.00
69. I believe you should ignore other people's faults and make an effort to get along with almost everyone.	0.84[a]	.18	.09
70. The best theory is the one that has the best practical applications.	0.41	−.12	−.09
71. Some people are so bossy that I feel like doing the opposite of what they tell me.	0.11	−.21	−.12[f]
72. I have a pretty clear idea of what I would try to impart to my students if I were a teacher.	1.00[a]	.25[c]	.04

APPENDIX. Rating of Items for Personal Adjustment, and Correlations of Items with Scores on the Preliminary 53-item Rational Scale, and With Observers' Ratings of Personal Adjustment (continued)

Items	Item Ratings	Correlations With	
		Preliminary Rational Scale	Observers' Ratings
73. When I start to work on something new I always take time to plan in advance the way in which I will work.	1.06[a]	.11	.03
74. I usually put a great deal of zeal and energy into my work.	1.31[a]	.49[c]	.14[c]
75. I work best when I have some particular problem which I must finish by a certain time.	0.91[a]	.02	.08
76. I would much rather do something by myself, even a difficult task, than have someone help me.	0.13	.00	.12[e]
77. As a rule I have difficulty in "putting myself into other people's shoes."	0.44	.08	.09
78. I do my best work when alone.	0.06	.02	−.05
79. I have sometimes pitied my father for not accomplishing what he set out to do.	−0.65[b]	−.18	−.01
80. I was taught to read before I started school.	0.27	−.01	.07
81. A person should enjoy what he has today and forget what he might have twenty years from now.	0.16	.03	−.05
82. I sometimes sleep in the nude.	−0.13	.06	.13[c]
83. I am usually rather short-tempered with people who come around and bother me with foolish questions.	−0.59	−.22	−.15[f]
84. In high school some of my school subjects seemed to be a complete waste of time.	−0.20	.05	.01
85. I have little sympathy for people who stick to their old ways and ideas when doing so makes for unhappiness.	0.55	.06	−.11

APPENDIX. Rating of Items for Personal Adjustment, and Correlations of Items with Scores on the Preliminary 53–item Rational Scale, and With Observers' Ratings of Personal Adjustment (continued)

		Correlations With	
Items	*Item Ratings*	*Preliminary Rational Scale*	*Observers' Ratings*
86. I would rather be on the entertainment committee than on the educational comittee of a club.	0.11	−.03	.08
87. I have always been a sort of "big brother" type.	0.66[a]	.17	.09
88. I would rather write an important scientific book than inherit $25,000.	0.15	.04	.04
89. Much of my work is far inferior to what I can really do.	−0.32	−.19	−.14[f]
90. Sometimes the world just doesn't seem to make any sense.	−0.04	−.23[d]	−.15[f]
91. If our professors would only agree a little better among themselves, academic work in our department would be more pleasant and rewarding.	−0.54	−.09	.06
92. It is hard for me to work intently on a scholarly problem for more than an hour or two at a stretch.	−0.04	−.22	−.09
93. When I sit down to study, it is hard to keep my mind on the material.	−0.68[b]	−.30[d]	−.15[f]
94. It is often hard for me to understand what the questions are driving at in a school test.	−0.60[b]	−.31[d]	−.10
95. Compared to your own self-respect, the respect of others means very little.	−0.45	.04	.04
96. A man ought to be physically disciplined.	0.25	−.07	−.07
97. Every boy ought to get away from his family while he is still in his teens.	−0.26	.07	−.07
98. Most women really want a man to push them around a little bit.	−1.32[b]	−.25[d]	−.04

APPENDIX. Rating of Items for Personal Adjustment, and Correlations of Items with Scores on the Preliminary 53-item Rational Scale, and With Observers' Ratings of Personal Adjustment (continued)

Items	Item Ratings	Correlations With Preliminary Rational Scale	Observers' Ratings
99. Every person ought to be a booster for for his own home town.	0.33	−.05	.00
100. Most theories are crackpot notions dressed up to look respectable.	−1.04[b]	−.31[d]	−.14[f]
101. Almost nobody wants war but there is an element of excitement about it which is in many ways preferable to peace.	−1.07[b]	−.29[d]	−.03
102. No governmnent can really be efficient.	−0.22	−.12	−.08
103. It irritates me when someone seems to be asking me for sympathy.	−0.59	.03	.11
104. In the morning I usually look forward with pleasure to the day's activities.	1.04[a]	.54[c]	.06
105. I often think of our present-day activities as just a tiny moment of time in the great stretch of history.	0.52	.08	−.05
106. I feel that most social affairs are a waste of time.	−0.98[b]	−.27[d]	−.17[f]
107. I often chat with clerks when they are waiting on me.	0.56	.32[c]	.09
108. Almost everyone is really friendly and kind at heart.	0.82[a]	.31[c]	.02
109. The feeling of "knowing everyone" that you get in a small town appeals to me.	0.46	.08	.07
110. Where sex is concerned, no woman can be trusted.	−1.31[b]	−.22	.01
111. I find discussions of politics boring.	−0.44	−.21	−.25[f]
112. I like people I can call by their first names almost as soon as I meet them.	0.70[a]	.22	−.03
113. I value being independent of other people.	1.25[a]	.24[c]	.05

APPENDIX. Rating of Items for Personal Adjustment, and Correlations of Items with Scores on the Preliminary 53-item Rational Scale, and With Observers' Ratings of Personal Adjustment (continued)

		Correlations With	
Items	Item Ratings	Preliminary Rational Scale	Observers' Ratings
114. It is hard for me to make quick decisions.	−0.24	−.37[d]	−.14[f]
115. I do not pay much attention to other people.	−1.07[b]	−.35[d]	−.20[f]
116. It is hard for me to talk freely about myself, even to my close friends.	−0.87[b]	−.27[d]	−.13[f]
117. If I found some money on the street I think I would probably keep it rather than try to find the owner.	0.11	−.15	.00
118. I would like to be able to read Greek and Latin with facility.	0.54	.07	−.08
119. My mood depends mostly on how I am doing in my work.	0.11	−.12	−.02
120. When I get hold of a newspaper I usually turn to the sports and comic sections before I read anything else.	0.11	−.08	−.04
121. It has sometimes been hard for me to know just what my employer really thought of me.	−0.28	−.15	−.13[f]
122. I get disgusted with myself when I can't understand some problem in my field or when I can't seem to make any progress on a research problem.	0.00	−.10	−.04
123. I get discouraged when I hear about another person's success.	−1.06[b]	−.36[d]	−.10
.124. When I see a crowd gathering, I usually go out of my way to see what it is all about.	0.34	.10	.05

246

TEST DEVELOPMENT

Appendix. Rating of Items for Personal Adjustment, and Correlations of Items with Scores on the Preliminary 53-item Rational Scale, and With Observers' Ratings of Personal Adjustment (continued)

		Correlations With	
		Preliminary	
	Item	Rational	Observers'
Items	Ratings	Scale	Ratings
125. Sometimes when I am not feeling well I am cross.	0.14	−.05	.05
126. I do many things which I regret afterwards (I regret things more or more often than others seem to).	−1.13[b]	−.40[d]	−.08
127. I am happy most of the time.	1.41[a]	.46[c]	.19[e]

Notes:
[a] Scored for true in the preliminary scale
[b] Scored for false in the preliminary scale
[c] Scored for true in the 40-item rational scale
[d] Scored for false in the 40-item rational scale
[e] Scored for true in the 40-item empirical scale
[f] Scored for false in the 40-item empirical scale

PART III

STATISTICS, PSYCHOMETRICS, AND TEST DATA

CHAPTER 7

Test Scores and Statistics

Mark L. Davison

Introduction

Test scores in and of themselves have limited meaning. If my son comes home on Friday and tells me he got 20 right on his spelling test, I don't know whether his score is good or bad. To evaluate the score, some frame of reference is needed. As discussed by Bracken (this volume), there are many possible frames of reference. For instance, one can compare my child's performance to that of other children in the class, a norm-referenced framework. If he spelled more words correctly than most other children, 20 is a good score according to this frame of reference. For a second frame of reference, one can compare his score to the highest possible score. If 20 is close to the maximum possible, then 20 is a good score. Or one can compare the score to grading standards set by the teacher. If 20 is above the minimum required by the teacher for an A or B, it is a good score. As a fourth alternative, one can compare his score of 20 to his score on Monday's practice test to see if there has been improvement.

This chapter discusses different kinds of test scores. Unlike raw scores, such as the number right on a spelling test, many of these scores are designed to be more interpretable than raw scores. The alternative scores have an explicit frame of reference that gives them meaning that raw scores, in and of themselves, do not carry.

This chapter begins by reviewing very basic statistics that are used in deriving some scores and in giving meaning to others. Next, the chapter reviews the concept of a raw score and its interpretation. The third section introduces norm-referenced scores, scores based on a comparison of the individual's performance to that of some specified norm group. Developmental scores are discussed next, followed by outcome-referenced interpretations and scaled scores. Finally, the chapter introduces two advanced topics—scaled scores, which includes equating, forms, and levels, and unidimensional item response theory.

Basic Statistics: A Review

This section presents a brief review of basic statistical concepts used in this chapter.

DISTRIBUTIONS

There are two kinds of distributions—empirical and theoretical. An *empirical distribution* refers to an actually observed set of scores. Such a distribution is described by a table or figure showing the possible scores and the frequency with which each occurred. Table 1 describes the empirical distribution of scores on a hypothetical depression inventory taken by 76 adolescents. The first column shows that the possible scores range from 0 to 20. The second column shows how many students achieved each score.

A distribution of scores may come from either a population or sample. A *population* refers to a collection of observations, often a group of people, who share some defining characteristic. All U.S. men or all pick-up trucks represent two examples of populations. A *random* sample is a subset of the observations drawn so that all observations in the population have an equal probability of being included. In statistics, random sampling is important because methods have been developed for logically inferring properties of a population from corresponding properties of a random sample. For instance, the arithmetic average of scores in a large random sample is a good estimate of the arithmetic average in the population.

Test developers often use the test scores of a representative sample as a reference group to which a client's test performance can be compared. Such a reference group is called a *norm group* or *norm sample*. A *representative sample* is a collection of observations that is like the population in all important respects except size. The "important respects" are those variables potentially

TABLE 1. Depression Inventory Scores of 76 Adolescents

Score	Frequency
20	1
19	2
18	1
17	4
16	7
15	11
14	9
13	6
12	5
11	7
10	5
9	3
8	1
7	4
6	3
5	3
4	1
3	2
2	1
1	0
0	0

related to test scores. These can include variables such as sex, region of the country, minority group composition, and socioeconomic status. If it is known or suspected that males and females have different mean test scores, then any representative sample would have the same proportion of males and females as does the population. Likewise, if cultural minorities have a different mean than the majority, any representative sample would have the same proportion of cultural minority and majority persons as does the population. In large-scale testing, one seldom obtains data on the entire population. Rather, one estimates population values from sample data.

The *centile rank* of a raw score equals the percentage of students in the distribution whose scores fall below the raw score. In Table 1, counting up from the bottom, one can see that 30 students received a score below 12. Five received a score of 12. Since the score 12 is considered to span an interval of one unit from 11.5 to 12.5, 50 percent of those with a score of 12 are counted as being above 12.0 (i.e., somewhere between 12.0 and 12.5), and 50 percent are counted as being below 12.0 (i.e., somewhere between 11.5 and 12.0). Therefore 32.5 people are counted as having scores below 12.0 (the 30 with scores of 11 or below plus 2.5 of the people with a score of 12), so the centile rank for a score of 12.0 is 43. Forty-three percent (32.5 of 76 people) have scores below 12.0.

In contrast to an empirical distribution, a *theoretical distribution* is a mathematical curve that specifies the proportion of observations at or below each possible test score. There are many such theoretical distributions, the most famous of which is the *normal* or *Gaussian distribution* shown in Figure 1. In a strict sense, theoretical distributions are just abstract mathematical equations. However, useful theoretical distributions, like the normal, are close approximations to some real empirical distributions. If the normal curve approximates a real empirical distribution, then for every score, its centile rank in the empirical distribution is roughly the same as the centile rank of the corresponding score in a theoretical normal distribution. The empirical scores are then said to be (approximately) normally distributed.

Central Tendency

At times we wish to highlight a particular feature of a distribution rather than describe the distribution completely in graphical or tabular form. Summary statistics do just that. Any single statistic has the same advantages and disadvantages of any summary—it highlights some features of the scores to the neglect of other features. The two features most commonly summarized are the central tendency and variability of scores.

Central tendency refers to the overall level of scores. Generally, are the scores high or low? As you probably know, there are three common measures of central tendency: the mode, the median, and the mean. The *mode* is the most frequently occurring score. In Table 1, the mode equals 15, the score with the highest frequency (11).

The *median* is the point below which 50 percent of the scores fall. In Table 1, the median is 13.0. Why is the median 13.0? The total frequency in Table 1 is 76, 50 percent of which is 38. The median, then, is the point below which 38 scores fall. At or below 12 there are 35 scores. At 13 there are 6 scores. Since the score 13 spans one score unit from 12.5 to 13.5, 3 of the 6 people with scores of 13 are considered to be below 13.0 (i.e., somewhere between 12.5 and 13.0) and the other 3 are considered above 13.0 (i.e., somewhere between 13.0 and 13.5). This means that there are 38 people below 13.0, 35 with scores of 12 and below plus 3 of the six with scores of 13. Hence, the median is 13.0.

FIGURE 1. Relationship of Various Norm-referenced Scores
to Areas Under a Normal Curve

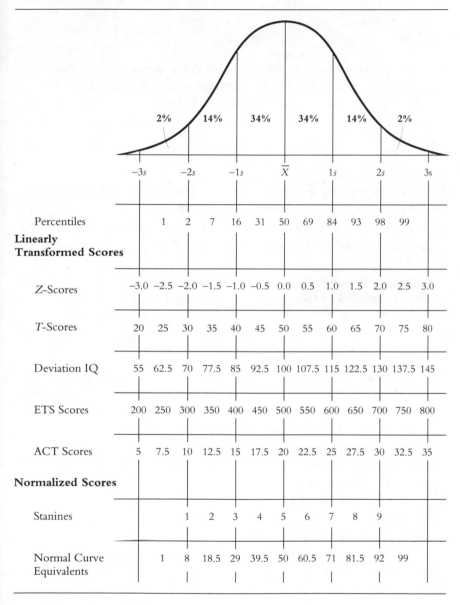

The *mean* is the arithmetic average. The symbols $\overline{X}$ and μ designate a sample and population mean, respectively. The formula for a sample mean is

$$\overline{X} = \frac{\Sigma X}{n} \tag{1}$$

where n equals the number of observations in the sample. In Equation 1, the symbol Σ is the summation sign designating that several values are to be added together. Specifically, ΣX refers to the sum of all the X scores. In Table 1, the sum of all 76 depression scores is 920, n is 76, so the mean, $\overline{X}$ equals 920/76 or 12.11.

Variability
Variability refers to the spread of scores. The higher the variability, the more widely scores differ. The simplest measure of variability is the range, the highest observed score minus the lowest observed score plus one. In Table 1, the highest and lowest observed scores are 20 and 2, so the range is 20 − 2 + 1 = 19.

In testing, the most common measures of variability are the *variance* and *standard deviation*. The sample estimate of the population variance is

$$s^2 = \frac{\Sigma(X - \overline{X})^2}{(n - 1)} \tag{2}$$

To compute a sample estimate of the population variance using Equation 2, subtract the mean $\overline{X}$ from each score, square each resulting number, add them together, and divide by the sample size minus one. For example, consider the eight reading test scores in Table 2. As shown at the bottom of the table, the mean of the eight scores equals 10. To compute their variance, first subtract the mean from each number to get the values shown in column $(X - \overline{X})$. Then square each of the resulting eight values to get the values shown in column $(X - \overline{X})^2$. Then add the values in column $(X - \overline{X})^2$ and divide by $n - 1$ to give the result shown at the bottom of column $(X - \overline{X})^2$. The result, 30.29, is the variance of the eight original scores.

Conceptually, the variance is an average, except that division is by $(n - 1)$ rather than n. That is, the variance is the average of the squared deviations about the mean—the average of the values $(X - \overline{X})^2$. Dividing by $(n - 1)$ insures that the sample value does not systematically under- or overestimate the population variance.

The *standard deviation* is the positive square root of the variance. For the eight reading test scores in Table 2, the variance is 30.29, so the standard

TABLE 2. Reading Test Scores X of Eight Fourth-grade Students

Student	X	$X - \overline{X}$	$(X - \overline{X})^2$
A	20	10	100
B	6	-4	16
C	7	-3	9
D	11	1	1
E	14	4	16
F	5	-5	25
G	13	3	9
H	4	-6	36
	$\sum = 80$		$\sum = 212$
	$\overline{X} = 10$		$s^2 = 30.29$

deviation is the positive square root of 30.29, namely $s = 5.50$. The higher the standard deviation, the more widely scores tend to deviate about the distribution's mean and, hence, the higher the variability of scores.

ESTIMATING THE POPULATION MEAN FROM SAMPLE DATA

If you were to draw two different random samples from the same population, you would probably get a different mean in each sample. Hypothetically, imagine drawing all possible random samples of size n from a population and computing the average for each sample. This process would generate a whole set of sample means, one mean for each possible random sample of size n. This set of sample means would have an arithmetic average that would equal the population mean μ for variable X. The set of all possible sample means for samples of size n would also have a standard deviation, which we call the *standard error of the mean*, $s_{\overline{x}}$.

If you draw just one random sample of size n, the appropriate estimate of the standard error of the mean is

$$s_{\overline{x}} = s\sqrt{n} \tag{3}$$

That is, one can estimate the standard error of the mean from knowledge of the standard deviation, s, and the sample size, n. In Table 2, if the eight reading scores come from a random sample of eight children in the population of fourth graders, the sample size is $n = 8$ and the standard deviation is $s = 5.50$, so the standard error of the mean is $s_{\bar{x}} = 5.50/\sqrt{8} = 1.94$. Given the sample data in Table 2, our best estimate of the population mean, μ, would be the sample mean, $\bar{X} = 10$. As an estimator of the population mean, the sample mean has a standard error of 1.94 units.[1]

If variable X is normally distributed, the standard error of the sample mean can be used to construct a confidence interval. When we draw a random sample of size n and compute the sample mean $\bar{X}$, we know that the obtained sample mean is unlikely to equal the population mean exactly. In many cases, it is useful to use the sample mean, $\bar{X}$, and the estimated standard error of the mean, $s_{\bar{x}}$, to find a range of plausible values in which the population mean probably falls. This range of plausible values for the population mean is called a confidence interval. The *95% confidence interval* is an interval constructed so that for 95 percent of the possible random samples one might draw, the population mean μ would be contained in that interval. It is estimated as the sample mean plus or minus 1.96 standard errors of the sample mean:

$$95\% CI = \bar{X} \pm 1.96 s_{\bar{x}} \tag{4}$$

For the data in Table 2, the sample mean is 10 and the standard error of the sample mean is 1.94. Therefore, the 95 percent confidence interval is $10 \pm (1.96)(1.94) = 10 \pm 3.80$. That is, the population mean is probably within 3.80 units of the sample mean 10. Therefore, the interval runs from 6.20 to 13.80. Given this data sample, numbers from 6.20 to 13.80 represent plausible values for the population mean. For the vast majority (95%) of random samples of size 8 that one could draw from this population, the sample mean is estimated to be within 3.80 [= (1.96)(1.94)] units of the population mean and, therefore, the population mean probably lies somewhere between 6.2 and 13.8.

In the two paragraphs above, the choice of 95 percent as the level of confidence was rather arbitrary. Why not 99 percent, or 90 percent, or 50 percent? In reporting results, researchers will differ in the level of confidence they require. The most commonly employed levels are 99 percent, 95 percent, 90 percent, and 68 percent. The 99 percent confidence interval is the sample mean plus or minus $2.58 s_{\bar{x}}$. Since in the vast majority of samples (99%), the population mean will be within $2.58 s_{\bar{x}}$ units of the population value, some researchers will report an interval that ranges from $\bar{X} - 2.58 s_{\bar{x}}$ to $\bar{X} + 2.58 s_{\bar{x}}$. A 90 percent confidence interval is the sample mean plus or minus $1.64 s_{\bar{x}}$. The 68 percent confidence interval is the sample mean plus or minus $s_{\bar{x}}$. As we shall see in the next section, a variation on the 68 percent confidence interval plays an important role in interpretation of test scores.

This variation of the 68 percent confidence interval is called a *score band,* discussed below.

ESTIMATING TRUE SCORES FROM A SAMPLE OF BEHAVIOR

Although more thorough discussions of reliability are found elsewhere (e.g., Hammer, this volume), it is worth noting that some reliability concepts are simple extensions of concepts, the mean and standard error of the mean, discussed in previous paragraphs.

In statistics the researcher often wants to estimate a population mean using a sample of observations. In testing, the examiner wants to estimate a client's true score from a sample of the client's behavior. The true score is, in fact, defined as a mean: the average score a client would obtain over repeated testings.

In statistics, the researcher knows that the sample mean is only an estimate of the population mean. Likewise, in testing, the examiner knows that the client's test score is merely an estimate of the client's true score. Just as a sample mean is unlikely to equal the population mean exactly, a client's test score is unlikely to equal the true score exactly.

In statistics, the standard error of the mean reflects the precision with which the population mean can be estimated from a sample mean. In testing, the standard error of measurement reflects the precision with which a client's true score can be estimated from the sample of behavior contained in a test.

In statistics, a sample mean and the standard error of the sample mean can be used to construct a confidence interval. This confidence interval is a plausible range of scores in which the population mean probably lies. In testing, the client's test score and the standard error of measurement, s_m, can be used to construct a confidence interval. This interval is an interval in which the client's true score probably lies.

In testing, a confidence interval for the client's true score is often called a *score band.* The 68 percent confidence interval is very common, but 68 percent is arbitrary and not the universal confidence level. It is equal to the client's test score plus or minus the standard error of measurement. Thus, a client with a score of 47 on a test with a standard error of measurement of 1.5 would have a score band of 45.5 to 48.5. This represents a range of plausible values for the client's true score. Unless otherwise specified, assume that a score band is a 68 percent confidence interval. That is, it is a band constructed so that 68 percent of the clients will have true scores within the score band calculated from their test score and the test's standard error of measurement.

While most score bands are 68 percent confidence intervals, some people may prefer other levels of confidence. A 99 percent confidence band for the true score can be obtained by taking the client's test score plus or minus $2.58s_m$. A 95 percent confidence interval can be constructed by taking the client's test score plus or minus $1.96s_m$. A 90 percent confidence interval can be constructed by taking the client's test score plus or minus $1.64s_m$. Implicit in any statement about the confidence level of any score band (68%, 90%, 95%, or 99%) is an assumption that the errors of measurement are normally distributed.

CORRELATION AND PREDICTION

So far, we have talked only about summarizing a feature of one distribution of scores, X. In statistics we frequently want to summarize the association between two sets of scores, X and Y. The *Pearson product-moment correlation coefficient*, r_{xy}, is an index of the strength and direction of association between two variables.

Correlation

The correlation coefficient, r_{xy}, ranges between -1.00 and $+1.00$. The sign of the correlation coefficient indicates the direction of the association. That is, if the sign is positive, people with higher scores on test X tend to be the ones who have higher scores on test Y and vice versa; there is a positive association between tests X and Y. If the sign of the correlation coefficient is negative, people with higher scores on test X tend to have *lower* scores on test Y and vice versa; there is a negative association between X and Y. If the correlation coefficient is zero, there is no consistent positive or negative association.

Table 3 shows three pairs of variables X and Y. In the left portion of Table 3, Y is the number of hours per day each child spends watching TV and X is his or her score on a mathematics anxiety scale. As you can see, there is a positive association between X and Y: $r_{xy} = .62$. Higher anxiety scores tend to co-occur with more extensive TV watching. In the middle panel of Table 3, Y is the number of hours per day spent on mathematics homework and X is the same mathematics anxiety score. There is a negative association between X and Y here: $r_{xy} = -.48$. Lower anxiety scores tend to co-occur with more homework and vice versa. The right panel illustrates little or no relationship. High anxiety scores tend to co-occur with high, medium, and low amounts of music practice per day: $r_{xy} = .05$.

The absolute value of a correlation coefficient indicates the strength of the relationship. Values near zero indicate no relationship, whereas values near

TABLE 3. A Comparison of Math Anxiety With Hours of TV, Hours of Homework, and Hours of Music Practice of Junior High Students

Student	(X) Math Anxiety	(Y) Hours of TV	(X) Math Anxiety	(Y) Hours of Homework	(X) Math Anxiety	(Y) Hours of Music Practice
1	72	1.00	72	.25	72	0.50
2	65	1.00	65	.00	65	1.00
3	64	.50	64	.20	64	0.25
4	58	.50	58	.00	58	0.50
5	57	.50	57	.25	57	0.00
6	51	.75	51	.00	51	0.50
7	43	.75	43	.25	43	1.00
8	40	.25	40	.25	40	1.00
9	37	.50	37	.00	37	0.00
10	33	.30	33	.50	33	0.25
11	30	.55	30	.50	30	0.50
$\overline{X}$	50.00	.60	50.00	0.20	50.00	0.50
s	14.23	.25	14.23	0.19	14.23	0.37
	$r = .62$		$r = -.48$		$r = .05$	

1.00 or −1.00 indicate a very strong relationship. Correlation coefficients of .50 and −.50 would indicate relationships of equal strength but opposite direction. As you can see from examining the three correlations in Table 3, the mathematics anxiety scores are most strongly associated with number of homework hours ($r_{xy} = .62$). They are least strongly related to hours of musical practice ($r_{xy} = .05$). In strength, the association with watching TV ($r_{xy} = .48$) is stronger than the relationship to musical practice but weaker than the relationship to homework.

Table 4 illustrates computation of the correlation coefficient. Expressed as a function of means and standard deviations, the formula for the correlation coefficient is as follows:

$$r_{xy} = \frac{\Sigma(X - \overline{X})(Y - \overline{Y})}{(n - 1)s_x s_y} \tag{5}$$

where $\overline{X}$, $\overline{Y}$, s_x, and s_y are the means and standard deviations of variables X and Y. Table 4 shows the data for the math anxiety and hours of homework scores

TABLE 4. Calculation of a Correlation Coefficient Using
Math Anxiety and Hours of TV Collected From Junior High Students

Student	Math Anxiety (X)	Hours of TV (Y)	$(X-\overline{X})$	$(X-\overline{X})^2$	$(Y-\overline{Y})$	$(Y-\overline{Y})^2$	$(X-\overline{X})(Y-\overline{Y})$
1	72	1.00	22	484	.40	.16	8.80
2	65	1.00	15	225	.40	.16	6.00
3	64	.50	14	196	−.10	.01	−1.40
4	58	.50	8	64	−.10	.01	−0.80
5	57	.50	7	49	−.10	.01	−0.70
6	51	.75	1	1	.15	.02	0.15
7	43	.75	− 7	49	.15	.02	−1.05
8	40	.25	−10	100	−.35	.12	3.50
9	37	.50	−13	169	−.10	.10	1.30
10	33	.30	−17	289	−.30	.09	5.10
11	30	.55	−20	400	−.05	.00	1.00

$$\overline{X} = 50.00 \quad \overline{Y} = 0.60 \qquad \Sigma = 2026.00 \qquad \Sigma = .62 \quad \Sigma = 21.90$$
$$s = 14.23 \quad s = 0.25 \qquad s^2 = 202.60 \qquad s^2 = .06$$

from Table 3. To compute the correlation between X and Y, first one must compute the mean and standard deviation of both variables, the steps for which are shown in columns 2 through 7 of Table 4. Then for each observation, one must compute a product $(X-\overline{X})(Y-\overline{Y})$ as shown in column 8. The sum of the values in column 8 is the numerator of the value in Equation 6. To compute the correlation, one must substitute the sum of column 8, the sample size n, and the standard deviations into Equation 6:

$$r_{xy} = \frac{\Sigma(X - \overline{X})(Y - \overline{Y})}{(n - 1)s_x s_y} = \frac{21.90}{(10)(14.23)(.25)} = .62 \qquad (6)$$

Plotting Relationships

Relationships between variables can be represented as in Figures 2 through 6, which show the number of people who obtained each combination of X and Y scores in a hypothetical sample. Plots showing values of Y on the vertical axis and values of X on the horizontal axis are said to portray the *regression of Y on X*. For instance, the lowest cell in Figure 2 shows that one person received a score of 15 on measure X and a score of 2.0 on Y. Two people received a score of 20 on X and a score of 2.6 on Y. Figure 2 depicts a strong positive relationship for which r_{xy} = .89. An equally strong negative relationship is depicted in Figure 3, r_{xy} = −.89. In Figure 4 there is no relationship and r_{xy} = 0. Figure 5 depicts a moderate, positive relationship, for which r_{xy} = .48. A weak, negative relationship is shown in Figure 6, r_{xy} = −.30. In research on testing, modest relationships like those in Figures 5 and 6 are more commonly encountered than strong relationships like those in Figures 2 and 3.

Prediction

When there is a nonzero correlation between X and Y, either of the two measures can be used to predict the other. For our purposes, let's discuss the prediction of Y from variable X. In that case, X is said to be the *predictor* test and Y the *criterion* measure. To predict Y from X, one must first use data to establish what the function relating X to Y has been in the past. That is, one must draw a random or representative sample of observations for which data on both X and Y are available. Once we have used data to establish the relationship between X and Y, then for any subsequent observation for which predictor test data are available we can predict performance on Y, albeit with possibly imperfect accuracy.

In trying to establish the function relating X to Y, we might begin by plotting the data from our sample, as in Figure 7. Look at the observations for which $X = 20$. There are 11 such observations. Of the people with X scores of 20, 3 had Y scores of 2.5, 5 had Y scores of 2.6, and 3 had Y scores of 2.7. The mean of these 11 Y scores is 2.6. In other words, for people with a score of 20 on X, the average Y score was 2.6. Given this relationship in our data, it seems reasonable to predict that people who have X scores of 20 will achieve Y scores of approximately 2.6.

In general, for any value of X, the predicted Y score, Y', would be the average Y score of people with the given value of X. As discussed above, for $X = 20$, $Y' = 2.6$ because in our data the average Y score is 2.6 for people with an X score of 20. Or as another example, for people with scores of $X = 25$, the average of their Y scores is 3.1. So, for anyone with a predictor test score of 25, the predicted criterion score would be $Y' = 3.1$. By computing the average Y score, for each value of X, we could generate a table of values showing the predicted Y value for persons with every possible score on X, as shown in Table 5. And, if the relationship found in our data continued, then from someone's score on X (someone outside the sample displayed in Figure 7) we could predict their score on Y. The prediction would be imperfect because our prediction would be the average Y score for people in our sample with the given X score, and that average does not characterize every individual with the given X score.

FIGURE 2. Variable X Plotted Against Variable Y for a Sample in Which There Is a Strong Positive Relationship

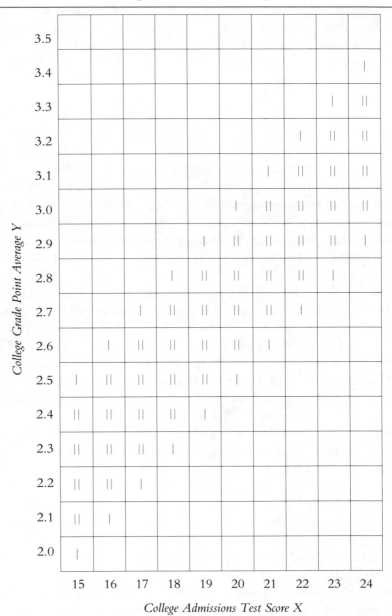

FIGURE 3. Variable *X* Plotted Against Variable *Y* for a Sample in Which There Is a Strong Negative Relationship

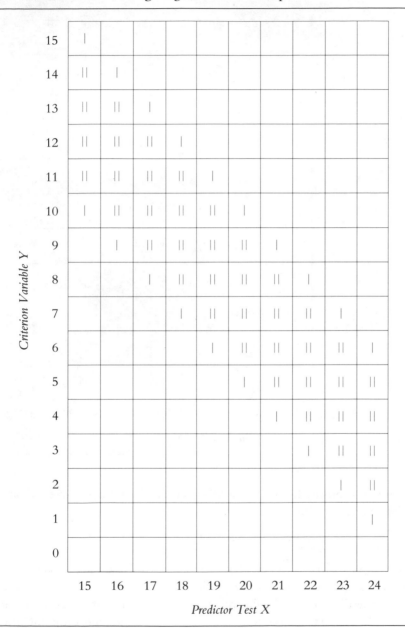

FIGURE 4. Variable X Plotted Against Variable Y for a Sample in Which There Is No Relationship

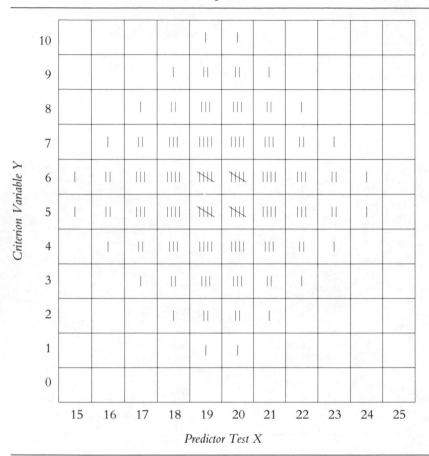

If the relationship between X and Y is linear, then the predicted Y values can be generated statistically. That is,

$$Y' = bX + a \qquad (7)$$

Here $b = r_{xy} s_y / s_x$ and $a = \overline{Y} - b\overline{X}$. That is, Y' can be expressed as a linear function of X. In that linear function, b is called the regression weight on the predictor, and it equals the slope of the line relating X and Y. The intercept of that line is a. Graphically, a is the point on the Y axis where the regression line intersects that axis; algebraically, it is the value of Y' when X equals zero. The slope

FIGURE 5. Variable *X* Plotted Against Variable *Y* for a Sample
In Which There Is a Moderate Positive Relationship

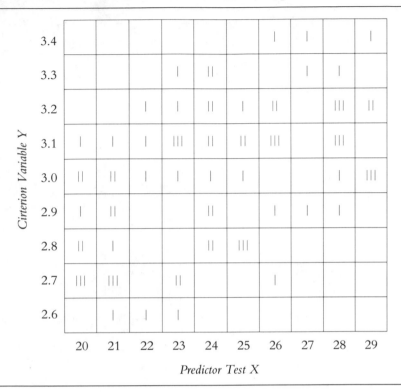

is a direct function of the correlation between *X* and *Y* as well as the standard deviations of the two variables: $b = r_{xy}s_y/s_x$. The intercept is a direct function of *b* and the means $\overline{X}$ and $\overline{Y}$: $a = \overline{Y} - b\overline{X}$.

In Figure 7, the correlation between *X* and *Y*, r_{xy}, equals .97 and the standard deviations are $s_x = 2.89$ and $s_y = .30$. Inserting these numbers into the formula for *b* yields $b = r_{xy}s_y/s_x = (.97)(.30)/2.89 = .10$. The means of *X* and *Y* are 24.50 and 3.05. Inserting these values into the formula for *a* yields $a = \overline{Y} - b\overline{X} = 3.05 - (.10)(24.50) = .60$. Thus, we arrive at the result that $Y' = bX + a = .10X + .60$. Notice that for $X = 20$, $Y' = .10X + .60 = (.10)(20) + .60 = 2.6$, which is the average of the *Y* values for people with *X* scores of 20 as shown in Table 5. Indeed, if you insert any *X* value into the formula $Y' = .10X + .60$, the result will be the *Y'* value in Table 5.

FIGURE 6. Variable X Plotted Against Variable Y for a Sample in Which There Is a Weak Negative Relationship

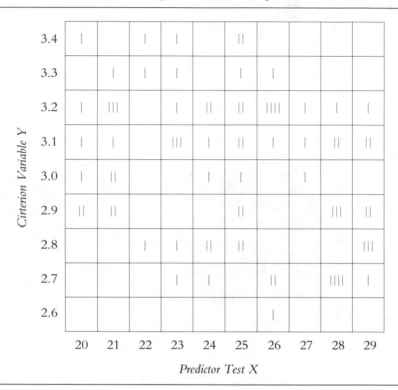

When the regression of Y on X is linear, the correlation between X and Y, their means, and their standard deviations can be estimated from a sample of data and used to estimate the slope and regression constants in the regression formula $Y' = bX + a$. The resulting regression equation can be used to generate predicted Y values for every predictor score X. Having empirically established the relationship between X and Y in the sample of data, then for any subsequent observation for which data on X is available, one can make a prediction about their score on Y.

For instance, in Table 5, X is a score on a hypothetical college admissions test and Y is the student's college GPA. Using data from some prior students, imagine that we have established the relationship shown in Table 5. A current college senior has taken the exam and has obtained a score of 25. Based on the test score, would we expect this student to do well? The predicted Y score

FIGURE 7. Hypothetical College Admissions Test Scores Plotted Against College Grade Point Averages

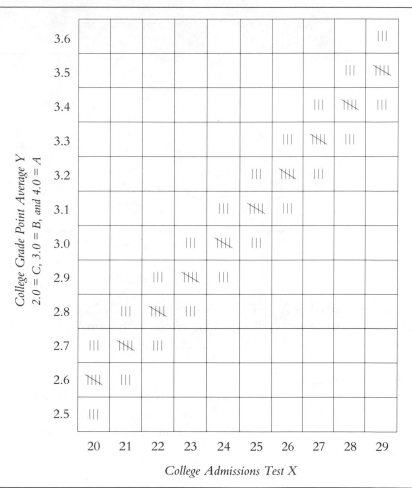

College Admissions Test X

would be 3.1. That is, in our experience (meaning our sample of data), students with test scores of 25 averaged a GPA of 3.1—about a B average.

The squared correlation coefficient, r_{xy}^2, equals the proportion of variance in Y that can be predicted from X. In the example of Figure 7, the correlation between X and Y equals .97, indicating that 94 percent $[(.97)^2 = .94]$ of the variance in Y can be predicted from X. Conversely, 6 percent of the variance

TABLE 5. Predicted Criterion Score, Y',
for Each Possible Predictor Test Score

Predictor Test Score X	Predicted Criterion Score Y'
20	2.6
21	2.7
22	2.8
23	2.9
24	3.0
25	3.1
26	3.2
27	3.3
28	3.4
29	3.5

in Y is unexplained by X. In Figure 5, $r_{xy} = .48$; so only 23 percent $[(.48)^2 = .23]$ of the variance in Y can be predicted from $X;$ the remaining 77 percent of the variance cannot be explained by X.

Standard Error of Estimate
In the example of Figure 7, our predictions would not be accurate for every student. That is, the predicted Y value is the average for students with a given X score, and not every student with the given X score achieves the average value.

How can we characterize the accuracy of our predictions? One way is to use the *standard error of estimate*, s_e, the standard deviation of Y scores for a given X score. Again, in Figure 7, note that there are 11 people with an X score of 20. Three have Y values of 2.5, five have Y values of 2.6, and three have Y values of 2.7. The standard deviation of these 11 Y values {2.5, 2.5, 2.5, 2.6, 2.6, 2.6, 2.6, 2.6, 2.7, 2.7, 2.7} is .08. That is, .08 is the standard deviation of actual Y scores about their average for the given value of $X = 20$.

The standard error of estimate is used as an index of predictive accuracy. If s_e equals 0, then everyone with the same X score has the same Y score, and we can predict Y perfectly from X. Larger values of s_e indicate that even for people with the same X scores, the Y scores vary widely. Consequently, we cannot predict Y very accurately from knowledge of X.

If for every value of X in Figure 7 you were to calculate the standard deviation of Y scores about their mean, you would find that the standard error of estimate, s_e, equals .08 for every value of X. These scores are said to be homoscedastic. *Homoscedasticity* means that the standard error of estimate is the same for every value of X. *Heteroscedasticity* means that the standard error of estimate varies across values of X. Figures 5 and 6 depict heteroscedastic relationships.

If scores are homoscedastic and the relationship between X and Y is linear, then the s_e is the same for all values of X, and it can be estimated from knowledge of the correlation between X and Y and the standard deviation of Y: In sufficiently large samples, $s_e = s_y \sqrt{1 - r^2_{xy}}$. In Figure 7, we found that the correlation between X and Y is .97 and the standard deviation of Y was .30. Inserting these into the formula yields $s_e = s_y \sqrt{1 - r_{xy}^2} = .30 \sqrt{1 - .97^2}$ = .08, the same value we obtained by computing the standard deviation of the Y scores for people with X scores of 20.

When the scores are heteroscedastic (and perfect homoscedasticity is rare), the formula $s_e = s_y \sqrt{1 - r_{xy}^2}$ provides a composite estimate of the standard error. In practice, the standard error of estimate is calculated from the standard deviation of the criterion variable, s_y, and the correlation, r_{xy}, using the formula $s_e = s_y \sqrt{1 - r_{xy}^2}$. This formula uses the data from all observations in the sample to yield an aggregate index of the accuracy with which Y can be predicted from X.

As can be seen from the formula $s_e = s_y \sqrt{1 - r^2_{xy}}$, for a fixed value of s_y, the standard error of estimate will decrease as the correlation between X and Y increases. The higher the correlation between X and Y, the more accurately Y can be predicted from X.

Before moving on, it is worth noting that the correlation coefficient r_{xy} and the standard error of estimate are closely related to two reliability concepts —the reliability coefficient, $r_{xx'}$, and the standard error of measurement. Since the reliability of a test equals the correlation of a test X with an alternate form of itself, X', reliability is usually written as the correlation between X and X'. The standard error of estimate, s_e, indicates the error in predicting Y from X. Correspondingly, the standard error of measurement, s_m, indicates the error in predicting a client's true score from her or his observed test score. Just as the standard error of estimate, s_e, depends on the correlation coefficient, r_{xy}, the standard error of measurement, s_m, depends on reliability, $r_{xx'}$.

Confidence Interval for Y

The standard error of estimate can be used to calculate a confidence interval about a predicted score. The 68 percent confidence interval is $Y' \pm s_e$; the 95 percent confidence interval is $Y' \pm 1.96s_e$, the 99 percent confidence interval is $Y' \pm 2.58s_e$, and so forth. Using the data in Figure 7, we estimated the regression equation to be $Y' = .10X + .60$. For anyone with a predictor score, X, that equals 25, the regression equation would yield a predicted value, Y', of 3.1. Since the standard error of estimate is .08, the 68 percent confidence interval would be $Y' \pm s_e$, which is the interval 3.02 to 3.18. The 95 percent confidence interval would be $Y' \pm 1.96s_e$, which is the interval 2.94 to 3.26; and the 99 percent confidence interval would be $Y' \pm 2.58s_e$, which is the interval 2.89 to 3.31. Each of these intervals is a range of plausible values for the client's college achievement, given our information about his or her test score. The higher the confidence level, the wider the interval, and the more likely that the client's actual achievement will fall in the interval. Implicit in any statement about the confidence level (68%, 95%, or 99%) is an assumption that the errors of estimate are normally distributed.

Multiple Regression

Equation 7 uses a single predictor variable, X, to predict the criterion variable Y. When more than one predictor variable is used, the regression is called a *multiple regression* and the coefficient is called the *multiple correlation coefficient, R*. With more than one predictor—say three predictors—Equation 7 becomes

$$Y' = b_1X_1 + b_2X_2 + b_3X_3 + a \tag{8}$$

where Y' is the predicted criterion score for a client with scores X_1, X_2, and X_3 on the predictor variables, a is the intercept constant as before, and b_1, b_2, and b_3 are regression weights on the three predictors. R is the correlation between the criterion variable Y and an optimally weighted linear combination of the several predictor variables. R^2 is the proportion of variance in Y that can be predicted from the several predictor variables. In sufficiently large samples, the standard error of estimate is $s_e = s_y\sqrt{1-R^2_{xy}}$.

SUMMARY

Statistics involve distributions of scores. An empirical distribution can be described by listing the scores and the frequency with which each occurred in some sample or population. The mean, median, and mode can be used to describe the overall level or central tendency of scores in a distribution. Measures of variability such as the range, variance, or standard deviation are used to summarize the spread of scores. The standard error of the mean is the standard deviation of the sample mean $\overline{X}$ for all possible samples of size n. It is used to construct confidence intervals for the population mean μ. In reliability theory, the concepts of true score, standard error of measurement, and score bands are extensions of the corresponding statistical concepts population mean, standard error of the sample mean, and confidence .intervals.

The Pearson correlation coefficient indexes the direction and strength of association between two variables. The strength and direction of association between two variables can be displayed as in Figures 2 through 7. If the relationship between two variables is linear, then predicted criterion scores can be expressed as a linear function of predictor test scores. The slope and intercept constants can be calculated from sample estimates of means, standard deviations, and the correlation for the two variables. The standard error of estimate indicates how widely actual criterion scores vary around their predicted values. Using a client's predicted criterion score, Y', and the standard error of estimate, a confidence interval for a client's actual score on the criterion variable can be computed. When more than one predictor variable is used to predict the criterion, the regression is called a *multiple regression* and the correlation coefficient is called a *multiple correlation coefficient*.

Types of Test Scores

RAW SCORES

Raw scores on tests can be computed from client responses in many ways. Since raw test scores are usually derived by adding the client's scores on each item, this section will begin by discussing test item scores. For scoring purposes, test items can be divided into dichotomous and polychotomous types. A *dichotomous* item is one on which a client can receive one of only two possible scores. The two scores may be any two numbers. Usually, however, one of the two scores is assigned a point value of 1 and the other is assigned a point value of 0. A *polychotomous* item is one on which there are two or more possible scores.

Dichotomous Items
One type of dichotomous item is called a *right/wrong scored* item because the response is scored either right or wrong. In assigning points, a correct response often receives 1 point and an incorrect response receives 0 points. If the examiner assigns points as just described and adds the number of points the client received for each item, the total will equal the number of items the

client answered correctly. Such raw scores are sometimes called *number correct* scores to differentiate them from other types of scores.

For some dichotomous items, there are no correct or incorrect answers. As an example, a test assessing introversion/extroversion might ask, "Do you enjoy loud parties?" If the client is forced to choose between two possible answers "Yes" or "No," the item is a dichotomous item, but there is no correct answer. How this item is scored will depend on how the test author has defined a high score: Does a high score mean high on extraversion? Or does a high score mean high on introversion? If the test author wants a high score to mean high on extraversion, then 1 point would be given to the extroverted response, "Yes," and 0 points to the introverted response,"No." On the other hand, if the author has defined a high score to mean high on introversion, then 1 point would be assigned to the introverted response, "No," and 0 points to the extroverted response, "Yes."

On tests containing dichotomous items with no correct or incorrect answer, the test author often must define the meaning of a high score and the test user must be aware of this definition. Scores are assigned to items so that 1 point is given to the *positive response,* the response characteristic of people at the defined high end of the attribute being measured, and 0 points are given to the *negative response,* the response characteristic of people at the defined low end of the attribute being measured. This means that from one question to the next the same response will sometimes receive 1 point and sometimes 0. For instance, on our extraversion/introversion test, if a high score means high on extraversion, then for the question, "Do you like loud parties?" the answer "Yes" would be the positive response indicative of extraversion. "Yes" would receive 1 point. But for the item "Do you like to read a good book on weekends?" the answer "No" would be the positive response indicative of extraversion. On this item "No" would receive 1 point and "Yes" would receive 0 points.

As with dichotomous right/wrong scored items, the raw score on the test is usually the sum of item scores. That is, the raw score would be the number of items on which the client had given the positive response.

Polychotomous Items

A *polychotomous item* is one for which there are two or more possible scores. For instance, on an individually administered intelligence test, a question might ask "What does this expression mean? 'A penny saved is a penny earned.'" Depending on the quality of the client's explanation, the examiner might assign 3, 2, 1, or 0 points to the response. Since the client might earn any one of several possible point values, the item is a polychotomous item.

On a typical performance test, such as a test of introversion/extroversion, a polychotomous item might state, "I like loud parties." To answer the item, the client would need to choose one of four possible responses: "Very true of me," "True of me," "Somewhat true of me," or "Not at all true of me." The client might receive 1 point for responding "Not at all true of me," 2 points for "Somewhat true of me," 3 points for "True of me," and 4 points for "Very true of me."

If the test has no right or wrong answers, the test author may need to define the high score. Does a high score mean high on introversion? Or does it mean high on extroversion? On a given item, the largest number of points is given to the answer most indicative of people at the defined high end of the attribute being measured. The smallest number of points is given to the answer indicative of people at the defined low end of the attribute being measured. This means that from one question to the next the same answer will receive a different number of points. Again, imagine a test of extraversion/introversion that assigns from 1 to 4 points to a client answer and that forces the client to choose one of four possible answers to each item: "Very true of me," "True of me," "Somewhat true of me," or "Not at all true of me." The test author wants high scores to designate high levels of extraversion. To an item that read "I like loud parties," the answer "Very true of me" would receive 4 points because it is the most extroverted answer; the "Not at all true of me" answer would receive 1 point because it is the introverted answer. On the other hand, to an item that read "I like to read a good book on weekends," the 4-point answer would be "Not at all true of me" because this is the most extroverted response; "Very true of me" would receive only 1 point because it is the most introverted response.

How are raw test scores derived from item scores? Most commonly, the raw score is simply the sum of the client's separate item scores.

PERCENTILE SCORES AND PERCENTILE BANDS

As discussed at the beginning of this chapter, raw scores usually have little meaning in and of themselves. Therefore, they must be compared to some frame of reference, and other types of scores are often useful in such comparisons. For instance, the raw score can be converted to a percentile score.

Percentile Scores
A client's *percentile score* is the percentage of people in some norm group with raw scores equal to or less than that of the client. For instance, if a client's raw

TABLE 6. Depression Inventory Scores of Adolescents Expressed as Percentiles, z-scores, T-scores, Deviation IQ Scores, ACT Scores, Stanines, Normalized T-scores and Normal Curve Equivalents

Raw Scores	Percentiles	z-scores	T-scores	Deviation IQ	ACT Scores	Stanine	Normalized T-scores	NCE
20	99	2.0	70	129	30	9	80	99
19	97	1.7	67	126	29	9	80	90
18	95	1.5	65	122	27	8	69	85
17	92	1.2	62	118	26	8	68	80
16	85	1.0	60	115	25	7	63	72
15	73	0.7	57	111	24	6	59	63
14	60	0.5	55	107	22	5	54	55
13	50	0.2	52	104	21	5	51	50
12	43	0.0	50	100	20	5	49	46
11	35	−0.2	48	96	19	4	48	42
10	27	−0.5	45	93	18	4	45	37
9	22	−0.7	43	89	16	3	43	34
8	19	−1.0	40	85	15	3	42	31
7	16	−1.2	38	82	14	3	41	29
6	11	−1.5	35	78	13	2	39	24
5	7	−1.7	33	74	11	2	37	19
4	5	−2.0	30	71	10	2	34	15
3	3	−2.2	28	67	9	1	32	10
2	1	−2.5	26	63	8	1	28	1
1	1	−2.7	23	60	7	1	20	1
0	1	−2.9	21	56	5	1	20	1

score is 43 and percentile score is 75, this means that 75 percent of the norm group had a raw score of 43 or below.

In practice, percentile scores are not actually computed from a client's raw score, but rather they are compared to values that have been computed and prepared in a table by the test author. Table 6 contains an example of such a score conversion chart. For each possible raw score on the test, Table 6 shows the corresponding percentile score. Once the client's raw score is computed, the percentile score is obtained by looking it up in the appropriate conversion chart. For instance, Table 6 shows that a client with a raw score of 15 should receive a percentile score of 73. A client with a raw score of 7 should receive a percentile score of 16. Even where computer scoring is used, the computer takes the client's raw score and finds the corresponding percentile score in a conversion chart stored in the computer's memory.

Percentile Bands

Converting to a percentile score can aid interpretation of a raw score. The standard error of measurement can also help. As discussed above, the raw test score is merely an estimate of the client's true score. The score band around the test score gives a range of plausible values for the true score.

In many tests the score report includes percentile bands rather than raw score bands. To understand what a percentile band is, imagine that a person gets a raw score of 47 on a test with a standard error of measurement equal to 1.5. Then the client's raw score band ranges from 45.5 to 48.5 (i.e., 47 ± 1.5). To convert this raw score band to a percentile band, one must find the percentile score corresponding to raw score 45.5 (say, 71%) and the percentile score corresponding to raw score 48.5 (say, 82%). The client's percentile band would range from 71 to 82. That is, if the client's true score lies between 45.5 and 48.5, then between 71 percent and 82 percent of the norm group have scores that fall below the client's true score.

Figure 8 shows how such percentile bands are often reported. Note the black bar graph in the middle of the figure. These bars represent percentile bands. For the Vocabulary test, the top bar, the band stretches from 70 to 95. From knowledge of the client's raw score and the test's standard error of measurement, it is estimated that the client equals or exceeds 70 percent to 90 percent of the norm group.

Percentile bands such as those in Figure 8 are sometimes used in comparing a client's performance on two or more scales in the same test. Where the percentile bands for two tests heavily overlap, the range of percentile scores is much the same for the two scales, and there is little justification for saying the client ranks higher in one area. If the percentile bands have no overlap, then the range of plausible values is somewhat different, and it is possible that the client ranks higher in one of the two areas. For instance, in Figure 8, the client's percentile bands in Vocabulary and Reading Comprehension do not overlap, and, therefore, the difference in the client's Vocabulary percentile and Reading Comprehension percentile is worth noting. On the other hand, the client's percentile band for Number Operation heavily overlaps the band for Problem Solving, so there is little reason to believe that his rankings are different in these two mathematics areas.

FIGURE 8. Individual Report Form From the Adult Basic Learning Examination

ADULT BASIC LEARNING EXAMINATION (ABLE)   INDIVIDUAL REPORT

INSTRUCTOR : MR COHEN	LEVEL : 2	FOR
PROGRAM : ROCKDALE COMMUNITY	FORM : E	
NORMS : COMBINED	DATE : 10/07/89	MIKE HANLON

TESTS	NP	RS	SS	NCE	PR-S	GE	LEGEND
VOCABULARY	32	25	691	71.8	85-7	10.0	NP Number Possible
							RS Raw Score
READING COMPREHENSION	48	37	676	52.1	54-5	8.5	SS Scaled Score
							NCE Normal Curve
SPELLING	30	25	670	55.3	60-6	6.8	Equivalent
							PR Percentile Rank
LANGUAGE	30	26	683	62.3	72-6	9.0	S Stanine
							GE Grade Equivalent
TOTAL LANGUAGE	60	51	674	58.7	66-6	7.4	DNA Did Not Attempt
							* Indicates RS is
NUMBER OPERATIONS	36	24	675	55.9	61-6	7.5	below COMBINED
							nat'l mean on
PROBLEM SOLVING	30	18	684	57.0	63-6	8.5	TEST/SKILL.
TOTAL MATHEMATICS	66	42	677	57.5	64-6	7.9	

PR BANDS	1	5	10	20	30	40	50	60	70	80	90	95	99

VOCABULARY
READING COMPREHENSION

SPELLING
LANGUAGE
TOTAL LANGUAGE

NUMBER OPERATIONS
PROBLEM SOLVING
TOTAL MATHEMATICS

TEST/SKILL CLUSTER	NP	RS	TEST/SKILL CLUSTER	NP	RS
VOCABULARY	32	25	NUMBER OPERATIONS	36	24
			Concepts of Numbers	7	5
READING COMPREHENSION	48	37	Computation	29	19
Functional Reading	24	23			
Educational Reading	24	14 *	PROBLEM SOLVING	30	18
Literal Comprehension	24	17 *	Determining an Outcome	14	5 *
Inferential Comprehension	24	20	Recording and Retrieving	4	4
			Geometric Concepts	4	1 *
SPELLING	30	25	Measuring	8	8
Sight Words	6	6			
Structural Principles	12	10			
Phonetic Principles	12	9			
LANGUAGE	30	26			
Punctuation	11	9			
Capitalization	7	6			
Applied Grammar	12	11			

Norm-Referenced Scores and Interpretations

The percentile score is the most widely known norm-referenced score, but there are others. A *norm-referenced score* implicitly compares the client's raw score to the raw scores of people in a specified norm group. Such scores fall into two major categories: linearly transformed scores and normalized scores.

Linearly Transformed Scores

There is a class of norm-referenced scores called *linearly transformed scores* because they can be expressed as linear functions of the raw score. Linearly transformed scores are normally distributed in the norm group *if and only if* the raw scores are normally distributed in the norm group.

Z-SCORES. One example of a linearly transformed score is the z-score or standardized score. Z-scores are computed so that they have a mean of 0.0 and variance of 1.00 in a specified group, which in testing is often a norm sample. To compute a z-score, one must know the client's raw score as well as the mean $\overline{X}$ and standard deviation s of raw scores in the norm sample:

$$z = (X - \overline{X})/s$$

The z-score indicates in standard deviation units how far the client's raw score lies above or below the norm group mean. A negative z-score indicates that the raw score falls below the norm group average; a positive z-score indicates that the raw score falls above the norm group average.

The raw scores, and hence the z-scores, on a test need not be normally distributed. If they are, however, one can use the z to approximate a client's percentile rank using information such as that in Figure 1. Figure 1 shows the percentile rank corresponding to selected z-scores. For instance, it shows that someone whose raw score lies one standard deviation above the mean (i.e., someone with a z-score of 1.00) has a percentile score of 84. Someone whose raw score lies 1.2 standard deviations below the mean (i.e., a z-score of −1.2) has a percentile score between 7 and 16.

No matter how the raw scores are distributed in the norm group, the sign of a z-score indicates whether the client's raw score was above or below the norm group average. The absolute value of the z-score indicates how far above or below. If and only if the raw scores are normally distributed, the interpretation of the z-score can be extended to include approximation of the client's percentile score.

While z-scores have the advantage that they place the client relative to the mean of a reference group, z-scores have a number of disadvantages. Most importantly, some z-scores are negative, and clients readily misinterpret negative scores. Consequently, other linearly transformed scores have been devised to avoid negative scores.

T-SCORES. One such score is the T-score, which has a mean of 50 and a standard deviation of 10. A client's T-score is related to his or her z-score as follows:

$$T = 10z + 50$$

One can quickly discern whether the client's raw score is above or below average by noting whether the associated T-score is above or below 50. Further, one can tell how far the raw score is above or below average by discerning how far the T-score is above or below 50.

If raw scores are normally distributed in the norm group, one can approximate a client's percentile score using Figure 1. A client with a T-score of 60, which is one standard deviation above the mean, has a percentile score of 84. A client with a T-score of 38, 1.2 standard deviations below the mean, has a percentile score between 7 and 16.

Figure 9 shows a client report for the *Strong Interest Inventory* (SII), which uses T-scores (called "Standard Scores" in the report form shown in Figure 9). Note in the right-hand panel that the two scores for each occupation are T-scores, which place the client's raw score with respect to samples of females and males in the specified occupation. On the Bus Driver scale, for instance, the client's T-score, 24, puts him well below average as compared to the sample of male bus drivers. The second T-score, 28, indicates his raw score was well below the average for female bus drivers.[2]

DEVIATION IQ SCORES. The deviation IQ Score (*DIQ*) is another score that is similar to z but avoids negative numbers. *DIQ*'s have a mean of 100 and a standard deviation of approximately 15 in the norm group to which they refer. They are related to z-scores as follows:

$$DIQ = 15z + 100$$

By noting whether a client's *DIQ* is above or below 100, one can quickly discern whether the raw score was above or below average with respect to the norm group. How far above or below 100 indicates how far the raw score differed from average. If the raw scores are normally distributed, Figure 1 can be used to approximate the client's percentile score.

FIGURE 9. *Strong Interest Inventory* Profile Report

STRONG INTEREST INVENTORY OF THE
STRONG VOCATIONAL INTEREST BLANKS

PAGE 1

PROFILE REPORT FOR: STEVE
DATE TESTED: 08/25/91

ID:
AGE: 34   SEX: M
DATE SCORED: 8/26/91

SPECIAL SCALES: ACADEMIC COMFORT 65
INTROVERSION-EXTROVERSION 41

TOTAL RESPONSES: 325   INFREQUENT RESPONSES: 8

GOT		
R	Average	
I	Average	
A	Average	
S	Average	
E	Mod. Low	
C	Average	

OCCUPATIONAL SCALES

STANDARD SCORES

			F	M	VERY DISSIMILAR	DISSIMILAR	MODERATELY DISSIMILAR	MID-RANGE	MODERATELY SIMILAR	SIMILAR	VERY SIMILAR

REALISTIC

F M

GENERAL OCCUPATIONAL THEME - R
30 40 50 60 70
Average 49
F
M

15 25 30   40 45 55

BASIC INTEREST SCALES (STANDARD SCORE)

AGRICULTURE Mod. High 59 F M
NATURE Mod. High 58 F M
ADVENTURE Average 51 F M
MILITARY ACTIVITIES Average 54 F M
MECHANICAL ACTIVITIES Mod. Low 47 F M

			F	M
(CRE)	RC	Marine Corps enlisted personnel	(CRS)	18
RC	RC	Navy enlisted personnel	34	21
RC	RC	Army officer	43	29
RI	RIC	Navy officer	46	35
R	R	Air Force officer	44	26
(C)	R	Air Force enlisted personnel	(C)	16
R	R	Police officer	36	19
R	R	Bus driver	28	24
R	R	Horticultural worker	37	34
RC	R	Farmer	24	25
R	RCS	Vocational agriculture teacher	32	19
RI	R	Forester	41	35
(IR)	RI	Veterinarian	(IR)	22
RIS	(SR)	Athletic trainer	21	(SR)
RS	R	Emergency medical technician	28	18
RI	RI	Radiologic technologist	25	23
RI	R	Carpenter	27	5
RI	RI	Electrician	33	10
RIA	(ARI)	Architect	38	(ARI)
RI	RI	Engineer	44	30

INVESTIGATIVE

F M

GENERAL OCCUPATIONAL THEME - I
30 40 50 60 70
Average 54
F
M

15 25 30   40 45 55

BASIC INTEREST SCALES (STANDARD SCORE)

SCIENCE Average 55 F M
MATHEMATICS Very High 65 F M
MEDICAL SCIENCE Average 45 F M
MEDICAL SERVICE Average 48 F M

			F	M
IRC	IRC	Computer programmer	44	38
IRC	IRC	Systems analyst	49	41
IRC	IR	Medical technologist	37	27
IR	IR	R & D manager	51	38
IR	IR	Geologist	44	33
IR	(I)	Biologist	34	(I)
IR	IR	Chemist	38	32
IR	IR	Physicist	29	20
IR	(RI)	Veterinarian	32	(RI)
IRS	IR	Science teacher	33	30
IRS	IRS	Physical therapist	33	27
IR	IRS	Respiratory therapist	38	33
IC	IR	Medical technician	30	23
IC	IR	Pharmacist	36	23
ISR	(CSE)	Dietitian	36	(CSE)
(SI)	ISR	Nurse, RN	(SI)	20
IR	I	Chiropractor	29	27
IR	IR	Optometrist	40	37
IR	IR	Dentist	35	20
I	IA	Physician	39	36
(IR)	I	Biologist	(IR)	34
I	I	Mathematician	43	32
IR	I	Geographer	56	46
I	I	College professor	47	50
IA	IA	Psychologist	42	41
IA	IA	Sociologist	42	41

ARTISTIC

F M

GENERAL OCCUPATIONAL THEME - A
30 40 50 60 70
Average 53
F
M

15 25 30   40 45 55

BASIC INTEREST SCALES (STANDARD SCORE)

MUSIC/DRAMATICS Mod. High 56 F M
ART Average 44 F M
WRITING Mod. High 57 F M

			F	M
AI	AI	Medical illustrator	15	7
A	A	Art teacher	-1	19
A	A	Artist, fine	26	17
A	A	Artist, commercial	22	23
A	A	Interior decorator	14	27
(RIA)	ARI	Architect	(RIA)	26
A	A	Photographer	29	32
A	A	Musician	33	33
AR	(EA)	Chef	18	(EA)
(E)	AE	Beautician	(E)	23
AE	A	Flight attendant	28	33
A	A	Advertising executive	28	39
A	A	Broadcaster	28	37
A	A	Public relations director	30	29
A	A	Lawyer	50	43
A	AS	Public administrator	51	45
A	A	Reporter	35	37
A	A	Librarian	46	44
AS	AS	English teacher	30	42
(SA)	AS	Foreign language teacher	(SA)	45

Consulting Psychologists Press, Inc.
3803 E Bayshore Road
Palo Alto, CA 94303

71   1   O E

OTHER LINEARLY TRANSFORMED SCORES. The *Scholastic Aptitude Test* and other tests published by the Educational Testing Service (ETS) use a score with a mean of 500 and a standard deviation of 100.[3] Scores on the ETS scale are related to the z-score as follows:

$$ETS = 100z + 500$$

Whether such a score lies above or below 500 indicates whether the client's raw score was above or below the norm group average. If raw scores were normally distributed in the norm group, then the client's percentile score can be approximated from information such as that in Figure 1.

The American College Testing Program, publisher of the ACT college admissions test, uses scores with a mean of 20 and standard deviation of 5.

$$ACT = 5z + 20$$

Whether a score on their test lies above or below 20 indicates whether the corresponding raw score was above or below average. Using Figure 1, percentile scores can be approximated if the raw scores are normally distributed in the norm group.

While the z-score is well known, it is seldom if ever used in psychological testing because such scores can be negative. Commonly used alternatives to the z-score, called *linearly transformed scores,* include the T-score, deviation IQ score, and the ETS and ACT scores. From inspection of such scores, one can quickly discern whether and how far the corresponding raw score was above or below average. If the raw scores are normally distributed, any of the linearly transformed scores can be converted into percentile scores. Linearly transformed scores have the same distributional shape as raw scores and are normally distributed if and only if the raw scores are normally distributed. Since linearly transformed scores are expressed relative to the mean and standard deviation of a norm group, users must understand the nature of the norm group to properly interpret the scores.

Normalized Scores

Normalized scores are like linearly transformed scores in two respects. Normalized scores have a fixed mean and standard deviation in a norm group; therefore, by looking at a client's normalized score, one can quickly conclude whether the corresponding raw score is above or below the corresponding norm group average. Normalized scores are usually found using a conversion chart such as that in Table 6.

Normalized scores differ from raw scores in two important but related respects. No matter how the raw scores are distributed in the norm group, normalized scores will be normally distributed. As a result, from knowledge of a client's normalized score, one can always approximate the percentile score. Whereas linearly transformed scores are directly related to z-scores, normalized scores are directly related to percentile scores. The stanine and normal curve equivalent are the most common normalized scores.

THE STANINE SCORE. The *stanine score* is a one-digit whole-number score that ranges between 1 and 9. Stanines have a mean of 5 and standard deviation of 2.0. Each stanine score is assigned to those whose percentile scores fall in the specified range. Specifically, a stanine of 1 is assigned to those with percentiles at or below 4, stanine score 2 to those with percentile scores between 5 and 11, stanine 3 to percentiles between 12 and 23, stanine 4 to percentiles between 24 and 40, stanine 5 to percentiles between 41 and 60, stanine 6 to percentiles between 61 and 77, stanine 7 to percentiles between 78 and 89, stanine 8 to percentiles between 90 and 95, and stanine 9 to percentiles of 96 and above.

If necessary, the range of percentile scores in which a client's raw score must fall can be determined using the stanine score. Often, however, stanines and percentile scores are reported together. In Figure 8, for example, the client's stanine scores are given in the PR–S column as the number after the hyphen.[4] The client's percentile score, called the *percentile rank,* is given to the left of the hyphen in the PR–S column. On the Vocabulary Subtest, for instance, the client received a raw score (column RS) of 25, which converts to a stanine of 7 and a percentile score of 85.

THE NORMAL CURVE EQUIVALENT SCORE. The *normal curve equivalent* (NCE) is a normalized score that ranges from 1 to 99. NCE scores have a mean of 50 and standard deviation of 21.06. If need be, you can convert the NCE into an approximate percentile score using Figure 1. As in the score reporting form of Figure 8, however, the percentile score is often reported along with the NCE.

NORMALIZED T-SCORE. While stanine and NCE scores are the most common forms of normalized scores, there are others, including the *normalized T-score.* The normalized T-score, like its unnormalized counterpart, has a mean of 50 and a standard deviation of 10. However, the normalized T-score is derived in such a way that it is always normally distributed in the norm group.

Like linearly transformed scores, normalized scores convey the client's performance relative to a norm group. Normalized scores are more directly related to percentile scores, whereas linearly transformed scores are more directly related to z-scores. Consequently, a client's approximate percentile score can always be derived from a normalized score using a normal curve chart, such as that in Figure 1.

Conversion Tables

Like percentile scores, an examiner seldom actually computes any of the scores above. Rather, most test publishers provide a conversion table, similar to that in Table 6, which allows the examiner to convert each raw score into the linearly transformed and normalized scores used by that particular test. For instance, for a client with a raw score of 19, the examiner could read from Table 6 the corresponding NCE, 90, or the corresponding T-score, 67. A client with a raw score of 12 would receive a NCE of 46 and a T-score of 50.

Concluding Remarks

In order to properly interpret norm–referenced scores, one must understand what the norm group is. The norm group must be fully described in a manual accompanying the test, and the chosen norm group should be appropriate. Proper interpretation of norm–referenced scores requires careful study of manuals accompanying tests, particularly those sections that describe the various reference groups. Workshops provided by test publishers and authors should explain the norm groups. Conversion tables provided by the test publisher aid the examiner in determining clients' linearly transformed and normalized scores.

DEVELOPMENTAL SCORES

Grade–equivalent and age–equivalent scores are *developmental scores*. Developmental scores implicitly compare the client's raw score to the average raw score (median or mean) of people at various developmental levels.

Grade-equivalent Scores

A person's *grade-equivalent score* denotes the grade and month at which the average raw score is the same as the client's raw score. On the score report of Figure 8, the client has a raw score of 25 and a grade equivalent (GE) of 10.0 on the Vocabulary subtest. That is, a raw score of 25 is approximately equal to the average raw score of people just beginning tenth grade (the 0th month of grade 10). On the Language subtest, his grade equivalent of 7.4 indicates that his raw score, 51, roughly equals the average raw score of people in the fourth month of seventh grade.

Age-equivalent Scores

An *age-equivalent score* denotes the age and month of people for whom the average score is approximately the same as the client's raw score. For instance, if a person had an age-equivalent score of 5-10 (i.e., an age-equivalent score of 70 months), the client's raw score approximately equaled the average raw score of children in the tenth month of their 5th year—that is, children who are 70 months old.

Equivalent scores, both age and grade, are norm-referenced in a sense. That is, if a client's grade-equivalent score is 10.0, this means his or her raw score equals the average score of beginning tenth-grade students in some reference group. As with norm-referenced scores, one must understand the reference group to properly interpret the scores. For instance, if the median achievement level of tenth graders rises over a five-year period, the raw score needed to achieve a grade-equivalent score of 10.0 on a given test will rise. Even for tests with the same content, grade-equivalent scores will not have the same meaning unless the two tests are normed using representative samples from the same population.

Criticisms of Grade- and Age-equivalent Scores

Many professionals have severely criticized grade- and age-equivalent scores (Anastasi, 1988; Cronbach, 1984). Such scores are open to many misinterpretations, some of which will be discussed here. First, age and grade equivalents are not performance standards. That is, a grade-equivalent score of 4.0 is not the level at which every fourth-grade child is expected to perform. Likewise, an age-equivalent score of 10–0 is not some minimum acceptable level for 10-year-old children.

Second, grade- and age-equivalent scores are not equal interval scales relative to raw scores. To improve performance one grade-equivalent unit can require more raw score points at some levels than others. That is, to go from GE 1.0 to GE 2.0 may take many more raw score points than to go from GE 5.0 to GE 6.0. In general, as one moves up the grade- or age-equivalent scale, a change of one unit requires fewer and fewer raw score points (e.g., see Salvia & Ysseldyke, 1988).

Third, the standard deviation of grade- or age-equivalent scores can vary from one test to another or from one grade to another. For instance, Sax (1989) reports much wider standard deviations for the GE scores of fourth graders in language than in math for the *SRA Survey of Basic Skills*. Because the variance of language GE scores is wider, a higher proportion of students would have language GE scores 1.0 to 2.0 grades discrepant from their grade placement than would have math GE scores 1.0 to 2.0 grades discrepant from their grade placement. As a rule, the variance of equivalent scores increases with age and grade. Consequently, it is more common to find older students, say eighth graders, with GE scores 2.0 grades below their grade placement than to find younger students, say third graders, with GE scores 2.0 grades below their grade placement.

Fourth, people of different age or grade levels but with identical age- or grade-equivalent scores may have very different patterns of abilities. For instance, consider a fourth grader and a seventh grader with a reading grade equivalent of 7.0 on one of the well-known educational achievement test batteries. One must remember that the fourth and seventh grader probably took different levels of the exam. The fourth-grade version of the reading exam would focus on material taught in fourth grade or below. The seventh grader would be tested on material taught in seventh grade and below. The fourth-grade child with a grade equivalent of 7.0 probably has a very proficient knowledge of skills tested on the fourth-grade exam, largely skills taught in fourth and lower grades. The child may not, however, be proficient at skills taught in fifth and sixth grade to which she or he has never been exposed and which are appropriately not tested on the fourth-grade exam. Without checking to see if the child has mastered them, wholesale skipping of fifth- and sixth-grade work would be unwise. The seventh grader, however, may have achieved his grade equivalent of 7.0 with partial mastery, not only of material taught in grade four and lower, but also items taught in fifth through seventh grades. The fact that the two have the same grade-equivalent score can mask the fact that their areas of reading proficiency differ.

Fifth, age- and grade-equivalent scores are often derived through interpolation between ages or grades included in the norm group and, sometimes, through extrapolation beyond age or grade levels in the norm group. Age- or grade-equivalent scores reached through extrapolation should be viewed skeptically at best. Where age and grade equivalents are reported, the test user should be familiar with the age and grade limits of the norm group.

Mental Age

Another developmental concept is that of mental age, popularized by Alfred Binet, author of the first major intelligence test. Binet's items were scaled in terms of difficulty expressed as the youngest age at which a majority of children could first pass the item. Items were then grouped by their difficulty level. An examinee would be assigned a *mental age* equal to the highest difficulty level at which the client could pass a prescribed number of the items.

For instance, if an examinee passed all of the items intended for eight-year-olds but failed most of the items at the next level of difficulty, the examinee would receive a mental age score of 8.0 (or 96 months). Later, mental ages were converted to ratios by dividing mental age by chronological age. For instance, a child who was 84 months old with a mental age of 96 months would have an intelligence quotient of $96/84 = 1.14$. The ratios were called IQ's and, to eliminate decimals, were multiplied by 100 (i.e., 114, not 1.14). Such IQ scores—mental age divided by chronological age—had a number of undesirable properties and have largely been replaced in today's tests of mental ability by the deviation IQ score. While the quotient itself has not survived, the acronym IQ, for intelligence quotient, is still (regrettably) in use.

OUTCOME AND OTHER FRAMES OF REFERENCE

Besides norm-referenced and developmental scores, there are other bases for evaluating test performance. Conceptually the simplest, perhaps, is to interpret it with respect to cutoffs established by "experts." We have all encountered cutoffs established by teachers—45 to 50 is an A, 40 to 44 a B, and so forth. For most published tests, it is difficult to find a rational basis for setting such cutoffs. Consequently, test publishers are reluctant to do so. For tests that employ them, wise application requires an understanding of the rationale behind the cutoff.

Some test users use what Brown (1983) calls *outcome referencing*. In outcome referencing, the score is interpreted with respect to expected performance on a future success criterion. The expected level of success is determined empirically. This system seems most natural when the test was designed to predict future performance and the test has substantial criterion-related validity for that performance. Outcome-referenced interpretations are often based on expectancy tables, such as that in Table 7.

In Table 7, the outcome or criterion variable is college grade point average (GPA). The predictor variable is a high school student's score on the ACT Assessment. For various ranges of test scores, the table shows the percentage of students in this sample who received GPA's of 3.0 to 4.0, 2.0 to 2.9, and 1.9 or lower. In the highest test score interval, 32 or higher, 93 percent of the sample received a 3.0 GPA or better, 6 percent carried a GPA between 2.0 and 2.9, and only 1 percent had less than a C average (1.9 or below). Contrast this with the lowest test score interval, 17 or lower, in which the majority (64 %) had less than a C average, 33 percent had GPAs between 2.0 and 2.9, and only 3 percent had a GPA above 3.0.

TABLE 7. The Distribution of College Grade Point Averages for Students Falling in Various ACT Test Score Intervals

Test Score	College Grade Point Average		
	3.0–4.0	2.0–2.9	0.0–1.9
32 or higher	93	6	1
30–31	58	39	3
28–29	34	55	11
26–27	19	56	25
24–25	14	49	37
22–23	5	47	48
20–21	4	45	51
18–19	2	42	56
17 or lower	3	33	64

Note: GPA is expressed on a scale where A = 4.0, B = 3.0, and so on. Entries are percentages of students.

From *Principles of Educational and Psychological Testing*, Third Edition, by Frederick G. Brown. Copyright © 1983 by Holt, Rinehart, and Winston, Inc. Reprinted by permission of the publisher.

A client with a score of 28, for instance, would correspond to a score group in which 34 percent received a B or better average, 55 percent were in the B to C range, and 11 percent failed to maintain a C average. Expectancy tables show the test interpreter how people with scores like that of the client have performed in the past.

Such outcome data for test scores should not be interpreted blindly. Intelligent interpretation of Table 7 requires some knowledge of the sample. Were these students well prepared for college? In what kinds of majors were these students? Even if one fully understands the nature of the sample, relating the experience of the sample to the particular client requires careful interpretation. One needs to understand the particular situation of the client. Does the client need to work substantial numbers of hours in order to afford college? What was the client's high school performance, and how well did his or her high school coursework prepare him or her for college? Using the past experience of a sample to interpret test scores of a unique client requires a thorough understanding of the client's circumstances, a scientific understanding of the data on which the expectancy table is based, and sensitive professional judgment.

TABLE 8. Raw to Scaled Score Conversion Table for Primary 1 and Primary 2 Levels of the Reading Comprehension Test in the *Stanford Achievement Test Battery*

	Scaled Score	
Raw Score	Primary 1	Primary 2
40	611	690
39	588	667
38	562	640
37	547	624
36	536	612
35	526	602
34	519	593
33	512	586
32	506	579
31	500	573
30	495	567
29	490	561
28	485	556
27	481	551
26	477	546
25	472	542
24	468	537
23	464	532
22	460	528
21	456	524
20	453	519
19	449	515
18	445	511
17	441	506

SCALED SCORES, EQUATING, FORMS, AND LEVELS

There is one score in Figure 8 that has not yet been explained, the score in column SS. Scaled scores are often found on tests for which there are several forms or levels, particularly ability tests (note the form and level designation of the test in Figure 8). What is meant by different forms or levels of a test?

Forms and Levels of a Test

Forms of a test are versions that are as identical as we can make them in length, content, administration procedures, item type, scoring, and difficulty (if it is an ability test). Two forms of a test should have approximately equal means and variances. Try as one will, however, the two forms will seldom be interchangeable. Their means and variances will differ at least somewhat, making direct comparison of raw scores from the the two forms inappropriate. Scaled scores adjust for the (hopefully small) remaining differences between the forms. In Figure 8, for instance, if one were to compare this performance to that of someone who took a different form, one would compare the scaled scores rather than the raw scores.

Whereas forms of tests are deliberately matched on features such as content and difficulty, levels of a test differ systematically. *Levels* are versions of a test designed for populations differing in age, education, or level of the construct measured. A depression inventory might have an adolescent level and an adult level because the symptoms of depression differ for adolescents and adults. An achievement test battery would have different reading test levels for different grades. Individually administered intelligence and aptitude tests use one level of items for children and a different level for teenagers and adults. Scaled scores permit comparison of individuals who took different levels of a test.

Scaled Scores

Table 8 shows part of a conversion chart for the Reading Comprehension test in the *Stanford Achievement Test Battery*. For each raw score from 17 to 40 on Primary Level 1 and Primary Level 2, the table gives a corresponding scaled score. Note that a raw score of 40 corresponds to a scaled score of 611 on Primary 1 and 690 on Primary 2. The publisher has determined that it takes a higher level of ability to get 40 correct on Primary 1 than on Primary 2 because the items on Primary 2 are harder than those on Primary 1; consequently, a higher scaled score is assigned to someone who receives 40 correct on Level 2 than is assigned to someone who obtains 40 correct on Level 1. Note that the same scaled score (506) is associated with raw scores of 32 on Primary 1 and 17 on Primary 2. It has been estimated that the same level of ability is required to correctly answer 32 items on Level 1 or 17 items on Level 2.

To derive scaled scores, the test publisher must use one of several equating methods (Allen & Yen, 1979; Crocker & Algina, 1986). Such methods are not above criticism. When one wants to compare two performances, it is best to use the same version of the test where possible. Potential errors due to inaccurate equating can then be avoided. Where two versions must be employed, however, scaled scores are useful. There are three major types of equating methods for deriving scaled scores: equipercentile, linear, and item response theory based equating.

Equating

In *equipercentile equating,* two raw scores from different versions of a test correspond to the same scaled score if they have the same percentile rank in a norm group. For instance, if 60 percent of the people in the norm group have raw scores equal to or less than 21 on Form A and 60 percent have raw scores equal to or less than 19 on Form B, then the same scaled score would be assigned to raw scores of 21 on Form A and 19 on Form B. Irrespective of which version they were given, people with equal scaled scores are people with equal percentile ranks. (Since stanines, normalized T-scores, and normal curve equivalent scores are derived directly from percentile ranks, people with equal scaled scores will also have equal stanines, normalized T-scores, and NCE scores.)

In *linear equating,* two raw scores from different versions of a test correspond to the same scaled score if they are the same number of standard deviations above or below the mean in some norm group. Linearly derived scaled scores are so named because they are linearly related to the raw scores. For instance, if raw scores of 21 and 19 on Forms A and B are both one standard deviation below the mean (i.e., $z = -1$), then both would be assigned the same scaled score. Irrespective of the version of the test, people with equal scaled scores will have equal z-scores in the norm group. If raw scores on two versions of a test are distributed identically in the norm group, except for their means and variances, then linear and equipercentile equating will yield the same result. That is, any two raw scores assigned the same scaled score via equipercentile equating will be assigned the same scaled score via linear equating.

In *item response theory based equating,* two people taking different versions of the test are assigned the same scaled scores if they have equal estimated probabilities of correctly (or positively) answering each item. Currently, item response theory based equating is most commonly applied to tests composed of dichotomously scored items. As discussed more fully below, an item response theory is a set of mathematical assumptions about how the properties of an item and the trait level of the person combine to influence the probability of correctly answering an item. If the items satisfy the assumptions of the model, one can score test responses so that a person's score allows one to estimate the probability that the person can positively answer any item.

FIGURE 10. Item Response Curves Conforming to the Rasch Model

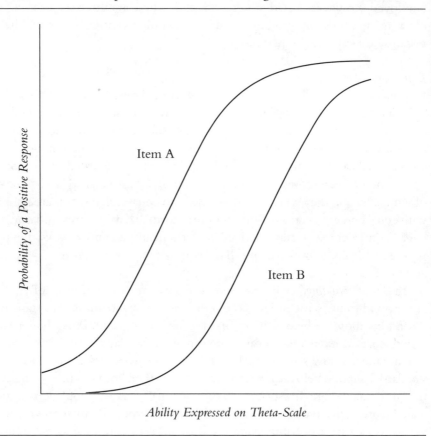

Ability Expressed on Theta-Scale

Note: Curves show the probability of a positive response at each trait level.

Equal scores are assigned to people with equal probabilities of positively answering items.

Not all tests report scaled scores. Unless a test has multiple forms or multiple levels, there is no need to do so. Where scaled scores are used, however, they are designed to facilitate comparisons of performance across forms or levels of the test. For any equating to be legitimate, the versions of the test must measure the same construct. No equating method can adjust for the fact that two tests measure different attributes.

Unidimensional Item Response Theory

Item response theory (IRT) has many potential applications in testing. First and foremost for our purposes is the application to test scoring and test equating. At present, the most practical item response theories apply only to dichotomous items. Hereafter, the term positive response refers to the correct response if the item has right and wrong answers. For items with no right or wrong answers, the positive response is the response characteristic of people at the high end of the trait being measured.

An *item response theory* is a mathematical model of how client scores on the trait being measured are related to the probability of positively answering the item. The IRT models in use posit that a person's response to an item is a function of only one measured trait or ability. The various IRTs further posit a particular mathematical function that relates the probability of positively answering an item to properties of the item, as represented in the model by *item parameters,* and to the person's position along the measured trait or ability.

To illustrate such a mathematical function, consider the simplest IRT, the *Rasch model,* named after the Danish mathematician Georg Rasch (1966; Wright & Stone, 1979). Figure 10 shows the mathematical function in the Rasch model for two test items.

Each curve shows the probability of positively answering the item at each trait level. The curve on the right, Item B, corresponds to a more difficult item. To reach any probability of positively answering, it takes a higher trait level for item B than for item A. The Rasch model is the simplest IRT model because it assumes that items vary in only one characteristic—their difficulties.

As should be evident from Figure 10, IRT focuses on the relationship between trait level and the probability of positively answering each item. For trait scores to be directly related to the probability of correctly answering an item, the scores must be expressed on a special scale, sometimes called the *theta scale.* Consequently, IRT leads to a different way of scoring tests.

Rather than expressing scores as the number of items answered positively, those using IRT work with scores expressed on their special theta scale. The relationship between these two kinds of scores is curvilinear, as illustrated in Figure 11. The scaled scores in Table 8 represent ability scores expressed on a theta scale (after a linear transformation to eliminate negative numbers). For Primary Levels 1 and 2 in Table 8, Figure 11 shows the relationship between scores expressed on the theta scale and the number correct score. A

FIGURE 11. Raw Score Plotted Against IRT Theta-Scale Scores

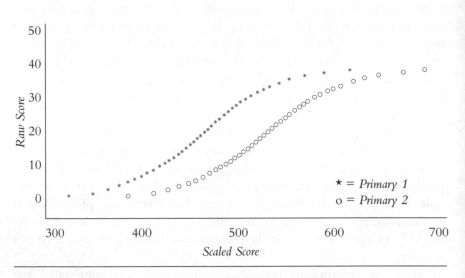

disadvantage of theta scores is that theta scores are not related in any simple way to item scores. Conversion tables, such as Table 8, or computers must be used to estimate IRT test scores. Despite the complexity of IRT scoring, however, simple number right scores and complex theta scores have a strong, positive relationship. That is, as illustrated in Figure 11, people who answer more items correctly have higher theta scores.

In equating two versions (two forms or two levels) with the Rasch model, the test developer first estimates the difficulty of each item on the two versions. These item difficulties are expressed on IRT's special theta scale. By adjusting for differences in difficulties of items on the two tests, it is possible to score each test on the theta scale so that scores from the versions are comparable. Even though they may have taken two versions of the test, two people with the same estimated trait level have the same estimated probability of answering any item positively.

In order to apply item response theory, the test developer must create test versions whose items satisfy the assumptions of IRT. That is, the items must all be unidimensional, measuring the same trait. Further, the IRT must accurately characterize the relationship between trait levels and the probabilities of positively answering each item.

If the test versions do satisfy IRT assumptions, then the versions can be equated in a logical manner. Scores from the equated versions will be comparable in the sense that two people who have equal estimated trait levels but took different versions of the test have equal estimated probabilities of positively answering any item. Furthermore, scores from the equated versions will also satisfy the linear and equipercentile equating criteria. No matter what versions of the test are involved, people with equal trait scores have equal percentiles in any norm group, and their raw scores are equal numbers of standard deviations above or below the mean of any norm group. Because versions equated with IRT also satisfy linear and equipercentile equating criteria, IRT leads to a very strong form of equating when the necessary IRT assumptions can be met.

Conclusion

The diverse types of test scores mirror the diverse frames of reference used by test developers to give meaning to raw scores. Norm-referenced scores are closely linked to some basic statistical concepts. Linearly transformed scores, such as *T*-scores and deviation IQ scores, are expressed relative to the mean and standard deviation of a reference group. A percentile score is the centile rank of the client's raw score in the reference group. Normalized scores, such as stanines or normal curve equivalent scores, are directly related to the percentile score. Proper interpretation of linearly transformed and normalized scores requires understanding the composition, size, and datedness of that norm group.

Developmental scores include age-equivalent, grade-equivalent, and mental age scores. While still popular, age- and grade-equivalent scores have been heavily criticized in recent years and are subject to misinterpretation.

For tests with substantial predictive validity, an expectancy table can be used to show the distribution of outcome scores for each predictor test score interval. Combined with an understanding of the client's unique circumstances, such a table can be a useful aid to test score interpretation.

Scaled scores appear on tests with different forms or levels and facilitate comparison of performance across the different forms and levels. To derive scaled scores, the test developer must employ some form of test equating—usually linear equating, equipercentile equating, or item response theory based equating.

Any test score should be interpreted with respect to that score's standard error of measurement, which expresses the score's precision. Unless the test has perfect reliability, the client's observed score is unlikely to equal his or her true score exactly. A score band expresses a range of plausible values in which the client's true score probably lies. A percentile band expresses a range of plausible values in which the percentile of the client's true score probably lies.

Professional test interpretation relies on scientific data such as that on the reliability of the test and the composition of any norm groups. To this data, the skilled professional must add information about the client's unique circumstances. The art of professional test interpretation is the art of facilitating enhanced client self-understanding through professional use of the data about a test, the client's responses to the test, and information about the client's unique circumstances.

Endnotes

1   This method of estimating the standard error of the mean was designed for the situation in which the sample was drawn using a purely random sampling technique. The samples used in testing are often drawn using a combination of random and representative sampling techniques, in which case the estimate of the standard error will be approximate.

2   The SII has male and female scales for each occupation. The female T-score is based on the female occupational sample and the male T-score is based on the male occupational sample.

3   A sample taking the test in 1941 is the SAT reference group in which the mean is 500 and the standard deviation is 100. At the time this was written, the mean scores of the current test takers are below 500 on both the math and verbal sections of the exam.

4   Stanine assignments in Figure 8 differ slightly from the description given here. Boundaries between stanines are one point lower, so that a stanine of 1 is assigned to percentiles below 4, stanine 2 to percentiles between 4 and 10, stanine 3 to percentiles between 11 and 22, and so forth.

References

Anastasi, A. (1988). *Psychological testing* (6th ed.). New York: Macmillan.

Allen, M. J., & Yen, W. M. (1979). *Introduction to measurement theory.* Monterey, CA: Brooks/Cole.

Brown, F. G. (1983). *Principles of educational and psychological measurement* (3rd ed.). New York: Holt, Rinehart, & Winston.

Crocker, L., & Algina, J. (1986). *Introduction to classical and modern test theory.* New York: Holt, Rinehart, & Winston.

Cronbach, L. J. (1984). *Essentials of psychological testing* (4th ed.). New York: Harper & Row.

Rasch, G. (1966). *Probabalistic models for some intelligence and attainment tests.* Copenhagen: The Danish Institute for Educational Research.

Salvia, J., & Ysseldyke, J. E. (1988). *Assessment in special and remedial education* (4th ed.). Boston: Houghton Mifflin.

Sax, G. (1989). *Principles of educational and psychological measurement and evaluation* (3rd ed.). Belmont CA: Wadsworth.

Wright, B. D., & Stone, M. (1979). *Best test design.* Chicago: MESA Press.

CHAPTER 8

EXAMINING TEST DATA USING MULTIVARIATE PROCEDURES

Patricia B. Jones & Darrell L. Sabers

Introduction

Once a test, instrument, or battery has been developed that hopefully measures the construct(s) of interest, the next step is to determine whether the measurements conform to the expectations that guided the construction of the instrument. Univariate data analysis techniques consider only one, or at most two, variables at a time; for example, the student *t* test and bivariate correlational analysis are examples of univariate techniques. In contrast, multivariate procedures attempt to examine structure of data by considering many variables simultaneously. Examples of multivariate techniques include factor analysis, canonical correlation, and multidimensional scaling.*

Although many statistical methodologies could be used to examine test data structure, we will limit our treatment to those multivariate techniques that we find most useful in analyzing structure of test data. Huberty and Barton (1989) have described types of multivariate analyses:

> Multivariate data analysis methods may be partitioned into interdependence methods and dependence methods. Interdependence methods include factor analysis, cluster analysis, and multidimensional scaling—

---

*Frequently, the term *univariate* is used to refer to techniques analyzing a single dependent variable, while multivariate techniques analyze multiple dependent variables. We do not make that distinction here.

methods that typically deal with a single variable set. Dependence methods typically involve two sets of variables, and sometimes one set is denoted the predictor variables and the other set is denoted the criterion variables. These methods include multiple correlation analysis, canonical correlation analysis, multivariate analysis of variance (MANOVA), and discriminant analysis. (p. 158)

The methods we typically use for examining structure in a set of test data are the interdependence methods, so those will be the ones introduced in this chapter. However, the data in the second part of this chapter could be analyzed by dependence methods as well, especially using canonical correlational analysis. Our goal is to cover the multivariate methods most likely to be encountered by the person reading about test development. Because the techniques are complex, we present a descriptive, nonmathematical approach. Readers who wish additional information should consult the list of references at the end of this chapter. Dillon and Goldstein (1984) provide a particularly good overview of a variety of multivariate techniques. Gnanadesikan (1977) gives a readable, although somewhat more mathematical, presentation of multivariate analysis. Additional texts that treat each of the techniques in more detail will also be specified as the topics are introduced.

Suppose, then, that we have developed an instrument following the techniques and sound advice appropriate for proper test development. To illustrate, we will use the *Guilford-Zimmerman Interest Inventory* (GZII; Guilford & Zimmerman, 1989). The GZII is a self-report measure that consists of ten scales with 15 items each and presents a profile of interest related to major occupations. Respondents rate activities on a 4-point scale (0 = Definite dislike, 3=Definite like). A score is provided for each scale in the battery by summing the ratings for items in each category. The ten areas represented by the items in the scale and a short description of each construct are presented in Table 1.

In situations where an instrument such as the GZII is being developed to meet prespecified criteria, it is advisable first to administer it to a sample of subjects who closely resemble those for whom the test is likely to be used in practice. Once this pilot testing is done, the test developer should examine the data to see whether the battery meets the criteria that guided its construction. Usually these criteria specify a certain structure for the instrument. When a test is designed to assess a single construct or trait (e.g., reading ability, attitude toward political activism, or depression) that has been defined in a fairly narrow manner, then the test is said to be *unidimensional*. If, on the other hand, we wish to develop a battery designed to measure multiple

TABLE 1. GZII Scales and Descriptors

	Scale	Descriptor
Na	Natural	Interest in being outdoors
Me	Mechanical	Interest in machines and tools
Sc	Scientific	Interest in research in any area of science
Cr	Creative	Interest in devising new ideas, replacing conventional ideas
Li	Literary	Appreciation of written or spoken language
Ar	Artistic	Appreciation of beauty in the fine arts
Se	Service	Interest in helping others
En	Enterprising	Interest in business transactions
Le	Leadership	Interest in leading or directing others
Cl	Clerical	Interest in office work

constructs or a complex construct having a number of facets, the battery should provide evidence of having more than one dimension or, in other words, should be *multidimensional.* Usually we expect to have a multidimensional battery consisting of unidimensional tests. A battery such as the GZII is expected to measure multiple aspects of interests, and we would expect (or at least hope) that it would appear to be multidimensional. On the other hand, we might expect each of the GZII scales described in Table 1 to show evidence of unidimensionality because the constructs that they assess are defined in a fairly narrow manner.

The dimensionality of a test has important implications for the researcher constructing a test. If a test battery that is intended to measure different constructs shows evidence of unidimensionality, there is a high degree of redundancy among the tests that comprise the battery. If all tests measure the same construct, administering the entire battery is a waste of resources. For example, if an achievement battery that consists of two tests designed to measure verbal and quantitative skills shows evidence of unidimensionality, there is little need to administer both tests; whatever the tests measure, it is probably not just verbal skill or just quantitative skill. Unidimensionality is an important requirement for tests for which a single score will be reported. It is also necessary when item response theory is used to place the items on a single scale.

When a battery is designed to measure different constructs, it should provide evidence of multidimensionality. Items that measure the same construct should appear to be highly related to each other; items measuring different constructs should show substantially lower relationships. When a battery is multidimensional, a single score is not as informative as a score for each test would be. Below are shown hypothetical scores for three students who each received a total score of 100 on a battery consisting of two tests, one measuring verbal achievement and one measuring quantitative achievement. Each test has a mean of 50 and standard deviation of 10.

Student	V	Q	T
A	50	50	100
B	65	35	100
C	35	65	100

Student A scored at the mean on both tests. While B scored substantially above the mean on the verbal test, B's quantitative score is much lower. Similarly, C shows evidence of substantial strength on the quantitative portion, but is quite weak in the verbal skills tested by the battery. The implications for instruction might be quite different for the three individuals; a single total score would mask this fact.

Dimensionality in a test is not a constant; it is a function of the context in which the test is given. A test may appear to be unidimensional in one setting or with one group of individuals and multidimensional in another. For example, a set of mathematical questions consisting of a mixture of word problems and short proofs may appear unidimensional when given to a group of students who are of fairly similar reading abilities. However, when some students are hampered by inadequate reading or verbal skills, the items may be differentiated along another dimension that measures verbal skill. For this reason, it is important to determine the dimensionality of a test or battery whenever it is administered, particularly when there is reason to suspect that the population to whom the test was originally administered differed in some important respect from the population with whom it is currently being used.

The question is, how do we find out whether a test is unidimensional or multidimensional? A substantial body of literature discusses a variety of techniques used for assessing dimensionality. There is no agreement on what procedures are best for looking at dimensionality. We use examination of the matrix of intercorrelations (which includes the multitrait multimethod approach addressed later in this chapter), exploratory factor analysis, cluster analysis, and multidimensional scaling for analyzing the structure of a data set. As mentioned above, many other techniques are available, but the ones we cover represent a variety of techniques that use substantially different assumptions and models. We like to use a variety of techniques because each method helps to shed additional light on the information provided by the others. When we can reach similar conclusions through all the techniques, we assume that the structure we see does not depend on the method we use to find it. When our conclusions about the structure of the data depend on the technique we use, we are forced to consider whether there is something about the technique that causes questionable conclusions (e.g., the model employed by the technique might be inappropriate for our data) or whether the data are too unreliable to permit accurate statements about the structure of the battery.

Examining the battery should consist of two phases. First, our questions are about the structure of the measure in the sample to whom it was administered during development. Is the battery unidimensional or multi-dimensional? How many dimensions are there? Are the dimensions approximately as expected? That is, do items that were developed to be related to each other demonstrate the expected relationship? Secondly, we seek information regarding how the measures in the battery agree with other measures designed to assess the same constructs. These two phases are considered separately in the two parts of this chapter.

Part 1: Examining the Structure of the Battery

INSPECTION OF THE MATRIX OF INTERCORRELATIONS

To look at the structure of the test battery, it is necessary to have some way of assessing relationships among tests or items within a test. One statistic that measures the closeness or proximity of two objects is the *correlation coefficient*. There are several types of correlation coefficients, and the one to use depends on assumptions about the nature of relationships between the objects being measured and the type of scale with which those objects are measured. For example, a *Pearson product-moment correlation* is appropriate when the relationship between the objects (in this case, tests) is linear and the scores being correlated are on an equal interval scale. In the verbal test scores above, A scored 15 points lower than B and C scored 15 points lower than A. At first glance, their scores seem to be equally spaced. However, if A does not know as much more than C as B does than A, the scores are not on an equal interval scale. This could happen if the difficulties of items on the test were not evenly spaced. With scores of this type, a Pearson product-moment correlation may not accurately represent the magnitude of the relationship between the tests. Depending on the nature of the scales, we may consider using other measures of association that would be more appropriate. Examples of these are the

TABLE 2. Matrix of Intercorrelations of GZII Scales

Scale	Na	Me	Sc	Cr	Li	Ar	Se	En	Le
Na									
Me	34								
Sc	26	66							
Cr	26	28	57						
Li	21	−20	11	51					
Ar	20	−34	−17	28	48				
Se	18	−34	−16	02	35	35			
En	10	20	02	06	−06	−01	−10		
Le	−05	02	02	15	21	−05	09	54	
Cl	13	07	−06	−22	−02	11	12	20	−03

Note: Decimals omitted

Spearman rank-order coefficient, the phi coefficient, the tetrachoric correlation, or Kendall's tau-B.

It is a good idea to inspect a matrix consisting of measures of association between tests or items for evidence of the expected relationships. In practice, we usually work with Pearson correlations, even when the data may not strictly meet the assumptions required for the coefficient.

It would be useful to look at an actual set of data to illustrate the techniques presented in this chapter. The editors of this book have provided us with data from administration of the GZII to a sample of 232 subjects, most of whom were included in the norming sample for the GZII. Scores on the ten scales were correlated and the results given in Table 2.

When we inspect the matrix, we notice high correlations for Sc-Me, Cr-Sc, Li-Cr, Ar-Li, and Le-En. These combinations represent interests that tend to appear jointly and are frequently required in combination for some occupations. For example, persons with an interest in scientific research often wish to know how things work, an interest measured by the Me scale. Similarly, persons with literary interests would be expected to display creativity. Negative correlations imply that a high degree of interest in one area tends to occur jointly with a low degree of interest in another. For example, mechanical interest tends to be negatively related to interests in literary, artistic, or service areas. On the other hand, mechanical interests are positively (although not highly) related to creative interests. Often when we attempt to look at the structure of a test or battery, we use a technique such as factor analysis as a data reduction technique. That is, we attempt to describe the structure of the test in terms of a smaller number of dimensions than might be suggested by the number of items in the test. It is common to do the same thing with tests in a battery. While it is a good idea to look for a parsimonious (i.e., involving as few variables as possible) explanation of the constructs under consideration, techniques of this sort by their very nature tend to wash out the differences among the objects that are being measured. Inspection of the correlation matrix tends to concentrate on pairwise structure, whereas more complex techniques tend to concentrate on structure that is common throughout a matrix such as that shown above.

FACTOR ANALYSIS OF THE GZII

Factor analysis has some advantages over visual inspection of the correlation matrix as a technique for exploring the structure of test data. Factor analysis is one of the more commonly used data-reduction techniques. A test consists of a number of items intended to measure one or more theoretical constructs. A reliable test should consist of items that overlap considerably, providing multiple assessments of the same trait—that is, the items should be internally consistent. Similarly, tests within a battery may share some essential components. For example, on achievement tests with a high reading content, test scores may be correlated because individuals with a high level of reading achievement would be expected to have a better chance of doing well across tests, whereas individuals with a low level of reading achievement might be handicapped in their performance in general. The common components or latent variables that underlie the items or tests are called *factors,* and the statistical technique used to find these components is called *factor analysis.* In the following explanation, we assume that we are factor analyzing a test or scale which consists of a set of k items Z_1, Z_2, ..., Z_k. Underlying these k items is a smaller set of p common factors F_1, F_2, ..., F_p which represent the constructs held in common by the items. Each item also has a unique factor U, which represents the part of the variance of the item not related to the common factors. We could express the relationship between each item and its factors as

$$Z_i = a_1 F_1 + a_2 F_2 + ... + a_p F_p + U_i \tag{1}$$

where the subscript i represents the ith item and the a represents weights given to each factor. These weights will differ for each item. For example, suppose we have a mathematics test that consists of three word problems. Successful performance on a problem requires good performance in both mathematics knowledge and reading achievement. Then, if Z_i represents a score on the ith item (i = 1, 2, or 3), F_m represents performance in mathematics knowledge and F_r represents performance in reading achievement, we might have a set of equations such as:

$$Z_1 = .4F_m + .6F_r + U_1$$
$$Z_2 = .8F_m + .3F_r + U_2$$
$$Z_3 = .7F_m + .1F_r + U_3$$

The weights differ from item to item because not every item is related to mathematics knowledge and to reading achievement to the same degree. Item 1 (Z_1) is more strongly related to reading achievement than the other two items; in fact, it is related more to reading achievement than to mathematics knowledge. The U's represent the unique components of the items that are not attributable to any factor. The weights described previously are called *factor loadings,* and the process by which these weights are obtained is factor analysis.

There are two approaches to factor analysis—*exploratory* and *confirmatory.* Exploratory factor analysis is most commonly used when little is known about the structure of the data. Most of the major computer analysis packages (such as SAS, SPSS, or BMDP) have one or more routines to do factor analysis. Confirmatory factor analysis, as represented by maximum-likelihood factor analysis, is used when the researcher wishes to test specific hypotheses about the structure of the data. Confirmatory techniques require prior knowledge of the structure of the data and that the data meet strict distributional assumptions (usually multivariate normality, meaning that the variables be jointly normally distributed. See Johnson & Wichern, 1988, for a more complete and technical description of multivariate normality). Confirmatory factor analysis is usually carried out using specially developed computer packages such as LISREL (Jöreskog & Sörbom, 1988) or EQS (Bentler, 1989). The technique is complex and beyond the scope of this book. Researchers who wish to use it are referred to Long (1983a, 1983b), Hayduk (1987), and Dillon and Goldstein (1984).

Factor analysis may be carried out on matrices of correlations or covariances. The covariance of two variables A and B, C_{AB}, is the product of the correlation between A and B, R_{AB}, and the standard deviations of each of the variables, S_A and S_B. In equation form, this is

$$C_{AB} = R_{AB} S_A S_B$$

When covariances are used as input to factor analysis, the standard deviations of the variables can affect the magnitudes of the factor loadings. In some applications, this may be useful and appropriate, but this approach may be of questionable value in psychometric applications since the scaling of the variables is arbitrary. In such a situation, then, we use a matrix of standardized covariances, which reduces to the intercorrelation matrix in the above application since the standard deviation of a standardized variable is 1.0. Because of this, only the magnitudes of the intercorrelations will affect the variable loadings in a factor analysis of psychometric variables. When a matrix of correlations is factor analyzed, the factor loadings (the a's in formula 1) can be examined to show which factors are most heavily influenced by each item. By examining which items load most heavily on each factor, we can attempt to interpret the meaning of the factors.

As stated earlier, a factor model assumes that there are fewer factors than items. In practice, we could have as many factors as items, but this would not provide us with a simpler explanation of the structure underlying the data. We therefore select only the most important factors to interpret, important being defined by some criterion which we have yet to specify. To determine how many factors should be extracted, we usually examine the eigenvalues of the correlation matrix that are output by the procedure. Each eigenvalue represents the amount of variance that corresponds to a given factor. The largest eigenvalue represents the amount of variance corresponding to the first factor, the next largest represents the amount corresponding to the second factor, and so on. The sum of the eigenvalues of a matrix equals the sum of the diagonal elements of the matrix. When the matrix analyzed is an item correlation matrix, the eigenvalues add up to the number of items; each eigenvalue corresponds to the amount of total standardized variance in the data accounted for by the factor it represents. If the items are highly intercorrelated, there may be one or two eigenvalues substantially greater than the rest. One technique used to determine how many factors are appropriate is the *scree test* in which eigenvalues are plotted on the Y-axis against the corresponding factor number on the X-axis. A sharp break in the slope of the plot suggests that factor numbers including and to the right of the break consist of random error, whereas factor numbers to the left of the break consist of common variance. Figure 1 presents the scree plot of the eigenvalues obtained in the factor analysis of the GZII. In Figure 1, there appear to be two locations where we might infer that a break occurs—either after two or after four factors. Most researchers would choose to interpret four factors given this scree plot.

Another technique for selecting factors is to accept only factors with eigenvalues greater than a specified cutoff value (the value of 1.0, which represents the mean of the eigenvalues in this case, is often selected). With

FIGURE 1. Scree Plot of Eigenvalues From Table 3

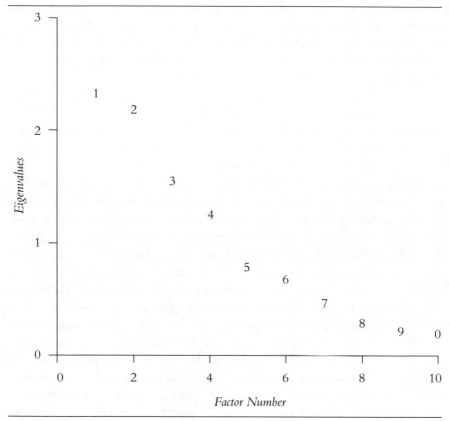

the set of eigenvalues in Figure 1, there would be four factors selected by this technique.

There are several methods of extracting factors from the correlation matrix; here we discuss the two techniques most commonly used: *principal components* and *principal factors*. In the principal components approach, the eigenvalues of the correlation matrix are computed and a cutoff value of 1.0 is often used to select how many principal components are interpreted. In the principal factors approach, an estimate is made of the *communality* of each variable with the other variables. The communality of a variable may be considered to be that portion of the variable's common variance that is attributable to the common factors (i.e., those shared across variables) rather than unique factors (which we often think of as error). One technique for estimating the communality of a variable is to calculate the squared multiple correlation for the variable when it is predicted by all other variables in the analysis. These communalities are substituted for the diagonal elements (i.e., the 1's) in the correlation matrix, yielding a *reduced* correlation matrix. The eigenvalues of the reduced matrix are calculated, and the average of the eigenvalues is used to select how many principal factors are interpreted. The two techniques are essentially the same in the way they are carried out—only the elements on the diagonals of the matrix and sometimes the criteria for choosing the number of factors are different. Although theoretical distinctions often are made between principal components analysis and factor analysis, the two procedures are quite similar in their execution and often yield comparable results. Also, statistical packages will differ to some extent from the procedures described here in how they extract and select factors. The sum of the eigenvalues for a principal components analysis will equal the sum of the diagonal elements in the full correlation matrix, or the total number of variables in the analysis (since there will be as many 1's in the diagonals as there are variables). However, while the sum of the eigenvalues for a principal factors extraction will equal the sum of the diagonal elements of the matrix, it will seldom sum to the total number of variables in the analysis since the communalities in the diagonal will seldom equal 1.0 (it would be unusual to find no unique variance for a variable). Reduced matrices can also yield negative eigenvalues, hindering the interpretation of eigenvalues as variance accounted for.

In factor analysis, we can consider factors as axes in a multidimensional space. The factor loadings for each item can be considered coordinates representing the location of the items in a space represented by the factors. In our discussion of the mathematics items above, we initially began with a three-dimensional space, with each item representing an axis. Then we reduced the space to one with two dimensions, with each dimension being represented by a factor (unique factors, the U's, are considered unimportant and therefore discarded). The items are plotted with the weights representing the coordinates in the two-dimensional factor space in Figure 2.

Note that the distance between the items is not the focus of the analysis (i.e., factor analysis is not a distance model). Rather, the angular separation of the items is of primary interest. The angular separation of the items may be found by plotting a vector between the origin and each item; the cosine of this separation represents the correlation of the items. Such a model is called a *vector product model*. While this concept may be confusing, it is important to understand that two items close to each other may not be related to the same factor; they may just be close to the origin on different factors. The concept of a distance model will be explained in more detail when we cover

FIGURE 2. Three Hypothetical Mathematics Items Plotted in Two-dimensional Factor Space

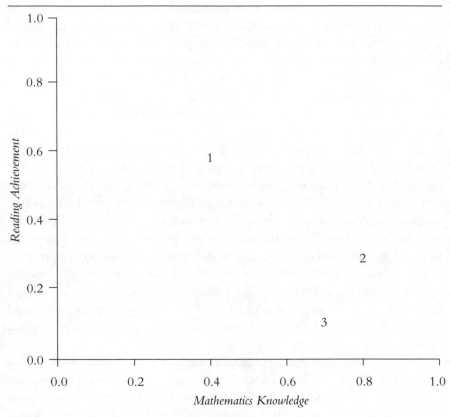

multidimensional scaling. Once a subset of factors is selected, the axes represented by the factors can be rotated to search for alternate, more meaningful, and possibly simpler interpretations of the factors. When the axes are rotated, the loadings (coordinates of the items) will change. How to rotate the factors depends on personal preference and theory about the structure. A varimax rotation is frequently chosen because it tends to maximize the loading of each variable on a single factor, thereby increasing interpretability of the factors. That is, interpretability is enhanced when each variable has a high loading on only one factor and each factor has variables with high loadings.

TABLE 3. GZII Principal Components Analysis:
Eigenvalues and Proportion of Variance

Factor	Eigenvalue	Proportion
1	2.3538	.2354
2	2.2233	.2223
3	1.5385	.1538
4	1.2786	.1279
5	.7937	.0740
6	.6830	.0683
7	.4515	.0452
8	.2873	.0287
9	.2331	.0233
10	.2111	.0211

There is no single solution to a factor analysis. There may be many possible weightings for several reasons: differing extraction methods, differing criteria for selection of factors, and differing rotation techniques. It is a good idea to try several approaches and to compare results. For example, we often do both a principal components and a principal factors extraction with varimax and oblique rotations (in oblique rotations, the angles between the axes are not 90 degrees). If the same variables have approximately the same loadings on a given factor under both varimax and oblique rotations, the structure may be considered stable and not method dependent. It is also a good idea to look at both rotated and unrotated loadings. For example, since a varimax rotation is intended to accentuate the differences between factors, information about a single factor that is held in common among the items or test will tend to be lost after rotation. If varimax and oblique rotations yield substantially different factor loadings, this suggests that the factors should not be considered orthogonal. This can be checked by examining the correlations between the factors that are output by the analysis. In this case, the intercorrelations of at least some of the factors will be moderate or high.

We carried out a principal components analysis of the GZII using PROC FACTOR in SAS. This package presents the eigenvalues for the full correlation matrix (in principal components analysis) and the reduced correlation matrix (in principal factors), allowing the researcher to assess the adequacy of each technique. The eigenvalues and proportion of total (standardized) variance accounted for by each factor are shown in Table 3.

TABLE 4. GZII Principal Components Analysis: Initial Loadings

Variable	1	2	3	4
Sc	81	−28	−24	−01
Cr	80	28	−19	−29
Me	68	58	−02	24
Ar	07	79	−04	14
Li	39	75	−04	14
Se	−07	69	07	20
En	27	−12	85	−01
Le	26	10	76	−43
Cl	−05	05	38	75
Na	54	19	−04	54

Note: Decimals omitted

Because there are 10 variables in the data set, we expect 10 eigenvalues (and thus 10 factors). How many of the factors to keep and rotate is the subjective judgment we must make. The scree plot for this analysis was previously presented in Figure 1.

Inspection of the eigenvalues reveals that there are two factors of approximately equal strength that account for approximately 46 percent of the total variance. The next two factors are also approximately equal in strength. Together, the first four factors account for 74 percent of the variance. Most researchers would choose four factors (there are four eigenvalues greater than 1.0), so we start with four factors to see if the solution is interpretable.

The loadings of the unrotated factors are shown in Table 4 with scales grouped according to the factor with which they have their highest loadings. The first factor appears to consist of qualities that would be associated with a preference for scientific research; the second factor is associated with an interest in the arts. The third factor seems to be related to the business world (enterprising, leadership, and, to a lesser extent, clerical), and the fourth seems to be a mixture of the clerical and natural interests with a fairly large negative loading for the leadership variable. Based on the values of the eigenvalues and the interpretability of the factors discussed above, it seems reasonable to assume that there are four factors present that account for most of the variance in the data. We could call these four factors investigative, aesthetic, business, and clerical. When the factors are rotated orthogonally, the loadings remain quite similar to the unrotated loadings, but the structure becomes somewhat

TABLE 5. Factor Loadings of Four Rotated Principal Components: Varimax Rotation

Variable	1	2	3	4
Sc	88	−11	00	−09
Me	79	−43	09	21
Cr	71	43	13	−35
Na	54	31	−07	49
Li	21	81	12	−10
Ar	−07	79	−06	12
Se	−20	67	−02	20
Le	00	11	90	−15
En	08	−11	84	27
Cl	−07	05	09	84

Note: Decimals omitted

clearer. Table 5 shows the loadings of each scale on the four rotated factors, with the scales again regrouped according to the factor with which the highest rotated loading is obtained. We can see that Cr, while retaining a substantial loading on the first factor, loads more heavily on the second factor than it did prior to rotation. Creativity would be expected to be an important component of interests in both science, as represented by the first factor, and artistic pursuits as represented by the second factor. On the other hand, it would not be particularly related to an interest in clerical areas.

We also could rotate the factors obliquely, that is, allow the factors to be correlated. However, when we did so, the largest correlations between the factors were −.14 and .13 (for the factor 2/4 pairing and factor 1/3 pairings, respectively). These correlations are quite small, and we conclude that an orthogonal rotation makes sense. The patterns of factor loadings remained essentially the same, so we conclude that appearance of the structure is not dependent on the method of rotation used. In fact, it appears that rotation does not give results that differ substantially from the unrotated solutions. However, sometimes we find rather different results when comparing methods of rotation.

There are many books that discuss factor analysis. Monographs by Kim and Mueller (1978a, 1978b) present a short introduction to the topic. Two widely used texts are those by Harman (1976) and Gorsuch (1983). Researchers who wish to pursue factor analysis in detail are advised to consult these books.

CLUSTER ANALYSIS OF THE GZII

Cluster analysis is frequently used to classify tests into groups in such a way that the differences among the tests within a group are small relative to the differences between the groups. Unlike factor analysis, in which several factors may account for portions of the variance of a single test, in the most commonly used approaches to cluster analysis, each test may belong to only one group. However, the factor analysis model assumes an additive model— that the variance of a variable is explained by a weighted sum of parts of the factors—which may not be appropriate. Furthermore, factor analysis is carried out using a matrix of Pearson correlation coefficients or tetrachoric correlations, which may be based on inappropriate assumptions about the nature of the data they represent. Unlike exploratory or confirmatory factor analysis, cluster analysis is not based on the additive model and allows use of more general distance measures (such as Euclidean or geometric distance) or measures of association that represent the relationships among the tests but are based on less restrictive assumptions than correlations.

There are two main types of techniques for classifying tests in cluster analysis. *Hierarchical techniques* group clusters beginning with individual tests in successive stages until a single cluster is achieved (agglomeration) or partition a single large cluster consisting of all tests in successive stages until each cluster contains an individual test (division). By examining the groupings at each stage of the cluster analysis, the order in which tests and clusters join, and the intracluster distances, the researcher can gain information about the relationships among the tests. *Nonhierarchical techniques* usually allocate tests to a specified number of clusters set by the researcher. Use of nonhierarchical techniques usually requires some knowledge about the number of clusters that could reasonably be expected; it may be thought of as a confirmatory technique, although there is no good measure of the adequacy of the clustering. As in factor analysis, many algorithms exist for each approach, and results may vary depending on the clustering technique chosen. For this reason, it is a good idea to try several clustering approaches to look for method dependence. For additional information on cluster analysis, consult Everitt (1980), Hartigan (1975), Sneath and Sokal (1973), or Aldenderfer and Blashfield (1984).

Although we could approach cluster analysis with some expectations based on literature about the GZII or the results of our factor analysis above, we prefer to act in an exploratory mode and begin with an agglomerative approach. For this analysis, we used CLUSTER in SPSS, in part because it includes both an icicle plot and a dendrogram as part of its output. The *icicle*

FIGURE 3. Vertical Icicle Plot of GZII
Using Average Linkage Clustering Criterion

	Se	Ar	Li	Cr	Cl	Le	En	Sc	Me	Na

```
      Se   Ar   Li   Cr   Cl   Le   En  Sc  Me  Na
1    XXXXXXXXXXXXXXXXXXXXXXXXXXXXXXXXXXX
2    XXXXXXXXXX   XXXXXXXXXXXXXXXX
3    XXXXXXXXXX   XXXXXX   XXXXXX
4    XXXXXXXXXX  X   XXXX   XXXXXXX
5    X   XXXXXXX  X   XXXX   XXXXXXX
6    X   XXXXXXX  X   XXXX   XXXX   X
7    X   X   XXXX  X   XXXX   XXXX   X
8    X   X   X   X  X   XXXX   XXXX   X
9    X   X   X   X  X   X   X   XXXX   X
```

plot is a compact schematic way of showing the order in which objects were joined together. Before the analysis begins, there is an *X* for each object that is to be clustered. As objects join in clusters, the space between them is filled in. When an agglomerative approach is used, vertical icicle plots such as that shown in Figure 3 are read from the bottom up. The first line of the icicle plot, which appears at the bottom of the plot, will show *N*–1 clusters where *N* is the total number of objects; the second (above the bottom line) will display *N*–2 clusters; the top line will display a single cluster. Figure 3 shows a vertical icicle plot for the GZII. Note that the number of clusters present at each stage of the analysis appears to the left of the plot.

On the first step, Sc and Me are joined into a single cluster, while on step two, Le and En join to form another cluster. On step three, Li and Cr form yet another cluster that is widened to include Ar on the fourth step. Note that the icicle plot only tells us the order of the clustering and presents no details regarding the compactness of the clusters. For this, we use the dendrogram.

The *dendrogram* presents information regarding the value of the within-cluster distances as clusters join and is read from left to right. The dendrogram presents the order of clustering, much as the icicle plot does, but it gives additional information regarding homogeneity within the clusters. At the beginning of the cluster analysis, each scale is in a cluster by itself. For the GZII, we begin with ten individual clusters. The within-cluster distance is the distance of each scale to the center of the cluster. At this point, then, the within-cluster distance is necessarily zero since each scale is at the center of its own cluster. When another scale joins the cluster, the within-cluster

FIGURE 4. Dendrogram of GZII Clustering Using Average
Linkage Clustering Criterion

Rescaled Within-cluster Distance

```
        0           5          10          15          20          25
        + ————————— + ————————— + ————————— + ————————— + ————————— +
Me  - + ————————————————————————————————— +
Sc  - +                                   + ————————————————————————— +
Na  ——————————————————————————————————————+                          |
En  ————————————— + ——————————————————————————————————————————————— +   |
Le  ————————————— +                                                 + - +
Cl  ——————————————————————————————————————————————————————————————— +   |
Cr  ————————————— + ——————————————————————— +                           |
Li  ————————————— +                         + ——————————————————— +     |
Ar  ————————————————————————————————————————+                     + ——— +
Se  ——————————————————————————————————————————————————————————— +
```

distance increases. The less similar the objects joining the cluster, the greater
the increase in the within-cluster distance (and correspondingly, the greater
the decrease in the within-cluster homogeneity).

In Figure 4, we show the dendrogram for the cluster analysis of the GZII.
Note that the horizontal scale at the top of the figure shows the scaling of
within-cluster distances (standardized to a maximum value of 25 in SPSS).
The divisions on the vertical scale correspond to each test. When two or more
scales join, the figure terminates the line corresponding to the scale with a +.
By reading vertically on the scale, one obtains the within-cluster distance. For
example, Me and Sc are the first two scales to join. When they form a cluster
(i.e., at the point where their lines terminate in a +), the within-cluster
distance increases from zero (for each of the two separate clusters) to
approximately one. Since the most similar objects will be clustered first, it is
apparent that adding objects to clusters tends to increase their within-cluster
heterogeneity. Note that Na is the next object to join the Me–Sc cluster. It
is clearly quite different from the two scales in the cluster, because the within-
cluster distance increases from 1 to 15. Note also that the degree of similarity
between Me and Sc is substantially greater than the similarity of the other
scales which cluster early in the analysis: En–Le (within-cluster distance, 5)
and Cr–Li (within-cluster distance, 6). The dendrogram may be examined for
evidence about objects which belong together (small within-cluster distances)
and for areas where objects are clearly different (as evidenced by abrupt jumps

in the within–cluster distance). Note that no direct meanings should be attached to the rescaled within–cluster distance. All analyses will have the same scale range. What is important is the relative magnitudes of the distances.

Examining the dendrogram shows that the Sc–Me grouping is substantially more homogeneous than the other two clusters set up in the first three steps since its within–cluster distance (approximately 1) is much smaller than those for Le–En and Cr–Li (5 and 6, respectively). Adding other scales to clusters continues to decrease the within–cluster homogeneity substantially. Because Cl appears to be quite distinct from all the other scales, it is the last scale to join a cluster, and when it does the resulting cluster has a large within–cluster distance. The relative heterogeneity of the higher order clusters may be reflective of the situation we encountered in the factor analysis above in which a scale appeared to be related to several factors simultaneously. It appears quite reasonable that Cr should be related to both the Investigative and the Artistic factors. In a cluster analysis, we might expect Cr to be positioned somewhere between clusters for Ar–Li and Sc–Me. Forcing Cr into one of these clusters would increase the within–cluster distance substantially relative to the between–cluster distance. Note that a four-cluster solution contains the groupings (Se–Ar–Li–Cr) (Cl) (Le–En) (Sc–Me–Na). These are essentially the same groupings we obtained in the rotated four-factor solution above.

Several approaches have been developed to determine how clusters are formed; these include single linkage (nearest neighbor), complete linkage (farthest neighbor), and average linkage. To understand how clusters are formed by these approaches, consider objects A, B, and C, which are included in a set to be analyzed by cluster analysis. If B is closer to C than it is to A, B will join with C to form a cluster with any of the linkage techniques described here. With *single linkage* or *nearest neighbor analysis,* if A is closer to *any* object in a cluster that contains B and C (and possibly other objects) than it is to any other object, then it will join that cluster (again assuming no other objects or clusters are closer to each other). With *complete linkage* or *farthest neighbor analysis,* if A is closer to the most distant object in the cluster that contains B and C than it is to the most distant object in any other cluster, then it will join the cluster containing B and C (if there are no other clusters or objects that are even closer by this criterion). With *average linkage,* if A is closer *on the average* to objects B and C which are already in a cluster than it is to any other objects or clusters, then it will join the cluster consisting of B and C (assuming that no other objects or clusters are closer on the average to each other).

FIGURE 5. Vertical Icicle Plot of GZII
Using Single Linkage Clustering Criterion

	Cl	Le	En	Se	Ar	Li	Cr	Sc	Me	Na
1	XXXXXXXXXXXXXXXXXXXXXXXXXXXXXXX									
2	X	XXXXXXXXXXXXXXXXXXXXXXXXXXX								
3	X	XXXX		XXXXXXXXXXXXXXXXXXX						
4	X	XXXX		XXXXXXXXXXXXXX						X
5	X	XXXX	X		XXXXXXXXXXXXX					X
6	X	XXXX	X	X		XXXXXXXXXX				X
7	X	XXXX	X	X	X		XXXXXXX			X
8	X	X	X	X	X	X		XXXXXXX		X
9	X	X	X	X	X	X	X		XXXX	X

Average linkage techniques were developed to avoid the extremes of two other agglomerative techniques, single linkage and complete linkage; these techniques can provide quite different results. For this reason, it is a good idea to try several clustering techniques before accepting any solution.

In the cluster analysis presented in Figures 3 and 4, the criterion used was that of average linkage. We also tried a cluster solution using a single-linkage criterion. The vertical icicle plot for the single-linkage cluster analysis, presented in Figure 5, shows a quite different grouping for four clusters (Cl) (Le–En) (Se–Ar–Li–Cr–Sc–Me) (Na). The difference in the solutions obtained using average linkage and single linkage suggests that perhaps other clustering solutions should be examined before making conclusions about the structure of the data, particularly when the clustering solutions disagree substantially with theoretical predictions or with solutions using other techniques such as factor analysis.

MULTIDIMENSIONAL SCALING OF THE GZII

Multidimensional scaling (MDS) involves recovering the underlying structure of a set of data points given the interpoint distances. The approach may be compared to attempting to reconstruct a map showing locations of cities when only the distances between the cities are known. MDS scaling techniques attempt to recover the coordinates of data points when only the distances between the data points are known. However, in map recovery, we know that we are working with a coordinate set with two dimensions (say, latitude and longitude) whereas in MDS the number of dimensions from which the data were obtained is unknown. In the data we are examining in this chapter, the *points* may be considered to be the scales. We have a measure of distance or proximity between the scales, the correlations between the scales. On a road map, proximities are measured such that a high value implies that points are far apart; such proximity measures are called *dissimilarities*. When we use correlations, high values imply that the points are quite close together; these proximity measures are called *similarities*. The researcher should be careful to specify whether a similarity or a dissimilarity measure is used.

In MDS, we first specify the number of dimensions of the space and state whether distance measures represent similarity or dissimilarity. Then, using the matrix of proximity measures (such as the intercorrelation matrix given above for the GZII), the MDS algorithm attempts to find the coordinates in a space having the specified number of dimensions that will do the best job of reproducing the interpoint distances. However, in the most commonly used approach to MDS, we do not require that the recovered coordinates produce distances that are the same as the proximities input to the procedure; we only require that they be ordered the same. That is, MDS analyses assume that the distance measures are only ordinal, not equal interval or ratio. This particular type of MDS is called *nonmetric MDS*.

As seen in previous chapters, data are subject to both sampling and measurement errors. As a result, the proximity measures used for the MDS analysis do not perfectly represent the theoretical space that underlies the data, and an MDS solution is unlikely to represent the data adequately. Consequently, it is necessary to have a measure of the adequacy of an MDS solution to determine whether a spatial representation of a given number of dimensions accurately represents the structure in the data. One commonly used statistic is called *stress* (Kruskal, 1964). Unfortunately, little is known about the distribution of the stress statistic except that it decreases as the number of dimensions increases and that the magnitude of stress is related to the number of objects being scaled, the type of coefficient used, and the reliability of the data. As a result, there is no criterion for choosing how many dimensions in the solution are appropriate. Kruskal suggested that values of .20, .10, and .05 represent a poor, fair, and good fit, but these criteria may not be appropriate for the reasons stated above. Another technique for finding the appropriate number of dimensions is to plot the stress values against the number of dimensions in the solution much as we do in the scree test in factor analysis. When the plot flattens out, the number of dimensions at the break is generally considered to be appropriate. As is usually the case in data analysis, the researcher should look for the most parsimonious explanation of the data. In this case, parsimonious means the analysis that best reproduces the interpoint distances while retaining a minimum number of dimensions. Once the number of dimensions is chosen, the researcher examines the locations of the points in space to assess the structure of the space. It is tempting to think of the axes in an MDS solution as dimensions in the data. However, their orientation is arbitrary. Any other orientation of the axes in the same number of dimensions would produce the same ordering among the data points. As a result, we should not necessarily attempt to interpret the axes as meaningful. Rather, we should look for clusterings of items and the way in which the items are ordered in the space.

MDS has several advantages over other techniques. First, like cluster analysis, MDS is appropriate for a wide variety of measures of association that would not be appropriate for factor analysis. Secondly, it does not require the additive model described for factor analysis, so it can successfully reproduce structure that cannot be captured by a more restrictive model. Its emphasis on graphic description of data is very helpful to the researcher and can display structures that would be less clear with models emphasizing a more structured, mathematical model. MDS has an advantage over cluster analysis in that it is not required to classify scales into mutually exclusive groups.

There are drawbacks associated with MDS as well. As mentioned previously, the criteria for a good fit are not well known. While computer programs to run factor analysis and cluster analysis are readily available, they are less common for MDS analyses. In addition, the maximum number of dimensions in an MDS analysis is usually limited to six or fewer. Finally, because interpretation of the structure is quite subjective, there may be substantial room for disagreement among researchers regarding the structure present in the data. However, MDS frequently can and does clarify structure for the researcher. Researchers wishing more information on multidimensional scaling may wish to consult texts by Davison (1983), Schiffman, Reynolds, and Young (1981), or Coxon (1982).

The GZII data described above were used as input to the ALSCAL procedure in SPSS. While many measures of distance may be used for input to ALSCAL, we used the same correlation matrix used in the previous analyses. We requested MDS solutions in one, two, and three dimensions. Kruskal and Wish (1978) suggest that there be at least twice as many stimulus pairs (i.e., correlation coefficients) as parameters to be estimated to ensure a stable solution. The number of parameters to be estimated in an MDS analysis is the product of the number of dimensions in the solution and the number of objects (scales) being positioned in space, that is, the total number of coordinates to be calculated. Since there are ten scales, we have 45 correlation coefficients available and 10, 20, and 30 coordinates to estimate for one-, two-, and three-dimensional solutions. While we should get fairly stable

FIGURE 6. Two–dimensional MDS Plot of GZII Data

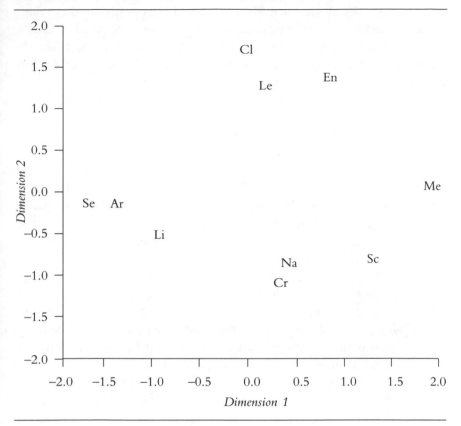

estimates for one or possibly two dimensions, we would expect less stability for three dimensions and results may be misleading. In fact, SPSS did issue a warning message that estimates in two and three dimensions were not reliable and should be interpreted with caution.

Stress values were .419, .192, and .051 for solutions in one, two, and three dimensions. This suggests that a three-dimensional solution permits us to best replicate the distances found in the correlation matrix. Because of the small coefficient-to-coordinate ratio for a three-dimensional solution, we would expect the positions of the scales in those three dimensions to vary considerably if the experiment were replicated. However, we will proceed to interpret these results and compare the findings to our previous findings, albeit with caution.

A one-dimensional solution is clearly not acceptable. Looking at the two-dimensional solution presented in Figure 6, we see that Se, Ar, and Li occupy the same region of space, suggesting that these areas are substantially similar to each other. We also see that Na, Cr, Sc, and Me occupy another region of space (but that Cr is also positioned near Li). Similarly, Cl, Le, and En occupy another region. It is interesting to note that the scales appear to be positioned on the periphery of an elliptical shape, which is what would be expected if the scales represented fairly dissimilar constructs.

While the overall locations of the scales in the space is reasonable, a closer examination of the positions reveals some discrepancies which should cause concern to the researcher who would attempt to interpret positions in a two-dimensional space. For example, Se and Ar are closer together than any other two scales, although their correlation (.35) is substantially smaller than the correlations between Sc and Cr (.57), Sc and Me (.66), and En and Le (.54). The misrepresentation of the distances between Cr, Sc, and Me is a matter of concern. In light of these problems and the relatively high stress coefficient of .19, a three-dimensional MDS solution would appear to be more reasonable and, hopefully, more interpretable.

A graphical representation of the three-dimensional solution is given in Figure 7. The low value of the stress coefficient suggests that this solution represents the differences in the data well. (However, note the objections voiced above, namely the small coefficient-to-coordinate ratio.) Here the configuration of the points suggests that they lie on the surface of a sphere or ellipsoid. On the surface we could find overlapping regions that correspond to groupings involving (Na, Me, Sc, Cr, Li), (Li, Ar, Na, Se), (En, Le), and (En, Cl). Note that although Cl is positioned near En, and En is positioned near Le, Cl is quite distant from Le. However, Se is quite close to Ar as it was in the two-dimensional solution.

When a structure such as the one described above is encountered in MDS, it suggests that factor analysis may do a poor job of representing the data, since the scales tend to be widely dispersed in the MDS space. Had the data clustered more tightly into distinct regions, it would appear that a factor solution might be meaningful.

We should mention that the intent of the GZII developers was to produce a battery of ten scales representing different interests. We should not expect the scales to cluster closely or to be represented well by four factors. The more each scale appears unique, the better the goal of construction was met. Additional information comparing the statistical approaches described in Part 1 may be found in MacCallum (1974), Reckase (1981), and Jones (1987).

FIGURE 7. Three-dimensional MDS Plot of GZII Data

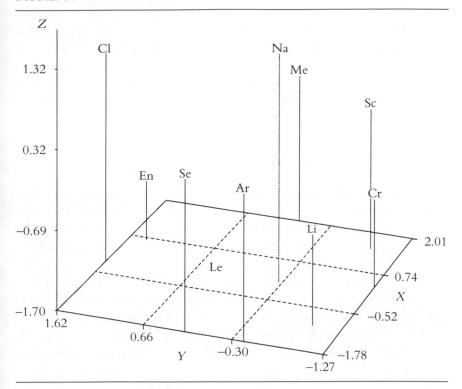

Part 2: Validation With External Criteria

After a test is developed, it is often of interest to determine how the test compares with other instruments or criteria. It is hoped that these comparisons will enhance the interpretation of test results by gaining meaning through what is already known about the criteria. Often the criteria used are other test batteries measuring similar traits.

Typically, a matrix of correlations between components of the test being investigated and the criterion measures is inspected to assist in understanding what the test measures. We start this part of the chapter by discussing the multitrait multimethod (MTMM) approach to examining such a correlation matrix, discussing the type of judgments made in the interpretation. We then proceed to statistical methods of making the same judgments. The amount of space devoted to the MTMM approach is not intended to indicate that this method is recommended; rather, it is chosen as the best way to introduce the type of thinking involved in examining structure of batteries and test validation. In most cases, two or more of the other approaches would be recommended. However, since the correlation matrix is the initial output from the correlations between all the variables (tests) included, visual inspection of the matrix (using MTMM type thinking) is a common first step in examining structure.

Multitrait Multimethod Matrix

The *multitrait multimethod matrix* (MTMM) is a generic approach to the study of relationships between two batteries intended to measure the same traits with different methods. MTMM is a systematic way to examine the correlation matrix visually, and we consider it under the approach of inspection of the correlation matrix. To provide a context for discussing this approach, we describe a fictitious situation in which a group of students attempted to produce a battery similar to the *Cognitive Abilities Test* (CogAT; Thorndike & Hagen, 1983). One of the students had read Cronbach's (1971) suggestion that if a test plan and description are clear, another group of authors should be able to produce an alternate measure following the original plan. According to Cronbach, the degree to which the methods produce similar results indicates the adequacy of the test specifications. The CogAT is a battery of three separate tests, providing the students three opportunities to demonstrate that they can follow the specifications provided by the authors. Any differences in the tests produced by the two teams indicate either that inadequate specifications have led to different methods being used to measure the traits assessed by the batteries, or that the two teams were not equally capable of developing tests and therefore their products were different.

This example presents an unusual case for examining test validity because typically there is an intention to find a substantial difference in the methods. However, this example is the type of situation for which the MTMM approach was designed. In our example, the students hope to find little difference in the methods so that their proficiency in test development is supported.

In the present example, we need to determine correlations between the CogAT tests and the tests built by the students to indicate the relationship between the two batteries. We will refer to the CogAT as Method 1, and to the students' battery as Method 2. We will then want to investigate the relationship between scores examinees obtain when tested by these two

TABLE 6. Coded Data for Interpreting the Multitrait Multimethod Matrix

		Verbal		Quantitative		Nonverbal	
		M1	*M2*	*M1*	*M2*	*M1*	*M2*
Verbal	M1	A					
	M2	B	A				
Quantitative	M1	C	E	A			
	M2	E	D	B	A		
Nonverbal	M1	C	E	C	E	A	
	M2	E	D	E	D	B	A

Note: M1 represents Method 1; M2 represents Method 2.
  A represents a reliability coefficient.
  B represents a multimethod monotrait correlation.
  C represents a monomethod multitrait correlation for method one.
  D represents a monomethod multitrait correlation for method two.
  E represents a multimethod multitrait correlation.

methods. Since this is a textbook example, we have no trouble finding a middle school where the faculty agrees to test a large sample of pupils with both batteries. Because the amount of sampling error in the statistics we use to describe the relationships between measures (such as the correlation coefficient) depends on sample size, it is recommended that the examination of structure be done with a sample exceeding two hundred cases.

Table 6 presents the format of a MTMM where we will present the correlation coefficients for examining the relationships between the CogAT and the students' battery. Instead of correlation coefficients, the entries in Table 6 are letters chosen to describe the order of the magnitude of the coefficients we expect to obtain from testing the pupils with the batteries. If the students have constructed a parallel battery and the results are as expected, the entries should be ordered approximately $A > B > C$ or $D > E$ as indicated by the letters in Table 6. The key under Table 6 provides a guide to understanding the types of correlations in the MTMM.

The elements on the diagonals of Table 6 represent the internal consistency reliability coefficients determined by the method referred to as coefficient alpha. The *A* in Table 6 indicates that we expect reliabilities to be higher than correlations between tests; that is, it is reasonable to expect within-test agreement to exceed between-test agreement. If the students have done a good job following clear specifications, the coefficients represented by B in the table can be considered correlations between alternate forms of the same tests. If the tests were perfectly parallel and no additional error were introduced by the separate administration of the students' battery, the B correlations would equal the reliabilities (A's) of the separate tests. Because these B correlations represent different measures of the same trait, they are called *multimethod monotrait correlations*.

The correlations represented by C or D are monomethod multitrait coefficients; that is, they represent correlations between different traits measured by CogAT or by the students' battery. It is difficult to predict whether the C or the D coefficients should be greater, but both sets should be lower than the B's. It is desirable to have monomethod multitrait correlations that are lower than the multimethod monotrait correlations to demonstrate that different traits are measured within a battery. If B correlations are not higher than C and D correlations, it may be that each battery consists of one single trait and that the traits differ across batteries (i.e., both batteries could be unidimensional but measure different traits). If CogAT really measures three different traits, the C coefficients will be lower than the B's, because different measures of the same trait would correlate higher than different traits measured with a common method. Also, if the students' battery really measures three different traits, the D's will be lower than the B's. Expecting the C's to be higher than the D's is based on the hope that the students did a better job of avoiding method similarity in the tests in their battery.

The E coefficients represent the multimethod multitrait correlations, which should be the lowest in the table. Differences in methods and differences in traits measured should work concurrently to lower the relationships between scores on these measures. If the tests in these batteries are to be used for profile analysis to determine strengths and weaknesses of students, the E's should be much lower than the B's and the A's. It is not important that the E's be much lower than the C's or D's, because if the batteries are good alternate forms it would make little difference which battery was used.

It is a good idea to describe one's expectations for a correlation matrix prior to obtaining and interpreting the results. Too often the data from an analysis have been used to confirm a hypothesis when, in fact, the hypothesis was suggested when the data were observed (of course, you can't tell this from reading an article where authors introduce the topic by presenting their expectations as though derived from the literature review). An advantage of the MTMM over undirected inspection of the correlation matrix is that the expectations are stated prior to looking at the data. Now that we have described what we want to see in the correlation matrix, we can look at Table 7, which presents the hypothetical data from the study.

TABLE 7. Fictitious Data for Multitrait Multimethod Matrix

		Verbal		Quantitative		Nonverbal	
		M1	M2	M1	M2	M1	M2
Verbal	M1	93					
	M2	90	92				
Quantitative	M1	78	75	94			
	M2	76	80	89	92		
Nonverbal	M1	72	70	78	74	92	
	M2	70	75	75	79	88	90

Note: Decimals omitted
M1 represents Method 1; M2 represents Method 2.

Table 7 presents the correlations between the three tests in the CogAT (Method 1) and in the students' battery (Method 2) for 300 middle school students. The elements on the diagonals of the table are the reliability coefficients.

Our first question is whether the B coefficients are almost equivalent to or only slightly lower than the corresponding A's. For example, for the verbal test, the .90 is found to be only slightly lower than the reliabilities of the two tests (.93 for Method 1, .92 for Method 2). Likewise, the other two B coefficients are very close to the reliabilities to which they are compared. This is what we would expect if the students have prepared a battery that contains three tests approximately parallel to those in the CogAT.

A problem arises when one asks how we determine what is meant by "approximately equivalent" or "very close" when comparing a coefficient with the reliabilities. There is no exact answer, but there are some guidelines. One approach is to compare the coefficient with the square root of the product of the reliabilities. If the coefficient is approximately equal to this geometric mean of the reliabilities, we conclude that the two tests are good alternate forms measuring the same trait. The same approach used to determine what we mean by "approximately equivalent" for the B's can be used when comparing the other coefficients to the reliabilities, although it is more common just to compare the rest of the correlations with the B's.

The major question to be asked for persons evaluating the adequacy of the CogAT as a battery would be whether the C's are sufficiently lower than the B's. Consequently, the students ask whether the D's are lower than the B's, and perhaps also whether the D's are lower than the C's. Again, we do not have exact criteria for determining what is *sufficiently lower,* but we might insist that they not be judged to be *very close* by the above guidelines. Since the C's and D's are too low for the tests to be considered good alternate forms for measuring the same traits, we should probably conclude that they are low enough to represent measures of different traits. If these coefficients were similar in magnitude to the B's, we would certainly suspect that all three tests in the batteries were measuring only one trait. In fact, one reviewer of the CogAT has seen similar correlations and concluded that since there is little uniqueness offered by the quantitative test an argument may be presented for deletion of this test from the CogAT (Ansorge, 1985).

All techniques of examining the MTMM require making a subjective judgment that the difference between the B's and other coefficients is (or is not) great enough to indicate validity for the use of separate tests in the battery. Like all analytical methods, MTMM is more appropriate for providing information to make an appraisal than for giving absolute answers. In the example we have used here, we found that there were more between-trait differences than between–method differences. That is, the correlations between traits (for same methods) were lower than the correlations between methods (for same traits). This finding was necessary for us to consider the CogAT and the student battery to be measures of the same three traits. Had the B's been lower than the others, we would have made a definite conclusion that we did not have good batteries for measuring three traits. But we are left without an answer regarding how good the battery is or whether the differences among the traits are enough for separate use. That type of judgment is not one where we will easily find agreement. Because each situation where a test battery may be developed is unique in some respects, there is no good rule of thumb to assist in determining whether the difference between types of coefficients is great enough. The decision is based on a comparative rather than an absolute judgment. A competing battery with lower correlations among its tests (for the same population with the same reliabilities) may be preferred if it exists. However, the results may indicate that cognitive ability as measured by multiple choice tests has such a strong general factor that it is unlikely to find relatively independent measures of its verbal, quantitative, and nonverbal components.

There are two types of evidence sought in the MTMM approach to examining a correlation matrix. The first type is *convergence,* or *convergent validity,* and is found when two tests that should be highly correlated exhibit such a correlation. The second type is *divergence,* or *discriminant validity,* and is found when two tests that should correlate lower exhibit such a correlation. *Correlate lower* always has a relative rather than an absolute meaning.

TABLE 8. SII General Occupational Themes and Brief Descriptors

	Theme	Descriptions
SR	REALISTIC	Robust, rugged, practical, direct, persistent
SI	INVESTIGATIVE	Strong scientific orientation, task oriented
SA	ARTISTIC	Creative, prefer unstructured situations
SS	SOCIAL	Sociable, responsible, humanistic, verbal
SE	ENTERPRISING	Strong leaders, aggressive, confident
SC	CONVENTIONAL	Conscientious, efficient, prefer structure

Most examinations of correlation matrices do not have such a clear structure as the one presented above because most batteries that are correlated do not represent alternate forms. In the more usual case, there is some agreement expected in the tests included in the batteries but there are also some differences expected. We will now examine the correlation matrix obtained between the GZII and another battery, the *Strong Interest Inventory* (SII; Hansen & Campbell, 1985). These two batteries are not intended to be alternate forms, but they are based on theories that have some similarities. The fourth edition of the SII, used to obtain the scores analyzed in this chapter, contains 325 items to which the respondent indicates "like," "indifferent," or "dislike." The results are analyzed by computer and presented in an extensive profile; for the purposes of this chapter, we are concerned only with the six scales that correspond to six general occupational themes, as shown in Table 8. These themes can be arranged in the hexagon shown in Figure 8 with the types most similar to each other falling next to each other, and those most dissimilar falling directly across the hexagon from each other.

The correlation matrix presented in Table 9 resulted from the administration of the GZII and the SII to a sample of 232 adults. With an initial glance at Table 9, we are confronted with 120 coefficients. Some of these coefficients are expected to show convergence and others are expected to show divergence, but which coefficients should show convergence is not as apparent as in the simpler example with the data in Table 7. There are six scales in the SII with which to compare the ten in the GZII. None of the ten scales in the GZII is intended to serve as an alternate form of any theme in the SII. Even though there is a scale labeled Enterprising in the GZII and a theme (scale) labeled ENTERPRISING in the SII, the content included in each is sufficiently distinct that there is no expectation of equivalence across batteries. Because of the similarity between the batteries, we will use the convention of presenting the themes from the SII in all capital letters, and we

FIGURE 8. Hexagonal Relationships Among SII Scales

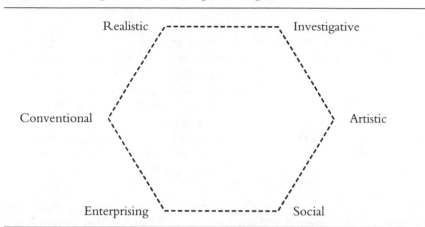

will refer to both themes and scales with the term scales. The abbreviations for the scales in the SII are given in Table 8—note that they all begin with a capital S and the second letter is also capitalized to differentiate these scales from those in the GZII.

There is enough overlap in the descriptions of what is intended to be covered by some of the scales in each battery that some high correlations across batteries are expected. Some correlations across the batteries should demonstrate convergence, but not all to the same degree. Also, not all the remaining coefficients are expected to show the same degree of divergence. The intercorrelations among the scales in the SII are expected to approximate the values indicated in Table 10 for the standardization sample of that battery (none of the data from our sample of 232 were included in the standardization of the SII). The expectation is that some scales within the GZII will have moderate intercorrelations because they were not developed in a manner to ensure independence from each other.

A comparison of the intercorrelations between Tables 9 and 10 shows that there is far from perfect agreement. For example, SE and SI correlated .13 in the standardization sample but only −.05 in our data. However, correlations based on only 200 subjects can fluctuate as much as .20 over repeated samples from the same population. The subjects for the norming studies of the GZII and the SII were drawn from different populations, so we should not be surprised by even greater differences. Note that some of the correlations are very close (e.g., SI and SR correlate .59 and .60 in the two samples), others are not, and there are 15 comparisons to make. When we look also at the GZII

TABLE 9. Correlations Between GZII and SII Measures

	Na	Me	Sc	Cr	Li	Ar	Se	En	Le	Cl	SR	SI	SA	SS	SE	SC
Na	90															
Me	34	96														
Sc	26	66	95													
Cr	26	28	57	89												
Li	21	−20	11	51	94											
Ar	20	−34	−17	28	48	92										
Se	18	−34	−16	02	35	35	94									
En	10	20	02	06	−06	−01	−10	94								
Le	−05	02	02	15	21	−05	09	54	91							
Cl	13	07	−06	−22	−02	11	12	20	−03	94						
SR	60	77	54	25	−04	−12	−15	22	03	11	91					
SI	26	47	79	48	19	−02	−03	05	07	−07	59	90				
SA	22	−17	00	45	62	76	31	−07	00	−04	06	20	93			
SS	19	−22	−08	01	33	26	64	03	22	19	08	13	33	89		
SE	04	−02	−18	−10	06	16	08	65	53	28	13	−05	11	32	85	
SC	10	25	16	−08	−02	00	−01	38	19	67	37	29	01	27	47	91

Notes: Decimals omitted
Reliabilities on diagonals: GZII=alpha, SII=two-week test-retest
Abbreviations:
GZII: Na = Natural, Me = Mechanical, Sc = Scientific, Cr = Creative,
    Li = Literary, Ar = Artistic, Se = Service, En = Enterprising,
    Le = Leadership, Cl = Clerical.
SII: SR = Realistic, SI = Investigative, SA = Artistic, SS = Social,
    SE = Enterprising, SC = Conventional.

correlations, there are too many coefficients to inspect visually with any degree of comfort.

The difficulty in determining what is meant by enough convergence and divergence with so many coefficients supports the need for statistical methods to assist in interpreting the correlation matrix. The rest of the methods discussed in this chapter—factor analysis, cluster analysis, and multidimensional scaling—are statistical methods for examining the correlation matrix. These methods of analysis reduce (but don't completely avoid) the subjective judgments one must make in determining whether a set of correlations indicate whether two scales go together or diverge. Our approach to data analysis involves using more than one method in an attempt to see how the structure of the data emerges in a consistent pattern across analyses.

TABLE 10. Intercorrelations Between the
General Occupational Themes (SII) From the Standardization Sample

Scale		SR	SI	SA	SS	SE
SR	REALISTIC					
SI	INVESTIGATIVE	60				
SA	ARTISTIC	09	34			
SS	SOCIAL	26	28	22		
SE	ENTERPRISING	30	13	09	39	
SC	CONVENTIONAL	35	32	-03	39	50

Note: Decimals omitted

FACTOR ANALYSIS OF THE COMBINED DATA SET

We again present the principal components solution with varimax rotation because there were few differences between the principal components and the principal factors solutions to the combined data set. The eigenvalues for the principal components solution are given below Table 11. Because we are comparing the GZII with the six scales in the SCII, we want to examine a six-factor solution. However, the eigenvalues suggest that four- and five-factor solutions should be examined as well. Because the four-factor solution was not very interpretable, we present the loadings for the five- and six-factor solutions in Table 11.

We examine the observed loadings in Table 11 to make decisions about the pattern of convergence and divergence, beginning with the six-factor solution. Factor 1 has five loadings that indicate some degree of convergence (as indicated by the asterisks), with Sc and SI showing the highest loadings. Note that in the correlation matrix in Table 9 these two scales correlated .79, the highest correlation between scales in the table. Thus, the comparable loadings of these two scales is not surprising, and scales with such high loadings are often referred to as *marker variables* because they help mark or explain what construct (trait) the factor is measuring. From the hexagonal relationships expected among the SII scales, the loading of SR is not surprising. Me and Cr appear to have much in common with these scales, although both of these are also seen to have moderate loadings on other factors.

Factor 2 also has two marker variables (SA and Ar) and another high loading (Li), and this is the other factor on which Cr has a moderate loading.

TABLE 11. Six- and Five-Factor Solutions
(PCA with Varimax Rotation) for GZII and SII

	6 Factors						5 Factors				
	1	2	3	4	5	6	1	2	3	4	5
Sc	92*	−02	−06	−01	−09	15	89*	−01	−02	−16	−06
SI	88*	10	00	09	09	13	83*	10	04	−07	13
Cr	63*	56*	09	−27	−09	06	56*	56*	11	−37	−07
Me	61*	−27	08	11	−31	51*	80*	−23	06	16	−30
SA	06	89*	−01	01	16	08	06	89*	−01	01	16
Ar	−22	87*	−02	12	10	08	−18	88*	−04	17	10
Li	21	73*	08	−11	30	−10	11	72*	11	−20	32
En	00	−02	85*	18	−17	17	09	−01	82*	24	−18
Le	15	−01	85*	−14	21	−16	05	−02	86*	−21	21
SE	−16	10	80*	33	11	08	−10	10	79*	37	09
Cl	−10	01	03	89*	08	08	−03	00	07	85*	09
SC	24	−04	30	86*	08	04	26	−06	36	72*	11
SS	02	17	16	19	86*	06	03	17	16	19	86*
Se	−14	23	−04	00	85*	04	−13	24	−05	04	84*
Na	13	20	−01	00	17	88*	51*	29	−11	32	14
SR	54*	−09	12	19	−05	72*	82*	−03	07	33	−06

Note: Decimals omitted
* Values greater than average loading
Eigenvalues for these analyses were: 3.72, 3.23, 2.65, 1.55, 1.10, .97, .62, and less.

Factor 3 has three scales with high loadings on it and all other loadings .3 or less. Factors 4 and 5 each have only two marker variables loading substantially. Factor 6 has two marker variables (Na and SR), and this is the other factor on which Me has a moderate loading.

The five-factor solution has one substantial difference from the six-factor solution; that is, the scales that comprised the sixth factor are combined with the first factor. Thus, the five-factor solution has a first factor that has so many variables with high loadings that they do not seem to define an interpretable factor. Given the multidimensional nature of this factor, it is not surprising that the four-factor solution was even more difficult to interpret. At this point, it seems reasonable to make a tentative conclusion that six factors best describe the combined set of scales.

Note that a factor seems to be composed of parts of the scales because each scale has some loading on the factor. In this respect, it is not possible to say

FIGURE 9. Dendrogram Using Average Linkage
for Combined Data Set (SII and GZII)

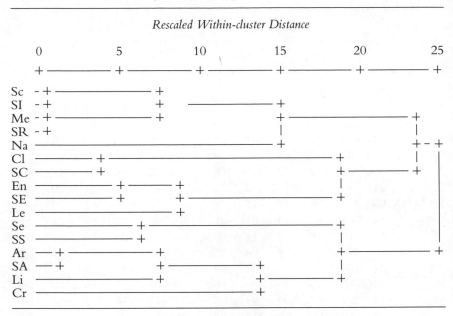

Rescaled Within-cluster Distance

how the scales group together because each scale may group partially with different sets of scales. Therefore, we turn to cluster analysis (CA), where each scale is assigned in its entirety to a set.

CLUSTER ANALYSIS OF THE COMBINED DATA SET

Figure 9 presents a dendrogram showing the results of a cluster analysis. This can be compared with the vertical icicle plot in Figure 10 to examine the differences in these two displays of essentially the same information. We mentioned earlier that the dendrogram shows the homogeneity within each cluster. However, the vertical icicle plot is usually read to examine the cluster membership for a specified number of clusters. Because the six scales in the SII present criteria for interpreting the GZII, it seems reasonable to examine the composition of the sets in the six-cluster solution. Viewing the row numbered 6 in the icicle plot shows that four of the clusters each contain one of the SII scales, one cluster has two SII scales, and one cluster contains only the single scale Na. Not surprisingly, the two SII scales that cluster together are SR and SI, the most highly intercorrelated scales in that battery. Note that

FIGURE 10. Verticle Icicle Plot Using Average Linkage for Combined Data Set (SII and GZII)

```
   SS  Se  Cr  SA  Ar  Li  Na  SR  Me  SI  Sc  SC  Cl  Le  Se  En

 1 XXXXXXXXXXXXXXXXXXXXXXXXXXXXXXXXXXXXXXXXXXXXXXXXX
 2 XXXXXXXXXXXXXXX  XXXXXXXXXXXXXXXXXXXXXXXXXXXXXXX
 3 XXXXXXXXXXXXXXX  XXXXXXXXXXXX  XXXXXXXXXXXX
 4 XXXX  XXXXXXXXXX  XXXXXXXXXXXX  XXXXXXXXXXXX
 5 XXXX  XXXXXXXXXX  XXXXXXXXXXXX  XXXX  XXXXXXX
 6 XXXX  XXXXXXXXXX  X  XXXXXXXXXX  XXXX  XXXXXXX
 7 XXXX  X  XXXXXXX  X  XXXXXXXXXX  XXXX  XXXXXXX
 8 XXXX  X  XXXXXXX  X  XXXXXXXXXX  XXXX  X  XXXX
 9 XXXX  X  XXXX  X  X  XXXXXXXXXX  XXXX  X  XXXX
10 XXXX  X  XXXX  X  X  XXXX  XXXX  XXXX  X  XXXX
11 X  X  X  XXXX  X  X  XXXX  XXXX  XXXX  X  XXXX
12 X  X  X  XXXX  X  X  XXXX  XXXX  XXXX  X  X  X
13 X  X  X  XXXX  X  X  XXXX  XXXX  X  X  X  X  X
14 X  X  X  X  X  X  X  XXXX  XXXX  X  X  X  X  X
15 X  X  X  X  X  X  X  X  X  XXXX  X  X  X  X  X
```

in the ten-cluster solution for a previous step, the scales separated into different clusters, each one grouping with one scale from the GZII.

For some purposes, the ten-cluster solution may be the one providing the most information on the relationships between the two batteries, and this demonstrates one advantage of cluster analysis over factor analysis. Factor analysis will not produce a factor with only one scale loading on it (although it can produce a factor on which only one scale has a high loading), whereas cluster analysis can produce a cluster of only one scale. In the ten-cluster solution, all GZII scales cluster by themselves or with a single scale from the SII.

Examining the composition of the clusters reveals that cluster analysis yields somewhat different information than factor analysis about the structure of the batteries. For example, compare the six-cluster solution with the previous six-factor factor analysis solution. Because there are five clusters and a singleton in the six-cluster solution, it is obvious that we will not find good agreement with six factors. Factors 3, 4, and 5 correspond well with clusters in either the five- or six-cluster solutions. Factor 2 corresponds fairly well with the second cluster in either solution, except that Cr had loaded higher with factor 1 than with factor 2 in the six-factor factor analysis. The big cluster in the five-cluster CA corresponds to the first factor of the five-factor factor analysis except for the absence of Cr. Because the first factor in the five-factor factor analysis was the combination of the first and sixth factors of the six-factor solution, all factors are thus accounted for. However, just as there was no clear description of dimensionality in the factor analysis, there is no clear picture in the cluster analysis. We should not be surprised by the similarity of cluster analysis and factor analysis results, because both methods analyze the same data (the correlation matrix). However, the agreement among the approaches is with respect to the ambiguity of the structure. Given the ambiguity with regard to structure of the data set, the researcher who would report only one outcome describing the structure might be misleading the reader.

Of course, when the investigator finds that the two methods of analysis do not agree or do not clearly describe the structure of the data, there is no judge to make the case clear. Fortunately, MDS is another method to turn to for a third picture. We now go to MDS in hopes of finding additional information regarding the structure of the data set from the combined batteries.

MDS ANALYSIS OF THE COMBINED DATA SET

The data set consisting of the responses to the GZII and the SII was analyzed using MDS as described above for the GZII data set. The matrix of correlations was larger in this case, making a three-dimensional solution more feasible. Stress coefficients were .397, .177, and .083 for solutions in one, two, and three dimensions. While a case might be made for the two-dimensional solution, a three-dimensional solution appears to provide a better fit for the data, particularly in view of our previous interpretation of the MDS analysis of the GZII data.

The three-dimensional plot is presented in Figure 11. The configurations of the GZII scales remain quite close to their positioning in the analysis for the GZII alone. The SII scales are located more or less as expected. For example, SA appears close to Li, Cr, and Ar; SR, SI, Sc, Me, and Na are close together; SE, En, Cl, and SC are together in another region.

A closer inspection of the plot reveals some unexpected discrepancies. SA appears to be closer to Li than to Ar, which is surprising given their titles and descriptors. However, an inspection of the correlation matrix reveals that the correlation between SA and Li is .62, and that for SA and Ar is .76. This discrepancy between the ordering of the actual fitted distances and the distances implied by the correlation matrix increases the magnitude of the

FIGURE 11. Three-dimensional MDS Plot of Combined Data

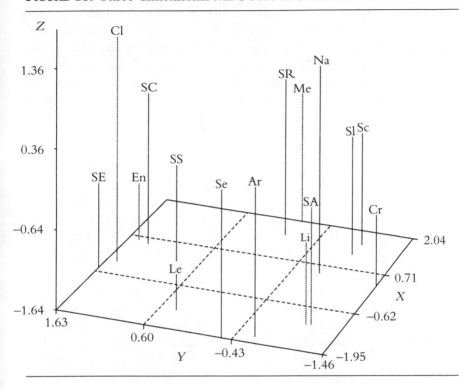

stress coefficient; the stress value, on the other hand, is small enough that we can consider the configuration fairly well fitted.

SI is located near Sc, as would be expected, and SS is located in the same region as Se. It is somewhat surprising that En is located about as close to SC as it is to SE and again, an inspection of the correlation matrix reveals a discrepancy between the ordering of the interpoint distances as represented by correlations and the ordering of the distances in the MDS configuration. This problem has been noted in research, and it has been suggested that MDS is better for scaling large distances than smaller ones; that is, the overall configuration may be fairly accurate with regard to regional separation, but discrepancies may be expected to occur in the positioning of fairly similar objects in the space. It may be, therefore, that it is better to look at the large-scale features of an MDS analysis than to attempt to interpret relative positions within narrow areas of the configuration. When the graph is viewed from this perspective, it is clear that the scales of the SII are quite similar to their GZII counterparts and that they group largely as would be expected. It is also interesting to note that a plot of dimensions 1 and 2 as derived from the three-dimensional graph follows a circular configuration similar to the hexagon described above for the SII. In situations such as those presented by the GZII and the combined data, a factor analysis will misrepresent the relationships among the variables. While the scales are intercorrelated, they test differing facets of interests, and it may not be worthwhile to attempt to combine the scores from either interest inventory into the type of additive score implied in the factor model.

Summary

These approaches to data analysis, while by no means the only techniques that could be used, represent a variety of methods for eliciting information about relationships in the data. Techniques such as factor analysis and regression analysis (not discussed in this chapter) are based on models using strict mathematical relationships and require restrictive assumptions about the nature of the data analyzed. On the other hand, when the data fit the model, these techniques can be highly informative, particularly in an analysis when we are concerned with a parsimonious explanation for structure in data. We have seen that factor analysis suggested that four constructs appeared to account for the relationships among the scales in the GZII and that these constructs were meaningful and interpretable. Five or six interpretable constructs appeared with the factor analysis of the combined scales. The cluster analyses provided results similar to those found in the factor analyses, but because cluster membership cannot be shared, the differences among scales tended to be exaggerated and relationships were somewhat distorted. The three-dimensional MDS solutions suggested that the constructs could be positioned in meaningful regions which represented some of the factors obtained in the factor analysis. However, the dispersion of the scales throughout the space suggested that each scale tended to represent a distinct construct with substantial overlap between the constructs represented by the GZII and the SII. The presence of a reduced number of factors was attributable primarily to the fact that the constructs are interrelated and that single-item factors are not usually produced in a conventional factor analysis. It is important to note that the results of the MDS analysis tended to agree with the test developers' expectations in developing the GZII.

These conclusions have implications for test construction. A researcher who wishes to score individuals on the four constructs obtained in the factor analysis could combine weighted scores from the scales to obtain a broad view of the person's interests. However, the MDS analysis shows that the scales do not cluster into tight regions, suggesting that they may represent distinct areas which should be treated separately.

It should be remembered that there is no single right answer in a statistical analysis. Different techniques may yield differing solutions. Which solutions are appropriate depends on the assumptions about the data and the appropriateness of the models used. Furthermore, there is no guarantee that any of the models yield meaningful conclusions. The researcher should always be guided by theory and careful interpretation of the results in the light of personal experience.

References

Aldenderfer, M. S., & Blashfield, R. K. (1984). *Cluster analysis.* Sage University Paper series on Quantitative Applications in the Social Sciences, 07-044.

Ansorge, C. J. (1985). Review of Cognitive Abilities Test, Form 3. In J. V. Mitchell (Ed.), *The ninth mental measurements yearbook* (pp.350–352). Lincoln: The Buros Institute of Mental Measurements, University of Nebraska Press.

Bentler, P. M. (1989). *EQS: Structural equations program manual.* Los Angeles: BMDP Statistical Software.

Coxon, A. P. M. (1982). *The user's guide to multidimensional scaling.* Exeter, NH: Heinemann Educational Books.

Cronbach, L. J. (1971). Test validation. In R. L. Thorndike (Ed.), *Educational measurement* (2nd ed., pp. 443–507). Washington, DC: American Council on Education.

Davison, M. L. (1983). *Multidimensional scaling.* New York: Wiley.

Davison, M. L. (1985). Multidimensional scaling versus components analysis of test intercorrelations. *Psychological Bulletin, 97,* 94–105.

Dillon, W. R., & Goldstein, M. (1984). *Multivariate analysis: Methods and applications.* New York: Wiley.

Everitt, B. (1980). *Cluster analysis.* New York: Halsted.

Gnanadesikan, R. (1977). *Methods for statistical data analysis of multivariate observations.* New York: Wiley.

Gorsuch, R. (1983). *Factor analysis* (2nd ed.). Hillsdale, NJ: Erlbaum.

Guilford, J. S., & Zimmerman, W. S. (1989). *The Guilford-Zimmerman Interest Inventory.* Palo Alto, CA: Consulting Psychologists Press.

The authors wish to express their appreciation to Mark Davison for his helpful comments on an earlier version of this chapter.

Hansen, J. C., & Campbell, D. P. (1985). *Strong Interest Inventory*. Palo Alto, CA: Consulting Psychologists Press.

Harman, H. H. (1976). *Modern factor analysis*. Chicago: University of Chicago Press.

Hartigan, J. (1975). *Clustering algorithms*. New York: Wiley.

Hayduk, L. A. (1987). *Structural equation modeling with LISREL*. Baltimore: Johns Hopkins University Press.

Huberty, C. J., & Barton, R. M. (1989). An introduction to discriminant analysis. *Measurement and Evaluation in Counseling and Development, 22*, 158–168.

Johnson, R. A., & Wichern, D. W. (1988). *Applied multivariate statistical analysis*. Englewood Cliffs, NJ: Prentice-Hall.

Jones, P. A. B. (1987). Assessment of dimensionality in dichotomously scored data using multidimensional scaling (Doctoral dissertation, University of Arizona, 1987). *Dissertation Abstracts International, 49* (01B), 157. Publication No. AAC8804177.

Jöreskog, K. J., & Sörbom, D. (1988). *LISREL VII: A guide to the program and applications*. Chicago: SPSS.

Kim, J., & Mueller, C. W. (1978a). *Introduction to factor analysis*. Sage University Paper series on Quantitative Applications in the Social Sciences, 07-013.

Kim, J., & Mueller, C. W. (1978b). *Factor analysis*. Sage University Paper series on Quantitative Applications in the Social Sciences, 07-014.

Kruskal, J. B. (1964). Nonmetric multidimensional scaling: A numerical method. *Psychometrika, 29*, 1–27.

Kruskal, J. B., & Wish, M. (1978). *Multidimensional scaling*. Sage University Paper series on Quantitative Applications in the Social Sciences, 07-011.

Long, J. S. (1983a). *Confirmatory factor analysis*. Sage University Paper series on Quantitative Applications in the Social Sciences, 07-033.

Long, J. S. (1983b). *Covariance structure models: An introduction to LISREL*. Sage University Paper series on Quantitative Applications in the Social Sciences, 07-034.

MacCallum, R. C. (1974). Relations between factor analysis and multidimensional scaling. *Psychological Bulletin, 81*, 505–516.

Reckase, M. D. (1981). *The formation of homogeneous item sets when guessing is a factor in item responses*. Office of Naval Research Report 81-5.

Schiffman, S. S., Reynolds, M. L., & Young, F. W. (1981). *Introduction to multidimensional scaling: Theory, methods, and applications*. New York: Academic Press.

Sneath, P., & Sokal, R. (1973). *Numerical taxonomy*. San Francisco: Freeman.

Thorndike, R. L., & Hagen, E. (1983). *Cognitive Abilities Test* (Form 3). Chicago: Riverside.

PART IV

SPECIAL TOPICS
IN TESTING

CHAPTER 9

COMPUTER-ASSISTED PSYCHOLOGICAL ASSESSMENT

Kevin L. Moreland

Introduction

The use of machines to process psychological test data is not a recent innovation (Fowler, 1985). A progression from the early practice of hand scoring materials to the use of a variety of mechanical and electronic scoring machines to the current use of digital computers has freed successive generations of beleaguered secretaries and graduate students from the laborious process of hand scoring psychological tests. The first information concerning scoring machines for the *Strong Vocational Interest Blanks*® (SVIB) appeared in 1930. In 1946 Elmer Hankes, a Minneapolis engineer, built the analog computer that was the first automatic scoring and profiling machine for the SVIB. In 1962 National Computer Systems linked an optical scanner with a digital computer and began scoring both the SVIB and the *Minnesota Multiphasic Personality Inventory* (MMPI; Campbell, 1971). Most automated test scoring still employs optical scanning and digital computer technology.

In the late 1950s, a group of psychologists and psychiatrists decided there would be advantages to interpreting tests by computer. Thus, the first computer-assisted test interpretation (CATI) system was developed at the Mayo Clinic in Rochester, Minnesota (Rome, Mataya, Pearson, Swenson, & Brannick, 1965). In 1965, the Roche Psychiatric Service Institute (RPSI) initiated the first national mail-in MMPI CATI service. The 1980s witnessed the development of well over a hundred CATI systems for a variety of tests of all sorts.

Output Issues

In this chapter we will provide an overview of the types of computerized assessment products and services currently available. First we will discuss the output side of computer-assisted psychological assessment (CAPA)—in other words, the types of reports that are generated. Next we will discuss the evaluation of computer-assisted test interpretations (CATIs), including validity studies—perhaps the most talked-about topic in CAPA today. This is followed by a discussion on input, or the various ways psychological assessment data can be entered into a computer. Next we address a controversial issue relevant to CAPA: computerized test administration. The chapter ends with advice on how to use CAPA products.

As a prospective consumer of CAPA, you should ask yourself some questions about output before deciding to buy. What kind of assessment information do you need? You shouldn't think about the computer while deciding on the type of assessment to be done—for example, evaluation of vocational interests of young adults for purposes of career counseling. Obviously, you need to deliver the assessment service your client needs regardless of whether computer assistance is available or not.

Once you decide on what type of assessment to do, think about what form you need the assessment information in. There are several output options available. The best option depends primarily on the amount of information you need to accomplish the assessment task at hand. Time may also be a factor. The more detailed the computer-assisted report, the less time and effort you'll have to spend dealing with the test results. In reading what follows, keep in mind that the taxonomy of report types is merely a heuristic device. In practice, reports are often a combination of the types discussed below; in particular, interpretive reports ordinarily report scores, too. CAPA systems can be usefully characterized along two lines: (a) the amount of information they provide and (b) the method used to develop them.

BASIC SCORING REPORTS

Simple Scoring Reports
These reports present exactly what their name implies: test scores. The scores may be listed or they may be drawn on a profile. Some instruments—notably

vocational interest inventories with well over 100 scales, such as the *Strong Interest Inventory*—are much too long to score by hand. Thus, computer-generated scoring reports are a necessity for those assessment tools. Even in cases where it is possible to score a test by hand, scoring reports by computer will be desirable when you want to make use of a large number of scores. One can, for example, get by with hand scoring the 13 scales that have been a part of the basic profile on the *Minnesota Multiphasic Personality Inventory* (MMPI) since it was first published. On the other hand, many clinical practitioners make use of the scores on special scales that have subsequently been developed. It takes roughly one minute to hand score and plot one scale on the revised MMPI (MMPI-2). That costs about 17 cents if the scoring and profiling are done by an employee who makes ten dollars an hour. With some scoring reports well under five dollars each, use of only about 20 scales will make computer scoring cost effective. In contrast, if a private practitioner who bills 80 dollars an hour hand scores and profiles the basic MMPI-2, it will cost about 17 dollars.

Extended Scoring Reports

Zachary (1984) defined *extended scoring reports* as "usually involving the addition [to a scoring report] of detailed statistical output but little or no case-specific narrative" (p. 9). Increasingly, computer-generated test profiles include statistical significance tests and statistical confidence intervals plotted around test scores. These kinds of data make it possible to identify especially meaningful scores and meaningful differences among scores at a glance. They should also increase a user's confidence that those scores are in fact important. Statistical significance tests are undoubtedly superior to "clinical rules of thumb" when it comes to accurate interpretation of test scores. And who has time to hand calculate confidence intervals—especially for tests with dozens of scales? (On the other hand, as Zachary was careful to point out, it is still up to the assessor to determine the practical significance of the reported statistical significance.)

The possibilities for reports of this kind are numerous. For example, different confidence intervals could be reported for use in comparing different scales on the same test or to compare scores on a scale administered more than once (see Dudek, 1979). Jackson (1984) provides statistical indices of similarity between *Jackson Vocational Interest Survey* profiles and mean profiles for a number of occupational clusters and college majors (see Figure 1). George Huba, Gale Roid, Robert Zachary, and their former colleagues at Western Psychological Services (WPS) pioneered these kinds of reports, developing them for everything from neuropsychological batteries to measures of self-esteem.

FIGURE 1. Extended Scoring Report
for the *Jackson Vocational Interest Survey*

```
RESPONDENT CASE, M.          123456789    MALE     27-MAR-84    PAGE 6

          SIMILARITY TO COLLEGE AND UNIVERSITY STUDENT GROUPS

                             FEMALES       MALES
AGRICULTURE                  -0.67         -0.57 (VERY LOW)
ARTS & ARCHITECTURE          -0.18         +0.08 (LOW)
BUSINESS                     +0.53         +0.65 (VERY HIGH)
EARTH AND MINERAL SCIENCE                  -0.72 (VERY LOW)
EDUCATION                    +0.64         +0.65 (VERY HIGH)
ENGINEERING                  -0.53         -0.61 (VERY LOW)
HEALTH, PHYSICAL EDUC.
  & RECREATION               -0.40
HUMAN DEVELOPMENT            +0.39         +0.70 (VERY HIGH)
LIBERAL ARTS                 +0.71         +0.77 (VERY HIGH)
SCIENCE                      -0.66         -0.60 (VERY LOW)
NURSES                       +0.17
MEDICAL STUDENTS             +0.08         -0.12 (VERY LOW)
TECHNICAL COLLEGE                          -0.43 (VERY LOW)

               SIMILARITY TO OCCUPATIONAL CLASSIFICATIONS

BELOW ARE RANKED THE OCCUPATIONAL CLASSIFICATION FOUND TO BE SIMILAR TO
YOUR INTEREST PROFILE.  A POSITIVE SCORE INDICATES THAT YOUR PROFILE SHOWS
SOME DEGREE OF SIMILARITY TO THOSE ALREADY WORKING IN THE OCCUPATIONAL
CLUSTER, WHILE A NEGATIVE SCORE INDICATES DISSIMILARITY.

SCORE     SIMILARITY          OCCUPATIONAL CLASSIFICATION
+0.78     VERY SIMILAR        COUNSELORS/STUDENT PERSONNEL WORKERS
+0.74     VERY SIMILAR        TEACHING AND RELATED OCCUPATIONS
+0.74     VERY SIMILAR        OCCUPATIONS IN RELIGION
+0.71     VERY SIMILAR        ADMINISTRATIVE AND RELATED OCCUPATIONS
+0.68     VERY SIMILAR        OCCUPATIONS IN LAW AND POLITICS
+0.60     VERY SIMILAR        PERSONNEL/HUMAN MANAGEMENT
+0.57     SIMILAR             OCCUPATIONS IN SOCIAL WELFARE
+0.55     SIMILAR             OCCUPATIONS IN SOCIAL SCIENCE
+0.55     SIMILAR             OCCUPATIONS IN PRE-SCHOOL & ELEMENTARY TEACHING
+0.50     SIMILAR             SALES OCCUPATIONS
+0.50     SIMILAR             OCCUPATIONS IN MERCHANDISING
+0.49     SIMILAR             CLERICAL SERVICES
+0.48     SIMILAR             OCCUPATIONS IN WRITING
+0.44     SIMILAR             OCCUPATIONS IN ACCOUNTING, BANKING AND FINANCE
+0.05     NEUTRAL             SERVICE OCCUPATIONS
+0.03     NEUTRAL             OCCUPATIONS IN MUSIC
+0.02     NEUTRAL             ASSEMBLY OCCUPATIONS-INSTRUMENTS & SMALL PRODUCTS
-0.30     NEUTRAL             OCCUPATIONS IN ENTERTAINMENT
-0.24     NEUTRAL             OCCUPATIONS IN COMMERCIAL ART
-0.35     DISSIMILAR          PROTECTIVE SERVICES OCCUPATIONS
-0.38     DISSIMILAR          AGRICULTURALISTS
-0.39     DISSIMILAR          MILITARY OFFICERS
-0.41     DISSIMILAR          OCCUPATIONS IN FINE ART
-0.58     DISSIMILAR          SPORT AND RECREATION OCCUPATIONS
-0.59     DISSIMILAR          MATHEMATICAL AND RELATED OCCUPATIONS
-0.62     VERY DISSIMILAR     MACHINING/MECHANICAL & RELATED OCCUPATIONS
-0.63     VERY DISSIMILAR     HEALTH SERVICE WORKERS
-0.65     VERY DISSIMILAR     OCCUPATIONS IN THE PHYSICAL SCIENCES
-0.65     VERY DISSIMILAR     CONSTRUCTION/SKILLED TRADES
-0.68     VERY DISSIMILAR     MEDICAL DIAGNOSIS AND TREATMENT OCCUPATIONS
-0.71     VERY DISSIMILAR     ENGINEERING & TECHNICAL SUPPORT WORKERS
-0.76     VERY DISSIMILAR     LIFE SCIENCES
```

FIGURE 2. The Mayo Clinic Descriptive Report for the MMPI

Sex: Male Education: 20 Age: 34 Marital Status: Married Outpatient
MMPI Code: 27" 5' 8064-391/-KLF/

D	2 Severely depressed, worrying, indecisive, and pessimistic
Pt	7 Rigid and meticulous. Worrisome and apprehensive. Dissatisfied with social relationships. Probably very religious and moralistic
MfM	5 Probabably sensitive and idealistic with high esthetic, cultural, and artistic interests
Sc	8 Tends toward abstract interests such as sciences, philosophy, and religion
Si	0 Probably retiring and shy in social situations
Pa	6 Sensitive. Alive to opinions of others
Pd	4 Independent or mildly nonconformist
Hy	3
Ma	9 Normal energy and activity level
Hs	1 Number of physical symptoms and concerns about bodily functions fairly typical for clinic patients

Consider psychiatric evaluation

INTERPRETIVE REPORTS

Interpretive reports, known as computer-assisted test interpretations (CATIs), include those that are descriptive, screening, and consultative.

Descriptive Reports

Descriptive reports may be distinguished from other types of CATIs by two factors: Each scale on the instrument is interpreted without reference to the others, and comments on any one scale are usually quite cryptic. These interpretations often involve no more than an adverb modifying the adjectival form of the scale name. Such an interpretation of a high score on a depression scale might, for example, read: "Ms. Hall reports that she is very depressed." At first glance, this kind of report may seem so simple-minded as to be relatively useless. Not so. This type of report can be especially helpful when a test has many scales or when a large number of tests need to be interpreted in a short time period. They allow you to quickly and easily identify the most deviant scales. This kind of report is most helpful if an instrument contains scales reported in terms of different types of standard scores (e.g., Ripley & Ripley, 1979) or different normative samples (e.g.,

Hansen, 1987). The MMPI report developed at the Mayo clinic was the first report of this type (see Figure 2).

Screening Reports
Screening reports, like descriptive reports, are cryptic. They are distinguished from descriptive reports in that relationships among scales are usually considered in the interpretation, and the interpretive comments are not usually couched in terms of a single scale name. The *Minnesota Report: Personnel Screening System for the MMPI* (University of Minnesota, 1984) is a screening report in this sense. The main body of that report is very cryptic—five 6-point rating scales. None of the rating scales corresponds directly to an MMPI scale, however. In fact, the rating on each of the five scales is determined by the configuration of a number of MMPI scales. The rules governing the Content Themes presented in that report are also complex. The comment that the client "may keep problems to himself too much" results from consideration of the following set of rules:

- Lie and Correction scales are greater than the Infrequency scale and

- The Infrequency scale is less than 55T and

- The Depression, Paranoia, Psychasthenia, and Schizophrenia scales are less than 65T and

- The Conversion Hysteria scale is greater than 69T or

- The Need for Affection subscale is greater than 63T or

- The Conversion Hysteria scale is greater than 64T, and the Denial of Social Anxiety subscale or the Inhibition of Aggression subscale is greater than 59T or

- The Repression scale is greater than 59T or

- The Brooding subscale is greater than 59T

Screening reports are most helpful in situations where the same decision can be reached by multiple paths. Take the example of screening candidates for emotional fitness for law enforcement jobs. A screening report like the Minnesota Personnel Screening Report may deem a candidate's emotional fitness "suspect" if he or she (a) seems to be a thrill-seeking individual, (b) is so obsessive that he or she is unlikely to respond promptly and properly to emergencies, or (c) may have a drinking problem. Because of this multifaceted approach to the assessment problem, such reports are also likely to be most helpful when they are truly used for screening rather than for making final decisions. They are too deliberately cryptic to be used for the latter. Further investigation, triggered by a screening report, may lead one to discover that a suspect candidate is a recovered alcoholic who has refrained from alcohol consumption for ten years.

Consultative Reports

Dahlstrom, Welsh, and Dahlstrom (1972) contrasted *consultative reports* with screening reports in the following fashion: "The intent [of consultative reports] is to provide a...detailed analysis of the test data in professional language appropriate to communication between colleagues" (p. 313). In other words, consultative reports are designed to mimic as closely as possible the reports generated every day by human test interpreters. Well-developed reports of this type are characterized by the smoothly flowing prose and detailed exploitation of the data that would be expected from an expert human consultant (see Figure 3). Indeed, the chief advantage of these reports is that they can provide a consultation from someone who has spent years studying and using the instrument in question—an expert to whom an assessor would not ordinarily have access. RPSI's system for the MMPI produced the first CATIs of this type. These are the types of reports most typically thought of as computer-assisted test interpretations.

Evaluating CATIs

SCIENTIFIC EVALUATION

If you elect to use the computer to administer or score tests, assessing the adequacy of a CAPA product is straightforward. However, before putting any faith in a CATI, you should ask some more questions. The empirical data available at the time of this writing offer little guidance in choosing CATI systems. Data are unavailable except in the case of a handful of tests, and most of those data are suspect (see below). Although discussion of the nature of scientific data bearing on your choice of a CATI system may be more academic than practical at this time, the quality and quantity of such data are clearly on the increase. In this section we will describe the kinds of scientific data that are becoming increasingly available and the different approaches to evaluating them.

FIGURE 3. The *California Psychological Inventory* Configural Analysis
Supplement, a Consultative Computer-assisted Test Interpretation

---

                    C P I   CALIFORNIA PSYCHOLOGICAL INVENTORY

    SAMPLE   MALE   07-02-91

                                                      Page 12

                    CPI Configural Analysis Supplement

                       by Loring W. McAllister, Ph.D.

        The remaining sections are based closely upon the Practical
    Guide to CPI Interpretation, Second Edition (McAllister, 1988).
    Interpretive hypotheses will be presented in two sections. In the
    first section, hypotheses are presented for individual CPI scales and
    indices. In the second, the hypotheses presented are based on
    configurations of two or more scales. In general, comments will be
    restricted to those scales or configurations on which Mr. Sample has
    obtained extreme scores.

        The interpretive hypotheses that follow are designed for use by
    the human services professional who is interested in a brief and
    practical approach to interpreting the CPI. These comments are
    likely to be particularly valuable in the areas of vocational and
    career counseling as well as in clinical settings.

    Hypotheses based upon individual scales
    _____

        Sociability (57)
            He is likely to be outgoing and sociable although not
            necessarily gregarious. He enjoys people and likes to
            participate in group activities; he is comfortable in
            meeting people.
        Social presence (57)
            He is likely to have high energy and activity levels and
            to demonstrate a sense of urgency and enthusiasm. He
            comes off well in social settings, and projects an air of
            confidence and poise.
        Empathy (55)
            He is probably friendly and adaptable. He exhibits some
            insight in understanding interpersonal behavior and is
            viewed by others as reasonably perceptive and observant.
            He is usually easy to have around.

        Responsibility (33)
            He is likely to appear flashy and may not be a consistent
            performer. He may have difficulty completing tasks, is
            not patient with detail or routine, and may be impulsive.
        Socialization (35)
            He is likely to be willing to take risks. He has strong
            viewpoints and will normally share them with others; he
            can be outspoken and somewhat opinionated. He tends to
            question rules and customs, and may demonstrate some
            rebellious tendencies in behavior. He may become
            defensive in the face of criticism. His ethical
            standards may appear idiosyncratic.

    CPP

Actuarial Approach

In 1956 Paul Meehl called for a good "cookbook" for test interpretation. He was advocating the *actuarial* approach to prediction and description defined by Sines (1966) as "the empirical determination of the regularities that may exist between specified psychological test data and equally clearly specified socially, clinically, or theoretically significant nontest characteristics of the persons tested" (p. 135). This approach to CATI development can best be illustrated through the example of one such system.

Unlike the MMPI and most other popular psychological tests developed prior to the computer age, Lachar's CATI system for the *Personality Inventory for Children* (PIC) was developed without considerable clinical lore concerning the meaning of the PIC scales (Lachar, 1987). Incidentally, Fowler (1987) considers the concurrent development of test and interpretive system an ideal strategy, since test development efforts enrich the evolving interpretation system.

Efforts to compile a database that would allow the development of empirically supported interpretive guidelines were initiated before the PIC was published. Criterion data collection forms (see Lachar & Gdowski, 1979, Appendix A) were accepted by the staff of an active teaching service as performing clinically meaningful functions. An application form was filled out by the child's parents, a form was mailed to the child's school for teacher observations, and a final form was completed by the psychiatry resident or psychology intern who conducted the initial evaluation of the child and parents. Collection of data using these three forms resulted in an actuarial analysis of the PIC scores of 431 children and adolescents (Lachar & Gdowski, 1979).

Development of Lachar's CATI system for the PIC first focused on the correlates of each scale on the basic PIC profile (Lachar & Gdowski, 1979). The actuarial database that provided the interpretive paragraphs and paragraph assignment to scores was generated in two phases. In the first phase, the external criterion variables were correlated with each of 20 profile scales to develop scale correlates. In the second phase, each identified correlate was studied to determine the relationship between the correlate and ranges of scores on the PIC scales. Rules for correlate assignment were then developed (see Table 1). A similar analysis determined frequent patterns of elevated scores and allowed the development of narrative paragraphs that reflected the elevation of two or more profile scales.

It is easy to see that this system conforms to Sines' (1966) definition of an actuarial system. It is also easy to understand Meehl's (1956) enthusiasm for the actuarial approach to test interpretation: The interpretations are, ipso

TABLE 1. Actuarial Correlates of the *Personality Inventory for Children* Delinquency Scale

Description[a]	Correlations[b]	Base Rate	T-score Ranges								Decision Rule	True Positive Rate
			30–59	60–69	70–79	80–89	90–99	100–109	110–119	>120		
Impulsive behavior	.25, .39	68[c]	40	57	61	72	76	72	84	100	>79T	79%
Temper tantrums	.27, .25	43	18	42	40	38	44	63	64	69	>99T <60T	66%
Involved with police	.44, .49	17	0	4	6	10	21	19	58	63	>109T	47%
Dislikes school	.18, .38	39	28	28	28	30	48	55	63	70	>89T	61%
Mother inconsistent in setting limits	.26, .30	59	27	45	61	59	64	82	89	67	>99T <60T	79% 63%

[a] Clinician ratings
[b] *n*s = 215 and 216, respectively
[c] Percentage of children rated as displaying the characteristic

facto, valid within known limits. The question one must ask when considering using an actuarial CATI system is, Will this system generalize to the population I work with? That is, was the developmental population different from your population along some dimension (e.g., severity of psychopathology) that may have an important impact on the validity of the CATIs? For example, several studies have cast doubt on the generalizability of the actuarial interpretation system for the *Halstead-Reitan Neuropsychological Battery* (HRNB) published by Russell, Neuringer, and Goldstein in 1970 (Anthony, Heaton, & Lehman, 1980; Goldstein & Shelly, 1982; Swiercinsky & Warnock, 1977). This is not too surprising considering that the key approach was developed in a hospital serving only veterans of the United States armed forces—a rather select population.

Despite the thorny issue of system generalizability, combining computerized scoring and computer-assisted actuarial interpretation would seem to be a marriage made in assessment heaven. Unfortunately, this relationship remains in the courtship stage. In spite of the fact that this is the way CATI systems *should* be developed, I am aware of only three such systems: that for the PIC, that for the *Marital Satisfaction Inventory* (Snyder & Hoover, 1989; Snyder, Lachar, & Wills, 1988), and that for the *California Psychological Inventory* (Gough, 1990). This is undoubtedly due to the expense and difficulty of developing actuarial CATI systems. After Meehl published his want ad, there were several major attempts to produce actuarial cookbooks for the MMPI (e.g., Gilberstadt & Duker, 1965; Marks & Seeman, 1963). These herculean efforts have fared poorly outside the settings in which they were developed. Application of the complex profile classification rules necessary for actuarial interpretation causes the bulk of the tests to go unclassified (e.g., Payne & Wiggins, 1968). Although ignoring some of the classification rules allowed a greater number of tests to be classified, Payne and Wiggins still could not classify all of their sample. That is to say nothing of the decrement in validity that has been shown to occur when the actuarial correlates are generalized to populations differing in base rates of psychopathology, demographic characteristics, and other important factors (cf. Fowler & Athey, 1971; Gynther & Brilliant, 1968; Palmer, 1971). This state of affairs led some psychologists who were determined to exploit the advantages of computer-assisted test interpretation, such as Fowler (1969), to advocate the "automated clinician...until the actuary comes" (pp. 109–110).

Computer-assisted Clinical Approach

The essential difference between the automated actuarial and *computer-assisted clinical* approaches is that the former method assigns interpretive statements on the basis of their statistical association with test data, while statements chosen by the latter approach are a function of human decision making. The individual who devises the statements and assignment rules in the computer-assisted clinical approach typically makes use of available actuarial data but, as suggested by the fate of the actuarial cookbooks discussed above, is sometimes forced to rely on his or her practical experience to insure that all tests are interpreted (Fowler, 1969). Fowler assumed that even though practical experience must sometimes be resorted to, the individual developing the interpretive statements usually possesses greater experience and, presumably, expertise than the average psychologist. (Unfortunately, however, the advent of microcomputers has made that assumption less tenable than it was when Fowler was writing [cf. Moreland, 1987].) Although undoubtedly not as good as actuarial interpretation, computer-assisted clinical interpretation has an advantage over human interpretation when large and varied populations are involved. Fowler (1969) noted that computers can store tremendous volumes of material and can retrieve them more rapidly and reliably than humans. Thus, while the average psychologist is typically limited in the research literature and population samples to which he or she is exposed and the information that can be retained, the expert human CATI developer can see to it that the computer adjusts for relevant demographic and other nontest variables.

The promise of the "automated clinician" has been realized in a number of studies, some employing psychological tests (e.g., Goldberg, 1970) and some involving other types of data (e.g., DeDombal, 1979; McDonald, 1976; but see Blois, 1980, and Kleinmuntz, 1968, for counter-examples). It comes as no surprise, then, that "automated clinicians" to interpret psychological tests have proliferated. Most current CATI systems use this method of computer-assisted clinical prediction. Thus, most of the available CATI systems need to be validated, just as tests do.

Validating Computer-assisted Clinical CATI Systems

Efforts to validate computer-assisted clinical CATI systems have involved several research designs. Studies of computer-assisted clinical systems developed to interpret the HRNB have been the most sophisticated, using "hard" neurological data (e.g., computed axial tomography studies) as criterion measures (Adams, Kvale, & Keegan, 1984; Anthony, Heaton, & Lehman, 1980; Heaton, Grant, Anthony, & Lehman, 1981). Studies of CATI systems for objective personality inventories—by far the most frequently automated tests—have been considerably less sophisticated. A few studies have compared

CATIs with human interpretations (e.g., Johnson, Giannetti, & Williams, 1978; also see Vale & Keller, 1987). Labeck, Johnson, and Harris (1983) asked three experts to rate the quality and accuracy of the interpretive rules and interpretive statements for the CATI system developed by Labeck. I believe you can use *positive* results of these kinds to justify using a CATI system. On the other hand, you would not necessarily want to reject a CATI system on the basis of negative results from studies like these. The criteria in these studies are based on the clinical judgment of human test interpreters and may, therefore, provide a poor standard against which to judge the validity of computer-assisted interpretations. The validity of clinicians' interpretations is often low enough that a CATI can be at serious variance with them and still be quite accurate (cf. Graham, 1967).

CUSTOMER SATISFACTION STUDIES. Most of the published studies of CATI validity have involved asking the recipients of CATIs to rate the accuracy of interpretations on the basis of their knowledge of the test respondents (see Moreland, 1987). Though disparaged as *customer satisfaction studies* by some writers (Lanyon, 1984), these studies are considered promising by other experts (e.g., Adair, 1978)—especially if slightly modified (see Moreland, 1987; Snyder, Widiger, & Hoover, in press). The customer satisfaction studies have been overwhelmingly supportive of CATIs, as indicated by the median accuracy rating of 78.5 percent found in one review (Moreland, 1987). Reviewers appear to agree that one should be skeptical of this figure because of what Webb, Miller, and Fowler (1970) characterized as the lack of information on the base rate accuracy of the reports. Webb and his colleagues were concerned that raters characterized reports as accurate not because they were pointed descriptions of assessees, but because they contained glittering generalities—so-called *P. T. Barnum statements* (Snyder, Shenkel, & Lowry, 1977).

Consider the following statements:

■ You have a tendency to worry at times, but not to excess.

■ You have found it unwise to be frank in revealing yourself to others.

■ Your sexual adjustment has presented problems to you.

In a now classic study, Forer (1949) got a room full of personnel managers to accept these statements (and others) as very good descriptions of their personalities. Forer had no personal information about the personnel directors—he simply wrote statements in a way he thought would make them applicable to virtually everyone. The Barnum effect is a very robust phenomenon, having been demonstrated many times under varying experimental conditions, including using computer-generated statements (cf. Baillargeon & Danis, 1984; O'Dell, 1972). Recently, those doing customer satisfaction studies of CBTI validity have begun to try to control for the Barnum effect. For example, Moreland and Onstad (1985) attacked this problem by having clinicians rate two CATIs—one of which was closely matched to the genuine CATI but was, nevertheless, bogus—for each test respondent. This procedure yielded an *incremental* validity (defined as genuine bogus) figure of 41 percent. This figure is encouraging, but it doesn't provide you with the same degree of comfort as Lushene and Gilberstadt's (1972) customer satisfaction rating of 93 percent! Eyde, Kowal, and Fishburne (1990) recently demonstrated significant differences in the accuracy of *genuine* reports on the same patient produced by different MMPI CATI systems.

The upshot of the foregoing is that customer satisfaction studies will be of no use in selecting a CATI system unless they have controlled for the Barnum effect. Fortunately, appropriately controlled customer satisfaction studies are appearing at an increasing rate (e.g., Guastello & Rieke, 1990).

EXTERNAL CRITERION STUDIES.   The second major approach to validating CATI systems makes use of *external criterion studies* (Moreland, 1985, 1987). A few researchers have asked consumers of CATIs to complete sympton checklists or Q-sorts based on the computer-generated reports and have subsequently compared those ratings with analogous ones made by individuals familiar with the test respondent. The external criterion studies have typically dealt with the base rate accuracy problem by comparing the accuracy of report-based ratings with "stereotypical patient" ratings or by intercorrelating report-based ratings with randomly chosen criterion ratings. These studies have been plagued by very small samples of test respondents, CATIs, raters, and criterion variables, calling into question the generalizability of the results. Because these problems seem insurmountable, I believe that this approach to CATI validation should be abandoned in favor of customer satisfaction studies that control for the Barnum effect. I am aware of no studies of this type since my own trouble-plagued effort in 1983. On the other hand, Snyder, Widiger, and Hoover (1990) have recently endorsed the external criterion approach to CATI validation. Hence, results of such studies may soon be available to help in decisions regarding computer-assisted clinical systems. Table 2 outlines methodological considerations in assessing validity studies of CATIs.

TABLE 2. Methodological Considerations
in Validity Studies of Computer-assisted Test Interpretations

---

1. Did raters have prior experience with the interpretive systems under study?
2. Were raters given experience with the rating system prior to the beginning of the study?
3. Was the sample of raters representative of those using the interpretation in applied contexts?
4. Was the sample of test respondents unbiased?
5. Was the content of the criterion instruments representative of the content covered by the interpretive system?
6. Were ratings completed keeping the appropriate time frame in mind? For example, the adequacy of inferences about transient affective states should not be rated on the basis of observations conducted weeks after the test was administered.
7. Was discriminant validity of the interpretations assessed? This can be accomplished in *customer satisfaction studies* by obtaining ratings of both genuine and bogus reports (see Moreland & Onstad, 1985) or genuine reports generated by different CATI systems (see Eyde et al., 1990); multireport-multirating intercorrelations can be used for this same purpose in *external criterion studies* (see Chase, 1974).
8. Was *inter*rater reliability assessed?
9. Was *intra*rater reliability assessed?
10. Was reliability of the interpretations themselves, across time, assessed?
11. Could raters indicate contradictory elements of interpretations?
12. Could raters indicate useless elements of interpretations?
13. Could raters indicate when interpretations omitted significant information?
14. Were interpretive statements produced by different rules assessed independently? Ideally, if different rules produce different paragraphs, accuracy ratings should be obtained for each paragraph.

From "Computer-based Test Interpretation: Problems and Prospects" by K. L. Moreland, 1985, *Journal of Consulting and Clinical Psychology, 53*, pp. 823–824. Copyright 1985 by the American Psychological Association. Reprinted by permission.

PRACTICAL EVALUATION

In deciding whether to use computer-assisted interpretations in testing, it is wise to consider four sources of data that have a direct bearing on the adequacy of assessment tools: (a) the credentials of the system author, (b) documentation of the system, (c) scholarly reviews of the system, and (d) brief trials.

Credentials of the System Author

Find out who developed the CATI system and investigate that individual's qualifications. Asking the following questions may be helpful:

- Can you find out anything about the system developer that suggests that he or she probably has at least as much—and preferably more— expertise with the test to be interpreted as you do?

- Has the developer done practically applicable research on the test in question?

- Has he or she written a textbook on the interpretation of the test in question?

- Does the system author present professionally approved (e.g., eligible for continuing education credits) workshops dealing with the test's use?

- Has the developer authored other CATI systems?

- Has he or she authorized previous publications or done consulting in the general area of CATI?

- Does the system author have credentials indicating special expertise as a practitioner? For example, is a clinical psychologist a diplomate of the American Board of Examiners in Professional Psychology?

If the answer to all of these questions is no, one would be well advised to look elsewhere for a CATI system.

Documentation of the System

Documentation providing decision rules for interpretive statements is almost unheard of because most CATI developers are concerned lest their work be stolen (for exceptions, see Lachar, 1974; Lachar & Alexander, 1978). However, the general interpretive approach is usually documented. That is, the developer explains something like this: "CPI system X generates its interpretations from one, two, three, and four scale elevation patterns at four different levels of scale elevation." The consumer should use the available documentation to try to determine whether the CATI system is orthodox. Some systems use idiosyncratic test scoring methods; the use of unorthodox norms is particularly common. Unusual interpretive logic is also fairly common. Such departures from orthodoxy dictate a need for extra caution. A significant minority of CATI developers appears to be creative people with the strong belief that their unorthodox scoring approach or unusual interpretive logic is superior to mainstream approaches. They are seldom able to empirically document the utility of their special approach to the instrument. In most cases, a list of the references consulted to guide development of the system is available. Are the references articles published in peer-reviewed professional journals or other highly credible sources, or are they unpublished research reports? One should be especially wary of the latter, discounting them unless copies can be obtained for evaluation.

Scholarly Reviews of the System

Good sources for reviews of CATI systems are *The Mental Measurements Yearbook* (e.g., Conoley & Kramer, 1989) and journals such as *Computers in Human Behavior* and *Journal of Personality Assessment. The Independent Practitioner,* the newsletter of the American Psychological Association's Division of Independent Practice, includes a regular column on computer-assisted practice which almost always discusses new developments in computer-assisted testing. New sources of information about computer-assisted psychological assessment are appearing rapidly. Reviewers may be given proprietary information about the system that will not be made available to outsiders (e.g., the rules used to choose the interpretive statements included in reports). One caution: Check the reviewer's credentials. It is difficult to find knowledgeable reviewers who don't have a conflict of interest. If you have no reason to believe that the reviewer has an edge on you by virtue of previous experience or access to secret information, you're probably better off trusting your own judgment.

Brief Trials

You should try out CATI systems you are thinking of using on a set of cases. The set of cases should be as large and diverse as possible. The cases should preferably be clients from your files about whom much is known and for whom you need not rely on the CATI in making practical decisions. Insofar as possible, these trials should conform to the methodological guidelines presented in Table 2. In particular, you need to take steps to make sure you don't fall prey to the Barnum effect. For example, if you're trying the CATI system with new clients (perhaps because you have not routinely used the test in question before), don't look at the CATI until you have a good deal of other information about the client. In any case, it's wise to *write down,* as precisely as possible, what you expect a CATI to say before you look at the CATI. My experience has been that it's easy to waffle on the accuracy and comprehensiveness of CATI statements unless you have written expectations to keep you honest. Implementing these suggestions will be costly and time consuming in the short run. However, choosing the wrong CATI system will be more costly and time consuming in the long run.

Input Issues

METHODS OF INPUT

Once you've determined that there is a computer output report that will meet your assessment needs, you can turn to the issue of getting the test data into the computer. There are several means of entering test data into a computer. All have important implications for the cost of computer processing and the time it takes to receive results.

Central Processing
Most central test processing requires that paper-and-pencil tests be completed by the respondent in the usual fashion. The answer sheets are then mailed to a remote, central location, read into the computer by an optical scanner, and processed. The report of test results is returned to the examiner in the same fashion. Modern twists on this technology include orally reporting raw scores by telephone and receiving an oral report of the results, and sending data back and forth via fax machines.

ADVANTAGES. With the increasing availability of inexpensive (under $1000) microcomputers and inexpensive optical scanners (under $4000), computerized test processing is being decentralized. Nevertheless, the demise of central processing is nowhere in sight; central processing remains the cheapest method of obtaining computer-generated test results. Central test processing is attractive when test results are not needed quickly or when a large number of tests needs to be processed, as when administering academic achievement tests and vocational interest inventories. When clients are being seen only once a week, central processing provides test results quickly enough. When tests are used for personnel selection, time is often not at a premium; however, the number of protocols to be processed at one time is frequently large. Virtually all major test publishers in the United States maintain a central processing service for one or more of their tests.

DISADVANTAGES. Central processing is cheap in the short run because it requires no up-front outlay for computer equipment. However, the low price of increasingly powerful, multipurpose microcomputers suggests that central processing, with its associated mailing costs, will not maintain this advantage for long. Indeed, a recent national survey of mental health practitioners in private practice reported that nearly 60 percent own a computer and another 15 percent plan to buy one in the near future (Psychotherapy Finances, 1988). Central processing also forces one to stay with tests that have a fixed item sequence. This means one cannot use modern tests that use statistical information to determine the number and sequence of items administered.

Teleprocessing

Like central processing, teleprocessing makes use of a remote computer. Unlike central processing, raw test data are always entered locally (e.g., in a private practitioner's office) and test results are printed locally. In between, raw test data are transmitted to the computer over the telephone, processed, and test results returned via telephone. Teleprocessing is a relatively new means of processing test data, having been commercially available for less than ten years.

ADVANTAGES. You may find teleprocessing to be an attractive alternative to central processing because test results are available in minutes. It is an attractive alternative to local processing (see the next section) because start-up costs are very low. The only equipment needed is a data communications terminal. Such terminals which do nothing but transmit, receive, and print data can be purchased for a few hundred dollars. By contrast, micro-computers powerful enough to allow local test processing cost about twice as much as a data communications terminal. However, you can, if you wish, teleprocess using practically any microcomputer in lieu of a data communications terminal. This permits you to take advantage of the nonassessment capabilities of microcomputers without being locked into a small number of brands and models of microcomputer; software used for local test processing is typically available only for the most popular microcomputers (see below). A final advantage of teleprocessing is that it allows you to obtain services other than test processing. For example, some services conduct literature searches.

DISADVANTAGES. One disadvantage of teleprocessing is the charge for the telephone call to the central computer. Fortunately, these charges tend to be modest, and they vary according to the test, type of report desired, and the teleprocessing service being used. Most telephone charges vary between about 50 cents and two dollars. These telephone charges may increase the test processing charges considerably if a large volume of testing is done.

In considering a teleprocessing service, keep in mind that there is always a charge for the call, though it may be hidden in the charge for test processing. The major disadvantage of teleprocessing is that such services are still uncommon. A few test publishers whose customers need immediate results (e.g., inpatient psychiatry services) have teleprocessing services, but most large educational test publishers do not have them because their customers do not need immediate turnaround, although they do need to process very large numbers of tests.

Local Processing

With local test processing, nothing has to be sent through the mail or over the telephone to receive computer-generated test results. Local processing involves the use of a microcomputer and possibly a scanner. A microcomputer used for local test processing can also be used for teleprocessing, but need not be.

ADVANTAGES. The major advantages of local processing are local control and flexibility. A local system will never be unavailable owing to routine maintenance at an inopportune moment. If an optical scanner isn't working, the test responses can always be entered via the keyboard. If for any reason the local system cannot be used to process tests in a timely fashion, one may fall back on teleprocessing or central processing. Another advantage of local processing is that the user has available a computer that may be used for other applications, such as accounting programs and word processing.

The ability to administer tests via the computer is another advantage usually touted for local test processing. Use of *computer-adaptive* tests—tests where the item to be administered is chosen on the basis of the examinee's responses to previous items (Weiss & Vale, 1987) — mandates computerized administration. At present, I am aware of no commercially available test batteries that are computer adaptive (Vale & Prestwood, 1988). Computer adaptations of conventional tests are common.

Local test processing software is plentiful. One reason for this is that local software is available that performs test interpretation but does not administer or score the test. (Test scores developed by hand or by using other computer software are entered into the interpretive program. Data entry may be automated, that is, the two computer programs may "talk" to each other, or it may be done by hand via the computer keyboard.) This is the case because the test items and scoring information are owned by the test developer or publisher and cannot be legally copied into computer software without the owner's permission—permission that is seldom forthcoming. This means that there is generally a selection of local interpretive software for a given instrument for a given application (e.g., clinical assessment, personnel screening), whereas mail-in and teleprocessing services, because they inevitably score the test, are usually available only from the test publisher. And most publishers offer only one interpretive system for a given test for a given application.

DISADVANTAGES. The cost disadvantage of local processing vis à vis central processing and teleprocessing has already been mentioned. Other than this, the only potential disadvantages of local processing have to do with on-line test administration. One significant disadvantage is that on-line test administration monopolizes the computer for long time periods. Some individuals can take the MMPI-2 on-line in 45 minutes; others may take as long as two hours. This is probably not a good use of the computer, given that a competent clerk can enter all 567 MMPI-2 responses from an answer sheet in less than five minutes. An optical scanner can process an answer sheet in less than five seconds.

The second potential disadvantage of on-line test administration has to do with the technical and psychometric properties of such administrations. In the abstract, computer administration of tests appears to be a nonissue— procedures for computer administration of tests are developed in the same way that administration procedures for conventional tests are developed. This is true in principle, but most assessment tools that are currently available for on-line administration were developed for conventional administration. Therefore, as a practical matter, one must be concerned that factors indigenous to on-line administration but irrelevant to the purposes of the test may alter test performance. These computer-linked factors may change the nature of the task so dramatically that the computer-administered and conventional versions of a test cannot be said to be measuring the same construct. For example, scores on a test of divergent thinking, where respondents list different uses for common objects within a time limit, will depend heavily on typing ability if administered using a computer keyboard, but will be completely independent of typing skill if administered in the usual fashion. In such cases normative, reliability, and validity data cannot be generalized from the conventional to the computer-administered form of the test.

On-line Test Administration

You need to be able to judge for yourself when nonequivalence may be a concern. At present, most software publishers do not address this issue. In this section, therefore, I will discuss this issue and review the related literature.

Effects of Item Presentation

There are a number of reasons to believe that differences may be found between computer-assisted and conventional item presentation. First, the computer presents items only a few at a time. On conventional tests, respondents often have access to all the items at the same time, allowing respondents to skip around looking for questions they can answer. This may give those taking conventional tests an advantage not shared by those taking a computer-administered version, as when a later question provides a clue to the answer for an item that was skipped. Skipping around in a personality inventory may create a more consistent response pattern than would otherwise be the case. For example, individuals who describe themselves as "depressed" may be more likely to endorse "sad and blue" if allowed to look back at the first response. The computer ordinarily does not permit such item interconnections.

Another difference between administration methods is that the computer usually requires a response—though not necessarily an answer—to each item. The test respondent who wishes to skip an item usually must make a key stroke to do so. As just noted, the computer does not present an entire test at once, so the respondent has no way of knowing how many items are on the test. On many conventional tests, the respondent can see all the items, and the prospect of answering them all may lead to hurried answers or even omissions. Administration by computer may lead to more careful attention to items, which may affect the meaning of responses, thus affecting the test scores.

In both of these instances, it is reasonable to suppose that automated administration is likely to be psychometrically superior to conventional administration. Unfortunately, if that is the case it will also be the case that scores will differ enough from conventional administration to make data developed in that mode inapplicable when the instrument is computer-administered.

Effects of Item Type

Evidence suggests that certain types of items may function differently depending on the mode of administration, regardless of how carefully they were adapted for computer administration. Greaud and Green (1986) found large differences in scores on speeded tests between computerized and paper-and-pencil administrations. Their tests involved very simple arithmetic problems, so it is not surprising that the time needed to record a response—a variable that differed greatly for the two administration modes—significantly affected scores. Hoffman and Lundberg (1976) found the two modes to be equivalent for multiple-choice and true-false items; however, the computer presentation of items requiring matching responses resulted in significantly lower scores, different numbers of changed responses, and different patterns of changed responses.

There is also evidence that rather subtle differences between on-line and conventional test administrations can produce large differences in test results generated by the two modes. Studies of on-line administration of the MMPI indicate that providing an explicit "cannot say" response option often produces a greater number of item omissions than is found when the option is less obvious (Honaker, 1988). Allred and Harris (1984) reported that a similar phenomenon occurs when the *Adjective Checklist* is administered by computer and respondents must actively reject an adjective rather than passively fail to endorse it.

Effects of Item Content

The content of items may also have an effect. Over 25 years ago, Smith (1963) hypothesized that "confession-type" questions might be answered most honestly on the impersonal computer. This is not a very appealing hypothesis where comparisons with apparently impersonal questionnaires are concerned. There is no a priori reason to believe that questionnaires are any more invasive than computers. Moreover, Skinner and Allen (1983) found no differences between respondents' willingness to describe their alcohol and illegal drug use on a paper-and-pencil questionnaire or on a computer. Three studies, on the other hand, have found some evidence that this is the case (Evan & Miller, 1969; Hart & Goldstein, 1985; Koson, Kitchen, Kochen, & Stodolsky, 1970). To further confuse the picture, one study of on-line administration of the MMPI found patients producing more pathological scores when the test was administered in the conventional fashion than when it was computer-administered (Bresolin, 1984).

Despite these inconsistencies, the bulk of evidence on computer adaptations of paper-and-pencil questionnaires points to the conclusion that nonequivalence is typically small enough to be of no practical consequence, if it is present at all (see Beaumont & French, 1987; Blankenship, 1976; Harrell & Lombardo, 1984; Katz & Dalby, 1981a, 1981b; Lukin, Dowd,

Plake, & Kraft, 1985; Ridgway, MacCulloch, & Mills, 1982; Wilson, Thompson, & Wylie, 1982). Rezmovic (1977) found that computer administration caused extreme scorers to become even more extreme, suggesting that nonequivalence of questionnaires may occur mainly at points in the distribution of scores where measurement is already imprecise. The only consistent finding in the literature is that provision of an obvious "cannot say" response option on the computer changes MMPI and CPI scores (Honaker, 1988; Scissons, 1976). This seems to be due to the change in the response format between computer-administered and conventional versions of the tests. When care is taken to keep the two administration formats as similar as possible, this problem disappears (Honaker, 1988).

These conclusions can only be tentative because of the paucity of studies. Furthermore, only a few of these studies took individual differences into account. There is some evidence—both direct and indirect—that individual differences may be important. As noted, Rezmovic (1977) found mode effects mainly for extreme scorers. Koson et al. (1970) found that only their female subjects tended to be more honest on the computer. In addition to this direct evidence, there is a growing body of literature on attitudes toward computer-administered tests as well as affective reactions engendered by computerized test administration.

Effects of Attitudes and Affective Reactions
Individuals generally respond favorably to being questioned by a computer; indeed, many prefer interaction with a computer to conventional assessment (see Bresolin, 1984; Honaker, 1988; Rozensky, Honor, Rasinski, Tovian, & Herz, 1986). People have rated interacting with the computer at least as relaxing as other methods of assessment (Honaker, 1988; Skinner & Allen, 1983), even if the computer initially was somewhat more anxiety-provoking than paper-and-pencil questionnaires (Lushene, O'Neil, & Dunn, 1974). However, a significant minority of subjects in these same studies report a persistent negative reaction to computerized test administration. The elderly compose one demographic group that appears to be, in general, uncomfortable being questioned by a computer (Carr, Wilson, Ghosh, Ancil, & Woods, 1982; Volans & Levy, 1982). It is reasonable to speculate that such negative reactions may adversely affect the quality of the computer-administered assessments.

In summary, most data indicate that if a computer-administration procedure is comparable to the conventional one, comparable scores will be obtained. Furthermore, most people like taking tests on a computer. On the other hand, you need to be familiar with the different types of test equivalence and their respective implications for the use of interpretive data. Hofer and Green (1985) provide a brief, practical synopsis of this complicated topic and other issues discussed in this chapter.

Conclusion

SUMMARY OF INPUT ISSUES

Assuming you don't need technology-dependent information (i.e., information generated by a computer-adaptive test), a variety of options may be available. You can now ask, How quickly do I need the test results? If you need immediate results, you will next need to consider the volume of assessment to be done. Do you process enough tests that you will want to avoid the telephone charges of a teleprocessing system? Regarding the company you are thinking about dealing with, is it financially sound? Are they going to be there when you need help? Like other high technology businesses, the CAPA industry is highly competitive, and companies that are here today may be gone tomorrow (cf. Larson, 1984). Some CAPA companies have already gone out of business. Does the company employ computer professionals to do their programming? Do they employ a full-time tests and measurement expert? What kind of technical support do they provide? Do they have a toll-free telephone number you can call if you have questions about one of their products? How knowledgeable is their customer service staff?

USING CAPA PRODUCTS

CAPA products are like surgeons' scalpels: They can be used well and help people achieve a better life, or they can be used poorly and do harm to individuals. Following a few simple rules will help to ensure that your use of CAPA products is always helpful.

Computerized Test Administration
Sound out your client before settling on computerized test administration. See if they feel comfortable using the computer. If they are uneasy about it, try to make them more receptive, but if a client remains reluctant administer the test in the conventional fashion. In any case, extra care should be taken to insure that people understand what they are expected to do and are able to respond appropriately. Johnson and White (1980) found that senior citizens who received one hour of training in the use of a computer terminal

before testing scored significantly higher on the *Wonderlic Personnel Test* than those who received no training. It may be useful to develop samples of different item types for acquainting subjects with automated test administration. Equipment and other testing conditions are important to the quality of any assessment, but computer administration requires special attention to see that testing conditions are optimal. Equipment must function properly, and devices for responding must be clear.

COMPUTER-ASSISTED TEST INTERPRETATIONS

If the CATI system selected is fundamentally sound, then good CATI use comes from knowing when one should be especially skeptical of CATIs. The limits of an actuarial system's utility are relatively easy to identify. Knowledge of the population used to develop the actuarial correlates will provide reliable clues about the system's limitations. Take, for example, Lachar and Gdowski's (1979) interpretive system for the PIC. Most of the actuarial data used in the system were developed at a comprehensive psychiatric facility in the midst of a large city; many of the children were ethnic minorities, were from poor families, and many had severe problems. This information should make the potential consumer at an exclusive, private residential center specializing in play therapy for neurotic problems proceed with caution.

It is more difficult to decide when to be skeptical of the reports generated by a computer-assisted clinical interpretation system. The following set of suggestions based on the clinical judgment literature may be useful:

- *Low-probability events.* One cannot depend on a CATI, or any other single measure, to confirm the presence or absence of a low base rate event. Suicide attempts are one example of such low probability events.

- *Rare score combinations.* The more unusual the combination of scores on a multiscale test, the more likely it is that the CATI author had to rely on his or her personal experience with the test and nonempirical clinical lore to develop an interpretation. No matter how experienced the developer, he or she will undoubtedly have less experience with uncommon score combinations than with common ones. Indeed, if a combination is sufficiently rare, the developer may have neither personal experience nor clinical lore to use in developing an interpretation and instead may have generalized from the general interpretive strategy for the instrument.

■ *Many deviant scores.* CATIs are more likely to be off the mark when based on extreme scores, particularly if the system uses coarse groupings. Many CATI systems for multiscore inventories group profiles solely according to the one or two most deviant scales; a child whose PIC profile includes elevations only on the Achievement and Development scales probably differs greatly from a child who also has a high Delinquency score.

■ *Scores near cutoffs.* The rigidity and reliability of the CATI system becomes a hindrance when scores are near interpretive cutoffs. A difference of one point on one scale of a multiscale test can some-times make a big difference in a CATI. For example, if scores on the MMPI-2 Depression and Hysteria scales are 70T and all others are lower, a CATI is likely to emphasize the use of repression, somatization, and other externalizing, hysteroid psychological defense mechanisms. If, on the other hand, the Hysteria score drops to 69T, a CATI is likely to emphasize depression, worrying, self-depreciation, and other internalizing symptoms of psychological disturbance.

■ *Unusual response sets or styles.* Many of the currently extant CATI systems deal poorly with the test respondent who, with or without malice aforethought, responds to the test in an unusual way. For example, an individual who obtains a high score on the Lie scale of the MMPI-2 may be characterologically unable to own up to faults. Hence, the remainder of the MMPI-2 scores are unlikely to present an accurate picture of the individual's problems. Most MMPI-2 CATI systems deal appropriately with this problem (i.e., they indicate that the test is unlikely to yield an accurate picture of the assessee), but some do not. Furthermore, none of the Halstead-Reitan CATI systems cited in this chapter have provisions for detecting those who are motivated to look bad in an effort to be compensated for an injury.

Final Note

It is most important that CAPA consumers use sound professional judgment and not acquiesce to computer-generated assessment results. The computer is likely to replace the professional for many, but not all, assessment functions (see Meehl, 1954, for instances in which the assessment professional is indispensable). Until Meehl's (1956) interpretive cookbooks (i.e., actuarial systems) are the rule rather than the exception, assessment professionals will have to be especially circumspect in their use of CAPA products (cf. Eyde & Kowal, 1987).

References

Adair, F. L. (1978). Computerized scoring and interpreting services (Re: Minnesota Multiphasic Personality Inventory). In O. K. Buros (Ed.), *The eighth mental measurements yearbook* (Vol. 1, pp. 940–942, 945–949, 952–953, 957–960). Highland, NJ: Gryphon Press.

Adams, K. M., Kvale, V. I., & Keegan, J. F. (1984). Performance of three automated systems for neuropsychological interpretation based on two representative tasks. *Journal of Clinical Neuropsychology, 6,* 413–431.

Allred, L. J., & Harris, W. G. (1984). *The nonequivalence of computerized and conventional administrations of the Adjective Checklist.* Unpublished manuscript, Johns Hopkins University.

Anthony, W. Z., Heaton, R. K., & Lehman, R. A. W. (1980). An attempt to cross-validate two actuarial systems for neuropsychological test interpretation. *Journal of Consulting and Clinical Psychology, 48,* 317–326.

Baillargeon, J., & Danis, C. (1984). Barnum meets the computer: A critical test. *Journal of Personality Assessment, 48,* 415–419.

Beaumont, J. G., & French, C. F. (1987). A clinical field study of eight automated psychometric procedures: The Leicester/DHSS Project. *International Journal of Man-Machine Studies, 26,* 311–320.

Blankenship, L. L. (1976). Computer-conducted assessment of life-change psychological stress. *Dissertation Abstracts International, 37,* 2495B. (University Microfilms No. 76–24, 045)

Blois, M. S. (1980). Clinical judgment and computers. *New England Journal of Medicine, 303,* 192–197.

Bresolin, M. J., Jr. (1984). A comparative study of computer administration of the Minnesota Multiphasic Personality Inventory in an inpatient psychiatric setting. *Dissertation Abstracts International, 46,* 295B. (University Microfilms No. 85–06, 377)

Campbell, D. P. (1971). *Handbook for the Strong Vocational Interest Blank.* Stanford CA: Stanford University Press.

Carr, A. C., Wilson, S. L., Ghosh, A., Ancil, R. J., & Woods, R. T. (1982). Automated testing of geriatric patients using a microcomputer-based system. *International Journal of Man-Machine Studies, 17,* 297–300.

Chase, L. L. S. (1974). An evaluation of MMPI interpretation systems. *Dissertation Abstracts International, 35,* 3009B. (University Microfilms No. 74–26, 172)

Conoley, J. C., & Kramer, J. J. (1989). *The tenth mental measurements yearbook.* Lincoln, NE: Buros Institute for Mental Measurements.

Dahlstrom, W. G., Welsh, G. S., & Dahlstrom, L. E. (1972). *An MMPI handbook: Vol. 1. Clinical applications.* Minneapolis: University of Minnesota Press.

DeDombal, F. T. (1979). Computers and the surgeon: A matter of decision. *The Surgeon, 39,* 57.

Dudek, F. J. (1979). The continuing misinterpretation of the standard error of measurement. *Psychological Bulletin, 86,* 335–337.

Evan, W. M., & Miller, J. R. (1969). Differential effects of response bias of computer vs. conventional administration of a social science questionnaire. *Behavioral Science, 14,* 216–227.

Eyde, L. D., & Kowal, D. M. (1987). Computerised test interpretation services: Ethical and professional concerns regarding U.S. producers and users. *Applied Psychology: An International Review, 36,* 401–417.

Eyde, L. D., Kowal, D. M., & Fishburne, F. J., Jr. (1990). The validity of computer-based test interpretations of the MMPI. In S. Wise & T. B. Gutkin (Eds.), *The computer as adjunct to the decision-making process.* Lincoln, NE: Buros Institute of Mental Measurements.

Forer, B. R. (1949). The fallacy of personal validation: A classroom demonstration of gullibility. *Journal of Abnormal and Social Psychology, 44,* 118–123.

Fowler, R. D. (1969). Automated interpretation of personality test data. In J. N. Butcher (Ed.), *MMPI: Research developments and clinical applications* (pp. 105–126). New York: McGraw-Hill.

Fowler, R. D. (1985). Landmarks in computer-assisted psychological assessment. *Journal of Consulting and Clinical Psychology, 53,* 748–759.

Fowler, R. D. (1987). Developing a computer-based test interpretation system. In J. N. Butcher (Ed.), *Computerized psychological assessment: A practitioner's guide* (pp. 50–63). New York: Basic Books.

Fowler, R. D., & Athey, E. B. (1971). A cross-validation of Gilberstadt and Duker's 1-2-3-4 profile type. *Journal of Clinical Psychology, 37,* 238–240.

Gilberstadt, H., & Duker, J. (1965). *A handbook for clinical and actuarial MMPI interpretation.* Philadelphia: W. B. Saunders.

Goldberg, L. R. (1970). Man vs. model of man: A rationale, plus some evidence, for a method of improving on clinical inferences. *Psychological Bulletin, 73,* 422–432.

Goldstein, G., & Shelly, C. (1982). A further attempt to cross-validate the Russell, Neuringer, and Goldstein neuropsychological keys. *Journal of Consulting and Clinical Psychology, 50,* 721–726.

Gough, H. G. (1987). *California Psychological Inventory.* Palo Alto, CA: Consulting Psychologists Press.

Graham, J. R. (1967). A Q-sort study of the accuracy of clinical descriptions based on the MMPI. *Journal of Psychiatric Research, 5,* 297–305.

Greaud, V. A., & Green, B. F. (1986). Equivalence of conventional and computer presentation of speed tests. *Applied Psychological Measurement, 10,* 23–34.

Guastello, S. J., & Rieke, M. L. (1990). The Barnum effect and the validity of computer-based test interpretations: The human resource development report. *Psychological Assessment, 2,* 186–190.

Gynther, M. D., & Brilliant, P. J. (1968). The MMPI K+ profile: A reexamination. *Journal of Consulting and Clinical Psychology, 32,* 616–617.

Hansen, J. C. (1987). Computer-assisted interpretation of the Strong Interest Inventory. In J. N. Butcher (Ed.), *Computerized psychological assessment: A practitioner's guide* (pp. 292–321). New York: Basic Books.

Harrell, T. H., & Lombardo, T. A. (1984). Validation of an automated 16PF administration procedure. *Journal of Personality Assessment, 48,* 638–642.

Hart, R. R., & Goldstein, M. A. (1985). Computer-assisted psychological assessment. *Computers in Human Services, 1,* 69–75.

Heaton, R. K., Grant, I., Anthony, W. Z., & Lehman, R. A. W. (1981). A comparison of clinical and automated interpretation of the Halstead-Reitan Battery. *Journal of Clinical Neuropsychology, 3,* 121–141.

Hofer, P. J., & Green, B. F. (1985). The challenge of competence and creativity in computerized psychological testing. *Journal of Consulting and Clinical Psychology, 53,* 826–838.

Hoffman, K. I., & Lundberg, G. D. (1976). A comparison of computer monitored group tests and paper-and-pencil tests. *Educational and Psychological Measurement, 36,* 791–809.

Honaker, L. M. (1988). The equivalency of computerized and conventional MMPI administration: A review. *Clinical Psychology Review, 8,* 561–577.

Jackson, D. N. (1984). *Jackson Vocational Interest Survey manual* (2nd ed.). Port Huron, MI: Research Psychologists Press.

Johnson, D. F., & White, C. B. (1980). Effects of training on computerized test performance in the elderly. *Journal of Applied Psychology, 65,* 357–358.

Johnson, J. H., Giannetti, R. A., & Williams, T. A. (1978). A self-contained microcomputer system for psychological testing. *Behavior Research Methods and Instrumentation, 10,* 579–581.

Katz, L., & Dalby, J. T. (1981a). Computer and manual administration of the Eysenck Personality Inventory. *Journal of Clinical Psychology, 37,* 586–588.

Katz, L., & Dalby, J. T. (1981b). Computer-assisted and traditional assessment of elementary-school-aged children. *Contemporary Educational Psychology, 6,* 314–322.

Kleinmuntz, B. (Ed.). (1968). *Formal representation of human judgment.* New York: Wiley.

Koson, D., Kitchen, C., Kochen, M., & Stodolsky, D. (1970). Psychological testing by computer: Effect on response bias. *Educational and Psychological Measurement, 30,* 803–810.

Labeck, L. J., Johnson, J. H., & Harris, W. G. (1983). Validity of an automated on-line MMPI interpretive system. *Journal of Clinical Psychology, 39,* 412–416.

Lachar, D. (1974). *The MMPI: Clinical assessment and automated interpretation.* Los Angeles: Western Psychological Services.

Lachar, D. (1987). Automated assessment of child and adolescent personality. In J. N. Butcher (Ed.), *Computerized psychological assessment: A practitioner's guide* (pp. 261–291). New York: Basic Books.

Lachar, D., & Alexander, R. S. (1978). Veridicality of self-report: Replicated correlates of the Wiggins MMPI content scales. *Journal of Consulting and Clinical Psychology, 46,* 1349–1356.

Lachar, D., & Gdowski, C. G. (1979). *Actuarial assessment of child and adolescent personality: An interpretive guide for the Personality Inventory for Children profile.* Los Angeles: Western Psychological Services.

Lanyon, R. I. (1984). Personality assessment. *Annual Review of Psychology, 35,* 667–701.

Larson, E. (1984, January). Many firms seek entry into software. *The Wall Street Journal,* p. 23.

Lukin, M. E., Dowd, E. T., Plake, B. S., & Kraft, R. G. (1985). Comparing computerized versus traditional psychological assessment. *Computers in Human Behavior, 1,* 49–58.

Lushene, R. E., & Gilberstadt, H. (1972, March). *Validation of VA MMPI computer-generated reports.* Paper presented at the Veterans Administration Cooperative Studies Conference, St. Louis.

Lushene, R. E., O'Neil, H.H., & Dunn, T. (1974). Equivalent validity of a completely computerized MMPI. *Journal of Personality Assessment, 38,* 353–361.

Marks, P. E., & Seeman, W. (1963). *The actuarial description of personality: An atlas for use with the MMPI.* Baltimore: Williams & Wilkins.

McDonald, C. J. (1976). Protocol-based computer reminders, the quality of care and the non-perfectability of man. *New England Journal of Medicine, 295,* 1351–1355.

Meehl, P. E. (1954). *Clinical versus statistical prediction: A theoretical analysis and a review of the evidence.* Minneapolis: University of Minnesota Press.

Meehl, P. E. (1956). Wanted—a good cookbook. *American Psychologist, 11,* 263–277.

Moreland, K. L. (1983, April). *A comparison of the validity of the two MMPI interpretation systems: A preliminary report.* Paper presented at the 18th annual symposium on Recent Developments in the Use of the MMPI, Minneapolis.

Moreland, K. L. (1985). Validation of computer-based test interpretations: Problems and prospects. *Journal of Consulting and Clinical Psychology, 53,* 816–825.

Moreland, K. L. (1987). Computerized psychological assessment: What's available. In J. N. Butcher (Ed.), *Computerized psychological assessment: A practitioner's guide* (pp. 26–49). New York: Basic Books.

Moreland, K. L., & Onstad, J. A. (1985). *Validity of the Minnesota Report: 1. Mental health outpatients.* Paper presented at the 20th annual symposium on Recent Developments in the Use of the MMPI, Honolulu.

O'Dell, J. W. (1972). P. T. Barnum explores the computer. *Journal of Consulting and Clinical Psychology, 38,* 270–273.

Palmer, W. H. (1971). Actuarial MMPI interpretation: A replication and extension. *Dissertation Abstracts International, 31,* 6265B. (University Microfilms No. 71–09, 128)

Payne, F. D., & Wiggins, J. S. (1968). Effects of rule relaxation and system combination on classification rates in two MMPI "cookbook" systems. *Journal of Consulting and Clinical Psychology, 32,* 734–736.

Psychotherapy Finances. (1988). Testing in private practice. *Psychotherapy Finances, 15,* 7.

Rezmovic, V. (1977). The effects of computerized experimentation on response variance. *Behavior Research Methods and Instrumentation, 9,* 144–147.

Ridgway, J., MacCulloch, M. J., & Mills, M. E. (1982). Some experiences in administering a psychometric test with a light pen and microcomputer. *International Journal of Man-Machine Studies, 17,* 625–678.

Ripley, R. E., & Ripley, M. J. (1979). *Career families: Interpretation manual for the World of Work Inventory* (rev. ed.). Scottsdale, AZ: World of Work.

Rome, H. P., Mataya, P., Pearson, J. S., Swenson, W., & Brannick, T. L.(1965). Automatic personality assessment. In R. W. Stacy & B. Waxman (Eds.), *Computers in biomedical research* (Vol. 1, pp. 505–524). New York: Academic Press.

Rozensky, R. H., Honor, L. F., Rasinski, K., Tovian, S. M., & Herz, G. I. (1986). Paper-and-pencil versus computer administered MMPIs: A comparison of patient's attitudes. *Computers in Human Behavior, 2,* 111–116.

Russell, E. W., Neuringer, C., & Goldstein, G. (1970). *Assessment of brain damage: A neuropsychological key approach.* New York: Wiley.

Scissons, E. H. (1976). Computer administration of the California Psychological Inventory. *Measurement and Evaluation in Guidance, 9,* 22–25.

Sines, J. O. (1966). Actuarial methods in personality assessment. In B. Maher (Ed.), *Progress in experimental personality research* (Vol. 3, pp. 133–193).

Skinner, H. A., & Allen, B. A. (1983). Does the computer make a difference? Computerized versus face-to-face versus self-report assessment of alcohol, drug, and tobacco use. *Journal of Consulting and Clinical Psychology, 51,* 267–275.

Smith, R. E. (1963). Examination by computer. *Behavioral Science, 8,* 76–79.

Snyder, D. K., & Hoover, D. W. (1989, August). *Validity of the computerized interpretive report for the Marital Satisfaction Inventory.* Paper presented at the annual meeting of the American Psychological Association, New Orleans.

Snyder, C. R., Shenkel, R. J., & Lowery, C. R. (1977). Acceptance of personality interpretations: The "Barnum effect" and beyond. *Journal of Consulting and Clinical Psychology, 45,* 104–114.

Snyder, D. K., Lachar, D., & Wills, R. M. (1988). Computer-based interpretation of the Marital Satisfaction Inventory: Use in treatment planning. *Journal of Marital and Family Therapy, 14,* 397–409.

Snyder, D. K., Widiger, T. A., & Hoover, D. W. (1990). Methodological considerations in validating computer-based test interpretations: Controlling for response bias. *Psychological Assessment: A Journal of Consulting and Clinical Psychology, 2,* 470–477.

Swiercinsky, D. P., & Warnock, J. K. (1977). Comparison of the neuropsychological key and discriminant analysis approaches in predicting cerebral damage and localization. *Journal of Consulting and Clinical Psychology, 45,* 808–814.

University of Minnesota. (1984). *User's guide for the Minnesota Report: Personnel Selection System.* Minneapolis: National Computer Systems.

Vale, C. D., & Keller, L. S. (1987). Developing expert computer systems to interpret psychological tests. In J. N. Butcher (Ed.), *Computerized psychological assessment: A practitioner's guide* (pp. 64–83). New York: Basic Books.

Vale, C. D., & Prestwood, J. S. (1988). *Manual for the Minnesota Clerical Assessment Battery.* St. Paul, MN: Assessment Systems Corporation.

Volans, P. J., & Levy, R. (1982). A re-evaluation of an automated tailored test of concept learning with elderly psychiatric patients. *British Journal of Psychology, 21,* 210–214.

Webb, J. T., Miller, M. L., & Fowler, R. D. (1970). Extending professional time: A computerized MMPI interpretation service. *Journal of Clinical Psychology, 26,* 210–214.

Weiss, D. J., & Vale, C. D. (1987). Computerized adaptive testing for measuring abilities and other psychological variables. In J. N. Butcher (Ed.), *Computerized psychological assessment: A practitioner's guide* (pp. 325–343). New York: Basic Books.

Wilson, S. L., Thompson, J. A., & Wylie, G. (1982).Automated psychological testing for severely physically handicapped. *International Journal of Man-Machine Studies, 17,* 291–296.

Zachary, R. (1984, August). Computer-based test interpretations: Comments and discussion. In J. D. Matarazzo (Chair), *Computer-based test interpretation: Prospects and problems.* Symposium conducted at the annual meeting of the American Psychological Association, Toronto.

CHAPTER 10

EXAMINEE FEEDBACK: PRACTICAL GUIDELINES

Baruch Nevo

Introduction

THE NECESSITY OF AN EXAMINEE FEEDBACK MECHANISM

Tests evoke a variety of emotions, thoughts, and attitudes in examinees that often negatively influence test performance. In considering how such potential negative influences can be minimized, experts in the field of education and psychological testing have recommended that the nonpsychometric features of tests be taken into account by those who design and administer tests.[*]

The reactions of examinees were recognized many years ago by test experts as a subject that requires attention and systematic study. As early as 1947, Mosier wrote that the term *face validity* implied that

> a test which is to be used in a practical situation should, in addition to having pragmatic or statistical validity, appear practical, pertinent and related to the purpose of the test as well; i.e., it should not only be valid, but it should also appear valid. (p. 191)

---

[*] This chapter is based, in part, on earlier studies by the author and his colleagues (Nevo, 1985, 1986; Nevo & Jager, 1990; Nevo & Sfez, 1985).

Two decades later, Fiske (1967) observed that examinee perceptions and reactions to tests were important insofar as they

> can affect responses to tests and thus contribute variance to scores. There appear to be few publications on subjects' perceptions and reactions to tests. Neither the immoderate critiques of testing written by laymen nor the moderate discussions by test experts offer systematic information on the topic. (p. 287)

And again, twenty years later, Baird (1987) wrote, "Considering the controversy concerning tests and their assumed importance, it is striking that there is so little information about the attitudes of test takers themselves" (p. 373). In addition, the American Psychological Association's guide for test users (1974, p. 65) stresses the importance of a nonhostile, respectful, and proper environment for the test situation.

In their influential textbooks on psychological testing, Anastasi (1988) and Cronbach (1984) discuss the importance of the face validity of the test and of examiner behavior for sound testing practice.

It is assumed either explicitly or implicitly by these and other authors that the conditions under which tests are administered, the behavior of the examiners, the face validity of the test, and the clarity of test instructions, as well as other nonpsychometric factors, are of major importance in testing. We can reasonably expect, therefore, that if these factors could be taken into account in designing and administering tests, the advantages would be felt in a number of spheres, namely in the (a) curtailment of measurement errors, (b) attraction of potential test users, (c) reduction of the incidence of dissatisfaction and resentment among examinees, particularly those who perform poorly, and (d) improvements in public relations between the testing industry and the public.

The design and modification of tests are usually undertaken on the basis of *hard* statistical data, obtained from the analysis of examinee responses to test items and considered either alone or in relation to performance of measurable tasks (*criterion*). Our purpose here is to show that there are other methods as well for obtaining useful information for the purpose of improving tests, with particular regard for the acquisition of feedback from test examiners. Although information of this kind is undoubtedly subjective, knowledge of the perspective of examinees is important and relevant to our purpose and can be used to improve tests and the testing process. After all, it is the examinees who actually submit to test procedures, and only they experience tests in any personal and immediate way. It is therefore highly likely that they would notice features about a test that may escape the attention of those who are responsible for the design, administration, interpretation, and use of tests.

The effort to develop examinee feedback mechanisms and their implementation on a regular basis can be justified on ethical, practical, and theoretical grounds. Ethically speaking, examinees should be given the opportunity to express their feelings and reactions; practically, it is useful to listen to what examinees have to say; and it is of some theoretical interest to learn about the reactions of examinees. Our concern here will be with the practical aspects of the issue. However, any effort to investigate examinee feedback must be systematic and carried out in conjunction with methodologically sound techniques that are determined in advance. The purpose of this chapter is to furnish some practical guidelines for the development, use, and interpretation of examinee feedback measures so that the readers who are either responsible for large-scale testing programs or are concerned practitioners will be able to apply examinee feedback procedures for purposes of their own.

BACKGROUND

As much as experts in the field may agree about the importance of assessing the reactions of examinees, relatively little has been done to develop systems for obtaining feedback from test takers (four exceptions are Baird, 1987; Davis, 1987; Fiske, 1967; Zeidner, 1987). The *Examinee Feedback Questionnaire* (EFeQ) was conceived as a tool to meet this need and will be used to demonstrate the various dimensions of feedback and their assessment. The first EFeQ employed by this author was designed with a specific test battery in mind: the *Inter-University Psychometric Entrance Examination*, which is one of the requirements for admission to the six universities in Israel. This examination was constructed and centrally administered by the National Institute for Testing and Evaluation (NITE). The entrance exam consists of a psychometric battery comprising five multiple-choice tests: General Knowledge, Figural Reasoning, Comprehension, Mathematical Reasoning, and English. All of the tests are of a multiple-choice type. The time allotted for the entire battery is about three and a half hours. The EFeQ is administered to either a sample of student candidates or to all examinees immediately upon their completion of the test battery.

Initially, ethical considerations figured most prominently in the minds of those working with the EFeQ: Their primary concern was giving examinees a chance to express their attitudes toward the test and to share their test experiences with test authorities. However, in time, the practical value of the questionnaire was recognized as furnishing a means of indirectly monitoring the quality of an exam, the conditions under which the exam was taken, and the procedures used in administering it. The questionnaire thus became a major tool for obtaining a perceptive understanding of examinee responses or reactions to the test situation. However, apart from the practical utility of the EFeQ, the questionnaire is a potentially rich source of information for research in the fields of social psychology, test anxiety, and cross-cultural psychology.

It should be noted that the questionnaire items for obtaining examinee feedback described in the following section need not be followed in detail. They are meant only to serve as a model for a variety of other examinee feedback questionnaires that could be developed by testing organizations, school superintendents, and teachers. It is a suggestive framework that readers are encouraged to use as a basis for designing questionnaires of their own, and it can be modified by adding or deleting items as necessary.

Examinee Feedback Instruments

FORMAT AND ADMINISTRATION

The sample items shown in Figures 1 through 9 were taken from versions of the EFeQ that were administered to college applicants (by NITE) in the period from 1983 to 1989. Although these items were designed with a specific context and audience in mind, we believe that with slight modification they could be made to apply to a great variety of tests, test situations, and examinee populations. Readers are encouraged to borrow ideas and formats from EFeQ and adjust them to their own needs and limitations.

A written statement at the head of examinee feedback inventories should introduce examinees to the questionnaire. For example:

> *This questionnaire is concerned with the test you have just taken. Your responses to the questionnaire are designed to help us improve the test in the future. The questionnaire is anonymous and your responses will not influence your test scores. Please answer all the items. Thank you for your cooperation.*

Characteristically, most versions of EFeQ we have used are made up of three sections, which we identify here as A, B, and C. In all versions of the questionnaire, section A consists of two parts:

- A set of items devoted to the behavior of examiners (see Figure 1)

- A set of items concerning testing conditions (see Figure 2)

FIGURE 1. Behavior of Examiners

How do you rate the behavior of the examiners during the test? Mark each box with a number from 1 to 5 according to the ratings defined below:

5 Excellent   4 Good   3 Satisfactory   2 Unsatisfactory   1 Poor

- ☐ Familiarity with test instructions
- ☐ Allowing questions from examinees
- ☐ Attention given to examinee requests
- ☐ Strictness in enforcing silence
- ☐ Silence maintained among examiners

FIGURE 2. Physical Conditions of Examination

How do you rate the physical conditions in which the examination was taken? Mark each box with a number from 1 to 5 according to the key provided below:

5 Excellent   4 Good   3 Satisfactory   2 Unsatisfactory   1 Poor

- ☐ Seating
- ☐ Temperature
- ☐ Quiet
- ☐ Lighting
- ☐ Crowding

Note: So that the data derived from the responses to Figures 1 and 2 above can be used effectively, examinee feedback answer sheets should be marked so as to allow identification of both the location of testing and the examiners.

FIGURE 3. Face Validity of Selection Methods

Apart from psychometric exams, there are also other methods for selecting university applicants. For each of the methods listed, please enter a number from 1 to 5 in the appropriate box according to the ratings defined below:

5 Very suitable   4 Suitable   3 Quite suitable   2 Unsuitable   1 Very unsuitable

- ☐ Psychometric exam
- ☐ Personal interview
- ☐ Matriculation GPA
- ☐ Achievement tests
- ☐ Letters of recommendation
- ☐ High school GPA
- ☐ Personality test
- ☐ Graphology test
- ☐ Palmistry
- ☐ Astrology

Note: The rankings for this item can be used as indices of face validity of college selection procedures. The personal interview is often ranked in first place in this regard. Studies of personnel selection are highly critical of personal interviews. Examinees are obviously unaware of this and appear to be convinced that personal contact is a necessary part of the selection process. The reason for this might be investigated further by introducing an additional item into the feedback inventories, or by conducting interviews of a sample of examinees. The findings may be of some interest to social psychologists, particularly in the field of attribution theory.

The items in Section B, which are changed periodically, may be classified as pertaining to one of three categories:

- *The test situation*
  This category concerns such subjects as clarity of exam instructions and convenience in using the answer sheet.

- *The test itself*
  These items address such issues as the face validity of the test (i.e., its perceived suitability as a selection device; see Figure 3); the perceived

FIGURE 4. Perceived Cultural Fairness of Examination

How do you rate the following tests in terms of cultural fairness? Mark each box with a number from 1 to 5 according to the ratings defined below:

5 *The test is fair to all cultural*   :   :   :   1 *The test is clearly unfair to one*
   and ethnic groups. It has   *or more cultural or ethnic groups.*
   no features that favor or are   *It contains many features that*
   biased against a particular   *put a particular subpopulation*
   subpopulation of test takers.   *of test takers at a disadvantage.*

☐ General Knowledge

☐ Figural Reasoning

☐ Comprehension

☐ Mathematical Reasoning

☐ English

☐ Entire Exam

degree of cultural fairness in the test (see Figure 4); the test's attractiveness to examinees; the perceived sufficiency of time allotted for completion of the test (see Figure 5); and the perceived difficulty of the test.

■ *The individual examinee*
   This category of items is concerned with topics such as preparation for the test (see Figure 6); self-assessment of performance on the exam; emotional responses to the test (see Figure 7); previous test experience; guessing (see Figure 8); and cheating (see Figure 9).

Section C consists of an open question in which respondents may discuss any subject of their own choosing concerning the exam. This may take the following form:

We are interested in any remarks or suggestions you might have for improving the exam. In the space allotted for this purpose below, you may write about whatever aspects of the test you feel may require improvement. Also, feel free to add positive aspects you regard as worthy of mention.

Responses to the open question often provide a wealth of feedback material. Some examinees use the space to explain their answers to the

FIGURE 5. Perceived Sufficiency of Time for Completion of Examination

---

Did you fail to complete any of the specific tests below because of insufficient time? You may mark more than one item.

☐ General Knowledge

☐ Figural Reasoning

☐ Comprehension

☐ Mathematical Reasoning

☐ English

How do you rate the amount of time allotted for each test? Mark each box with a number from 1 to 5 according to the ratings defined below:

5 *Far too much time*	4 *Too much time*	3 *Sufficient time*	2 *Too little time*	1 *Far too little time*

☐ General Knowledge

☐ Figural Reasoning

☐ Comprehension

☐ Mathematical Reasoning

☐ English

Note: In situations in which guessing is encouraged, examinees may tend to mark all items on the answer sheet during the few last seconds of every subtest. Thus, this kind of examinee feedback may furnish the only means in determining the time required by examinees to complete the test. The classic formulas based on the number of items omitted do not apply here.

multiple-choice items that preceded. Other examinees make evaluative judgments that are either favorable to the exam (e.g., "This was a brilliant test"; "You test people should be praised for what you have done") or unfavorable (e.g., "It was a frustrating experience"; "The school should be ashamed of putting students through all this"). Still others may bring up issues that were unanticipated by the designers of the feedback inventory.

In principle, there is no reason that data obtained from the open question should not be amenable to quantitative analysis. However, since the main part

FIGURE 6. Exam Preparation

How did you prepare for the psychometric tests? More than one answer may be given.

☐ 1. No preparation

☐ 2. By reading the information brochure

☐ 3. By solving sample questions and discussing them with friends

☐ 4. By reading books that prepare for the test

☐ 5. By special tutoring for the test

☐ 6. Other (specify) _____

What advice would you give a friend who is about to take a psychometric test? You may give more than one answer.

☐ 1. Not to prepare

☐ 2. To read the instruction brochure

☐ 3. To solve sample questions and discuss them with friends

☐ 4. To read books that help prepare for the test

☐ 5. To receive tutoring for the test

☐ 6. Other (specify) _____

Note: Discrepancies between ratings assigned to these two items may indicate a change of mind on the part of examinees regarding proper procedure for preparation. The reader should note that the first item concerns past experience, whereas the second item refers to the future.

of the EFeQ is dealt with quantitatively, some room can be left for subjective and interpretative processes to come into play.

Examinee feedback inventories are generally administered anonymously so that examinees feel they are free to answer without worrying that their responses might negatively affect their test scores. The disadvantage of anonymous administration is loss of data that would otherwise allow us to determine the relationship between examinee responses to the feedback questionnaire and personal background and performance on the psychomet-

FIGURE 7. Emotional Responses to the Test

Did the tests make you anxious? How do you rate the following tests in terms of the anxiety they induced? Mark each box with a number from 1 to 5 according to the ratings defined below:

5 *The test* *aroused* *an almost* *unbearable* *degree of* *anxiety,* *worry, and* *frustration.*	4 *The test* *aroused a* *high level* *of anxiety.*	3 *The test* *aroused* *anxiety.*	2 *The test* *did not* *arouse* *anxiety.*	1 *I was* *relaxed and* *felt no* *anxiety* *while taking* *the test.*

☐   General Knowledge

☐   Figural Reasoning

☐   Comprehension

☐   Mathematical Reasoning

☐   English

☐   Entire exam

---

ric test. Therefore, from time to time, examinees may be sampled and asked voluntarily to write their names on the questionnaire, as we have done in the past.

The EFeQ typically consists anywhere from 7 to 10 items; the required time to complete the questionnaire is approximately 5 to 10 minutes. Based on our experience, examinees tend to be highly receptive to the EFeQ and are cooperative in filling out the questionnaire. The rate of response to each EFeQ item is normally 80 percent or higher.

ADDITIONAL TOPICS

Examples of additional topics that might be profitably used by other examining organizations and that warrant measurement via examinee feedback procedures are listed on page 46.

FIGURE 8. Guessing

There are two policies regarding guessing on tests. One policy is to encourage guessing the right answer, even if the guess is completely at random or "wild." The other is to discourage guessing by announcing and implementing a procedure of correction for guessing by reducing test scores by a certain amount for each wrong answer.

We are interested in knowing which system you prefer. Before indicating your preference below, you should consider that although the policy of encouraging guessing may allow you to achieve a higher score (since no deductions are made for wrong answers), the other examinees benefit from the same rule. Hence there is no guarantee that you will come out ahead. You should therefore try to consider the other aspects of the issue.

☐ 1. I definitely prefer being encouraged to guess.

☐ 2. I prefer being encouraged to guess.

☐ 3. I have no preference: Both systems are equally acceptable to me.

☐ 4. I prefer that wild guessing be discouraged by point deduction.

☐ 5. I definitely prefer that wild guessing be discouraged by point deduction.

Note: The issue of guessing has been debated for half a century without a clear statistical advantage being established for either of these approaches to scoring. We should therefore perhaps leave the decision to the test takers.

FIGURE 9. Cheating Behavior

Did you cheat on this test? If the answer is yes, then in what way? You can mark more than one alternative.

☐ Yes—I illegally obtained a copy of the test prior to the examination.

☐ Yes—One of the examiners illegally helped me during the test.

☐ Yes—One or more of the other examinees helped me during the test.

☐ Yes—I helped one or more of the other examinees.

☐ Yes—I made illegal use of material I had with me during the test.

☐ I myself did not cheat, but I saw others cheating.

☐ No—I did not cheat in any way.

Note: Test takers will be reluctant to answer this item frankly unless they are completely convinced that the inventory is administered anonymously and there is no way in which any of the responses can be attributed to particular persons.

- Level of satisfaction with the test registration process

- Sources of information concerning exam content and testing dates and locations

- Clarity of test instructions

- Perceived difficulty level of the tests

- Attitudes toward computerized testing

- Prior experience with psychometric tests

- Examinee preferences regarding feedback on scoring

- Plans for taking the test a second time

- Level of correspondence between the test content and the content requirements or specifications as defined by the course instructor

- Examinee expectations or self-evaluations regarding test scores and outcomes

- Level of satisfaction with the test format (e.g., multiple-choice vs. essay type questions)

RELIABILITY INDICES

Establishing the reliability of a feedback inventory is of considerable importance, since one of its aims is to establish a bridge between examinee test reactions and practical procedures implemented by the questionnaire's users. The EFeQ typically consists of various items, each of which deals with a different issue. Therefore, the reliability of feedback inventories cannot be measured by the *internal consistency* procedures customarily used; they require a somewhat different approach. To give some indication of the expected reliability of examinee feedback inventoried, we will present results derived from a sample of 1,385 college applicants tested in 1983 who responded to a pilot EFeQ (Nevo, 1986; Nevo & Sfez, 1985). Three measures of reliability were used in this case:

- *Correlation between examinee rankings for two similar items.* In 1983 the rating of the face validity of the battery appeared twice, once at the beginning and once at the end of the EFeQ—the wording and context differing somewhat in each instance. The correlations between the two ratings across 1,385 respondents was .65.

- *Comparison of data from the open question and the multiple-choice part of the EFeQ.* The open question allowed for determining intraindividual consistency in still another way. Two hundred questionnaires were sampled at random, and the responses to the open question in each questionnaire were examined. In 120 questionnaires, the open responses had an immediate bearing on various items in the multiple-choice section. Each of these statements was then independently compared with the responses to the multiple-choice question, with a score of + given if the two corresponded, a score of − if they did not correspond, and a score of 0 in cases of uncertainty. Of a total of 120 questionnaires, 79 pairs received a score of +, 32 pairs received a score of 0, and no more than 9 pairs were marked as inconsistent −.

- *Test-retest reliability.* Three weeks following examination, letters were sent to 100 respondents who had filled out the EFeQ, asking them to respond to the same questionnaire once again. Replies were received from only 54 in this sample. Stability (test–retest) correlations were calculated for each item: The lowest correlation was .46, the highest was .88, and the median was .72.

These reliability findings are encouraging, although they are associated with a particular setting and sample of test takers. Even so, the phenomenon we are investigating (i.e., examinee reactions to tests) impresses us generally as being quite consistent and stable.

Guidelines for Developing and Applying Examinee Feedback Questionnaires

Some general guidelines for the development, administration, analysis, and application of examinee feedback questionnaires are presented here. These guidelines may be useful to organizations or individuals involved in large- or small-scale testing programs and are designed to provide systematic information about examinee reactions to such testing. An effort of this kind would require the following stages.

- *Stage 1: Reviewing the literature.* A review should be undertaken of studies and reports concerning the following: (a) examinee as well as public attitudes toward tests, (b) available feedback devices, and (c) self-reports of examinees concerning behavior during and after tests (Nevo, 1991; Nevo & Jäger, 1991).

FIGURE 10. Three-facet Map for Determining Feedback Requirements for an Organization

---

In an examinee feedback questionnaire, items can relate to the

A: Content		*B: Subject*
a_1 attitudes		b_1 test
a_1 feelings	[of respondents to the]	b_2 testee
a_2 behaviors		b_3 test situation

	C: Time
	c_1 before test
[in the time]	c_2 during test
	c_3 after test

- *Stage 2: Determining the feedback requirements of the organization.* Specific feedback needs can be identified by means of interviews with officials of the organization and examinees, as well as by analyzing newspaper articles and radio and TV interviews. The themes to be covered in the EFeQ can be subsumed under three general issues to which the self-reports of the examinees would be addressed. It would be best to present these issues in the frame of a three-facet map, as shown in Figure 10. Numerous items of interest could be proposed for each combination of these issues.

- *Stage 3: Designing a number of versions of the EFeQ.* When stages 1 and 2 are completed, a number of alternative versions of the questionnaire should be prepared. Each of these should consist of 7 to 10 questions, most of them multiple-choice. None of the versions should take longer than 10 minutes to complete.

- *Stage 4: Administering the EFeQ.* Examinee samples should be determined with the priorities of the testing organization in mind. The questionnaire should be administered to the respondents immediately following their completion of the test, resulting in an addition of 10 to 15 minutes to the time required by the testing procedure.

- *Stage 5: Analyzing data.* A quantitative analysis is then undertaken of the feedback data collected in stage 4, and the potential applications of the results are then considered. The analysis of data includes comparisons of the EFeQ responses by subpopulations, as well as comparisons across testing dates, so that shifts in examinee attitudes can be detected.

■ *Stage 6: Evaluation and changes in the EFeQ.* In this last stage, the feedback project is evaluated and decisions made regarding its improvements. It may be necessary to modify or reformulate some, or possibly even all, of the items.

Other Methods of Obtaining Examinee Feedback

A structured questionnaire such as the EFeQ is only one of the techniques that can be used to elicit information regarding the opinions, attitudes, and feelings of test takers toward a test. Other methods include feedback letters from test-takers (which is self-explanatory), group interviews, and individual interviews used primarily in psychodiagnostic testing and held immediately after testing. Both will be discussed in the next section.

GROUP INTERVIEWS

A group interview is less structured and its results less quantifiable than a standard questionnaire, but it is also more dynamic, flexible, and open and, in a sense, more innovative. Group interviews allow a free and spontaneous exchange of ideas and provide nonverbal information. From the point of view of the test taker, the group setting offers an opportunity for sharing feelings and ideas, thereby creating a sense of solidarity among people who have been exposed, as it were, to the same threatening situation.

The Interviewer's Behavior
Since interviewers aim to facilitate communication with subjects in order to uncover their responses to the test, they should be warm, accepting, and genuinely concerned. An interviewer should encourage free expression of ideas and feelings concerning a test, whether they be positive or negative. Moreover, the interviewer should not be defensive or critically evaluative; better results will be achieved by taking a nonevaluative approach, following the suggestions made by Dinkmeyer and Muro (1971) and by Ivey (1980).

The Interviewer's Guide
A practical guideline for implementing the group interview is presented here for interviewers.

THE OPENING ANNOUNCEMENT. Make certain that you know the location and suitability of the designated test room. A few minutes before the examination session is scheduled to end, enter the room, identify yourself to the examiner, and wait without interfering with the testing process until the examination is finished. Ask the examiner to introduce you and wait until he or she leaves the room. Then take a position in front of the class and make the following announcement:

> *The board of directors of this testing project wishes to learn about the reactions of examinees to the test. We think that such feedback could be of great value in improving our tests. One good technique to achieve this goal is group discussion. My task here today is to listen to your responses, ideas, and suggestions concerning the test you have just taken. I would like to ask some of you to volunteer to stay for the discussion. It will take about half an hour. We do not need everyone—10 to 12 people will do. Will those who are willing to stay please remain seated while the others leave.*

BEGINNING OF THE INTERVIEW. With the help of the interviewees, move the chairs to form a circle so that all participants, including yourself, can face each other. If you are not acquainted with the participants, or if they are unacquainted with one another, distribute name tags and ask the participants to write their first names only on the tags. Now say the following:

> *I would like to assure you that your participation in this discussion is in no way connected with your test results. That is why I have asked you to write only your first names. Please feel free to say whatever is on your mind, whether it is complimentary or critical. As to the content of our group discussion, I would appreciate it if you would openly express your attitudes, opinions, and feelings toward the test format, the content of the test, the clarity of the instructions, the registration process, and so on. May I suggest that the meeting be informal. In other words, there is no special procedure, and everyone can speak up at any time. I would like to have your permission to operate this tape recorder. I do not want to trust my memory regarding all the details of our conversation. However, if there is any objection I will turn it off. All right, we can begin now.*

INTERVIEWING TECHNIQUES. In conducting the interview, you should use interviewing techniques as described by Ivey (1980) and by Dinkmeyer and Muro (1971), namely:

- Maintain direct eye contact with the interviewees.

- Sit in a relaxed position that reflects attention and acceptance.

■   Follow the content suggested by examinees.

■   Pose open rather than closed questions.

■   Paraphrase main themes raised by examinees in regard to content and feeling.

■   Summarize main points that are made by one, or preferably more, people. (Once a good summary is achieved, the group will move to another topic.)

■   Make generalizations from one person's remarks in the hope that others will see the relevance of the discussion to their own ideas.

■   Emphasize similarities or differences of two or more interviewees. This will result in more involvement and greater participation on the part of those being interviewed.

THE INTERVIEW. A normal group will provide rich information within 20 to 30 minutes of conversation and with minimal intervention on your part. You may encounter, however, some problematic groups where unwanted developments may threaten to interfere with the interview. Here are some examples:

■   The group may concentrate too long on a single, relatively insignificant issue.

■   One or two participants may try to dominate the group.

■   The group may be apathetic and uninvolved.

It is best to tackle the first two problems by using a direct approach, that is, by openly defining the source of the difficulty. In a situation of general lack of interest, you may try to stimulate the group by asking provocative questions such as, Everything about this test was fine, wasn't it? Or you might read out a list of possible discussion topics to the group, including the following:

■   The registration process

■   Testing conditions

■   Clarity of instructions

■   Appeal of subtests

■   Sources of anxiety

■   Face validity

■   Cultural characteristics of items and subtests

■   Cheating

If the participants skip these topics, you can mention them once or twice, but you should be careful not to impose your own preferences on the feedback process.

SUMMING UP. It is your job to end the interview. Do so when you feel the participants are tired or when they start repeating themselves. Before sending them away, summarize what has been said in the meeting and thank them for their cooperation.

INDIVIDUAL INTERVIEWS:
EXAMINEE FEEDBACK IN THE PSYCHODIAGNOSTIC CLINICAL SETTING

Another semistructured procedure for obtaining examinee feedback is recommended with regard to psychodiagnosis. The number of individuals who undergo psychodiagnostic testing is generally smaller than the number who take group tests. Nevertheless, the first group is not a small one. Hundreds of thousands of children and adults are examined each year with currently available individual assessment devices: intelligence scales, projective techniques, personality questionnaires, and so on. The same considerations that were specified above as justifications for the use of examinee feedback (practical, theoretical, and ethical) exist here, and perhaps even more so. The responses of examinees to the psychodiagnostic tool are influenced by their emotions and cognitions as well as their attitudes toward the examiner, the environment, and the character of a particular test. In other words, not only can we obtain via examinee feedback important information regarding the instruments, the procedure, the psychodiagnostician and so on, but we can also gain better understanding and deeper insight into the individual person under diagnosis.

The format for securing examinee feedback in a psychodiagnostic setting should be different than the questionnaire format of group tests as has been described in the preceding section. It is much more natural to interview the examinee than to ask him or her to fill out a questionnaire. It is also natural for the psychodiagnostician to be the interviewer. This face-to-face interview can take place immediately after the administration of a battery of tests. Benziman (1986) proposes the following questions be asked by the psychodiagnostician:

- Did you like the seating arrangement, or would you have preferred a different position?

- How did you feel about the fact that I wrote down everything you said during the session? How did you feel about being videotaped throughout the whole session?

- Did you have any prior knowledge of the tests before taking them? What were your expectations regarding this psychodiagnostic session? Were you disappointed?

- Which part of the battery (or which test) did you like best? Why? Which part did you mostly dislike? Why?

- On the whole, did you find this experience disturbing, or was it a positive experience?

Every psychodiagnostician can eliminate some questions or add them, depending on the focus. Such an interview may turn into dialogue: The examinee may take advantage of the situation to ask the examiner some questions about the test or to express anxieties. This kind of a dialogue may add further insight to the process.

The atmosphere during the feedback discussion should be friendly, warm, and accepting. There is no need for the examiner to keep a "poker face." At this stage, the examiner is not expected to remain neutral or impersonal.

Conclusion

Examinee feedback inventories have contributed substantially to our understanding of examinee attitudes toward a variety of examinations. A few of the more important findings we have considered have already led to concrete changes in test administration. Some of the results have stimulated further research, while others are still under review.

Here are several examples of direct applications of EFeQ findings to the college aptitude test situation:

- Changing the answer sheet format to make it more congruent with examinee preferences

- Extending the time allotted for specific tests reported to be too speeded

- Placing smokers in special smoking areas or examination halls

- Deleting items of a subtest that were rated as culturally biased or unfair

- Replacing examiners who obtained very low ratings, and retraining other examiners whose behavior during the test was reported to be flawed in any specific domain

- Revising and tightening up security measures in order to minimize cheating

These are, of course, applications associated with a specific feedback device (EFeQ) and a specific tradition of its employment. Readers who use feedback mechanisms of their own may benefit from the procedure in different ways. Since the ratings of EFeQ items have no natural or absolute anchors, the questionnaire's value depends in part on the possibility of meaningful comparisons being carried out over time. For this reason, it would be desirable that a continuous, rather than one-shot design, be used whenever possible. The cost of an EFeQ survey need not be excessive for the examining institution. As noted, examinees are inclined to be receptive to requests to fill out the EFeQ. Most of them are not only cooperative, but also view the matter as being a token of the goodwill of the examiners. The question of whether the outcome justifies the effort is one that only the user can answer. Once the appropriate changes have been introduced, similar questionnaires can be used to evaluate examinee response to almost any kind of test.

Because feedback questionnaires are subjective, it is legitimate to ask whether they furnish an unbiased source of data. The objection might be raised that examinees might think they could improve their test scores artificially by responding to the items in the questionnaire in a way they regard as reflecting the wishes of the examiner or selection criteria of the institution. This could certainly be a serious factor in biasing the result. However, the probability of obtaining sincere answers is greatly increased if the EFeQ is administered anonymously. Apart from this issue, the EFeQ is not entirely free from biasing factors. For instance, examinees who feel they performed poorly may assign low ratings to EFeQ items and criticize the test in order to punish the system or rationalize their poor test performance. Nevertheless, we lose nothing by accepting such feedback as is, if only for the reason that it may indicate that greater effort has to be made by the examining institution.

Complaints by the examinee often cannot be dealt with in practical terms. But even if the criticism of examinees happens to be unjustified, giving them the sense that someone cares enough to listen can help to ease their resentment of what may appear to them as wrongful treatment. This applies not only to university entrance examinations but also to routine tests given in the classroom, as well as to professional and vocational proficiency tests. Feedback questionnaires can help to reduce postexamination stress in all these cases, in addition to fulfilling their primary function of assisting designers to improve tests and testing procedures.

We would recommend that, as a rule, test designers use the EFeQ in developing their own tests and that reports of examinee reactions be included in test manuals. It would be of benefit as well if test users employed the questionnaire and took into consideration the relevant findings derived from examinee feedback when developing test programs in the future.

References

American Psychological Association. (1974). *Standards for educational and psychological tests.* Washington, DC: Author.

Anastasi, A. (1988). *Psychological testing* (6th ed.). New York: Macmillan.

Baird, L. L. (1987). Do students think admissions tests are fair? Do tests affect their decision? *Research in Higher Education, 26,* 373–388.

Benziman, H. (1986). The psychodiagnostic experience: A call for systematic feedback procedures. In B. Nevo & R. Jager (Eds.), *Psychological testing: The examinee perspective.* Toronto: Hografe.

Cronbach, L. J. (1984). *Essentials of psychological testing* (4th ed.). New York: Harper Institute.

Davis, R. (1987, June). *When applicants rate the examinations: Feedback from 2,000 people.* Paper presented at the 10th annual meeting of the International Personnel Management Association, San Francisco.

Dinkmeyer, D. C., & Muro, J. J. (1971). *Group counseling: Theory and practice.* Illinois: Peacock.

Fiske, D. W. (1967). The subjects react to tests. *American Psychologist, 22,* 287–296.

Ivey, A. E. (1980). *Counseling and psychotherapy: Skills, theories and practice.* New York: Prentice-Hall.

Mosier, C. I. (1947). A critical examination of the concepts of face validity. *Educational and Psychological Measurement, 7,* 191–206.

Nevo, B. (1985). Face validity revisited. *Journal of Educational Measurement, 22,* 287–293.

Nevo, B. (1986, July). *The practical value of Examinee Feedback Questionnaires.* Paper presented at the International Congress of Applied Psychology, Jerusalem.

Nevo, B. (1991). The practical and theoretical value of examinee feedback questionnaires. In B. Nevo & R. Jäger (Eds.), *Educational and psychological testing: The test-taker outlook.* Toronto: Hogrefe.

Nevo, B., & Jäger, R. (Eds.). (1991). *Educational and psychological testing: The test-taker outlook.* Toronto: Hogrefe.

Nevo, B., & Sfez, J. (1985). Examinee feedback questionnaires. *Assessment and Evaluation in Higher Education, 10,* 235–243.

Zeidner, M. (1987). Essay versus multiple-choice type classroom exams: The students' perspective. *Journal of Educational Research, 80,* 352–358.

CHAPTER 11

ASSESSMENT OF RACIAL AND ETHNIC MINORITY STUDENTS: PROBLEMS AND PROSPECTS

Richard R. Valencia & Ruben Lopez

Introduction

The psychoeducational assessment of racial and ethnic minority students continues to be a subject fraught with issues regarding the routine aspects of referral, assessment, and intervention. These problems have been so severe that lawsuits by minority plaintiffs, in part, have helped to shape federal legislation mandating nondiscriminatory assessment and other significant provisions (Henderson & Valencia, 1985). Public Law 94–142, the Education for All Handicapped Children Act of 1975 (*Federal Register,* 1977), has been hailed by many as the most important educational legislation in the history of our nation. In brief, PL 94–142 is an omnibus federal legislation that focuses on the rights of all handicapped students to be provided a free and appropriate education. In the context of the present chapter, a particularly significant PL 94–142 provision is the requirement of nonbiased assessment. Despite the potential influence of PL 94–142 in providing better assessment and delivery of services in special education, there are wide gaps between what PL 94–142 mandates and the level of knowledge and technology presently available to the practitioner (e.g., school psychologist).

In this chapter our intent is to provide the practitioner with some thoughts on how the lacuna between legislative mandates and current knowledge and practice can be narrowed to provide more appropriate psychoeducational assessment of minority students. Specifically, we will provide (a) an overview of psychoeducational assessment issues with respect to minority students, (b) a discussion of perspectives and practices that could lead to nondiscriminatory assessment, and (c) a rationale for forging a link between researcher and practitioner.

In light of our focus on the assessment of minority students, the notions of *culture* and other terms such as *cultural differences* and *cultural diversity* occupy a central position in our discussion. Broadly speaking, *culture* is generally conceptualized as the particular traditions, values, norms, and practices of any people who share a common ancestry.[1] It is widely acknowledged that tests and other assessment tools measure samples of behavior. Furthermore, it is well known that culture influences behavior. Thus, in the context of psychoeducational assessment, the connection between measurement instruments and culture is clear: Assessment information, especially test data, gathered by school psychologists and other practitioners is—in varying degrees—culturally shaped. It is critical for educational practitioners to be aware of sociocultural diversity among the student population and to understand the potential influence of such differences in the process of collecting, interpreting, and using psychoeducational assessment data.

The target populations of students in our discussion will be elementary and secondary school-age black and Hispanic pupils. We focus on these two groups because of space limitations and in view of the fact that blacks and Hispanics accounted for approximately 88 percent of the total racial and ethnic minority 5- to 17-year-old population nationally in 1990 (United States Bureau of the Census, 1986).[2]

Before beginning our discussion, it must be noted that concerns of equity in assessment also exist in other domains. First, there is the issue of sex bias. Similar to the claim of discriminatory testing practices against racial and ethnic minority groups, criticisms have been directed toward test makers and users about test bias against women. Although the amount of research is slight, the measurement community has made some inroads in understanding whether specific tests are biased with respect to sex. A succint and worthwhile review of the empirical research on sex bias can be found in Jensen (1980; see also Berk, 1982).

Second, there is a burgeoning literature dealing with test bias, both racial/ethnic and sex bias, in college admissions, professional school admissions, and employment testing. Tests used for this purpose have become increasingly scrutinized for potential bias and unfairness. There has been—and continues to be—scrutiny by measurement experts, the courts, the government, psychologists, and other parties.[3] With respect to testing in the workplace, there is a growing concern about the increasing use of *honesty and integrity tests*—instruments that purportedly predict whether a prospective employee will behave dishonestly or engage in theft while on the job. Currently, there are over 40 such tests used by 5,000 to 6,000 companies in the United States (DeAngelis, 1990). Suffice it to say that independent researchers in the measurement community, as well as civil rights groups, are raising scientific and ethical issues about honesty and integrity tests.

Third, it is critical to note that issues of test bias and fairness have been of concern in other national settings. For example, Zeidner (1988) reports that the issue of discriminatory testing has recently emerged as one of the most hotly contested concerns in Israel. The Israeli lay, educational, and professional communities have all entered the debate. Zeidner notes that the elements of the fray in Israel, as well as some of the developing research findings, are remarkably similar to what has transpired in the United States over the last 15 years. We urge the reader to be vigilant about cross-cultural, cross-national testing issues and research, as such awareness may assist in a broader understanding of test bias and the adverse consequences of discriminatory testing.

Overview of Problems and Concerns: What the Practitioner Needs to Know

In this section we will provide an overview of problems and issues dealing with the psychoeducational assessment of racial and ethnic minority school-age students in the hope that future assessment of minority students will improve. We will cover (a) the move toward nondiscriminatory assessment, (b) test bias, (c) characteristics of an acceptable test, and (d) multiple data sources in assessment.

THE MOVE TOWARD NONDISCRIMINATORY ASSESSMENT

The history of minority assessment has been a troubled one, particularly in the area of test misuse and resultant abusive outcomes.[4] According to Valencia and Aburto (1991), criticisms of test misuse typically focus on two concerns:

> the issue of administering tests that lack good, intrinsic quality— that is, the administration of unreliable tests and tests that have not been validated for specific use... [and] the concern that tests are often used as the sole or major determinant in educational decision-making. (p. 206)

It would be informative here to revisit the early years of agitation for nondiscriminatory assessment. By having a sense of this history, the practitioner should be in a better position to evaluate contemporary concerns about the assessment of minority groups.

Although the history of assessing minority students has been controversial over the years, it has only been relatively recent that professional organizations have attempted to clarify discriminatory assessment issues. The Society of Social Issues (Division 9 of the American Psychological Association) in 1964 produced some guidelines for testing minority students (Deutsch, Fishman, Kogan, North, & Whiteman, 1964). Issues introduced by Deutsch et al. included, for example, test score variability, differential predictive validity, score interpretation, and sensitivity on the part of practitioners.

In the early 1970s, three major influences that helped shape subsequent improvements in the psychoeducational assessment of minority students were professional organizations, litigation, and legislation (Oakland & Laosa, 1977). Particularly influential was the litigation brought forth by plaintiff parents of minority children. Oakland (1974–75; cited in Henderson & Valencia, 1985) identified seven concerns that were brought to bear in minority-initiated lawsuits:

(a) discriminatory language assessment practices, (b) discriminatory tests (e.g., IQ tests), (c) poorly trained and insensitive psychologists, (d) overrepresentation of minority children in special education, (e) no systematic evaluations of children assigned to special education classes, (f) lack of consultation with parents regarding special education placement and student progress and (g) limited data sources and information in making placement decisions. (p. 344)

The combined influences of professional associations, victorious lawsuits brought forward by minorities (black, Mexican American, and native American children), and governmental legislation were highly instrumental in bringing about significant reform mandates in the psychoeducational assessment of minority students. By far, PL 94–142 is the single most important piece of legislative reform. The issue of inappropriate instruments (e.g., biased tests) is central to minority-initiated litigation and concerns. Thus, it is not surprising that of the nine major mandates in PL 94–142 (e.g., free and appropriate education; due process), three are especially pertinent to minority assessment. These are (a) the requirement of nonbiased, nondiscriminatory assessment, (b) the mandate of validation for specific use regarding tests and evaluation measures, (c) and the attempt to provide assessment in the student's native language, if possible.

In summary, a look back at the early period of reform efforts with respect to the psychoeducational assessment of minorities informs us that the demands of the law and what practitioners can truly do to implement more appropriate assessment for minority students makes for frustration. Yet, as Henderson and Valencia (1985) note (citing Reschly, 1980), attempts to narrow the mandate-practice gap can

> also be a stimulating challenge. School psychologists should look at special education legislation as a vehicle providing *legal authority* to move ahead with vigor toward the development and implementation of high quality assessment and more effective interventions for all children. (p. 348)

With this in mind, we now turn to one of the most important assessment issues with respect to racially and linguistically diverse students—the subject of test bias.

TEST BIAS

The issue of bias in educational testing, especially in intelligence measures, has produced controversial and protracted debates in both the legal and educational systems.[5] A major concern has been whether individual intelligence tests are culturally biased against racial and ethnic minority students. During the 1970s and 1980s, the test bias question concerning minority children was one of the hottest issues discussed in the literature on psychoeducational assessment. Practitioners, as well as the courts, legislative bodies, media, and public, have all become involved in one way or another. The debates have been emotional, acrimonious, contradictory, and scientifically confusing. So what is the practitioner to do? Our goal is to try to make sense of this perplexing state by asking two questions in the sections to follow: What is test bias? And what does the research literature have to say about test bias findings regarding minority students?

What Is Test Bias?

In the measurement community, a predominant conception is that test bias is an empirical, scientific, and quantifiable matter. For example, Jensen (1980) notes that bias is strictly statistical. It is typically defined as the systematic error of some true value (e.g., test scores) of individuals that are connected to group membership. In the present discussion, such membership would be along lines of race and ethnicity. Bias in the context of racial or ethnic membership is typically referred to as *cultural bias*. As such, the investigation of potential bias in intelligence tests, as an example, employs empirically defined and testable hypotheses as well as sophisticated statistical analyses.[6] For instance, if one were interested in examining possible content (item or subtest) bias in a cognitive test, the testable definition advanced by Reynolds (1982a) can be used:

> An item or subscale of a test is considered to be biased in content when it is demonstrated to be relatively more difficult for members of one group than another when the general ability level of the two groups being compared is held constant and no reasonable theoretical rationale exists to explain group differences on the same item (or subscale) in question. (p. 188)[7]

If test bias is conceptualized and defined as being purely objective and technical, what then is meant by charges that a particular test is unfair toward, for example, black students? Most measurement experts (e.g., Jensen, 1980) assert that the notion of test unfairness (and its opposite, test fairness) denotes subjective value judgment regarding how test results are used in the decision-making process (e.g., selection procedures). As such, test fairness/unfairness "belong more to moral philosophy than to psychometrics" (Jensen, p. 49). We agree with this conception—that is, fairness or unfairness can be looked at, perhaps even defined, as how people use test scores in decision-making matters.

Suffice it to say that although the above distinctions are important in that they help to diffuse emotionally laden debates over the conception of test bias and unfairness, there is not unanimity about the notions' meanings. For example, Shepard (1982) criticizes the distinctions between test bias and test unfairness along lines of confusion in everyday communication and awkwardness in the psychometric sense. Second, there are some scholars who argue that the dichotomized framework of bias and unfairness unduly blurs the critical connection between test instruments and their use. A case in point is Hilliard (1984), who argues:

> The important demonstration that is needed is not an empirical demonstration of test bias, but of test utility. None of the discussion over the presence or absence of bias should be allowed to obscure that central matter. (p. 166)

In summary, the topic of test bias is complex—and controversial. Attempts to define, measure, and interpret bias are unresolved issues in measurement and assessment (Reynolds, 1982b). Notwithstanding these problems, there have been major advancements in the study of test bias. Valencia and Aburto (1991) comment on this progress:

> In the last 10 years or so…a number of publications have appeared discussing statistical and methodological approaches for measuring test bias. This body of research—in both theoretical treatises and empirical investigations—has greatly enhanced the state of the art of test bias conceptualization, methodological detection, and interpretation.... Conceptualizing test bias as a psychometric notion has proven to be a valuable contribution. (pp. 214, 219)

In recent years, however, criticisms have been directed toward the strict statistical approach to understanding test bias. Specifically, the major reservation voiced has been that the current conceptualization of test bias within a psychometric paradigm is rather exclusive.[8] It is misleading to adhere to such exclusiveness, as tests do not operate in a vacuum, but have social consequences (e.g., Reschly, 1979). For the practitioner, it is important to realize that it is scientifically and ethically inappropriate not to connect testing and assessment with schooling and its consequences. The statistical notion of bias is helpful for our understanding, but alone it has little meaning. We think that the statistical psychometric definition of test bias (as defined above) is highly valuable in comprehending the interaction between group membership and test content. This conceptualization should be preserved. We also think, however, that the notion of test bias needs to be linked with test uses and consequences, particularly when elements of test unfairness may be present.

What Does the Research Literature Have to Say
About Test Bias Findings Regarding Minority Students?
Jensen (1980) concludes that the "currently most widely used standardized tests of mental ability—IQ, scholastic aptitude, and achievement tests—are, by and large, *not* biased against any of the native-born English-speaking minority groups" (p. ix). Let us take the case of the most frequently individually administered intelligence test designed for school-age children—the *Wechsler Intelligence Scale for Children - Revised* (WISC-R; Wechsler, 1974). There is ample evidence from a number of empirical test bias investigations employing a majority (i.e., white) and nonmajority (i.e., racial or ethnic minority) group that the WISC-R is nonbiased. The following examples of research studies, with their accompanying psychometric focuses, indicate that for the populations examined, the WISC-R is relatively nonbiased against black and Mexican American students (and in some cases, native American):[9]

- Reliability—see Dean (1980), Oakland and Feigenbaum (1979), and Sandoval (1979)

- Construct validity—see Dean (1979), Gutkin and Reynolds (1980, 1981), Oakland and Feigenbaum (1979), Reschly (1978), and Vance and Wallbrown (1978)

- Content (item and subtest) validity—see Jensen (1976), Reynolds (1980), and Sandoval (1979)

- Predictive validity—see Reschly and Reschly (1979), Reschly and Sabers (1979), Reynolds and Gutkin (1980), and Reynolds and Hartlage (1979)

Based on the available research, the school psychologist can be somewhat assured that when testing white and minority children, the WISC-R has comparable reliability, measures similar constructs with about the same accuracy, is relatively free of biased items and subtests, and does not have differential validity when predicting academic achievement.[10] Although these conclusions carry a broad-based credence, they should, nevertheless, be tempered with caution. The investigations from which such generalizations are made are limited in the populations studied. Puerto Rican and Asian American children are virtually absent as subjects in WISC-R bias research. Native American children have been vastly understudied. Investigations involving Mexican Americans and blacks, though comprising the bulk of the populations studied, are limited (with some exceptions) to normal (i.e., nonreferred) children.

Aside from the impressive body of WISC-R test bias research, an important issue to address is whether *other* prominent intelligence tests are also relatively free of cultural bias. As Valencia and Aburto (1991) note, there is a paucity of test bias research investigations other than those on the WISC-R. A case in point is the *Stanford-Binet Intelligence Scale* (i.e., the Terman & Merrill, 1973, version as well as the 1986 version). In his review, Reynolds (1982), for example, alludes to only a single differential predictive validity investigation of the Stanford-Binet (Bossard, Reynolds, & Gutkin, 1980).[11]

In addition to the very limited amount of test bias research on intelligence instruments other than the WISC-R, there is the issue of mixed findings involving such non–WISC-R studies. For example, Valencia and Rankin (1986, 1988, 1990) examined the *Kaufman Assessment Battery for Children* (K-ABC; Kaufman & Kaufman, 1983a) for potential cultural bias. The subjects were nonreferred fifth- and sixth-grade white and Mexican American students. The results of these K-ABC bias investigations underscore the complexity of test bias detection and interpretation, as the findings showed bias (against the Mexican American group) with respect to predictive validity and content validity, but not for reliability and construct validity. For the school psychologist, the implications of the Valencia and Rankin studies are that test bias research is not that explicit regarding bias detection and practical application. That is, although the K-ABC with respect to Mexican American upper-primary grade children was found to have comparable reliability and construct validity compared to their white peers, it is culturally biased with respect to predicting academic achievement and contains pervasive subtest and item bias (e. g., in the Achievement scale). Certainly, such inconsistent findings emphasize the vigilance school psychologists need to maintain when considering the administration of such instruments to minority children.

In summary, the last ten years have spawned a number of empirical investigations and theoretical treatises dealing with test bias. As such, the state-of-the-art with respect to test bias has grown considerably. Notwithstanding this development, a strong case can be made for the measurement community to push along further to engage in expanded test bias research. That is, "given the number of intelligence tests available and the variation in possible test bias research focuses and designs, there are indeed a large number of research investigations that are in the realm of possibility" (Valencia & Aburto, 1991, p. 214). Regarding the role and responsibility of the practitioner in administering acceptable tests to minority students, we now turn to this issue.

CHARACTERISTICS OF AN ACCEPTABLE TEST

How might the practitioner, in his or her day-to-day assessment activities, approach the question of seeking out and using tests that are acceptable for administration to minority children? Obviously, there is no clear-cut answer to this complex issue. Given the large cultural and linguistic diversity between and within racial and ethnic minority school-age populations, we can only offer broad-based suggestions. We present brief discussions on norms, reliability and validity, and the clinical utility of tests. Although the focus is on intelligence tests, our coverage needs to include psychoeducational tests in general.

Norms

A frequent criticism of standardized tests is that minority representation has been so small in the standardization sample that their minimal inclusion has little influence on eventual item selection (cf. Reynolds, 1983). Although it is preferable that minority populations be adequately represented in the norm group of a standardized instrument, their disproportionately low inclusion does not mean a priori penalization. For example, in the standardization sample (N = 1,032 children) for the *McCarthy Scales of Childrens' Abilities* (MSCA; McCarthy, 1972), 16.4 percent (n =170) were minority (Asian American, black, Pilipino American, native American, Puerto Rican, and Mexican American). Black children made up the vast percentage (91 percent, n =154) of the total minority norm group, and 14.9 percent of the total norm group. Mexican American children, on the other hand, comprised less than 1 percent of the total normative group (Valencia, 1990). Despite their virtual absence from the norming of the McCarthy, Mexican American English-speaking children (all from low socioeconomic status in various research studies) have performed identical (M = 100) on the *McCarthy General Cognitive Index* (GCI) compared to the McCarthy standardization mean of 100 (Valencia, 1988, 1990.)[12]

In light of the above, we urge school psychologists not to automatically rule out psychoeducational tests that fail to have ideal representation of minority group children in the standardization sample. With respect to the McCarthy, the normative group contained a minuscule percentage of Mexican American children and other non-black minority children, yet it "has earned a reputation as one of the best multiscore batteries for the psychoeducational assessment of young children [ages three to six or six and a half]" (Valencia, 1990, p. 253). The near exclusion of Mexican American children from the norming of the McCarthy and their subsequent impressive GCI performance, though a notable case, does not represent the ideal norming situation. Our recommendation to school psychologists is to seek out tests that have included proportional representation of minority children in the standardization sample.[13] For example, the K–ABC, which was normed on 2,000 children, included 550 minority children (27.5%) in the standardization sample (Kaufman & Kaufman, 1983b). Blacks, Hispanics, and other minorities comprised 15.6 percent, 7.8 percent, and 4.1 percent, respectively—proportions nearly identical to their percentages in the U. S. population based on 1980 census data. In addition, the K–ABC's norming shows further sensitivity to minority assessment by the inclusion of supplementary sociocultural norms (Kaufman & Kaufman, 1983b).[14]

The issue of having appropriate inclusion of children from all racial and ethnic groups in the development of test items as well as in the standardization group is only one aspect of sound norming. There are three factors that influence the adequacy of a test's norms: (a) the representative nature of the standardization sample (the factor that subsumes race and ethnicity, but includes other aspects such as age and sex), (b) the number of cases in the sample, and (c) the relevance of the norms to the purpose of psychoeducational testing (Salvia & Ysseldyke, 1988).

In light of this, where is the practitioner to obtain information on the normative sample used to develop the test? First, one may consult the test manual. Ideally, "reports of norming studies should include the year in which normative data were collected, provide descriptive statistics, and describe the sampling design and participation rates in sufficient detail so that the study can be evaluated for appropriateness" (American Educational Research Association, American Psychological Association, & the National Council on Measurement in Education, 1985, p. 33). Second, one can consult the *Mental Measurements Yearbook* (e.g., the *Ninth Mental Measurements Yearbook*; Mitchell, 1985), where test specialists offer test review summaries and critiques, providing insight into strengths and weaknesses about a particular instrument's norms, reliability, and other technical characteristics. Third, one can consult published scholarly literature on educational testing that provides overviews of norming and other qualitative aspects of various instruments. Such literature takes many forms, including journal articles (e.g., Valencia, 1988), chapters in handbooks (e.g., Valencia, 1990), sections in books (e.g., Salvia & Ysseldyke, 1988), and entire books (e.g., Kaufman & Kaufman, 1977). In short, information on the adequacy of norms is available, but one must seek it out. Exercise caution, however. Given that 28 percent of the tests listed in the *Eighth Mental Measurements Yearbook* were not normed appropriately in some significant aspect (Mitchell, 1984), we echo Salvia and Ysseldyke's admonishment that "in the marketplace of testing, let the buyer beware" (p. 107).

Reliability and Validity

Suffice it to say that the topic of test reliability and validity transcends the issue of nondiscriminatory assessment of minority children. Without reliable and valid tests, *all* students would be subject to inappropriate testing. Notwithstanding this truism, particular attention needs to be paid that tests have adequate internal consistency and are valid for specific use in the psychoeducational assessment of minority children.[15]

Racial and ethnic minority populations, given their cultural and linguistic diversity, present challenges to test measurement specialists in the establishment of adequate reliability and validity of tests. For example, due to many factors—opportunity to learn, familiarity with item content, limited English-speaking skills, cultural loading— minority children, compared to their white peers, tend to exhibit restricted range of performance on standardized tests (e.g., Valencia, 1985b). In that it is widely known that restricted variability

can depress correlation coefficients, test developers and users should be aware
of this measurement aspect when undertaking validity studies with minority
children. When depressed correlations (e.g., in a concurrent validity study)
are corrected statistically for range restriction, a more realistic appraisal of a
test's validity can be ascertained (such as seen in Valencia & Rothwell, 1984;
see also Valencia, 1990).[16]

As in the case for test norms, school psychologists and other practitioners
must seek out information about test reliability and validity. The sources of
information mentioned for norms also apply here—test manuals, journal
articles, the *Mental Measurements Yearbook* reviews, book chapters, and
complete books. Particularly relevant are empirical investigations published
in scholarly journals. By far, such studies account for the bulk of psychometric
research in which test reliability and validity information regarding minority
students can be found. For example, in Valencia's (1990) comprehensive and
integrated review of research on the McCarthy Scales, he lists over 36 journal
articles that examine, in part, the reliability and validity of the McCarthy with
respect to black, Mexican American, Puerto Rican, and native American
children.

Finally, it is important to mention that the vast majority of the empirical
literature investigating reliability and validity of various tests with respect to
minority populations has focused on single population studies. In such
studies, a single minority group (e.g., Mexican American) is administered
tests (e.g., two tests to examine concurrent or predictive validity or stability;
see, as cases in point, Valencia, 1984, 1985a, 1985b). The resultant correlations
are observed to see if the magnitudes are acceptable enough to conclude that
validity has been established, comparing the correlations to acceptable,
conventional measurement standards and/or by comparing them to correlations observed in the test manual. Notwithstanding the information provided
in single population validity studies, they are limited in scope regarding the
detection of cultural bias. As described earlier, test bias studies require a major
and minor group. In any event, single population studies are valuable in their
own right and can provide useful psychometric information for school
psychologists when assessing minority students. Valencia and Aburto (1991)
summarize matters this way:

> The comparison of two or more racial/ethnic groups is the preferred
> strategy in investigating cultural bias in mental and other tests. Yet,
> although single population validity studies cannot examine cultural
> bias directly, they are still valuable in providing insights if validity
> coefficients are of sufficient magnitudes to conclude that an instrument
> has clinical utility for a particular minority group. (p. 212)

Clinical Utility of Tests

Let us assume that a school psychologist has in his or her hands a test that has been adequately normed and is reliable and valid (perhaps even free of cultural bias). Does this mean that the test is appropriate and can be used in the assessment of minority children? Not necessarily. Indeed, knowing that a test is solidly normed and has psychometric integrity is important. For the school psychologist, however, a real concern is in the proverbial "proof of the pudding" (cf. Valencia, 1990). That is, does the test have utility in actual assessment? Can it, in the context of the present discussion, accurately assist in the identification of minority students who deviate below the norm to such an extent that special education services are necessary? Can such diagnosis lead to assessment information that, in turn, can be translated to direct educational remediation and/or intervention for minority children?

Clearly, it is this link between psychoeducational assessment and intervention with which school psychologists are most concerned. How can the process of collecting information on a student's background, current functioning, strengths, and weaknesses be brought to bear on helping the student grow cognitively and affectively? There is no easy answer. And, of course, the answer becomes even more difficult to address when cultural and linguistic diversity are brought into the picture. For example, are there any cultural or language differences operative that need to be considered during the process of assessment? How does one collect such data? How does this information become transformed with respect to direct intervention? These issues will be addressed in part in the upcoming section, "Promising Perspectives and Practices: Toward Nondiscriminatory Assessment."

In conclusion, the connections between assessment, particularly test data and intervention, remain troublesome in the field of school psychology. Cancelli and Duley (1985) describe this problem as such:

> The best indicator of the value of the change that occurs in school psychological assessment practices is the tightening of the link between assessment and intervention. Although the profession continues to make progress toward this goal, it sometimes seems to have lost its direction. The heavy emphasis still placed on assessment for special education decision making in the school highlights the misdirection. Placement is not the major purpose of assessment, and as school psychologists broaden their assessment activities, the potential impact of their expertise on helping children will increase. (p. 137)

As we continue our discussion through the remainder of this chapter, we will periodically return to this important need of bridge-building between assessment and intervention.

Multiple Data Sources in Assessment

In general, there is a need to implement the notion of *multiple data sources* in assessment (Valencia, 1982), sometimes referred to as *multifactored assessment* (Reschly, 1979). Furthermore, the requirement of multifactored assessment is suggested in the rules and regulations of PL 94–142. Despite the need for multiple informed sources in assessment, "the degree to which comprehensive assessment has been conducted, documented, and used in planning interventions must be recognized" (Reschly, p. 250). We dare say that one of the major obstacles to the use of multifactored assessment is the misconception that testing and assessment are synonymous. As a number of scholars have admonished, testing and assessment are *not* identical.[17] Certainly, psychoeducational testing is important in assessment. There is also no doubt that testing is commonplace in special education. Approximately 3 to 5 percent of public school students are referred by their teachers for psychoeducational assessment. Of those referred, about 92 percent are administered tests. Of those tested, approximately 73 percent are placed in special education (Salvia & Ysseldyke, 1988). Notwithstanding the significant and ubiquitous role of testing, it is impossible to defend the argument that a test in itself can provide a full psychoeducational assessment. Put more bluntly, no major educational decision should ever be determined on test scores singularly (Gronlund, 1985). In addition to testing, a well-rounded psychoeducational assessment should also include two other sources of diagnostic information—observations and judgments (Salvia & Ysseldyke).

Given that good assessment involves the collection of data from a variety of sources, including teachers, parents, and on the basis of psychometric evidence and medical diagnosis, what is the implication of multifactored assessment in the assessment of minority students? As Valencia (1982) comments, the use of multiple informed data sources in minority assessment has two advantages. First, such comprehensive assessment can provide multiple windows from which to view and understand the diversity that minority students possess by the nature of their background. Second, the use of multiple data sources can possibly minimize, perhaps even eliminate, inaccuracies in assessment. Reschly (1979) has identified three areas in which these problems have potential to surface: (a) instrumentation (i.e., cultural bias), (b) atmosphere (e.g., low expectations of the child as perceived by the school psychologist), and (c) use (e.g., dead-end classification that leads to reduced opportunities for growth). The use of comprehensive assessment with minority students can assist in reducing these problems by improving the credibility of the data collected and hopefully will lead to a reduction of bias in future assessment.

In closing, the use of multiple data sources in assessment can provide for more accurate and comprehensive assessment of minority students. Areas particularly important to assess are language dominance and proficiency, sociocultural variability, and adaptive behavior (cf. Reschly, 1979). School psychologists in their daily activities have considerable time in contact with students from culturally diverse backgrounds. Notwithstanding the amount of contact, most school psychologists appear not to be aware of the backgrounds of the students they serve. In that many practitioners have not experienced the ongoing circumstances of minority students, it is not surprising that the performance of these students has been interpreted through monocultural lenses. As such, the following advice from Henderson and Valencia (1985) may provide some direction:

> Nondiscriminatory psychological services are possible if school psychologists function as problem solvers. They must be open to multiple sources of evidence, sensitive to cultural influences on the performance of children in school, and willing to take the information provided by multiple data sources as the basis for *hypotheses* to be tested through instructional planning and evaluation. Assessment never provides facts. It provides only data to be interpreted from various perspectives. (p. 368)

Promising Perspectives and Practices: Toward Nondiscriminatory Assessment

In this section, we offer a number of practical ideas we believe have promise in the promotion of nondiscriminatory assessment. The following topics are discussed: (a) relevance of assessment to instruction and intervention, (b) cultural considerations, (c) language, (d) cognitive processes, (e) psychoeducational assessments, and (f) planning the assessment of minorities.

RELEVANCE OF ASSESSMENT TO INSTRUCTION AND INTERVENTION

First and foremost, psychological assessment of racial/ethnic and linguistic minorities conducted for educational purposes must be relevant to educational instruction and psychological interventions. Although the decreasing percentages of minorities in some special education placements may give the impression that schooling is improving for minority students, black and Hispanic students throughout the United States continue to do more poorly while in school, drop out of school more often, and graduate from school more poorly educated than students of other racial and ethnic groups in the United States.[18] Although changes in psychoeducational assessment alone cannot solve the school failure of some minority–group students, assessment can expose their educational needs and strengths.

Making school success the overriding concern of psychoeducational assessment makes the indiscriminant acceptance of psychometrically questionable and educationally irrelevant tests and procedures less likely. Of utmost importance, such a focus will help to correct the existing incongruency between assessment and instruction in special education. Enigmatically, interest in cognitive processing deficits and strengths that prevails in psychoeducational assessment is very much unrelated to directly remediating basic academic skills that dominate actual practice in special education.[19] An alignment between psychological assessment and instruction is imperative. Data show that concentrating on the instruction of deficient academic skills and their subcomponents consistently produces gains, while training and instruction focused on cognitive processes does not. Therefore, psychological assessment that mostly yields data about hypothetical cognitive processes should be discontinued (Ranes, 1990; Ysseldyke & Mirkin, 1982).

For many practitioners, the use of an intelligence test is equivalent to psychological testing. Given this unfortunate situation, it seems necessary to find some justification for administering an intelligence test to minorities. Within the perspective that psychological testing should be educationally relevant, the intelligence test derives its value from the fact that some such tests, as we described earlier, predict academic achievement reasonably well for some blacks and Hispanics. There are, however, many who question whether the time spent giving an intelligence test can be better invested. For example, Jensen (1980) writes:

> There is no routine use of IQ or aptitude tests in the schools for which well-designed scholastic achievement tests would not better serve the same purpose. The major aim of schooling is to inculcate certain types of knowledge and skills, the products of which can be termed "scholastic achievement." Children's progress in this endeavor should be periodically assessed by means of standardized tests of scholastic achievement, tests designed expressly to assess what the pupil has been taught in school, and the pupil's ability to understand and to apply what has been taught. (p. 716)

Peckham (1979) of the well-known *Larry P. v. Riles* court case makes the same point when he writes his opinion that in the educational settings as it related to E. M. R. classes, the child is already in school and already doing poorly, so it can be predicted without tests that the poor performance will continue in the absence of remedial attention. Indeed, past performance in school is a better predictor than tests of future school performance. (pp. 969–970)

In short, the importance of educational relevance goes beyond any particular psychological instrument. Presenting the conclusions of a panel of the National Academy of Sciences, Keller (1986) writes, "The purpose of the entire process—from referral for assessment to eventual placement in special education—is to improve instruction for children. Valid assessment, in our view, is marked by its relevance to and usefulness for instruction" (pp. 10–11).

CULTURAL CONSIDERATIONS

A plethora of terms, including *nonbiased, nondiscriminatory, least-biased, least-discriminatory, culture-free,* and *culture-reduced,* have been used to address cultural concerns about the assessment of minorities. Unfortunately, these terms have the potential to mislead the practitioner into believing mistaken conceptions of test bias and culture. It should come as no surprise that tests are intended to discriminate (i.e., measure assumed variability) and to be culturally oriented. Otherwise, they would have no practical value.

An example of advice about culture that is befuddling is the belief that what schools need to do to conduct culturally sensitive assessments is to hire experts as cultural consultants for each of the "cultures" represented in the school district. Depending on one's definition of culture, this could mean finding as many as 100 such experts. The real tragedy of such misdirected thinking is that it displays a profound ignorance that the salient culture of psychoeducational assessment is the school culture. A number of scholars have indirectly acknowledged that school culture is central to assessment by admitting that psychological tests are adequate predictors of academic achievement and then questioning measures of academic achievement themselves or the form of instruction provided.[20] Plainly, instruments and procedures used in schools should have something to do with schools. If they do not, inadvertently a student's school failure may be justified with the argument that there is an irreconcilable mismatch between the student's culture and that of the school. If such a mismatch does exist, the matter becomes one of school reform rather than assessment reform.

Regarding cultural generalizations about minorities, first of all, one must be extremely hesitant to apply group characterizations to individual students. As found in footnote number 70 in the *Federal Register*, Peckham (1979), in discussing *Larry P. v. Riles,* writes, "Admittedly 'black culture' is not easily defined and is not homogeneous in this country." Ogbu and Matute-Bianchi (1986) assert, "We wish to underscore the fact that both the Mexican-descent and Chinese-descent populations in the United States are large and extremely diverse" (p. 99). Generalizations about the culture of minorities may have their place in speculation about the high incidence of school failure in some minority groups (Bilingual Education Office, California State Department of Education, 1986). Such generalizations, however, should be assiduously minimized when considering the individual child or youth. Just as it is damaging to expect a language minority student (e.g., Mexican American) to learn English in a year, it is equally insulting to presume that all Mexican Americans can speak Spanish.

Due to the problematic nature of applying generalizations about minority groups to individuals, it is necessary in assessment to complement a norm-referenced perspective with an ideographic one. Such a perspective focuses on the student's *own* demonstrated skills and actual school and home experiences. Hence, as we discussed in an earlier section, information about the student's cultural background should be collected from as many sources as possible. Information from parents and teachers is indispensable. These data will provide a window to an individual student's actual culture. Be aware, however, that there are attending problems with such information.

For one, data such as birth and developmental histories as remembered by parents are notoriously imprecise and should not be assumed to have an invariable effect on school functioning (Stewart, 1983). Another problem directly related to psychoeducational assessment is that there are inconsistencies between parent and teacher ratings on adaptive behavior scales (Heath & Obrzut, 1986; Keller, 1986). Because of the numerous differences between home and school activities, this should not be surprising. It nevertheless contributes to making a student's eligibility for special education a numbers game. For instance, because parents, compared to teachers, tend to rate students as having better adaptive behavior (Heath & Obrzut, 1986), one can arbitrarily decide whose ratings to accept based on one's desire to find a student eligible. Parent's ratings will often show that a student is doing fine and, therefore, will not be qualified for special education. Teacher's ratings, on the other hand, will likely show the student to be eligible, consistent with the teacher's reasons for referring a student for assessment in the first place.

This very complication brings one back to the question of which culture is the focus of assessment in schools. The question is: In reference to what culture am I assessing a student's degree of adequate or inadequate functioning? If one does not choose an answer to this question, factors relevant to deciding such issues as whether a student's low achievement is the result of environmental, cultural, or economic disadvantage, will likely be disregarded. In this respect, Harris, Gray, Davis, Zaremba, and Argulewicz (1988) found that of a random sample of school psychologists, less than half said they take into consideration the PL 94–142 exclusionary factors concerning home environment, culture, and economic status pertaining to the specific learning disabilities category of special education.

To the question, What is the culture to which psychoeducational assessment refers, our opinion is that *psychoeducational assessment must primarily relate to the school culture.* In this respect, although it is essential to consider a student's home culture to determine the effects on school functioning, adaptation to the school culture is the primary issue of eligibility for special education. It is true that special education conditions, such as mental retardation and serious emotional disturbance, must, according to their definitions, be manifest in the home setting as well as at school, yet they must be clearly evident at school to be relevant to special education. All of the 11 handicapping conditions of the federal regulations in the United States include as part of their definitions the requirement that the handicap in question must have an adverse effect on school functioning.

Elliott (1987), in describing the success of educators using tests to place black children in special education in *PASE v. Hannon,* demonstrates the centrality of school culture to psychoeducational assessment by commenting:

> They [the defense] welcomed the plaintiffs' view that ability tests, school grades and achievement tests were all part of the same culture and virtually invited the plaintiffs to attack the criterion—that is, the schools.... The defense simply granted that school children in Chicago were not being trained for life in (at various times) Greece, China, Tasmania, or (in Judge Grady's final comparison) "another planet." (p. 198)

Identifying the referent culture of psychoeducational assessment as the school culture puts assessment into a realistic and somewhat manageable context. Consequently, this allows such controversial activities as labeling to be qualified by the fact that labels are primarily, if not exclusively, relevant to the school setting and should be applied cautiously, if at all, outside of that setting. Although not in the least minimizing the significance of cultural differences, looking at the school setting as the referent permits every aspect of the assessment process to be evaluated by the question, "What relevance does this activity have to the student's adaptation to the school culture?" This gives psychoeducational assessment a cross–cultural orientation. Assessment can be cross–cultural because of the common core of educational objectives held for all students. Otherwise, as some have concluded, the only way to assess the burgeoning racial and ethnic minority school population in the United States is to have entirely different assessments for each group—an impossible task. This does not imply, however, that schools should neglect the unique instructional needs of culturally and linguistically diverse minority children. Bilingual programs, for example, are indispensable to ensure the educational success of linguistic minorities (Cummins, 1984).

LANGUAGE

A highly pertinent aspect of a student's culture relevant to school functioning is the vehicle of culture—language. In particular, for the student whose home language is other than English, assessment of the home language and development in English is essential when investigating why a student is not learning (Garcia & Ortiz, 1988). In fact, in–depth assessment of a linguistic minority's language skills should precede any efforts to assist a limited–English-proficient (LEP) or non–English-proficient (NEP) student who is doing poorly in school. Do not, however, assume, for instance, a bilingual speech pathologist will be able to say with a high degree of sophistication whether a student is displaying low achievement because of a language difference or a language disorder. This is so because language assessment of Spanish-speaking and other LEP/NEP children in the United States is still in its infancy.[21] In addition, though the use of interpreters is assumed to be a reliable practice, Figueroa (1989) writes that there is "no substantive empirical evidence supporting the use of interpreters in psychological testing" (p. 19).

It is crucial to note that, as with psychological tests, there are many limitations with English language tests (Sommers, 1989). It should therefore not be surprising to find that measures of languages other than English often yield equivocal results or are simply nonexistent for students living in the United States. When standardized measures are unavailable, a qualitative measure, such as the *Student Oral Language Observation Matrix* (California State Department of Education, 1984), can provide a rough but useful estimate of a student's functioning in the native language.

In addition to assessing a student's primary language, a language minority student's pattern of English language development should be investigated. Such monitoring can be done by single subject assessment designs (Sugai,

1987). As noted by Cummins (1984), the most common error in evaluating a bilingual student's English skills is to assume that *basic interpersonal communicative skills* (BICS) are synonymous with a bilingual student's competency in dealing with decontextualized academic instruction (*cognitive/academic language proficiency*, CALP). Whereas a language minority may be able to interact at a basic conversational level (BICS) in a year or two, Cummins has found that it takes on the average five years for a student to be competent compared to English-speaking peers in cognitive academic English. Regarding the use of black dialect English in the assessment of black students, the findings have been contradictory and, consequently, inconclusive (Reynolds, 1982a).

COGNITIVE PROCESSES

Because of its popularity and ardent following, the *Learning Potential Assessment Device* (LPAD; Feuerstein, 1979) serves as an example of an experimental procedure that should be receiving more cautious advocacy than it is. There seems to be ubiquitous support for the LPAD and other forms of dynamic assessment in discussions of minority assessment as the most promising alternatives to traditional assessment practices (Duran, 1989). Without a doubt, the assumption that intelligence can be improved is irresistible. The notions of testing first, followed by teaching what a student did not know, and then finally testing again to find how well the student has profited from the instruction (test-teach-test) makes good sense. This is the sensible strategy of diagnostic teaching. Nonetheless, the adherents of dynamic assessment are realizing that the LPAD and its instructional program, *Instrumental Enrichment* (IE; Feuerstein, 1980), have yet to be shown adequately relevant to the classroom. Litz and Mearig (1989), proponents of the LPAD, in writing about the LPAD and IE admit that

> there remains difficulty in demonstrating meaningful transfer
> to academic performance. This connection may require more
> intense focus on "bridges" between IE and academic curricula,
> as well as attempts to assure association with a clearly defined
> and well-developed academic curriculum. (p. 84)

Recognizing the inadequacies of inferring the potential of basic academic skills from nonacademic skills tasks, Campione (1989) is developing a dynamic assessment system that consists of academic skills.

The point is that inferences about cognitive skills underlying academic performance will be more substantial if the instruments used to make inferences about cognitive skills consist of actual academic content or obvious analogues. For instance, if you want to determine whether a child has problems with letter and numeral reversals, choose something like the *Jordan Left Right Reversal Test* (Jordan, 1980). It requires the student to distinguish backwards letters and numerals from properly oriented ones in isolation, and then in the context of actual words, and finally in complete sentences. Although the *Boder Test of Reading-Spelling Patterns* (Boder & Jarrico, 1982) has been rightly criticized because it uses only word recognition and spelling and does not consider comprehension to infer reading disabilities, at least the instrument uses actual academic tasks to determine types of poor readers. The *Rosner Test of Auditory Analysis Skills* (Berninger, Thalberg, DeBruyn, & Smith, 1987) requires the student to segment and then blend words as is actually required in reading decoding. These instruments are not without their technical weaknesses. They nonetheless serve to exemplify instruments that make stronger inferences about academic deficits because they are more directly related to the academic skills themselves.

As with the whole notion of cognitive processes, there has not yet been evidence collected that indicates generalized processing styles within groups of minorities (Henderson & Valencia, 1985; Pearson, 1988). For all students, the validity of measuring and modifying cognitive processes awaits substantiation despite the efforts of many conceptualizers (cf. Arter & Jenkins, 1979; Ysseldyke & Mirkin, 1982). Until considerable improvements in the theories and assessments of cognitive processes occur, such factors should receive cautious, if any, consideration when assessing a minority student for educational purposes. Scholarly censure of process testing is vehement. Ysseldyke and Mirkin (1982) admonish:

> We concluded that, to date, there has been essentially no empirical support for the beliefs that process dysfunctions cause academic difficulties, can be reliably assessed, or can be remediated. Yet, as illustrated in our review of current assessment-intervention practices, such efforts predominate. We believe it is time for practitioners to attend more carefully to research findings and to discontinue practices for which there is very little support. (p. 409)

Regarding treatments based on cognitive processes, Howell (1986) notes,

> Research consistently indicated that the use of ATI (aptitude-treatment interaction) to select treatments does not work. In part, this is because available aptitude measures are inadequate and because treatment measures do not even exist. Validated scales for

determining the extent to which a reading program is auditory/ visual or simultaneous/sequential simply do not exist. (p. 326)

Fortunately, generating hypotheses about racial and ethnic minorities can be more effectively done by a task-analytic and ecological perspective.[22]

PSYCHOEDUCATIONAL ASSESSMENT: BEYOND INTELLIGENCE TESTING

Psychologists in the schools are often engaged in an identity crisis. This entails searching for ways in which they are distinctive from other assessment personnel found in schools. Generally, the role of psychologists is defined by the tests only they can use. Frankly, the arguments about restricting particular tests to psychologists are frequently insubstantial and plainly embarrassing. Based on observation by the second author (a practicing school psychologist), the *Bender Visual Gestalt Test* (Bender, 1938) was fought over for an entire school year in one school district. Had someone objectively analyzed the importance of this instrument to psychoeducational assessment, the conflict over its use would have been considered shameful. Nevertheless, intelligence testing by psychologists only has been for the most part never seriously questioned.

Suppose, however, that the use of intelligence tests for special education decisions is prohibited—as might occur in California. What unique contribution can the psychologist make in the schools, especially when involving minorities? Not only is this a serious question because of its implications on the employment of psychologists in schools, but the question also requires that psychologists themselves become aware of other psychological tests for assessing why a minority student is doing poorly in school.

Clearly, such a distinctive area of testing is that of socioemotional functioning (or personality). Useful school-related factors that fall under these are social skills, behavioral assets and problems, and self-perceptions. An example of a discrete area of socioemotional functioning is that of anxiety. The *Revised-Children's Manifest Anxiety Scale* (Reynolds & Paget, 1983) exemplifies a self-report instrument of anxiety that provides, in addition to national norms, separate norms for white and black children. The *Child Rating Scale* (Hightower et al., 1987) and the *Teacher-Child Rating Scale* (Hightower et al., 1986) may be appropriate for assessing minority students because these instruments are specifically oriented to school situations and concerns and may therefore be germane for children attending school in the United States—whatever their racial or ethnic backgrounds. One type of assessment commonly employed with minorities (Vasquez-Nuttall, 1987)—and that should *not* be used with them—involves the use of projective techniques. This type of instrument has been harshly criticized even when majority students are involved (Anastasi, 1988; Peterson & Batsche, 1983).

Another cross-cultural area of relevance to the school setting that can be assessed by psychologists is a student's work habits (Lloyd & Loper, 1986) and prevocational and vocational skills and interests (Hohensil, Levinson, & Heer, 1985). Another critical area to assess when trying to determine why a minority student is not adjusting to the school setting is the classroom environment.[23] This kind of assessment constitutes part of what some have called *ecological assessment*. Lastly, the school psychologist can make an important contribution by assessing the home environment and its relation to a student's school functioning—a connection that may yield the most important information in identifying the cultural factors related to a student's poor school performance and, more importantly, pinpointing cultural resources that may contribute to ameliorating a student's school failure (Erchul, 1987; Ogbu & Matute-Bianchi, 1986).

PLANNING THE ASSESSMENT OF RACIAL AND ETHNIC MINORITIES

Simply deciding how to begin conducting a psychological assessment with minorities is overwhelming in light of the confusing array of technical, philosophical, and social issues. If not for the projections and present reality of ever increasing numbers of minorities in schools throughout the United States, it might seem easiest and most ethical to avoid testing minorities altogether. However, as long as access to educational programs such as special education includes quantitative eligibility criteria, the use of tests yielding scores will undoubtedly continue.

Despite the need to recognize the complexities associated with the assessment of minority students, it is, however, advisable to begin the assessment of minorities with a modest and pragmatic outlook. The realities of working in schools will lead to this perspective, whether or not you decide to begin here. The practitioner soon realizes that many state-of-the-art models and recommendations are plainly unworkable in the school setting. For example, if you take our suggestion of collecting multiple sources of data and begin *without* a pragmatic framework for guidance, you will quickly fatigue, either by the task of gathering such information or by the effort of deciding what to do with it once it is obtained. The mistake of amassing too much data is as ineffective as getting too little.

Decide first what the purpose for testing is. Salvia and Ysseldyke (1978) identify five purposes for assessment in schools, which are applicable to all students—white as well as minorities:

- *Screening*—to decide whether a student is in need of further assessment

- *Eligibility*—to determine whether a student is eligible and in need of particular educational placement

- *Instructional planning*—to obtain data to plan the best instructional program for a student

- *Monitoring progress*—to determine progress of a student during an intervention

- *Program evaluation*—to decide whether the student's program is working

As discussed earlier, the term *assessment* implies that the process should not be limited to norm- or criterion-referenced tests. Systematic observations, for instance, in the settings of concern are also essential (Shapiro, 1987).

Because it has dominated litigation regarding the assessment of minorities in schools (Bersoff, 1982; Elliott, 1987), the issue of determining whether a student qualifies for special education will be used to briefly discuss how to plan the assessment of minorities for special education. It can be assumed that there are definitions or criteria for determining eligibility, if eligibility is a question at all. The definitions or criteria should provide the basic framework for assessing students' eligibility for special education, whether or not they are minorities. Although only implicit thus far, it is our belief that assessment is nondiscriminatory when it contributes to the educational success of the individual undergoing the assessment process (cf. Reschly, 1979; Valencia & Aburto, 1991).

Assuming that the educational program being provided to a minority student is appropriate (this may, however, not be the case; see Carnine & Kameenui, 1990; Cummins, 1984), it is best to start by analyzing the data that already exist in the school of the student being assessed. This is consistent with the fact that all the categories of special education—even the most controversial, such as mental retardation and specific learning disabilities—require that there be an adverse effect on school functioning. In the case of linguistic minority students, the information regarding language functioning must be considered first. This might include, if available, a language survey completed by the parents. The results of language tests that were likely used during the student's initial language assessment should also be reviewed. The norm-referenced achievement data (e.g., the *Comprehensive Tests of Basic Skills*, *The California Achievement Test*, or the *Spanish Assessment of Basic Education*) that may be available for any student should be reviewed. To avoid overrepresentation of minorities in a program, the disaggregated norms for racial and ethnic groups on these tests might be requested to ascertain a student's degree of achievement relative to other students of the same racial or ethnic group.

Criterion-referenced and competency and proficiency tests also provide useful existing data to consider. Grades on report cards should also be examined. Consideration of these data help to indicate how a student is doing on criterion measures used within a student's actual school environment. For the special education categories of mental retardation and specific learning disabilities, measures of academic achievement within the school setting should be deemed the critical markers of a student's eligibility for special education (Reschly, Kicklighter, & McKee, 1988).

From this essential base of information, it will be known if the student is failing or not in school. All other data collected when assessing a minority should be considered supportive, not primary. There are simply too many shortcomings in psychological tests. If (a) extremely low intellectual ability, (b) an ability-achievement discrepancy, or (c) a process deficit must be documented, use the most achievement-relevant instruments available. As we described previously, be vigilant about ascertaining whether the instruments used have appropriate norms and are psychometrically sound. For an impressive alternative, consider using curriculum-based measures to determine a student's skill levels and, if permitted, a student's eligibility for special education.[24] These are measures that consist of samples from the student's actual school curriculum. Until tests or procedures of cognitive processes are proven to have validity for instruction, the most significant test related to a minority student's school functioning are those related directly and specifically to the student's academic achievement (Carnine, Granzin, & Becker, 1988; Hoge & Andrews, 1987). To rest educational decisions on any other measure is distinctly unhelpful to students who are very likely in desperate need of assistance.

In the present section, we have attempted to identify and discuss a number of suggestions that psychologists in the schools can consider to improve the psychoeducational assessment of minority students. Suffice it to say that the implementation of these ideas is no easy task. As such, we contend that nondiscriminatory assessment can best be realized if research and practice are linked—a topic we cover in the concluding section.

Forging a Link Between Researcher and Practitioner

In the field of education, a common and ongoing concern is the need to link research with practice. This issue is particularly germane to special education regarding culturally and linguistically diverse students in light of the problems and potential solutions identified in this chapter. In this final section, we offer some suggestions as to how the researcher and practitioner can forge a tighter connection to serve more fully the needs of minority students. Our focus is on specific ideas that can be implemented—(a) scholarly collaboration, (b) local norming, and (c) research issues.

SCHOLARLY COLLABORATION

We know of no better way for the researcher and practitioner to forge links than to collaborate on scholarly work in special education that attempts to connect theory and research to practical concerns regarding the assessment of minority students. Such collaboration can take many forms. Examples include writing expository or empirically based works, serving on symposia at national, regional, or state meetings of professional organizations (e.g., American Educational Research Association), and codirecting research projects.

A case in point of researcher-practitioner collaboration is the present chapter. Valencia is a university professor, who by the nature of his work, teaches and engages in research dealing with minority schooling issues, particularly testing concerns. Lopez is a practicing school psychologist who interacts daily with students through his assessment activities. He has also written several articles (Lopez, 1987, 1989). Writing this chapter together has allowed us to learn from each other's discipline and scholarly background. Our collaboration has also given the present work on minority-related assessment issues a much sharper focus than had either of us written it alone.

In summary, scholarly collaboration by the researcher and practitioner has great potential for bridging the gap that exists between the current knowledge base and the ongoing needs in special education. Through shared scholarly undertakings, researchers and practitioners can assist in addressing the many assessment concerns school psychologists have about minority students.

LOCAL NORMING

An emerging concern being voiced by school psychologists is the need for local norming in order to understand more fully the relative performance of minority students on standardized tests. Given the widely acknowledged finding that certain minority-group students typically score lower on standardized instruments (especially achievement tests; see Valencia, 1991), school psychologists are often cautious about interpreting the meaning of such scores. Thus, there is growing interest at the local level to develop some semblance of normative performance. Although there have been attempts to develop pluralistic norming at broad levels (e.g., Kaufman & Kaufman, 1983a; Mercer & Lewis, 1978), very little research effort has gone into the development of local norms in the context of sociocultural diversity.

The rationale for the establishment of local norming (as deemed important by local school districts) is given considerable support by our nation's changing demography. Racial and ethnic minority groups are increasing at such dramatic rates that the social structure of the United States will fundamentally change in the near future. For example, by the year 2000 it is projected that blacks and Hispanics combined will comprise a clear majority in about one-third of our nation's 50 largest cities (Staff, 1989). In the ten most populated cities—as well as the four largest (New York, Los Angeles, Chicago, and Houston), blacks and Hispanics will comprise the majority population in six cities. One particular segment of the population that is growing at an unprecedented rate is the Hispanic group. It increased 38.6 percent (14.5 to 20.1 million) during the 1980s—a rate nearly *five times faster* than the rest of the U.S. population (Swibold, 1989). Regarding the youth population (newborns to 17-year-olds), Mexican American and other Hispanic youngsters will account for most of the overall youth population increase expected to occur between 1982 and 2020 (Pallas, Natriello, & McDill, 1988). Currently in California, the combined racial and ethnic "minority" in kindergarten to grade 12 (K–12) enrollment constitutes the majority (Watson, 1988). In the year 2030, the combined K–12 minority enrollment in California is predicted to reach nearly 70 percent, and the *single largest group* will be Hispanic students—comprising about 44 percent of the total K–12 population (Population Reference Bureau, 1985).

In light of the significant shifts along racial and ethnic lines, a strong case can be made for the value of developing and using local norms. In addition, the use of local norms can help to some degree in promoting nondiscriminatory assessment by encouraging sensitivity to sociocultural diversity—that is, by defining normality in the context of "comparing the performance with others who have had approximately the same opportunity to learn the materials in the test, the same motivation, and similar test-taking experience" (Mercer, 1979, p. 93).

The ideal situation for the development of local norms, we believe, is for researchers and practitioners to work together. Based on the demographic profile of the school district, specific assessment needs, the delivery of special education services, and other factors particular to the local district, the school psychologist and other practitioners can serve as valuable resources in helping shape the local norming. The researcher, with his or her technical expertise, can make an important contribution to the local norming effort as well.

RESEARCH ISSUES

A third way in which the researcher and practitioner can work together to help promote better assessment of minority students is in determining the subject of research areas or issues germane to a local school district. Such research topics can be raised jointly by researcher and practitioner or singularly by either person. There are many possible research ventures that are pertinent to the assessment of minority students. Examples include (a) development of assessment measures to identify gifted and talented minority students, (b) validity and reliability investigations of standardized tests, (c) test bias (i.e., cultural bias) investigations, (d) development of criterion-referenced tests, and (e) development of language assessment tests.

The major value of linking researcher and practitioner interests in re-search activities is that such work has the potential for immediate practical applications. Because most research is first published in scholarly journals, a great deal of these findings that have implications for practice may not be quickly accessible to practitioners. Having research topics driven by local needs has the potential to link research and practice in a more timely fashion. In closing, we highly encourage researchers and practitioners to work together in identifying, structuring, investigating, and applying research concerns consonant with the needs of local districts that have interests in promoting nondiscriminatory assessment.

Conclusion

As we have seen, the quest for nondiscriminatory assessment is no easy task. It is an issue filled with controversy, technical confusion, and, to some degree, very slow progress. Notwithstanding these problems, we believe that the psychoeducational assessment of minority students has considerable potential for improvement. In view of the nation's increasing sociocultural diversity, the goal of achieving nondiscriminatory assessment will become imperative. As discussed in the present chapter, researchers, test publishers, and practitio-ners all have a role and responsibility in meeting the challenge of nondis-criminatory assessment. Being sensitive to cultural diversity, advancing our technical knowledge, and linking research with practice should prove to be of great value in providing appropriate and equitable psychoeducational assessment of our nation's minority students.

Notes

1   See Henderson and Valencia (1985) for further discussion of the construct of culture and the educational implications between culture and competence.
2   Of the total national racial and ethnic minority population of 5- to 17-year-olds, blacks, Hispanics, and other minorities account for 52.4 percent, 35.9 percent, and 11.7 percent, respectively.

Regarding Hispanics in the general population, 1989 Bureau of the Census data showed that of the 20.1 million Hispanics, the largest segment is the Mexican-origin population (62.6%). In descending order, the other Hispanic populations are Central and South American (12.7%), Puerto Rican (11.6%), and Cuban (5.3%). Spanish and other Hispanics account for 7.8 percent of the Hispanic population (Miranda & Quiroz, 1989).
3   For examples of coverage of these testing concerns, the reader is referred to Bersoff (1984), Cronbach (1984), Jensen (1980), and the *Journal of Vocational Behavior* (1989).
4   For historical as well as contemporary perspectives, see Oakland (1977), Rueda (1991), Samuda (1975), and Valencia and Aburto (1991).
5   It is beyond the scope of this section to go into depth regarding the measurement and technical aspects of test bias. The reader is referred to the following comprehensive, but readable, sources: Berk (1982), Jensen (1980), Reynolds (1982a, 1983), and Reynolds and Brown (1984).
6   By definition, the study of test bias always involves a comparison of two or more populations. Typically, the design calls for a major group (i.e., white) and a minor group (i.e., racial or ethnic minority) (cf. Jensen, 1980).
7   For examples of research studies of test bias using testable definitions of various forms of validity, see Valencia and Rankin (1985—content validity; 1986—construct validity, and 1988—predictive validity).
8   See Henderson and Valencia (1985), Hilliard (1984), and Shepard (1982).
9   For a description and discussion of WISC-R test bias studies involving white and minority children, see Reynolds (1982, 1983) and Jensen (1980).
10 See Jensen (1980) and Reynolds (1982a) for brief reviews of studies involving intelligence measures other than the WISC-R.
11 In Bossard et al. (1980), which is the first regression analysis of test bias of the Stanford-Binet (black and white children studied), no differential predictive validity was found.
12 The GCI, an index of a child's global intellectual functioning, is considered to be an IQ analogue (Kaufman & Kaufman, 1977).
13 We also hope that test publishers who develop new tests in the future will heed the advice of having adequate inclusion of minority children in the national norm group. This is especially important in that minority popula-

tions are growing at rates much faster than the white sector. For example, in 1985 the combined minority school-age population (nationally) accounted for 20 percent of the total school-age population. By the year 2000, the projection is that minority children will comprise 33 percent of the total school-age population (American Council on Education, 1988). In short, for nationally standardized psychoeducational tests developed for school-age children around the turn of the century, the ideal norming situation would be for test publishers to include in their standardization sample one-third racial and ethnic minority children.

14 The sociocultural norms are designed for black and white children. Parental education (three levels) serves as the sociocultural reference group.

15 In addition, tests should have sound stability (i.e., test score consistency over time). The property of test stability should not be confused with reliability (i.e., the degee to which items are intracorrelated on a specific test at a specific point in time; see Jensen, 1980).

16 Corrected correlations allow inferences to be made about magnitude of the correlation coefficients beyond that of the restricted sample to the entire norm group. However, because the correlations are corrected (adjusted upward), they should be interpreted very cautiously.

17 See Cancelli and Duley (1985), Salvia and Ysseldyke (1988), and Valencia and Aburto (1991).

18 For discussion of these issues, see the following examples: Lopez (1989), MacMillan et al. (1988), Ralph (1989), and Valencia (1991).

19 See Algozzine, Morsink, & Algozzine (1988), and Jenkins et al. (1988).

20 Refer to the following works: Cummins (1984), Diaz, Moll, and Mehan (1986), and Jones (1988).

21 See Ambert (1986), Langdon (1989), and Metz (1988).

22 See Christenson and Ysseldyke (1989), Taylor (1988), and Ysseldyke and Mirkin (1982).

23 For a related discussion, see Christenson and Ysseldyke (1989), Lentz and Shapiro (1986), and Ysseldyke and Christenson (1987).

24 For discussion of curriculum-based measures, see Lopez (1987, 1989), Marston and Magnusson (1988), Shinn, Tindal, and Stein (1988), and Tindal, Wesson, Deno, Germann, and Mirkin (1985).

References

Algozzine, B., Morsink, C. V., & Algozzine, K. M. (1988). What's happening in self-contained special education classrooms? *Exceptional Children,* *55,* 259–265.

Ambert, A. N. (1986). Identifying language disorders in Spanish-speakers. In A. C. Willig & H. G. Greenberg (Eds.), *Bilingualism and learning disabilities: Policy and practice for teachers and administrators* (pp. 15–33). New York: American Library Publishing.

American Council on Education. (1988). *One-third of a nation: A report of the Commission on Minority Participation in Education and American Life.* Washington, DC: Author.

American Educational Research Association, American Psychological Association, and National Council on Measurement in Education Joint Committee. (1985). *Standards for educational and psychological testing.* Washington, DC: American Psychological Association.

Anastasi, A. (1988). *Psychological testing* (6th ed.). New York: Macmillan.

Arter, J. A., & Jenkins, J. R. (1979). Differential diagnosis-prescriptive teaching: A critical appraisal. *Review of Educational Research, 49,* 517–555.

Bender, L. (1938). A visual motor gestalt test and its clinical use. *American Orthopsychiatric Association Research Monograph*, No. 3.

Berk, R. A. (Ed.). (1982). *Handbook of methods for detecting test bias.* Baltimore, MD: Johns Hopkins University Press.

Berninger, V. W., Thalberg, S. P., DeBruyn, I., & Smith, R. (1987). Preventing reading disabilities by assessing and remediating phonemic skills. *School Psychology Review, 16,* 554–555.

Bersoff, D. N. (1982). The legal regulation of school psychology. In C. R. Reynolds & T. B. Gutkin (Eds.), *The handbook of school psychology* (pp. 1043–1074). New York: Wiley.

Bersoff, D. N. (1984). Social and legal influences on test development and usage. In B.S. Plake (Ed.), *Social and technical issues in testing. Implications for test construction and usage* (pp. 87–109). Hillsdale, NJ: Erlbaum.

Bilingual Education Office. (1986). *Beyond language: Social and cultural factors in schooling language minority students.* Sacramento, CA: Bilingual Education Office, California State Department of Education.

Boder, E., & Jarrico, S. (1982). *The Boder test of reading-spelling patterns: A diagnostic screening test for subtypes of reading ability.* New York: Grune & Stratton.

Bossard, M. D., Reynolds, C. R., & Gutkin, T. B. (1980). A regression analysis of test bias on the Stanford-Binet Intelligence Scale for black and white children referred for psychological services. *Journal of Clinical Child Psychology, 9,* 52–54.

California State Department of Education. (1984). *Individual learning problems for the limited English proficient students: A handbook for school personnel.* Sacramento, CA: Author.

Campione, J. C. (1989). Assisted assessment: A taxonomy of approaches and an outline of strengths and weaknesses. *Journal of Learning Disabilities, 22,* 151–165.

Cancelli, A., & Duley, S. (1985). The role of assessment in school psychology. In J. R. Bergan (Ed.), *School psychology in contemporary society* (pp. 119–139). Columbus, OH: Merrill.

Carnine, D. W., Granzin, A., & Becker, W. (1988). Direct instruction. In J. L. Graden, J. E. Zins, & M. J. Curtis (Eds.), *Alternative educational delivery systems: Enhancing instructional options for all students* (pp. 327–349). Washington, DC: National Association of School Psychologists.

Carnine, D. W., & Kameenui, E. J. (1990). The general education initiative and children with special needs: A false dilemma in the face of true problems. *Journal of Learning Disabilities, 23,* 141–148.

Christenson, S. L., & Ysseldyke, J. E. (1989). Assessing student performance: An important change is needed. *Journal of School Psychology, 27,* 409–425.

Cronbach, L. J. (1984). *Essentials of psychological testing* (4th ed.). New York: Harper & Row.

Cummins, J. (1984). *Bilingualism and special education: Issues in assessment and pedagogy.* San Diego, CA: College-Hill Press.

Dean, R.S. (1977). Reliability of the WISC-R with Mexican-American children. *Journal of School Psychology, 15,* 267–268.

Dean, R.S. (1980). Factor structure of the WISC-R with Anglos and Mexican-Americans. *Journal of School Psychology, 18,* 234–239.

DeAngelis, T. (1990, June). Task force, publishers meet on integrity tests. *APA Monitor,* pp. 6–7.

Deutsch, M., Fishman, J., Kogan, L., North, R., & Whiteman, M. (1964). Guidelines for testing minority group children. *The Journal of Social Issues, 20,*127–145.

Diaz, S., Moll, L. C., & Mehan, H. (1986). Sociocultural resources in instruction: A context-specific approach. In Bilingual Education Office, California State Department of Education, *Beyond language: Social and cultural factors in schooling language minority students* (pp. 187–230). Sacramento, CA: Bilingual Education Office, California State Department of Education.

Duran, R. P. (1989). Assessment and instruction of at-risk Hispanic students. *Exceptional Children, 56,* 154–158.

Elliott, R. (1987). *Litigating intelligence: IQ tests, special education, and social science in the courtroom.* Dover, MA: Auburn House.

Erchul, W. P. (Ed.). (1987). Mini-series on family systems assessment and intervention. *School Psychology, 16,* 427–526.

Federal Register. (1977, August). Education of Handicapped Children. Regulations Implementing Education for All Handicapped Children Act of 1975, pp. 42474–42518.

Feuerstein, R. (1979). *The dynamic assessment of retarded performers: The learning potential assessment device, theory, instruments, and techniques.* Glenview, IL: Scott, Foresman.

Feuerstein, R. (1980). *Instrumental enrichment: An intervention program for cognitive modifiabilty.* Glenview, IL: Scott, Foresman.

Figueroa, R. A. (1989, May.) Using interpreters in assessments. *Communique,* p. 19.

Garcia, S. B., & Ortiz, A. A. (1988, June). Preventing inappropriate referral of language minority students to special education. *New Focus,* (5).

Gronlund, N. E. (1985). *Measurement and evaluation in teaching* (5th ed.). New York: Macmillan.

Gutkin, T. B., & Reynolds, C. R. (1980). Factorial similarity of the WISC-R for Anglos and Chicanos referred for psychological services. *Journal of School Psychology, 18,* 34–39.

Gutkin, T. B., & Reynolds, C.R. (1981). Factorial similarity of the WISC-R for white and black children from the standardization sample. *Journal of Educational Psychology, 73,* 227–231.

Harris, J. D., Gray, B. A., Davis, J. E., Zaremba, E. T., & Argulewicz, E. N. (1988). The exclusionary clause and the disadvantaged: Do we try to comply with the law? *Journal of Learning Disabilities, 21,* 581–583.

Heath, C. P., & Obrzut, J. E. (1986). Adaptive behavior: Concurrent validity. *Journal of Psychoeducational Assessment, 4,* 53–59.

Henderson, R. W., & Valencia, R. R. (1985). Nondiscriminatory school psychological services: Beyond nonbiased assessment. In J. R. Bergan (Ed.), *School psychology in contemporary society* (pp. 340–377). Columbus, OH: Merrill.

Hightower, A. D., Work, W. C., Cowen, E. L., Lotyczewski, B. S., Spinell, A.P., Guare, J. C., & Rohrbeck, C. A. (1986). The teacher-child rating scale: A brief measure of elementary children's school problem behaviors and competencies. *School Psychology Review, 15,* 393–400.

Hightower, A. D., Cowen, E. L., Spinell, A. P., Lotyczewski, B. S., Guare, J. C., Rohrbeck, C. A., & Brown, L. P. (1987). The child rating scale: The development of a socioemotional self-rating scale for elementary children. *School Psychology Review, 16,* 239–255.

Hilliard, A. G. (1984). IQ testing as the Emperor's new clothes: A critique of Jensen's *Bias in Mental Testing.* In C. R. Reynolds & R. T. Brown (Eds.), *Perspectives on bias in testing* (pp. 139–169). New York: Plenum.

Hoge, R. D., & Andrews, D. A. (1987). Enhancing academic performance: Issues in target section. *School Psychology Review, 16,* 228–238.

Hohensil, T. H., Levinson, E. M., & Heer, K. L. (1985). Best practices in vocational assessment for handicapped students. In A. Thomas & J. Grimes (Eds.), *Best practices in school psychology* (pp. 215–228). Washington, DC: National Association of School Psychologists.

Howell, K. W. (1986). Direct assessment of academic performance. *School Psychology Review, 15,* 324–335.

Jenkins, J. R., Pious, C. G., & Peterson, D. L. (1988). Categorical programs for remedial and handicapped students: Issues of validity. *Exceptional Children, 55,* 147–158.

Jensen, A. R. (1976). Test bias and construct validity. *Phi Delta Kappan, 58,* 340–346.

Jensen, A. R. (1980). *Bias in mental testing.* New York: Free Press.

Jones, R. L. (1988). Psychoeducational assessment of minority group children: Issues and perspectives. In R. L. Jones (Ed.), *Psychoeducational assessment of minority group children: A casebook* (pp. 13–35). Berkeley, CA: Cobb & Henry.

Jordan, B. T. (1980). *Jordan left-right reversal test manual* (2nd ed.). Novato, CA: Academic Therapy.

Kaufman, A. S., & Kaufman, N. L. (1977). *Clinical evaluation of young children with the McCarthy Scales.* New York: Grune & Stratton.

Kaufman, A. S., & Kaufman, N. L. (1983a). *Kaufman Assessment Battery for Children.* Circle Pines, MN: American Guidance Service.

Kaufman, A. S., & Kaufman, N. L. (1983b). *K-ABC interpretive manual.* Circle Pines, MN: American Guidance Service.

Keller, H. R. (1986). In-school adaptive behavior: Assessment domains of behavior rating scales and child characteristics. *Journal of Psychoeducational Assessment, 4,* 1–12.

Langdon, H. W. (1989). Language disorder or difference? Assessing the language skills of Hispanic students. *Exceptional Children, 56,* 160–167.

Lentz, F. E., & Shapiro, E. S. (1986). Functional assessment of the academic environment. *School Psychology Review, 15,* 346–357.

Litz, C. S., & Mearig, J. S. (1989). Commentary: A response to Reynolds. *Journal of School Psychology, 27,* 81–86.

Lloyd, J. W., & Loper, A. B. (1986). Functional assessment of the academic environment. *School Psychology Review, 15,* 346–357.

Lopez, R. P. (1987). *Assessing black children for special education: Recommendations regarding the California State Department of Education's directive of December 3, 1986 titled "Larry P. litigation: Directive to state special educators."*

Unpublished report. Merced, CA: Merced City School District, Special Services Department.

Lopez, R. P. (1989). *Special education eligibility and assessment: A cross-cultural perspective.* Unpublished report. Sacramento, CA: California State Department of Education, Special Education Division.

Macmillan, D. L., Hendrick, I. G., & Watkins, A. V. (1988). Impact of Diana, Larry P. and PL 94-142 on minority students. *Exceptional Children, 54,* 426–432.

Marston, D., & Magnusson, D. (1988). Curriculum-based measurement: District level implementation. In J. L. Graden, J. E. Zins, & M. J. Curtis (Eds.), *Alternative educational delivery systems: Enhancing instructional options for all students* (pp. 137–172). Washington, DC: National Association of School Psychologists.

McCarthy, D. (1972). *Manual for the McCarthy Scales of Children's Abilities.* New York: Psychological Corporation.

Mercer, J. R. (1979). In defense of racially and culturally non-discriminatory assessment. *School Psychology Digest, 8,* 89–115.

Mercer, J. R., & Lewis, J. (1978). *System of multicultural pluralistic assessment. SOMPA.* New York: Psychological Corporation.

Metz, I. B. (1988). The relative importance of language and culture in making assessment decisions about Hispanic students referred to special education. *Journal of the National Association of Bilingual Education, 12,* 191–218.

Miranda, L., & Quiroz, J. T. (1989). *The decade of the Hispanic: A sobering economic retrospective.* Washington, DC: National Council of La Raza.

Mitchell, J. V., Jr. (1984). Testing and the Oscar Buros lament: From knowledge to implementation to use. In B. S. Plake (Ed.), *Social and technical issues in testing: Implications for test construction and usage* (pp. 111–126). Hillsdale, NJ: Erlbaum.

Mitchell, J. V., Jr. (Ed.). (1985). *The ninth mental measurements yearbook.* Lincoln: University of Nebraska Press.

Oakland, T. (1974–75). Assessment, education and minority-group children. *Academic Therapy, 10,* 133–140.

Oakland, T. (Ed.). (1977). *Psychological and educational assessment of minority children.* New York: Brunner/ Mazel.

Oakland, T., & Feigenbaum, D. (1979). Multiple sources of test bias on the WISC-R and the Bender-Gestalt test. *Journal of Consulting and Clinical Psychology, 47,* 968–974.

Oakland, T., & Laosa, L. M. (1977). Professional, legislative and judicial influences on psychoeducational assessment practices in schools. In T. Oakland (Ed.), *Psychological and educational assessment of minority children* (pp. 21–51). New York: Brunner/Mazel.

Ogbu, J. U., & Matute-Bianchi, M. E. (1986). Understanding sociocultural factors: Knowledge, identity, and school adjustment. In Bilingual Education Office, California State Department of Education, *Beyond language: Social and cultural factors in schooling language minority students* (pp. 73–142). Sacramento, CA: Bilingual Education Office, California State Department of Education.

Pallas, A. M., Natriello, G., & McDill, E. L. (1988, April). *Who falls behind: Defining the "at risk" population—current dimensions and future trends.* Paper presented at the meeting of the American Educational Research Association, New Orleans.

Pearson, C. A. (1988). Cognitive differences between bilingual and monolingual children on the Kaufman Assessment Battery for Children. *Journal of Psychoeducational Assessment, 6,* 271–279.

Peckham, R. F. (1979). Opinion, Larry P. v. Riles. *Federal Supplement 495,* 926–992.

Peterson, D. W., & Batsche, G. M. (1983). School psychology and projective assessment: A growing incompatibility. *School Psychology Review, 12,* 440–445.

Population Reference Bureau. (1985). *Population and California's future.* Washington, DC: Author

Ralph, J. (1989). Improving education for the disadvantaged: Do we know whom to help? *Phi Delta Kappan, 70,* 395–401.

Ranes, R. (1990, March). Working with visual, auditory preferences: Should you invest your effort elsewhere? *Communique,* p. 23.

Reschly, D. J. (1978). WISC-R factor structures among Anglos, blacks, Chicanos, and Native American Papagos. *Journal of Consulting and Clinical Psychology, 46,* 417–422.

Reschly, D. J. (1979). Nonbiased assessment. In G. D. Phye & D. J. Reschly (Eds.), *School psychology: Perspectives and issues* (pp. 215–253). New York: Academic Press.

Reschly, D. J. (1980). Assessment of exceptional individuals: Legal mandates and professional standards. In R. K. Mulliken & M. R. Evans (Eds.), *Assessment of children with low-incidence handicaps.* Washington, DC: National Association of School Psychologists.

Reschly, D. J., Kicklighter, R., & McKee, P. (1988). Recent placement litigation Part III: Analysis of differences in Larry P., Marshall, and S-1 and implications for future practices. *School Psychology Review, 17,* 39–50.

Reschly, D., & Reschly, J. E. (1979). Validity of WISC-R factor scores in predicting achievement and attention for four sociocultural groups. *Journal of School Psychology, 17,* 355–361.

Reschly, D. J., & Sabers, D. (1979). Analysis of test bias in four groups with the regression definition. *Journal of Educational Measurement, 16,* 1–9.

Reynolds, C. R. (1980, September). *Patterns of intellectual abilities among blacks and whites matched for "g."* Paper presented at the meeting of the American Psychological Association, Montreal.

Reynolds, C. R. (1982a). The problem of bias in psychological assessment. In C. R. Reynolds & T. B. Gutkin (Eds.), *The handbook of school psychology* (pp. 178–208). New York: Wiley.

Reynolds, C. R. (1982b). Methods for detecting construct and predictive bias. In R. A. Berk (Ed.), *Handbook of methods for detecting test bias* (pp. 199–227). Baltimore, MD: Johns Hopkins University Press.

Reynolds, C. R. (1983). Test bias: In God we trust; all others must have data. *Journal of Special Education, 17,* 241–260.

Reynolds, C. R., & Brown, R. T. (Eds.). (1984). *Perspectives on bias in testing.* New York: Plenum.

Reynolds, C. R., & Gutkin, T. B. (1980). A regression analysis of test bias on the WISC-R for Anglos and Chicanos referred to psychological services. *Journal of Abnormal Child Psychology, 8,* 237–243.

Reynolds, C. R., & Hartlage, L. C. (1979). Comparison of WISC and WISC-R regression lines for academic prediction with black and white referred children. *Journal of Consulting and Clinical Psychology, 47,* 589–591.

Reynolds, C. R., & Paget, K. D. (1983). National normative and reliability data for the revised children's manifest anxiety scale. *School Psychology Review, 12,* 324–336.

Rueda, R. (1991). An analysis of special education as a response to the diminished academic achievement of Chicano students. In R. R. Valencia (Ed.), *Chicano school failure and success: Research and policy agendas for the 1990s* (pp. 252–270). Basingstoke, England: Falmer Press.

Salvia, J., & Ysseldyke, J. E. (1978). *Assessment in special and remedial education.* Boston: Houghton Mifflin.

Salvia, J., & Ysseldyke, J. E. (1988). *Assessment in special and remedial education* (4th ed.). Boston: Houghton Mifflin.

Samuda, R. (1975). *Psychological testing of American minorities: Issues and consequences.* New York: Dodd, Mead.

Sandoval, J. (1979). The WISC-R and internal evidence of test bias with minority children. *Journal of Consulting and Clinical Psychology, 47,* 919–927.

Shapiro, E. S. (1987). *Behavioral assessment in school psychology.* Hillsdale, NJ: Erlbaum.

Shepard, L. A. (1982). Definitions of bias. In R. A. Berk (Ed.), *Handbook of methods for detecting test bias* (pp. 9–30). Baltimore, MD: The Johns Hopkins University Press.

Shinn, M. R., Tindal, G. A., & Stein, S. (1988). Curriculum-based measurement and the identification of mildly handicapped students. A research review. *Professional School Psychology, 3,* 69–85.

Staff. (1989, April). The biggest secret of race relations: The new white minority. *Ebony,* pp. 84, 86, 88.

Stewart, A. (1983). Severe perinatal hazards. In M. Rutter (Ed.), *Developmental neuropsychiatry* (pp. 15–31). New York: Guilford Press.

Sugai, G. (1987). Single subject research in bilingual special education. *Journal of the National Association of Bilingual Education, 12,* 65–84.

Swibold, D. (1989, October 12). U. S. Hispanic numbers rise 39 percent since 1980. *San Antonio Light,* pp. A1, A12.

Taylor, J. M. (1988). Behavioral assessment and special education evaluation: A successful and necessary marriage. In R. L. Jones (Ed.), *Psychoeducational assessment of minority group children: A casebook* (pp. 225–235). Berkeley, CA: Cobb & Henry.

Terman, L. M., & Merrill, M. (1973). *Stanford-Binet intelligence scale: Manual for the third revision, Form LM.* Boston: Houghton Mifflin.

Tindal, G., Wesson, C., Deno, S. L., Germann, G., & Mirkin, P. K. (1985). The Pine County model for special education delivery: A data-based system. In T. Kratochwill (Ed.), *Advances in school psychology* (Vol. 4, pp. 223–250). Hillsdale, NJ: Erlbaum.

U.S. Bureau of the Census. (1986). *Projections of the Hispanic population: 1983 to 2080* (Current Population Reports, Series P–25, No. 995). Washington, DC: United States Government Printing Office.

Valencia, R. R. (1982). Psychoeducational needs of minority children: The Mexican American child, a case in point. In S. Hill & B. J. Barnes (Eds.), *Young children and their families: Needs of the 90s* (pp. 73–87). Lexington, MA: Lexington Books, D. C. Heath.

Valencia, R. R. (1984). Concurrent validity of the Kaufman Assessment Battery for Children in a sample of Mexican American children. *Educational and Psychological Measurement, 44,* 365–372.

Valencia, R. R. (1985a). Predicting academic achievement with the Kaufman Assessment Battery for Children in Mexican American children. *Educational and Psychological Research, 5,* 11–17.

Valencia, R. R. (1985b). Stability of the Kaufman Assessment Battery for Children in a sample of Mexican American children. *Journal of School Psychology, 23,* 189–193.

Valencia, R. R. (1988). The McCarthy Scales and Hispanic children: A review of psychometric research. *Hispanic Journal of Behavioral Sciences, 10,* 81–104.

Valencia, R. R. (1990). Clinical assessment of young children with the

McCarthy Scales of Children's Abilities. In C. R. Reynolds & R. Kamphaus (Eds.), *Handbook of psychological and educational assessment of children: Vol. 1. Intelligence and achievement* (pp. 209–258). New York: Guilford Publications.

Valencia, R. R. (1991). The plight of Chicano students: An overview of schooling conditions and outcomes. In R. R. Valencia (Ed.), *Chicano school failure and success: Research and policy agendas for the 1990s* (pp. 3–26). Basingstoke, England: Falmer Press.

Valencia, R. R., & Aburto, S. (1991). The uses and abuses of educational testing: Chicanos as a case in point. In R. R. Valencia (Ed.), *Chicano school failure and success: Research and policy agendas for the 1990s* (pp. 203–251). Basingstoke, England: Falmer Press.

Valencia, R. R., & Rankin, R. J. (1985). Evidence of content bias on the McCarthy Scales with Mexican American children: Implications for test translation and nonbiased assessment. *Journal of Educational Psychology, 77,* 197–207.

Valencia, R. R., & Rankin, R. J. (1986). Factor analysis of the K–ABC for groups of Anglo and Mexican American children. *Journal of Educational Measurement 23,* 209–210.

Valencia, R. R., & Rankin, R. J. (1988). Evidence of bias in predictive validity on the Kaufman Assessment Battery for Children in samples of Anglo and Mexican American children. *Psychology in the Schools, 22,* 257–263.

Valencia, R. R., & Rankin, R. J. (1990). *Examination of content bias on the K–ABC with Anglo and Mexican American children.* Manuscript submitted for publication.

Valencia, R. R., & Rothwell, J. G. (1985). Concurrent validity of the WPPSI with Mexican American preschool children. *Educational and Psychological Measurement, 44,* 955–961.

Vance, H. B., & Wallbrown, F. H. (1978). The structure of intelligence for black children: A hierarchical approach. *Psychological Record, 28,* 31–39.

Vasquez-Nuttall, E. V. (1987). Survey of current practices in the psychological assessment of limited-English-proficiency handicapped children. *Journal of School Psychology, 25,* 53–61.

Watson, A. (1988, May 15). Changing classes: State's minority students to make a majority next fall. *San Jose Mercury News,* pp. 1A, 12A.

Wechsler, D. (1974). *Manual for the Wechsler Intelligence Scale for Children-Revised.* New York: Psychological Corporation.

Ysseldyke, J. E., & Christenson, S. L. (1987). Linking assessment to intervention. In J. L. Graden, J. E. Zins, & M. J. Curtis (Eds.), *Alternative educational delivery systems: Enhancing instructional options for all students* (pp. 91–109). Washington, DC: National Association of School Psychologists.

Ysseldyke, J. E., & Mirkin, P. K. (1982). The use of assessment information to plan instructional interventions: A review of the research. In C. R. Reynolds & T. B. Gutkins (Eds.), *The handbook of school psychology* (pp. 395–409). New York: Wiley.

Zeidner, M. (1988). Cultural fairness in aptitude testing revisited: A cross-cultural parallel. *Professional Psychology: Research and Practice, 19,* 257–262.

CHAPTER 12

RESPONSIBLE TEST USE

Lorraine D. Eyde & Ernest S. Primoff

Introduction

In this chapter we will review issues relating to test user competence in administering, scoring, and interpreting tests and discuss the need for test user qualifications, referring to the formal ethical principles and test standards developed by professional associations. We will also describe some of the results of a large-scale research project in which test user competencies for promoting good testing practices were identified.

Before tests may be used properly, they must be standardized and evidence for their reliability and validity documented. The *Standards for Educational and Psychological Testing* (AERA, APA, & NCME, 1985) provide guidelines on how tests should be validated. Test users need training and supervised experience to use tests appropriately and to evaluate tests for their validity. On the other hand, the public is continuously exposed to sets of questions and answers that look like tests but do not meet professional standards. These *pop tests* may be entertaining for readers, but they are unlikely to serve as sound tools for decision making.

On the basis of a few questions, the authors of one pop test, for example, claim to describe the personality and sexual attractiveness of others. Such unstandardized questions, which lack scientific documentation, are found in software such as the *Mind Prober,* which is sold to the general public (Eyde &

Kowal, 1985). Anyone may use the software to learn how to observe the behavior and understand the motivation of others, and unsophisticated test users may be tempted to exaggerate their own competence and overestimate the value of the tests, especially considering the inflated claims made in some of their promotional materials. For example, advertisements claim that it is possible to probe the minds of others using the *Mind Prober* and its offspring, *Dr. Shrink.* Inexperienced test users may be impressed by the apparent accuracy or face validity of pop software and are not trained to evaluate the claims made by their publishers. Let us examine some of the advertisements for the *Mind Prober. Psychology Today,* a publication designed to convey the science of psychology to the general public, carried *Mind Prober* advertisements in three issues, starting in September 1984 with this ad:

> Read Any Good Minds Lately? With the *Mind Prober* you can. In just minutes you can have a scientifically accurate personality profile of anyone. This new expert systems software lets you discover the things most people are afraid to tell you. The strengths, weaknesses, sexual interests and more.

InfoWorld, a newsweekly for microcomputer users, ran this *Mind Prober* ad in their November 19, 1984, issue:

> We'll Get You Inside Her Head, the Rest is Up to You. It's a situation every guy has faced. There she is. The perfect woman. Or close enough. The problem: How to insert yourself into her psyche...that's a tremendous advantage in figuring out how to get what you want from someone. Anyone. In a business situation. Or a personal situation. *Mind Prober.* It delivers the goods. What you do with them is up to you.

Not only are unsubstantiated claims made for this pop test, but the computer-based test interpretation could deliver bad advice. One reviewer offered this caution to readers: "Don't use this program to evaluate your 'significant other' unless you are prepared for a short relationship" (Lima, 1984).

The Need for Consumer Awareness

Tests, Advertising, and Critiques

Test takers and test users need to be aware of the merits of using tests as well as the potential problems. Tests have value, but problems are often ignored by publishers, particularly those of pop tests. Testing is big business, and unsophisticated buyers can use tests incorrectly. According to Neimark (1985), the Human Edge Corporation, which marketed the *Mind Prober*[*] and related products, reached 5 million dollars in sales in 1983. Even professionals may find that scientifically developed and documented tests, which are actively marketed in professional newsletters, journals, convention booths, and mailings, may not live up to their expectations on close examination.

Since 1938 it has been possible for test users to turn to the *Mental Measurements Yearbooks* for guidance in choosing tests. The *Yearbooks* were designed to provide "frank evaluations of tests by competent reviewers...[and] to assist test users in education, psychology, and industry to choose more discriminatingly from the many tests available" (Buros, 1978, p. xxxi).

TESTS AS DECISION-MAKING TOOLS

There are many ways appropriate tests can be used to help professionals make decisions about individuals or groups of individuals. Tests can be used to help in the process of making vocational decisions, placing children in special education classes, selecting and placing persons in particular kinds of jobs, diagnosing mental health problems, and in self-appraisal. In all these uses, tests must be properly administered, scored, and interpreted by an appropriately trained professional who knows how to use the test and is familiar with its limitations as well as his or her own limitations in using it. Professional associations, through their publications and governance structure, provide professionals with guidance in delivering professional services.

Tests are used in a variety of settings by a variety of professionals:

- *In schools.* Tests are most often used by teachers, educational diagnosticians, principals, school psychologists, educational researchers, and by public relations specialists who communicate test results to the media.

- *In employment settings.* Tests are developed by measurement specialists and personnel psychologists, but the key test users may be supervisors and managers who make decisions about selection, placement, and promotion.

- *In counseling settings.* In counseling centers, tests are used by counselors and counseling psychologists. Private practitioners may include marriage and family therapists, and pastoral counselors may use tests in their work with clergy, laypersons, and parishioners.

---

[*] Currently marketed by MINDWARE.

- *In mental health centers and clinical settings.* The test user group in this setting is primarily composed of clinical psychologists, psychiatrists, and medical specialists such as those who evaluate persons with speech, hearing, and language disorders.

- *By professional groups.* Many professional groups use certification exams to maintain their own standards and ethical codes and to ensure that members possess the most current body of knowledge and specialized skills required of the profession.

Professional Ethical Principles for Test Use

Many professional associations have formal ethical principles and committees that engage in the regulation of the ethical behavior of their members and require professional competence (see AACD, 1988; American Association for Marriage and Family Therapy, 1985; APA, 1190; ASHA, 1986; Eyde & Kowal, 1987; NASP, 1984). The ethical principles of the American Medical Association and the American Psychiatric Association are described in Eyde and Kowal (1987).

Three of these organizations have detailed ethical principles that relate to testing (AACD, APA, and NASP). These will be discussed below.

AACD TEST STANDARDS

The American Association for Counseling and Development devotes considerable attention to test use in its ethical standards, summarized as follows:

- Specific orientation or information must be provided to the examinee(s) prior to and following the test administration.

- AACD members must select a test considering its specific reliability, validity, and appropriateness for a given purpose.

- Statements to the public about testing must be accurate.

- AACD members must perform only those testing functions, which include computer-based interpretations, for which they are professionally prepared.

- In situations where a computer is used for test administration and scoring, AACD members are responsible for ensuring that the program properly provides clients with accurate test results.

- Tests must be administered under the same conditions established in their standardization.

- Test security is a professional obligation of AACD members.

- The purpose of testing and the use of results must be made known to the examinees prior to testing.

- Test data must be interpreted and communicated in keeping with the examinee's particular concerns and wishes.

- AACD members responsible for making decisions based on test results must have an understanding of educational and psychological measurement, validation criteria, and test research.

- Caution must be exercised in the interpretation of research instruments.

- Caution must be exercised in evaluating the test performance of individuals belonging to groups not represented in the norm group.

- When computer-based test interpretations are developed by AACD members to support the assessment process, the members must ensure that the validity of such interpretations is established prior to the commercial distribution of such computer programs.

- AACD members will avoid and prevent the misuse of obsolete test results.

- AACD members must respect the legal rights of test publishers.

NASP Ethical Principles

The National Association of School Psychologists, in their principles for professional ethics, stress the principles summarized below:

- School psychologists should recognize individual differences in students and strive to select appropriate procedures relevant to these individual differences.

- School psychologists should strive to obtain and present the most comprehensive and valid description of a student, combining observations, background information, and other pertinent data.

- School psychologists who use computerized services or other technical services for diagnostic, consultative, or information management purposes, should use them as tools and bear full responsibility for their use.

APA Ethical Principles and Test Standards

The American Psychological Association's ethical principles, since their inception in 1953 (Golann, 1970), have focused on preventing test misuse. Psychologists perform within the boundaries of their competencies. Many of the principles mentioned above are included by APA. In addition, the APA principles include the following requirements:

- Psychologists must not encourage inappropriately qualified persons to use psychological assessment through their teaching, sponsorship, or supervision.

- Computer-based test interpretations are to be used within the context of a professional consultation. Clinicians must use their judgment in interpreting the printouts to clients.

- Test developers must use established scientific procedures and observe relevant APA standards.

In addition to formal ethical principles that apply specifically to testing, a number of professional associations have test standards. These include the *Standards for Educational and Psychological Testing* (AERA et al., 1985) and *Responsibilities of Users of Standardized Tests* (AACD, 1978). These standards were developed by committees, building on the consensus of their membership and constituencies within the organizations.

Report on the Test User Qualifications Working Group Study

In addition to ethical principles and related standards, it is important to find out how tests are misused and empirically identify the behaviors that contribute to the misuse. Problems in testing are likely to result from the ways tests are used rather than from the tests themselves (Anastasi, in press). Systematically collected information on the misuse of tests was gathered by the Test User Qualifications Working Group (TUQWoG) and is described below.[*]

---

[*] The research was conducted by the Test User Qualifications Working Group (TUQWoG), a committee established by the Joint Committee on Testing Practices. The Joint Committee consists of the American Psychological Association (APA), the American Association for Counseling and Development (AACD), the American Speech-Language-Hearing Association (ASHA), the National Association of School Psychologists (NASP), and the National Council on Measurement in Education (NCME) (Eyde, Moreland, Robertson, Primoff, & Most, 1988).

These results should be used to make test users aware of their responsibilities and to teach them how to avoid test misuse (Anastasi, in press).

We will begin by describing the empirical basis of TUQWoG's research. Since proper test use is an aspect or function of a job, such as that of a psychologist, counselor, or speech therapist, two job analysis methods were used. In the first phase, the *critical incident method* (Flanagan, 1954) was used to identify observed misuse of tests by professional experts. The *job element method* (Primoff & Eyde, 1988) was used in the second phase to evaluate the extent to which each critical test user behavior is important to good test use and to arrange the most significant ones in the order of their importance for good test use.

Critical incidents of test misuse were collected from 62 experts on 48 tests from a list of commercially available tests. A list of 86 generic subelements(test user behaviors) was generated that apply to tests in general. We will discuss these generic subelements after we present a critical incident.

A Critical Incident of Test Misuse and the Resulting "Subelement"

Six critical incidents from this study are reported elsewhere (Eyde & Quaintance, 1988). We will use one for illustration purposes:

> An examiner responsible for administering a test procedure to job candidates knows one of the candidates personally. The examiner assists the candidate in attaining a good score on the selection instrument by coaching.

The test administrator in this incident succumbed to the personal pressures of friendship and failed to recognize that these pressures might affect the lives of the test takers. By giving a personal friend an advantage on this particular hiring measure, the test administrator has violated the civil rights of the other applicants (i.e., the right to equal employment opportunity). The subelement that resulted from identification of this critical incident is as follows:

> Refraining from helping a favored person get a good score.

Job Element Method for Evaluating "Subelements"

The significance of each generic subelement to tests in general was evaluated by 19 experts in testing from different disciplines, using the job element method. Each subelement was evaluated for four considerations:

- How many even barely acceptable (marginal) test users exhibit the subelement?

- To what extent does the behavior exhibited in the subelement imply superior test use?

- How much trouble would be expected if a test user does not exhibit the behavior described in the subelement?

- To what extent is the subelement or the behavior practical to expect in current test users?

The results that we report below are based on job element formulas in which the responses to these considerations are weighted (see Primoff & Eyde, 1988).

Screenouts

Subelements that cause considerable trouble if not exhibited by even barely acceptable or marginal test users, and are practical enough to expect, are considered absolute or minimum requirements for all test users, regardless of the type of test used. Such absolute requirements, termed *screenouts* when used to qualify persons for using tests, are usually simple, routine behaviors. The screenout requirements for test use appear in Table 1.

Failure to meet the screenout requirements might harm test takers or be detrimental to the testing process. A subelement such as, "Refraining from labeling people in personally derogatory terms like 'dishonest' on the basis of a test score that lacks perfect validity," if ignored, can cause great harm. Since no test has perfect validity—is perfect in its prediction of behavior—it is poor practice to categorize a person as "unintelligent," "incapable of higher education," or "dishonest" on the basis of a test score. Judges in court are not likely to permit a defendant to be called dishonest on the basis of a statistical probability. Even to imply that a test proved a person could not learn in a normal classroom can have unfavorable repercussions. In one case, a student was placed in a special education class because of obstreperous behavior. However, school officials, looking for an easy explanation, told the parents that the reason for the placement was a low test score. Test scores appeared more definitive than a teacher's judgment. Because test scores were used merely as an excuse for making a placement in a special education program, the usefulness of the test was denigrated. Because the administrators did not focus on the *behavior*, the parents missed the opportunity to help their child deal with the underlying problem. Eventually, complaints from the community concerning the use of test scores to place this student in a special

TABLE 1. Screenout Subelements for Avoiding Test Misuse

Refrains from using homemade answer sheets that do not align with strip keys

Does not photocopy copyrighted materials
(Note: This does not cover emergencies where a copy of the test is unexpectedly missing during a testing session)

Keeps keys and test materials under close security

Arranges test settings that allow for optimum performance by the test taker (adequate room, etc.)

Establishes rapport with examinees so as to obtain accurate scores

Makes sure examinees follow directions so that test scores will be accurate

Answers questions of test takers in greater detail than the manual if permitted

Avoids errors in scoring and recording

Does not assume that the same norms apply to different jobs

Gives interpretation and guidance to test takers in counseling situations

Refrains from labeling people in personally derogatory terms like "dishonest" on the basis of a test score that lacks perfect validity

Refrains from using tests as training tools
(Note: This does not apply to persons with difficulties in understanding and who are being tested to their limits)

---

education class led administrators to suspend the use of the test, even though test scores did not play a major role in the placement decision.

Elements of Good Test Use
Unlike screenouts, which are generally simple behaviors, *elements* are more comprehensive behaviors that include different levels. *Elements* may be treated as labels for sets of *descriptors* under which related *exemplifiers* may be classified. Elements are chosen from the listed subelements because they are behaviors that differentiate the superior test users from the barely acceptable ones to the greatest degree. Descriptors and exemplifiers are chosen from the list of subelements because they differentiate superior test users from barely acceptable ones to a moderate degree.

Table 2 presents the elements and the descriptors for each, under which are grouped related subelements that serve as exemplifiers. The first element is "Knowledge of the test and its limitations." The first descriptor is "Applying test theory and principles of interpretation," and the first exemplifier is "Understanding of standard scores and percentile scores."

ELEMENT I. "KNOWLEDGE OF THE TEST AND ITS LIMITATIONS." This element indicates that test use involves more than a matter of following a few simple rules. To teach students properly, a teacher should be aware of the intelligence of each student. But if a student has not been taught to read, test scores on an intelligence test involving printed materials are not a measure of that student's intelligence. Furthermore, a criterion-referenced test, which measures a person's performance in relation to a specified behavioral domain, based on the average subject matter taught at a particular grade in a school system, applies neither to students in an advanced program that covers high-level subject matter, nor to students in a class of semi-illiterate students who are being motivated and taught to acquire basic reading skills.

In many employment situations, workers with identical job titles do different kinds of work. Those doing the work with the highest intellectual demands are likely to perform best on intelligence tests and will be rated by their supervisors as being the most valuable to the organization. The validity coefficient for the test, that is, the relation of test scores to value of the employee to the organization, will be high. However, if work of a less complex nature must also be done, and if persons are selected by an intelligence test, the less complex work may be slighted. In an extreme example, some ferryboat attendants did clerical work, some closed gates, and some cleaned restrooms. Those doing clerical work were rated as most valuable; those cleaning were rated least valuable. Scores on an intelligence test were highest for those doing clerical work and lowest for those doing cleaning. This finding was interpreted as implying that the test was valid for persons with the highest test scores doing the most valuable work and with the lowest test scorers doing the least valuable work. However, this finding is spurious because persons with the same job title were lumped together, even though they were performing distinctly different tasks. When an intelligence test was used to select attendants, the new employees pointed out that the job descriptions read, "*may* clean toilets," not *must*. The attendants refused to do the cleaning.

The test user must have an appreciation for test statistics, for example, the size of the validity coefficient, but must also understand the relation of test content to the background of the particular individuals tested and to the complexities of life requirements at home, in school, and on the job.

TABLE 2. Significant Subelements Arranged as Elements, Descriptors, and Exemplifiers of Test Misuse

I. Knowledge of test and its limitations

   A. Applying test theory and principles of interpretation

      1. Understanding of standard scores and percentile scores
      2. Understanding norms and limitations
      3. Understanding the meaning of test scores in the pattern of evaluation
      4. Interpreting for the particular group tested
      5. Avoiding interpretation beyond test's limits
      6. Perceiving score on a test as representing only one period of time, subject to changes from experience

   B. Keeping up with the field and checking one's own interpretations with others

   C. Using multiple sources of convergent data

      1. Basing promotion/retention decisions and grades or classes on wider information than on test score
      2. Interpreting test scores to parents and teachers rather than simply transmitting scores labeling child without consideration of compensating strengths and actual school performance

   D. (In clinical situation) recognizing when a patient's state has been misdiagnosed or has changed and selecting suitable norms

   E. (In school situation) advising administrators on limitations of grade equivalent conversions and percentiles among different student populations (e.g., inflated city-wide grade equivalent reports due to policy of no out-of-level testing, and chance-level grade equivalent conversion well above actual grade equivalents for some examinees; use of school means for school effectiveness comparisons without regard for differences in student populations; combining scores across achievement tests; using grade equivalents or percentiles without regard for differences in normal populations)

   F. Interpreting elements (based on valid information) in each test that would be discriminatory against certain populations

II. Acceptance of responsibility for competent use of test

   A. Selecting tests appropriate to the measurement purpose and test takers

      1. Choosing test sufficient to sample behaviors for a purpose, e.g., neuropsychological testing
      2. Refraining from making evaluations from inappropriate test, e.g., clinical evaluation from nonclinical test

TABLE 2. Significant Subelements Arranged as Elements,
Descriptors, and Exemplifiers of Test Misuse (continued)

B. Restricting test administration to personnel qualified to do so

1. Refraining from helping a favored person get a good test score
2. Preventing individuals from reviewing actual test prior to administration
3. Following scoring instructions
4. Following timing instructions accurately, especially for short speeded tests
5. Giving standard directions as prescribed

C. Conducting appropriate training and maintaining quality control over operations for all users of tests and test results, for example, administrators, media personnel who disseminate test results, department heads, teachers, social workers, and psychologists

1. Using checks on scoring accuracy
2. Resisting pressures to amass higher scores than justified to make system look good
3. Using professional ethics

Descriptor A, "Applying test theory and principles of interpretation," requires understanding that norms used to interpret test scores apply to a specific group of persons in a particular situation. They indicate how persons perform at a particular time, and in a particular place, and they may vary as a result of societal changes (Anastasi, 1985). The same set of norms is not likely to apply to all persons in another situation. Also, norms for different tests are probably based on different populations and are not equivalent. Furthermore, test results must be interpreted in terms of other information, such as records of achievement and environmental deficiencies.

Descriptor B, "Keeping up with the field and checking one's own interpretations with others," is vitally important to all test users. At the beginning of this century, a *Washington Post* editorial ridiculed the idea that a mosquito might cause yellow fever. Today the transmission of this disease by mosquitos is widely accepted. Similarly, in the first decades of this century, it was considered necessary to post students' intelligence test scores in permanent records so that successive teachers might use them to avoid giving too high a grade to students with low intelligence test scores or too low a grade to students with high intelligence test scores. By posting IQ scores on student records, teachers were discouraged from exercising independent judgment in evaluating students. Today it is generally recognized that test scores should not be used in that way because they might bias teachers. Users of tests should receive in-service training, attend workshops on the tests they use, and discuss their interpretations with others to make sure they are not developing idiosyncratic, unsubstantiated views or using out-of-date procedures.

Descriptor C, "Using multiple sources of convergent data," is at the heart of assuring that a test result that is inapplicable to a particular person does not bias that person's chance to progress, be it in school, work, or psychotherapy. The test user should consider the specific characteristics of test takers, such as gender, age, anxiety level, cultural group, past educational or family history, and other life experiences that affect test scores and comparisons with the norm used in test interpretation.

The responsibility of the test user is especially important when a computer-based test interpretation is used. The computer-generated narrative is often based on unknown norms and algorithms (Eyde & Kowal, 1987). The narrative must not be substituted for the report prepared by a test user. To the extent that the test user knows the norms and algorithms on which the computer report is based, the test user may use the narrative as a suggestion of a possible interpretation. However, the necessity of considering test content, test research studies, and the characteristics of the test taker remains. The fact that the computer narrative is attractively reproduced should serve as a warning that one should not judge the contents of a package by its wrapping.

Descriptor D, "Recognizing when a patient's state has been misdiagnosed or has changed and selecting suitable norms," emphasizes that norms must be suitable for the test taker at the present time. Circumstances such as a changed emotional state or medical condition, new experience, or altered interest pattern may indicate that a norm previously applicable is no longer appropriate. This point applies generally to tests and is not confined to clinical work.

Descriptor E, "Advising administrators on limitations of grade equivalent conversions and percentiles among different student populations," points out the need to advise administrators on the proper use of test statistics. For example, if eight percent of a group have test scores at the mean and seven percent have scores one point below the mean, a difference of only two raw score points corresponds to a difference of 15 percentile points. Serious errors may arise if poorly informed administrators compare persons or groups on the basis of percentile points. Descriptor E is especially important in school situations where administrators may make poor citywide policies on the basis of misunderstood statistics. Such misleading use of statistics also applies to the many other settings in which descriptive statistics are used.

Descriptor F, "Interpreting elements in each test that would be discriminatory against certain populations," refers to a serious problem in testing: the fact that large numbers of certain minorities receive relatively lower test scores than do majority group members. There are many possible reasons for these test score differences, including differences in educational opportunities among test takers. A small part of the problem may result from the use of inappropriate test materials. A test in English cannot accurately measure the ability of a person who understands little English and speaks English as a second language. Test scores derived from analogies such as comparing president to congress and prime minister to parliament do not serve as accurate measures of thinking ability for persons with little knowledge of social studies. Another example of the impact of test materials on the test scores of minority and majority group members is given by Haynes (cited in Primoff & Eyde, 1988, p. 820) who developed job-relevant test materials for selecting clerks to process tax returns for the Internal Revenue Service. Originally, academic tests of spelling, reading, grammar, and arithmetic were used to select clerks, resulting in adverse impact—the selection rate was considerably lower for minority group members than for members of the majority group. When the test was based on the ability to detect infrequently occurring errors, identified through a job element analysis of the critical requirements of the job, adverse impact was reduced and employees showed a lower error rate in performing their work than did those selected through academic tests. By using a test dealing with error detection, the job performance of employees was improved and test score differences between minority and majority group members decreased.

ELEMENT 2. "ACCEPTANCE OF RESPONSIBILITY FOR COMPETENT USE OF TEST." This element emphasizes the necessity for test users to accept responsibility for their own competent use of tests as well as for competent use by all persons to whom they supply tests. This responsibility extends to selecting tests appropriate to the measurement purpose, restricting test administration to persons who have been trained to administer them properly, and providing appropriate quality control over the testing activities of all persons to whom they provide test materials. The situation where an authorized person orders tests from a publisher and turns them over to staff personnel to use as they please is likely to lead to test misuse. In one instance, a psychologist ordered a personality test and turned it over to an administrator for use in a trainee program. The administrator encouraged trainees to read the manual and disclose and discuss their personality characteristics. The testing process produced devastating results. Trainees thought they had discovered abnormal tendencies in themselves that they needed to overcome. One trainee, for example, needed psychotherapy to maintain stability.

REVIEW QUESTIONS BASED ON TUQWoG RESEARCH FOR TEST QUALITY ASSURANCE

In this chapter, we have discussed facets of TUQWoG's research. Now we direct the reader to a series of questions adapted from the data and organized according to the guidelines that Robertson (1992) derived from these data. These questions serve as review questions to heighten test users' awareness of potential problems in the use of tests. The quality of test interpretations made from test scores depends on how test users respond to relevant questions. The validity of test interpretations depends on actions taken during test administration and the test scoring process.

Test users should periodically review these guidelines and questions so that they continue to engage in good testing practices.

1. *Conduct testing and assessment activities within a broad context, avoiding placing undue emphasis on a single test score.*
   a. What kind of information is needed to aid in decision making?
   b. How may test scores facilitate the decision-making process? What are their limitations?
   c. Are the tests selected sufficient to sample the behaviors needed for decision making, for example, in neuropsychological testing?
   d. What kinds of nontest information are needed?
   e. When administering tests, has rapport been established to ensure that the test taker's scores are relatively accurate?
   f. Are you aware that a test score represents behavior at a specific time and that these behaviors change over time?
   g. Will you avoid making interpretations that extend beyond the validity and reliability of the test?

2. *Accept the professional responsibilities that accompany proper test use.*
   a. Are you carrying out your testing responsibilities in keeping with professional ethics?
   b. Are you taking proper actions regardless of pressures from managers or from persons who desire preferential treatment?
   c. Do you avoid photocopying copyrighted materials?

    d. Do you have the proper training and experience to administer, score, and interpret test scores to support your use of test data in decision making?

    e. Are you taking the proper precautions to safeguard the test items and scoring keys for the tests you are using?

    f. Do testing conditions allow for test takers to perform optimally?

    g. Are the tests administered according to standard directions, e.g., according to time limits?

    h. Are you making sure that quality control procedures exist and are used by all staff in your organization involved in using test score information?

    i. Has the test been accurately scored?

3. *Exercise the appropriate psychometric knowledge when interpreting test results.*

    a. Do you remind yourself that no single test result is perfectly accurate due to limitations in measurement devices and day-to-day changes in behavior?

    b. Do you recognize the significance of different types of documented validity of tests—content, criterion-related, and construct—when using test scores in decision making?

    c. Do you recognize how a test's reliability affects its validity?

    d. Do you understand and use standard error concepts when interpreting test results?

4. *Maintaining the integrity of test results.*

    a. Do you consider whether the use of a particular test in a local setting or situation meets the purpose for which the test was designed?

    b. When using tests in an educational setting, do you resist amassing higher test scores than justified to make a school system look good?

    c. Do you resist using a test developed for research purposes when making operational decisions using test scores?

    d. Are you sensitive to and use valid information in interpreting elements in each test which would be discriminatory against certain populations?

    e. When using tests for placing students in special programs for the gifted, do you consider measurement errors when setting cutoff scores?

    f. When interpreting test scores to parents and teachers, do you consider compensatory strengths and actual school performance rather than transmitting scores that label children?

5. *Exercise care in the selection and use of norm groups.*
   a. Are you careful not to assume that a norm developed for one population or job automatically applies to other populations?
   b. Are you sensitive to the pros and cons for using separate sex and racial norms?
   c. When using computer software for interpreting test results, are you alert to the need for detecting and rejecting unauthorized and unvalidated norms? Do you detect and reject errors and overstatements in narratives? Do you integrate computer printouts with other information rather than present the printout as a professional report?

6. *Provide interpretive feedback to test takers.*
   a. Are you willing and able to provide interpretation and guidance to test takers?
   b. Is there enough sufficiently qualified staff to provide adequate counseling?
   c. Are you able to interpret test results properly, keeping in mind the characteristics of the particular group tested?

Conclusion

In this chapter we have examined the ethical principles developed by professional associations to guide their members in competent use of tests. We have also highlighted some of the general requirements for the competent use of tests that grew out of TUQWoG's research on commercially published tests used in many settings for a variety of purposes.

To aid test users in applying our empirically based guidelines, we have presented a set of review questions. By examining these questions, test users with a minimum amount of education, training, and experience should be able to recognize that many considerations contribute to good test use. They should not engage in testing without responding to these elements of competency. On the other hand, experts with rich experience in testing are likely to recognize the nuances in these caveats. They should use the review questions to fine tune their use of test information in decision making. In order to prevent harm to test takers whose lives are affected by their test results, responsible test users who vary in expertise need to be competent in the administration, scoring, and interpretation of the tests they use.

References

American Association for Counseling and Development (AACD). (1978). Responsibilities of users of standardized tests. *Guidepost,* 5–8.

American Association for Counseling and Development (AACD). (1988). *Ethical standards.* Washington, DC: Author.

American Association for Marriage and Family Therapy. (1985). *Code of ethical principles for marriage and family therapists.* Washington, DC: Author.

American Educational Research Association (AERA), American Psychological Association (APA), & National Council on Measurement in Education (NCME). (1985). *Standards for educational and psychological testing.* Washington, DC: American Psychological Association.

American Psychological Association (APA). (1990). Ethical principles of psychologists (Amended June 2 , 1989). *American Psychologist, 45,* 390–395.

American Speech-Language-Hearing Association. (1986). *Code of ethics of the American Speech-Language-Hearing Association.* Rockville, MD: Author.

Anastasi, A. (1985). Some emerging trends in psychological measurement: A fifty-year perspective. *Applied Psychological Measurement, 9,* 121–138.

Anastasi, A. (in press). The Test User Qualifications project: Commentary. *American Psychologist.*

Buros, O. K. (1978). *The eighth mental measurements yearbook.* (Vol. 1). Highland Park, NJ: Gryphon Press.

Eyde, L. D., & Kowal, D. M. (1985). Psychological decision support software for the public: Pros, cons, and guidelines. *Computers in Human Behavior, 1,* 321–336.

Eyde, L. D., & Kowal, D. M. (1987). Computerized test interpretation services: Ethical and professional concerns regarding U.S.A. producers and users. In L. D. Eyde (Ed.), *Computerised psychological testing.* London: Erlbaum.

Eyde, L. D., Moreland, K. L., Robertson, G. J., Primoff, E. S., & Most, R. B. (1988). Test user qualifications: A data-based approach to promoting good test use. *Issues in Scientific Psychology.* Report of the Test User Qualifications Working Group of the Joint Committee on Testing Practices. Washington, DC: American Psychological Association.

Eyde, L. D., & Quaintance, M. K. (1988). Ethical issues and cases in the practice of personnel psychology. *Professional Psychology: Research and Practice, 19,* 148–154.

Flanagan, J. C. (1954). The critical incident technique. *Psychological Bulletin, 51*(4), 327–358.

Golann, S. E. (1970). Ethical standards for psychology: Development and revision, 1938–1968. *Annals of the New York Academy of Sciences, 169*(2), 398–405.

Lima, T. (1984, December 17). Psychological software. Mind Prober: The more you know someone, the better it works. *InfoWorld, 6,* 48–49.

National Association of School Psychologists (NASP). (1984). *Principles for professional ethics.* Washington, DC: Author.

Neimark, J. (1985, May). The cutting edge: Lesson from Jim Johnson, a master salesman and innovator. *Success!, 32,* 24–28.

Primoff, E. S., & Eyde, L. D. (1988). The job element method of job analysis. In S. Gael (Ed.), *The job analysis handbook for business, industry, and government* (Vol. II). New York: Wiley.

Robertson, G. J. (1992). The development, publication, and distribution of psychological tests. In M. M. Zeidner & R. B. Most (Eds.), *Psychological testing: An inside view* (pp. 159–214). Palo Alto, CA: Consulting Psychologists Press.

The authors acknowledge the assistance of Dorothea E. Johannsen and Lois C. Northrop in reviewing the chapter. The opinions expressed are those of the authors and are not necessarily official policy statements of the U.S. Office of Personnel Management.

CONTRIBUTORS

PAMELA BRADLEY is currently a research associate at the Institute of Personality Assessment and Research at the University of California, Berkeley, where she is also a doctoral candidate in personality psychology. She has developed research scales to measure political perceptions and perspectives on foreign policy. Her current research focuses on psychological integration and its mediation of personality type.

BRUCE BRACKEN earned his Ph.D. in school psychology at the University of Georgia. Currently professor in the Department of Psychology and the Center for Applied Psychological Research at Memphis State University, he has published widely in the area of psychoeducational assessment, including *The Psychoeducational Assessment of Preschool Children; The Bracken Basic Concept Scale,* a preschool test; and a companion curriculum, the *Bracken Concept Development Program.* Dr. Bracken also founded and edits the *Journal of Psychoeducational Assessment.*

MARK L. DAVISON is adjunct professor of psychology, professor of educational psychology, and chairman of the Educational Psychology Department at the University of Minnesota. He received his Ph.D. in psychology from the University of Illinois, Urbana-Champaign. He has published numerous journal articles and is a coauthor of *Multidimensional Scaling.* Dr. Davidson has been elected to *Who's Who in American Education.*

LORRAINE D. EYDE is a personnel research psychologist with the U. S. Office of Personnel Management. She holds a Ph.D. in psychology from Ohio State University, has earned a diplomate in industrial and organizational psychology, ABPP, and is a fellow of three divisions of the American Psychological Association. She has received APA's Committee on Women in Psychology's citation for Distinguished Leader for Women in Psychology and has published widely on such topics as job analysis, computer-based test interpretation, ethics, and interrelationships between work and family. Dr. Eyde helped to organize the Joint Committee on Testing Practices and serves as chair of its Test User Training Work Group.

HARRISON GOUGH is currently professor of psychology emeritus at the University of California, Berkeley, is author of the *California Psychological Inventory,* and is coauthor of the *Adjective Check List.* Dr. Gough received his Ph.D. in clinical psychology from the University of Minnesota, and was a long-time member of the Department of Psychology at Berkeley and the Institute of Personality Assessment and Research. He is the recipient of a Guggenheim Foundation Fellowship, two Fulbright Research Fellowships, and the Society for Personality Assessment's Bruno Klopfer Distinguished Contribution Award for work in personality assessment.

ALLEN L. HAMMER is a licensed psychologist and senior developer for Consulting Psychologists Press, Inc. He prepares training materials on test use and interpretation, with a special empahsis on the *Myers-Briggs Type Indicator* and the *Strong Interest Inventory.* He received his Ph.D. from Michigan State University, is coauthor of the *Coping Resources Inventory,* and is currently a member of TUQWoG, a working group of the Joint Committee on Testing Practices.

PATRICIA B. JONES holds joint appointments at the University of Arizona as adjunct assistant professor of educational psychology, principal research specialist, and adjunct lecturer in the College of Nursing. She received her Ph.D. in educational psychology with a minor in statistics from the University of Arizona. Her consulting specialties include multivariate analysis and statistical packages.

V. L. SCHWEAN KOWALCHUK completed her Ph.D. at the University of Saskatchewan. She is an assistant professor in the Department for the Education of Exceptional Children and an associate member in the Department of Psychiatry, University of Saskatchewan. Her current research program focuses on attention deficit disorders in children and adults.

RUBEN LOPEZ is a bilingual school psychologist for Merced City School District, California. He received his master's degree in counseling and training in school psychology from San Diego State University and has served on various committees and task forces related to multicultural and minority concerns for the California State Department of Education, the National Association of School Psychologists, and the California Association of School Psychologists.

KEVIN L. MORELAND is assistant professor in the psychology department at Fordham University and teaches courses in assessment and abnormal psychology. Prior to this, he spent six years as research and product development manager at National Computer Systems, where he assisted in the development of the MMPI-2™. Dr. Moreland obtained his Ph.D. in clinical psychology at the University of North Carolina. His research interest is computerized test interpretation, and he has published numerous articles and book chapters in this area.

ROBERT MOST is a publishing executive at Consulting Psychologists Press, Inc. He received his Ph.D. from Wayne State University, has authored numerous articles for scholarly publications, and is a member of TUQWoG, a working group of the Joint Committee on Testing Practices.

BARUCH NEVO earned his Ph.D. at the Hebrew University in Israel. He is currently associate professor of psychology at the University of Haifa, where he founded the university assessment and selection unit. From 1983 to 1987 he was the director of the Inter-University National Institute for Testing and Evaluation. Dr. Nevo's main interest areas are tests and measurement in psychology and education, human intelligence, and personnel psychology.

ERNEST S. PRIMOFF is retired from the U. S. Office of Personnel Management, where he worked from 1944 to 1979. He developed the job element method of job analysis, for which he received the U. S. Civil Service Commissioner's Award for Distinguished Service. His method, used in both the public and private sectors, focuses on competencies and has provided the foundation for upward mobility programs. Mr. Primoff published his first job analysis report in 1948 and continues to be active in his retirement, contributing to both books and journals on testing and job analysis, as well as presenting at professional meetings. He has most recently served as a consultant to two major projects, applying his job element method to study test user qualifications and to develop suitability criteria.

GARY J. ROBERTSON is vice president of test publishing at American Guidance Service in Circle Pines, Minnesota, where he has directed the test development and test publications department since 1976. He has published widely and was responsible for the development and publication of more than 25 educational and psychological tests. He is a fellow of the American Psychological Association and a member of the American Educational Research Association, the National Council on Measurement in Education, and the American Association for the Advancement of Science. Dr. Robertson received his Ph.D. from Columbia University where he studied with Professor Robert L. Thorndike.

DARRELL L. SABERS is professor of educational psychology at the University of Arizona where he teaches measurement, research, and statistics. He received his Ph.D. in educational measurement and statistics from the University of Iowa. His consulting specialties include analysis of data and test development.

D. H. SAKLOFSKE received his Ph.D from the University of Calgary in Canada. He is a professor in the Department of Educational Psychology and associate member in the Department of Psychology and Department for the Education of Exceptional Children, University of Saskatchewan. His research interests include individual differences, personality, intelligence, and cognitive processes.

RICHARD R. VALENCIA is an associate professor of educational psychology and speech communication at the University of Texas, Austin. His research interests focus on ethnic minority schooling, particularly issues of cultural bias in testing, academic/intellectual development of minority children, and the social and psychological foundations of minority schooling. His most recent work is an edited book, *Chicano School Failure and Success: Research and Policy Agendas for the 1990s*. Dr. Valencia served for three years as associate editor for the *Journal of Educational Psychology*.

MOSHE ZEIDNER is currently a faculty member of the School of Education, University of Haifa, Israel. His major research interests include personality and individual differences, test bias, and test attitudes and motivation. He has published widely in the United States and Europe and serves as a consultant and reviewer for the *Journal of Classroom Interaction*. Dr. Zeidner was a sabbatical fellow at the Program for Psychology in Education at Stanford and distinguished visiting professor at the Department of Psychology, San Jose State University. He is currently a member of the executive committee of the International Society for Test Anxiety Research.

CREDITS

Acknowledgment is made to the following authors and publishers for their gracious permission to reprint material from the following copyrighted sources:

CHAPTER 3
Influences on Testing and Test Results
D. H. Saklofske & V. L. Schwean Kowalchuk

Page 90 From "The Psychology of Educational Measurement" by S. Messick, 1984, *Journal of Educational Measurement, 21,* p. 216. Copyright 1984 by the National Council on Measurement in Education. Reprinted by permission of the publisher. Page 91 From *Assessment of Children* (3rd ed., pp. 535–536) by J. M. Sattler, 1988, San Siego: Sattler. Copyright 1988 by Sattler. Reprinted by permission. Pages 97–98 From *Psychological Testing* (6th ed., p. 35) by A. Anastasi, 1988, New York: Macmillan. Copyright 1988 by Anne Anastasi. Reprinted by permission of Macmillan Publishing Company. Pages 100–101 From *Essentials of Psychological Testing* (5th ed., p. 69) by L. J. Cronbach, 1990, New York: HarperCollins. Copyright 1990 by HarperCollins. Reprinted by permission. Page 101 From *Assessment of Personality* (pp. 195–196) by L. R. Aiken, 1989, Boston: Allyn and Bacon. Copyright 1989 by Allyn and Bacon. Reprinted by permission. Page 108 From *The Measurement Mystique* (p. 3) by S. T. Johnson, 1979, Washington, DC: Institute for the Study of Educational Policy. Copyright 1979 by the Institute for the Study of Educational Policy.

466 PSYCHOLOGICAL TESTING

CHAPTER 8
Examining Test Data Using Multivariate Procedures
Patricia B. Jones & Darrell L. Sabers

Pages 297–298 From "An Introduction to Discriminant Analysis" by C. J. Huberty and R. M. Barton, 1989, *Measurement and Evaluation in Counseling and Development, 22,* p. 158. Copyright 1989 by the American Association for Counseling and Development. Reprinted by permission. No further reproduction authorized without written permission of American Association for Counseling and Development.

CHAPTER 11
**Assessment of Racial and Ethnic Minority Students:
Problems and Prospects**
Richard R. Valencia & Ruben Lopez

Page 404 From "The Problem of Bias in Psychological Assessment" by C. R. Reynolds, 1982. In *The Handbook of School Psychology* (p. 188), edited by C. R. Reynolds and T. B. Gutkin, New York: Wiley. Copyright 1982 by John Wiley and Sons, Inc. Reprinted by permission. Pages 405, 410 From "The Uses and Abuses of Educational Testing: Chicanos as a Case in Point" by R. R. Valencia and S. Aburto, 1991. In *Chicano School Failure and Success: Research and Policy Agendas for the 1990s* (pp. 212, 214, 219), edited by R. Valencia, London: Falmer Press. Copyright 1991 by Falmer Press. Reprinted by permission. Page 414 From *Bias in Mental Testing* (p. 716) by A. R. Jensen, 1976, New York: Free Press. Copyright 1976 by Arthur R. Jensen. Reprinted by permission of Free Press, a division of Macmillan, Inc. Page 415 From "Opinion, Larry P. v. Riles" by R. F. Peckham, 1979, *Federal Supplement 495,* pp. 969–970. Copyright 1979 by Federal Supplement. Page 417 From *Litigating Intelligence: IQ Tests, Special Education, and Social Science in the Courtroom* (p. 198) by R. Elliott, 1987, Dover, MA: Auburn House. Copyright 1987 by Auburn House. Reprinted by permission of Greenwood Publishing Group, Inc., Westport, CT. Page 420 From "The Use of Assessment Information to Plan Instructional Interventions: A Review of the Research" by J. E. Ysseldyke and S. L. Christenson, 1987. In *The Handbook of School Psychology* (p. 409), edited by C. R. Reynolds and T. B. Gutkins, New York: Wiley. Copyright 1987 by John Wiley and Sons, Inc. Reprinted by permission. Pages 420–421 From "Direct Assessment of Academic Performance" by K. W. Howell, 1986, *School Psychology Review, 16,* p. 326. Copyright 1986 by the National Association of School Psychologists. Reprinted by permission of the publisher.

INDEX

Also Available From Consulting Psychologists Press

INDUSTRIAL AND ORGANIZATIONAL PSYCHOLOGY
Handbook of Industrial and Organizational Psychology, Volume 1
edited by Marvin D. Dunnette and Leaetta M. Hough
Handbook of Industrial and Organizational Psychology, Volume 2
edited by Marvin D. Dunnette and Leaetta M. Hough

PERSONALITY AND TYPE
Applications of the Myers-Briggs Type Indicator in Higher Education edited
by Judith A. Provost and Scott Anchors
The Character of Organizations: Using Jungian Type in Organizational Development by William Bridges
Gifts Differing, 10th Anniversary Edition by Isabel Briggs Myers with
Peter B. Myers
The Inner Image: A Resource for Type Development by William Yabroff
Katharine and Isabel: Mother's Light, Daughter's Journey by Frances Wright
Saunders
Portraits of Type: An MBTI Research Compendium by Avril Thorne and
Harrison Gough
Work, Play, and Type: Achieving Balance in Your Life by Judith A. Provost

CAREER COUNSELING
Dictionary of Holland Occupational Codes compiled by Gary D. Gottfredson,
John L. Holland, and Deborah Kimiko Ogawa
New Directions in Career Planning and the Workplace edited by Jean M.
Kummerow

EDUCATION AND CHILDREN
Building Self-esteem: An Elementary School Program by Robert W. Reasoner
Building Self-esteem in the Secondary Schools by Robert W. Reasoner and
Gail S. Dusa
Developing Motivation in Young Children edited by Stanley Coopersmith
Smart Plays: A Story About Safety for Young People by Frances S. Dayee
Treating Sexually Abused Children and their Families by Beverly James and
Maria Nasjleti
Type Tales: Teaching Type to Children by Diane Farris

*For further information on any of these titles, or to receive a CPP catalog,
please call 1–800–624–1765.*